S0-AAG-755

FLORIDA STATE
UNIVERSITY LIBRARIES

SEP 8 1998

TALLAHASSEE, FLORIDA

THE FIFTH TIGER

Thailand Development Policy Study

This study is one of several in the area of development strategies undertaken by the United Nations University's first research and training centre, the World Institute for Development Economics Research (UNU/WIDER), in furtherance of its mandate to help identify and meet the need for policy-oriented socio-economic research. The experience of post-World War II economic development in Thailand indeed presents valuable insights, which may be replicated with suitable adaptation in other countries in the region. It is therefore fitting that UNU/WIDER should undertake a comprehensive study of this type, the outcome of which is presented in this book. The study was carried out under the Institute's programme area Money, Finance and Trade—Reform for World Development. UNU/WIDER started its work in Helsinki in 1985.

THE FIFTH TIGER

A STUDY OF THAI DEVELOPMENT POLICY

ROBERT J. MUSCAT

United Nations
University Press

M.E. Sharpe

An East Gate Book

Copyright © The United Nations University Press, 1994

A publication of the United Nations University Press/World Institute
for Development Economics Research (UNU/WIDER), Helsinki, Finland

All rights reserved. No part of this book may be reproduced in any form without
written permission from The United Nations University Press.

First published in the United States in 1994 by M.E. Sharpe, Inc.,
80 Business Park Drive, Armonk, New York 10504, U.S.A.

First printed in Japan in 1994 by United Nations University Press, The United Nations
University, 53-70, Jingumae 5-chome, Shibuya-ku, Tokyo 150, Japan

ISBN (United Nations University Press): 92-808-0843-5
United Nations Sales No. E.94.111.A.2
ISBN (United Nations University Press): 92-808-0849-4 (pbk.)
United Nations Sales No. E.94.111.A.3 (pbk.)

HC
445
M867
1994

Library of Congress Cataloging-in-Publication Data

Muscat. Robert J.
The fifth tiger: a study of Thai development policy / Robert J. Muscat.
p. cm.
Includes bibliographical references and index.
ISBN 1-56324-323-7.—ISBN 1-56324-324-5 (pbk.)
1. Thailand—Economic policy.
2. Thailand—Politics and government.
I. Title.
HC445.M867   1994
338.9593—dc20
93-25775
CIP

Printed in the United States of America

The paper used in this publication meets the minimum requirements of
American National Standard for Information Sciences—
Permanence of Paper for Printed Library Materials,
ANSI Z 39.48-1984.

| BM (c) | 10 | 9 | 8 | 7 | 6 | 5 | 4 | 3 | 2 | 1 |
| BM (p) | 10 | 9 | 8 | 7 | 6 | 5 | 4 | 3 | 2 | 1 |

To
Chavalit Thanachanan
and
Snoh Unakul

CONTENTS

PREFACE

It is a pleasure to write a book about economic development in Thailand. At a time of uncertainty and self-doubt among economists over the ability of the discipline to offer secure policy prescriptions for many of the problems facing both the advanced industrial countries and the socialist countries in transition to market capitalism, there is a relatively high level of confidence that the profession knows good policy from bad when it comes to the large third category of nations, the less developed. That confidence derives from the analysis of past policy errors, crises, and disappointments in the pace of poverty alleviation, among large numbers of the less developed, on the one hand, compared with a smaller set of countries enjoying more successful outcomes, on the other hand. Thailand belongs to the smaller set, although its experience is not without its own failures and disappointments.

The writing of this work became possible when the World Institute for Development Economics Research decided that the Thai development policy experience merited a comprehensive study. My deep gratitude goes to WIDER and its director, Lal Jayawardene, for their generous financial support, and to the Thailand Development Research Institute, especially Executive Vice President Twatchai Yongkittikul, for their administrative and research support as the sponsoring institution. My gratitude also goes to the East Asian Institute of Columbia University—especially Jack Bresnan, Gerald L. Curtis, James W. Morley, and Andrew Nathan—for offering me an extended residence as visiting scholar.

To Dr. Puey Ungphakorn must go the greatest debt from anyone of my generation fortunate enough to have known him and to have learned from him. For an understanding of the events and policy issues of the seminal late 1950s and early 1960s, I owe much to the generosity of the late John Loftus and Khunying Supharb Yossundara, and to William Gilmartin.

My deepest thanks and appreciation for years of friendship, and for sharing with me their experience and judgment, go to Snoh Unakul, Chavalit Thanachanan, Kosit Panpiemras, Bunyaraks Ninsananda, Medhi Krongkaew, William J. Klausner, and John Eriksson. I owe a special debt to Snoh Unakul, who urged me to undertake this study, facilitated the arrangements, and gave so generously of his time and long experience in Thailand's policy processes.

There are many others who gave me important insights and encouragement, including George Abonyi, Akin Rabibhadana, Ammar Siamwalla, Anat Arbhabhirama, Anek Laothamatas, Chakramon Phasukavanich, M. R. Chandram S. Chandratat, Charad Cherdpongsathorn, Chirayu Isarangkun Na Ayuthaya, Richard Donor, Christopher Hermans, John Lewis, Jamie Mackie, Narongchai Akrasanee, Charles Myers, Nibhat Bhukkanasut, Theodore Panayotou, Phisit Pakkasem, Piyasavasti Amranand, Alek Rozental, Rungruang Isarangkura, Sanan Teekathananont, Santi Bang-Or, Jean-Christophe Simon, Sippananda Ketudat, Sompong Thanasaphon, Somsak Tambunlertchai, James Stent, Surachart Bamrungsuk, Surakiart Sathirothai, Tawat Yip In Tsoi, Thalerng Thamrong-Nawasawat, Thamarak Karnpisit, Thongroj Onchan, Peter Mytri Ungphakorn, Vijit Supinit, and Anthony Zola.

Finally, it is a pleasure to acknowledge Witit Rachatatanum for his research assistance, and Suvadee Kovatana and Beatrice Bridglall for their patience and competence in helping to prepare the manuscript.

To the institutions and all the individuals I have named goes much credit for this study's merits. Responsibility for its shortcomings and errors is entirely my own.

LIST OF TABLES

GLOSSARY AND ABBREVIATIONS

Glossary

changwat	province
amphur	district
baht (B)	Thai currency unit
rai	0.16 hectares; 0.4 acres
Isan	Northeast Thailand
Sangha	Buddhist hierarchy
Wat	Buddhist temple

Abbreviations

ASEAN	Association of Southeast Asian Nations
BOI	Board of Investment
BMR	Bangkok Metropolitan Region
CIPO	Center for Integrated Plan of Operations
CPT	Communist Party of Thailand
ESB	Eastern Seaboard
IBRD	International Bank for Reconstruction and Development, also known as the World Bank
IEAT	Industrial Estate Authority of Thailand
IFCT	Industrial Finance Corporation of Thailand
IMF	International Monetary Fund
JPPCC	Joint Public Private Sector Consultative Committee
NEDCOL	National Economic Development Corporation, Limited
NESDB	National Economic and Social Development Board
NFC	National Fertilizer Corporation
OECD	Organization for Economic Cooperation and Development
OECF	Overseas Economic Cooperation Fund
OPEC	Organization of Petroleum Exporting Countries

PAT	Port Authority of Thailand
PTT	Petroleum Authority of Thailand
SAL	Structural Adjustment Loan
TDRI	Thailand Development Research Institute
U.S. AID	U.S. Agency for International Development

CHRONOLOGY

June 1932	Revolution: Constitutional monarchy
	Government of Phraya Mano
October 1933	Coup attempt
March 1935	King Ananda succeeds after King Prachathipok abdicates
November 1938	Election: Government of Luang Phibunsongkhram
December 1941	Japanese invasion
August 1944	Government of Khuang Aphaiwong
August 1945	Government of Tawi Bunyakhet
September 1945	Government of M. R. Seni Pramoj
January 1946	Election: Second Khuang government
March 1946	Government of Pridi Phanomyong
June 1946	King Bhumibol succeeds upon King Ananda's death
August 1946	Election: Government of Thamrong Nawasawat
November 1947	Coup: Third Khuang government
January–April 1948	Election, coup, and second Phibunsongkhram government
October 1948	Coup attempt
February 1949	Coup attempt by Pridi
June 1951	"Manhattan" coup attempt
September 1957	Sarit Thanarat Group coup: Government of Pote Sarasin
December 1957	Election: Government of Thanom Kittikachorn
October 1958	Coup: Government of Sarit
December 1963	Second Thanom government
February 1969	Election: Third Thanom government
November 1971	Thanom coup: Fourth Thanom government
October 1973	Student uprising: Government of Sanya Dharmasakti
January 1975	Election: Second Seni government
March 1975	Government of M. R. Kukrit Pramoj
April 1976	Election: Third Seni government
October 1976	Coup: Thanin Kraivixien government

March 1977	Coup attempt
October 1977	Coup: Kriangsak Chomanan government
April 1979	Election: Second Kriangsak government
Mach 1980	Prem Tinsulanonda succeeds Kriangsak
March 1981	Second Prem government
April 1981	Yung Turks coup attempt
December 1981	Third Prem government
April 1983	Election: Fourth Prem government
September 1985	Coup attempt
July 1986	Election: Fifth Prem government
July 1988	Election: Chatichai Choonhaven government
February 1991	Coup: Interim government of Anand Panyarachum
March 1991	Election: Suchinda Kraprayoon government
May 1992	Anti-military crisis
June 1992	Second interim Anand government
September 1992	Election: Chuan Leekpai government

THE
FIFTH
TIGER

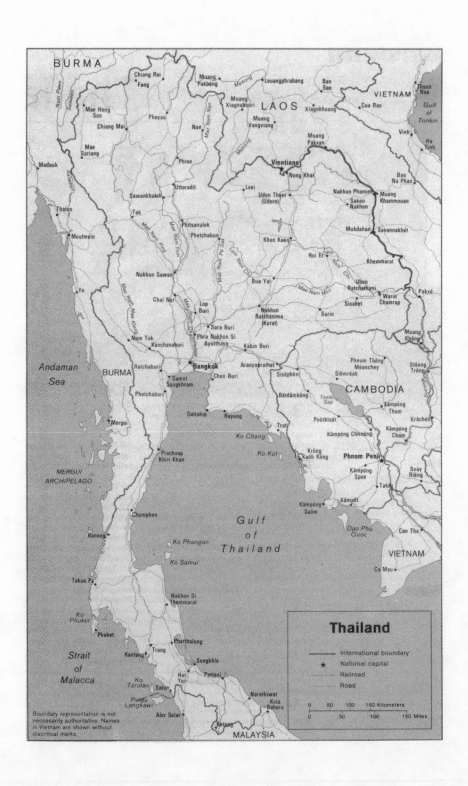

Thailand

International boundary
★ National capital
Railroad
Road

0   50   100   150 Kilometers
0   50   100   150 Miles

Boundary representation is not
necessarily authoritative. Names
in Vietnam are shown without
diacritical marks.

1

INTRODUCTION

Among the nonsocialist countries of East and Southeast Asia, their histories led to the adoption of trade-oriented market economies based on private ownership of the means of production. The reasons behind this common orientation differ from country to country. For example, Malaysia inherited a thriving capitalist economy from British colonialism; its continuation was implicit in the economic and political bargain between the Malay and Chinese communities on which the Malaysian polity rests. The economic orientation of Taiwan and South Korea was inherent in their responses to the security threats posed by mainland China and North Korea, respectively, and in their early economic and security dependence on the United States. Indonesia adopted a market economy policy after the Communist coup attempt in 1965. Thailand's route to a market economy was different still, as I shall explain in the body of this study. While the majority of countries of this region share a broad orientation that has contrasted sharply with socialist economics and with the highly protected, inward-looking policies that prevailed in much of the Third World in the postwar era, the development policies of the Southeast and East Asian countries have differed from one another in many respects. Their economic policy histories show substantial variation around the basic "model."

This region is of particular interest to students of modern economic development because the model has yielded more sustained and rapid economic growth than has been experienced by the developing countries that have pursued substantially different strategies. The super-performing economies—Taiwan, the Republic of Korea, Singapore, and Hong Kong—have become well known as the Four Tigers, or as the Asian NICs or Newly Industrializing Countries (Hong Kong, of course, is not a country). In the lead in the region has been Japan, the most super-performing economy of all. Behind the Tigers have been Indonesia, Malaysia, and Thailand, also growing relatively quickly, but not in the sustained

3

double-digit league. In the late 1980s Thailand did edge over into double-digit growth to become one of the fastest growing economies in the world.

The experience of Taiwan and Korea has deservedly commanded much attention. A considerable literature has accrued that analyzes the evolution of economic policy in these outstanding cases, drawing lessons that may be applicable to other developing countries. The Thai case has not received the attention it deserves. Like every country, Thailand has its unique history, culture, and resource endowment. The opportunities and threats it has faced in the postwar period have also had their unique characteristics. It differs from most developing countries in never having been colonized, in its long history of bureaucratic centralism, and in its unusual status as a major food exporter. In other important respects, however, Thailand's experience has been closer to that of the general run of developing countries than that of the Tigers, and it may contain lessons more readily applicable than those drawn from the economic management experience of the super-performers. Thailand has been more typical in its relatively modest (in relation to Korea and Taiwan in the 1950s and 1960s) volume of aid receipts; its high but not extraordinary levels of domestic saving and investment; its ethnic composition (less diverse than Malaysia, the subcontinent, or most of Africa and Latin America, but more diverse than homogeneous Japan, Taiwan, and Korea); in the extent of the threat to its survival (compared with Taiwan and Korea) and the pressures that threat put on government to press economic growth and industrialization; and in its character as a "soft" state, that is, a country where government has limited ability to impose its policy preferences or decisions on its citizens' economic (and other) behavior.

A primary objective of most nonindustrialized states has been to reduce poverty, to emulate the material, technical, and welfare achievements of the industrialized countries. (A few poor countries have been governed by regimes preferring stagnant isolation. Some larger number have been wrecked by governments predacious or malignant.) At different times over the past four decades or so, different schools of thought have risen, and fallen, regarding the most efficacious role for the state in the development process. In the 1950s and 1960s the dominant wisdom held that development required an active intervening state to overcome inadequacies of the private sector and of the operations of the market—for example, paucity of entrepreneurs, low domestic savings rates, technological weaknesses and other market information "failures," and small market size, inhibiting local industrial investment in the face of competing imports.

In the 1970s an international projection of this orientation, especially favored by Latin American economists, asserted that the world market system had enabled the already industrialized capitalist countries to erect an economic framework in which the less developed nations were locked into a dependent and essentially low-growth position. Throughout this postwar period, political motives aside, governments and economic managers in many developing countries were drawn to Marxist ideas and to "command" system models inspired by Soviet or Maoist experience.

The collapse of the command economies in the 1980s reinforced the palpable superiority of market systems and private property rights as a framework for modern human economic activity. Within this framework, however, there remains wide scope for greater or lesser government suasion or control over private economic decision making. In the early 1990s the argument has tended to crystallize. Analysts and advocates have clustered around two alternatives generally characterized as state minimalism versus market-friendly dirigism or intervention. Emphasizing the glaring inefficiencies and economic failures of government interventions over the years, the minimalists would limit severely the economic role of the state beyond that of watchdog over free-market rules of the game and provider of public goods (such as national defense and public education) not likely to be provided more efficiently, or equitably, by the private sector, a policy prescription commonly identified with the World Bank. The market-friendly dirigists point to the outstanding growth records of South Korea, Taiwan, and Japan as demonstrations of the superiority (or at least superior potential) of government guidance of the private sector, even its manipulation (e.g., through credit allocation), albeit well short of thoroughgoing command.

The political economy of decision making in Thailand has been the very opposite of that in Japan and the Asian NICs in one important respect: Thai governments normally *react* to the logic and pressure of economic conditions, waiting until they have built up a fair degree of consensus. These decision processes have generally reached the point of inaugurating policy adjustment well before macro conditions have gotten out of hand. But, for the most part, Thai governments have responded to pressures rather than attempting to shape the pattern of private-sector activity according to a technocratically predetermined set of objectives. In the Japanese and NIC models, government has played an initiating, leading, and directive role toward private investment and the evolution of the basic structural and comparative advantage characteristics of the economy.

The Thai experience stands between market-friendly dirigism (and its perverse cousin, market-inimical state intervention), on the one hand, and state minimalism, on the other. In this middle ground the Thai experience may be more apposite to the conditions of the large numbers of developing countries still struggling in the rear who are unlikely to be able to forge conditions conducive to the mandarin management at the heart of East Asian dirigism. The relative success of the Thai approach to economic affairs also serves as a demonstration that rapid growth in a "soft" state is feasible. In other words, the Thai experience (fluctuating between quasi-authoritarian and quasi-democratic episodes) stands, thus far, as a counter-instance to the proposition that has been put forward by some analysts that strong authoritarian governance and "hard" state economic intervention are necessary for developing countries to move onto a fast growth track.

Some writers have characterized Thai governments as passive with respect to economic policy, compared with the activism and initiatives of many other developing country governments.[1] At times, this "passivity" has taken the form of slow response to evident problems; as will be seen, this tardiness has been costly and merits criticism in some cases, but judicious (in retrospect) in other cases. There is another respect, however, in which apparent passivity, overlooked in development policy studies, has been a major part of the policy history. I refer to options that were rejected, policies and programs considered and discarded. As obvious as it may seem in 1994, after the collapse of the socialist command economies, the avoidance of bad policy (or rapid correction of bad policy, learning from palpable mistakes) has been one of the keys to sustained growth. The Thai economic policy record has been conspicuous for its avoidance of egregious resource allocation errors. Thus, to obtain a full understanding of Thai policy formation, this study will examine some important cases of what would otherwise be ignored as nonevents, that is, errors eschewed.

In any effort to describe and judge the policy experience of government over a long period of time, it is essential to distinguish between the more and the less important. Any day's reading of the Bangkok press would give one the impression (as would the press in any open society) that economic and related policies were the subject of heated debate in a sharply divided polity. There are always inconsistencies in policies and programs, and decisions that appear to be misguided, even unintelligent or venal. The basic policy history, however, is composed of those components that are the relatively powerful levers, the major determinants of an economy's performance, both short and long run. Among the determinants are the rules of the game respecting the roles of government and the private sector; public-sector performance in the provision of public goods and services; the extent and efficiency of market determination of prices and resource allocation decisions; government policies affecting the overall monetary and fiscal condition of the economy, the general price level, and the foreign exchange value of the currency; the climate for domestic and foreign investment; the underlying stability of the society; the health and education systems that build the stock of human capital; and development of the variety of technical, intellectual, and representational institutions that are essential to the functioning of a modern state and economy. In this study, I try to focus on the major determinants (while giving some sense of the deviations from the main thrusts), on the policy decision-making processes, and on the political and social forces working on these processes. In short, what did the Thais do, and why?

The Thai experience may also be instructive for the light it sheds on specific aspects of the development process, and on economic management of a relatively small international player that starts from a position of fledgling institutional capacities for the business of a modern state. Its "structural adjustment" experience in the 1980s, to correct macroeconomic imbalances resulting in part from the second "oil shock" in 1979, is particularly interesting in a comparative context. This study will review both macroeconomic and sectoral issues as part of a broad examination of the course of the economy over the post–World War II period. In addition, I shall examine some of the important interrelationships between economic and social change over this period. Thai intellectuals who are critical of the effects of modern development on Thai life frequently attribute the country's social ills to the economic technocrats who allegedly have led the society into a conception of progress that is material and acquisitive, at the expense of traditional values and purposes. It is incumbent upon anyone undertaking a broad analysis of Thailand's modern economic transformation to address these issues, and not presumptuously to assert that an economic framework alone is sufficient for considering the results that have flowed from a particular policy history.

The modern development of Thailand (and the other trade-oriented economies of the region) has been strongly influenced by the country's intellectual, economic, and security relationships with the industrialized world. At times, these influences have played important roles in the evolution of development policies of particular interest to this study. However, the major substance and contribution of foreign aid to Thailand's development has been in the creation of the institutional capacities required to develop and manage a modern state and in the education and training of Thai elites and professionals to lead and staff these institutions. By institutions, I refer to the panoply of public-sector functions needed to facilitate economic development and to the educational systems required for the creation of human capital. International technical assistance was particularly important in the 1950s and 1960s when these institutional capacities were, for the most part, initially designed and built up, and when overseas training of Thai technocrats and professionals was essential for "jump-starting" the institutional development process.

Many of these institutions, and the external aid projects assisting them, had "policy" functions in addition to programmatic responsibilities. That is to say, in their respective sectoral and subsectoral areas (e.g., teacher training, curriculum development, higher education faculties, population and family planning, communicable disease, mining, industrial finance, public administration, electric power generation and distribution, irrigation) these institutions played pivotal roles helping to define policies and public-sector objectives, and conducting policy-oriented research and pilot projects. Foreign technical aid was also critical for many of the operational agencies that in their formative years were receiving capital assistance for the initial expansion of transport and other infrastructure. Although the importance of sectoral institution-building and human capital formation processes for modern economic development cannot be overstated, my focus on broad development policy, especially its economic aspects, largely precludes extensive treatment of development management capacity at the sectoral level. The reader interested in fuller examination of Thailand's institutional development than is contained herein, and the role of foreign assistance, may refer to sources listed in the bibliography.

Finally, it is important to note that, for several areas of development policy, the country as a whole is too heterogeneous to be the proper unit of analysis. The pace and substance of social and economic change in Thailand have varied considerably from one part of the country to another. The overall policy frameworks adopted by Thai governments (respecting, for example, macroeconomic demand management or the external trade regime) have applied uniformly to all parts of the country. The effects of these general policies, however, have not been uniform, thanks to the substantial differences among regions. Some of the major policy issues, respecting public-sector programs and adjustments to macrolevel policies, have arisen out of the need to cope with these regional differences in resource endowment, rates of growth in income, production structure, and ethnic character. Among the most important of these inherent variations between regions has been their location on the map in relation to neighboring countries, especially affecting the Northeast, the region most directly exposed to the long-running instabilities in the former IndoChina states of Laos, Cambodia, and Vietnam.

Until recently, an adequate description of Thailand's economic geography could be based on a division of the country into four agroclimatic regions—Center, North, Northeast, and South. The Center largely comprises a flat alluvial plain not much above sea level. Much of the area is flooded for several months a year, naturally suitable for rice cultivation. The rivers flowing south into the Gulf of Thailand have given the Center a transportation system that has facilitated its traditional position as the country's "rice bowl" and producer of a rice export surplus. It was the ability of farmers in this region (and in similar flood plains elsewhere in Southeast Asia) to produce rice in excess of domestic needs, in response to growing export demand from the middle of the nineteenth century, that gave rise to the application of the term "vent for surplus" to describe the essential economic character of these regions.[2]

The principal theories of international trade describe the effects and gains from trade as arising out of the reallocation of domestic factors of production, within each trading partner economy, as each responds to the opportunities to focus on its own products of comparative advantage in production cost. The vent for surplus concept, in contrast, describes the process in which an agricultural region with underemployed land and labor applies these underemployed factors to expand production for export, without necessarily any change in technology or reallocation of factors in favor of a changed product mix. The Thai Central Plain experience was a classic example of this model.

The North is a region of mountains interlaced with north-south-oriented river valleys. Northern farmers have created a dense network of small local irrigation systems, mixing rice production with a variety of so-called upland crops. The

North is also home to numerous minority groups, commonly referred to as the Hill Tribes, who have practiced shifting cultivation for generations, best known to outsiders for growing poppy in the northerly areas that comprise Thailand's portion of the "Golden Triangle."

The long southern peninsula has a much wetter climate than the rest of the country. The main agricultural commodities have been tree crops, fruits, and rubber, with commercial fishing and tin mining as the other traditional main economic activities. Although rice is also produced in the South, it is relatively less important. The rhythm of economic activity in the South has thus been less seasonal than in the other regions of the country. The Northeast region, with about one-third of the country's area and population, has the poorest resource endowment. Rainfall is highly seasonal, and erratic from year to year. The soil is generally poor. Less than 15 percent of the arable land is believed to be irrigable.

For many decades Bangkok has been the primate city of Thailand. From the very start of the modern growth of industry, manufacturing facilities have been concentrated in Bangkok and its immediately surrounding suburbs. The locational structure of Thai industry, and the concentration of urban growth in the greater Bangkok region, have been the almost inevitable consequences of the country's geographic configuration—the bulk of trade (except for southern rubber and tin) moving south to the gulf for export, with imports off-loading at the head of the gulf. The centralized government, the seat of political power, and the headquarters of finance and commerce are all located at this geographic focus. The economies of concentration from this configuration are apparently enormous, reinforced by the traditional concentration in Bangkok of higher education, advanced medical services, the foreign community, the media, and other leading institutions and cultural centers.

The traditional fourfold (or fivefold if Bangkok is counted separately from the Central region) division of the country's socioeconomic geography is becoming an oversimplification. As the economy has diversified in the last twenty years, the large regions are becoming too diverse for treatment as homogeneous areas respecting agricultural, distributive, and other policy areas.

The evolution of Thai economic and social policy falls neatly into periods that coincide with the successive political periods marking the country's history. An understanding of this evolution can best be gained through recurrent examination of sectoral and macro policy issues in their successive political contexts. Thus, the plan of this book is chronological, starting with a review in chapter 2 of the historical background (up to World War II) and the emergence of characteristics and preferences in public policy that would carry over into modern development. Chapter 3 covers the first postwar period (1945–57), characterized by political instability and by potentially destabilizing economic objectives. Chapter 4 covers the period of autocratic rule ushered in by Marshal Sarit, a period of strong economic growth that set the fundamentals that have governed Thai development policy ever since. A popular reaction against the military's authoritarian rule gave birth to the "democracy period" (1973–76) with its focus on distributive justice, the subject of chapter 5. The democracy period ended abruptly in a violent reaction. Chapter 6 covers the period under Prime Minister Prem (1980–88) in which a restored political calm and social stability provided the framework for "structural adjustment," that is, the restoration of macroeconomic balance and the correction of policy distortions that had built up in the previous decade. The Prem years were followed by two relatively short, highly contrasted regimes. The first (1988–91) was a parliamentary-based government under which Thailand became perhaps the fastest growing economy in the world despite the government's inattention to economic policy. The second (1991 to early 1992) was an interregnum of technocratic government (put in place by a military coup) that picked up the process of policy reform left unfinished at the end of the Prem period. After an election in March 1992 that left unresolved constitutional issues regarding the political role of the military, the country fell into a crisis. Massive prodemocracy demonstrations were met by military force. The ensuing bloodshed brought down and discredited the military leadership. In a second election, in September 1992, the "prodemocracy" parties not associated with the military took power and restored civilian government. The social and economic forces gathering over the past three decades had erupted to propel the political system toward civilian, constitutional government. The crisis and its resolution appear to have been a major watershed. Chapter 7 concludes with a review of major social and economic issues of the 1990s and of the challenges to future economic and social management.

2

HISTORICAL ROOTS OF MODERN POLICY

The Old Order

People speaking Tai languages and dialects live over a wide area of Southeast Asia, southern China, Burma, and northeastern India. The total number of Tai speakers was estimated at seventy million in 1983,[1] of whom about fifty million lived in Thailand.

Although the history of Thailand before the fourteenth century is relatively obscure and the subject of much scholarly debate, there is general agreement on the broad outlines of a lengthy migration of Tai-speaking peoples from China down into Southeast Asia. Moving south in small groups, the Tai speakers met, fought, and intermixed with unrelated peoples like the Mons who already lived in the areas that would be dominated gradually by the Tai as the latter increased in numbers and linguistically and culturally absorbed the earlier inhabitants. Only in the mid-fourteenth century does the history of the various Tai principalities begin to emerge with some clarity. By common usage, the Tai who occupied the alluvial central plains of the Chao Phraya River were already known as Siamese. As the kingdoms on the central plain extended their suzerainty over wider areas occupied by principalities already speaking different forms of Tai, and over areas inhabited by people linguistically unrelated (such as the Khmer, the modern-day Cambodians) or even more distant both linguistically and culturally (such as the Moslem Malays in the peninsular south), the state of Siam gradually emerged. By the early nineteenth century, Bangkok exercised sovereignty over a large area that included present-day Cambodia and Laos and several Malay sultanates. Over the course of the nineteenth century, Siam lost most of these latter dependency areas to French and British colonial encroachment as modern Siam (the name was changed to Thailand in 1939) crystallized within its present borders. The modern-day term "Thai," referring to the citizens of Thailand, connotes a people and identity that developed over a long period of assimilation among the Tai, the earlier cultures, and the more recent immigrants from China and elsewhere.

The dominant principality that developed into the first extensive Siamese kingdom, a major power in Southeast Asia, was centered on the glittering capital city of Ayudhya. In 1767 the Siamese, weakened by internal rivalries, were unable to raise a Burmese siege. Ayudhya fell and was sacked and completely destroyed by the Burmese. The Thais recovered rapidly and established a reinvigorated state. A new capital was established at Thonburi near the mouth of the Chao Phraya River, then moved in 1782 to Bangkok on the opposite bank. The second monarch of the new state, King Ramathibodi (or Rama I, 1782–1809), was the first of the Chakri dynasty, the royal line that has continued as head of state up to the present time.

Modern Thai history begins with (more accurately, was initiated by) King Mongkut in the middle of the nineteenth century. Given the central role played by the monarchy, it will be useful to the reader unfamiliar with Thai history to note the monarchs and dates of the dynasty:

Mongkut (Rama IV)	1851–1868
Chulalongkorn (Rama V)	1868–1910
Vajiravudh (Rama VI)	1910–1925
Prajadhipok (Rama VII)	1925–1935 (abdicated)
Ananda Mahidol (Rama VIII)	1935–1946
Bhumibol Adulyadej (Rama IX)	1946–

Thailand's modern history—certainly its modern economic history—can be dated precisely from 1855, the year King Mongkut concluded a treaty with Great Britain that established the basis for commercial relations between the two countries. Named after the British negotiator, who became a close friend of the king, the Bowring Treaty opened Siam to foreign trade after a long period of virtual closure to Western contact and set the pattern for similar treaties with other Western nations. When Mongkut ascended the throne at the age of forty-seven, after twenty-seven years in the Buddhist monkhood, he had a reputation as a man of powerful intellect, learned in foreign languages and in Western science, a Buddhist reformer, an admirer of Western civilization. Above all, he and his closest modern-minded associates realized that the traditional Siamese polity and economy would have to change in fundamental ways for the country to be able to avoid losing its independence to European colonialism.

During Mongkut's seventeen years of rule and his son Chulalongkorn's lengthy forty-two year rule, from the mid-eighteenth century until shortly before the First World War, Siamese statecraft faced three principal issues: maintenance of independence, internal political consolidation, and development of economic and administrative strength. These three essential objectives were interrelated.

The consolidation of central control over previously loosely governed outlying regions was vital in order to reduce the opportunities that loose integration created for territorial encroachment by France on the east from Indochina, and by Great Britain on the west and south from Burma and the Malay sultanates. Administrative reforms and the development of key central institutions would be necessary to give Bangkok the capability to exercise more effective and extended internal management. A growing economic and commercial base would be required to finance the state's expanding functions and to avoid the financial weakness or misadventure that had undermined independent states elsewhere and opened the way to European intervention.

By the time of King Chulalongkorn's death in 1910, these three broad objectives can be said to have been met. Based on a policy of close association with and accommodation to Great Britain, Siam's independence had been maintained in an era when large areas of Asia and Africa were falling under colonial rule. To develop and sustain its position as a buffer between British and French possessions, Siam had to relinquish suzerainty over large outlying Cambodian, Lao, and Malay jurisdictions. Under the Bowring and subsequent treaties the monarchs granted extraterritorial rights over the legal treatment of the respective foreign nationals. The treaties also fixed the rules for foreign trade and inland commerce, greatly reducing the scope for an independent Siamese fiscal or trade policy. In addition to putting restraints on the government's ability to mobilize financial resources, the treaties eliminated state trading and most government and private monopolies. In effect, the treaties established a free-trade regime under which infant-industry protectionism was precluded.

It is important to note that the provisions of the Bowring Treaty were negotiated within the general context of European colonial advance in Asia, but not under any direct duress. In fact King Mongkut entered into the treaty quite willingly, brushing aside opposition from nobles and officials to provisions that were detrimental to their interests. Regardless of how one interprets the motivations for the foreign economic policies of Rama IV and Rama V (I will touch on this below), these policies did contribute to sustaining the integrity of the Thai state.

Toward the end of King Chulalongkorn's reign the treaties were renegotiated to eliminate the extraterritorial and financial restrictive provisions. Starting from a social configuration, worldview, and technological level utterly different from contemporary Europe, the Chakri monarchs had launched a broad process of modernization and state consolidation. The study of Western science had been introduced. Slavery and corvée labor were eliminated. Large-scale immigration of Chinese labor had been undertaken to provide manpower for the construction of railway, irrigation, and other projects. A central administration had been created, based on a powerful bureaucracy. Under the stimulus of foreign trade, the country's export capacity had grown steadily based on a vast expansion of rice production and on the extraction of tin from the southern peninsula and teak from the northern provinces.

Between the end of the First World War and the coup that ended the absolute monarchy in 1932, Thailand was severely shaken first by a deep drought and later by the effects of the world economic depression. In sharp contrast with the adulation enjoyed by Chulalongkorn, Kings Vajiravudh and Prajadhipok suffered a loss of confidence and authority and were unable to provide a sense of direction so characteristic of Rama IV and Rama V, in a period when problems of short-run economic instability dominated over the issues of long-run modernization and development. It was only in the decade after the Second World War that Thailand, still with a very low per capita income and an economy similar in many respects to the legions of Third World states only beginning to emerge from colonialism, entered on the path of modern economic growth and change that is the subject of this book.

My purpose for the remainder of this chapter is not to recount Thailand's economic history in any detail before World War II. Rather I shall try to identify the salient characteristics of the historical period that appear to have had strong continuing influence in recent years and that may be helpful in an attempt to understand the dynamics of contemporary Thai development policy processes and policy content. Some of these characteristics become evident immediately when one confronts the paradox that leaps out from even the briefest account of the century prior to World War II. After a century of independence and purposive modernization, why was Thailand still such an underdeveloped country? Why was independent Thailand less developed—lower income per capita, lower literacy, undeveloped educational system, more rudimentary economic infrastructure, lower productivity agriculture, and so on—compared with Malaysia and with the Philippines, two colonies that achieved independence only after the war? Why had Japan, also never colonized, developed so much more rapidly than Thailand?

The sense of lost development opportunity has been felt by Thai scholars most acutely in the comparison with Japan because of certain striking historical similarities. Both countries closed themselves off from contact with the West in the middle of the eighteenth century. Both countries were reopened at almost the same time in the mid-nineteenth century, Japan by the Treaty of Kanagawa with Commodore Perry in 1854 and Thailand, as noted above, by the treaty with Sir John Bowring of Great Britain in 1855. The two countries also appear to have shared some broadly similar characteristics significant for economic development:

> Both countries maintained their political independence; both were characterized by a homogeneous culture, awareness of national identity, a high degree of authority enjoyed by the central government, and an early realization by the rulers that it was imperative for national survival to learn Western methods. Even in more direct economic facts there were similarities, especially in that both had ample markets abroad for the principal foreign exchange earner (silk for Japan and rice for Thailand).[2]

At the same level of historical and social generality, however, one can also point to major differences. Japan started the Meiji Restoration period with a more literate and better educated populace, a more unified polity, more highly developed commerce, and the samurai class that was readily transformed into an industrial entrepreneurial class. The modernization process in Japan was forced at a much higher pace, under the imperatives of a geopolitical perception very different from that of the Chakri monarchs in Thailand. Japan was an island nation under a policy regime that envisaged an expansion of national power in the region and the rapid development of naval capability to challenge czarist Russia. Thailand was surrounded by French and British colonial inroads. France and Britain had effectively eliminated any further military threat from Thailand's traditional rival neighbors, but military confrontation with the European powers was recognized as futile and even self-defeating for Thai independence (as it had been, in fact, for the Burmese, who lost their independence after crossing the Indian border to attack the British in 1824). The Thais faced the problem of coping through diplomacy, territorial concessions, maneuvering between and playing off the French and British, and avoiding provocative acts that could serve as *casus belli*. While Rama IV and Rama V carried out policies of modernization, such as legal and administrative reform, reentering trade with the West, education of the elite in British schools, investment in rail transport and other infrastructure supportive of the trade expansion, and development of a greater tax base, the pace was gradual. There is no indication that the Chakri monarchs ever conceived of a Japanese option—creation of modern armed forces with external conflict capabilities, based on a forced-pace adoption of Western industrial and military technologies—as a feasible strategy for maintaining independence. Whatever may have been the relative importance of geopolitical, cultural, administrative, dynastic, or other factors,[3] the resulting economic policy is clear. Assisted by British financial advisers, successive Thai governments modernized slowly and undertook what can only be described as preliminary programs for turning the machinery of government into an engine of development, supplemented limited domestic investment funds with very modest foreign borrowing, and thereby engendered (and limited) a development process that brought about very gradual social and technological change between the Bowring Treaty and the end of the absolute monarchy in 1932.

Before turning to an examination of the policy content of this long period, I should note that my conclusion—that the monarchy, at least up until the death of Chulalongkorn in 1910, served the national interests of Thailand well—follows the mainstream view of historians, but is a view that has been challenged in recent years. I have noted the costs incurred in maintaining Thai independence, in terms of territory ceded and economic growth foregone. Needless to say, there is no way of knowing what might have been if Siam had resisted the restrictive provisions of the Bowring Treaty or had then, or later, in other ways, attempted to loosen these constraints earlier or to promote more rapid internal modernization and economic expansion. Nevertheless, the critics of the mainstream view, more or less explicitly assuming that Siam could have developed more rapidly without loss of independence, interpret the conservatism of past economic policies as having been promoted by deliberate monarchical resistance to more rapid change, designed as much to protect royal power as to parry external powers. In the most trenchant exposition of this revisionist interpretation, Benedict Anderson argues that the Chakri policies were centralizing and "absolutizing" rather than "modernizing," class-based rather than nation-state building (evidenced by the encouragement of Chinese immigration that led to commerce being in Chinese rather than ethnic Thai hands; and by the employment of large numbers of foreign advisers, some of whom wielded great influence if not actual power), and colonial (or "colonial-style") rather than independent or indigenous in character.[4]

Since there is little dispute about the essential facts of this period, one cannot avoid the impression that this debate is mainly semantic, hanging on the looseness of definition of the terminology and the seeming plausibility of alternative characterizations of history's inevitable ambiguities and anomalous features. Thus, the scholar John Girling turns the same Chakri policies on their head and draws the opposite conclusion from Anderson's: "the Thai elite associated with Chulalongkorn adopted certain practices of colonialism primarily in order to *escape* colonialism" (original emphasis).[5] Furthermore, rather than disparaging the economic expansion of the period, Girling is impressed at its extent and notes that the expansion was made possible by policies that were national in effect even if "dynastic" when viewed from a twentieth-century perspective:

> To improve and extend royal authority, to maintain kingly power in a changing, uncertain, even hostile environment: these, of course were dynastic rather than "national" aims, at least in the modern or democratic sense. Chulalongkorn, like Louis XIV, might well have declared, "*L'Etat, c'est moi*" ("I am the state"). Unlike Louis XIV, however, Chulalongkorn did *not* lead his country into ruinous wars for the sake of dynastic ambitions. On the contrary, he was spared the possibility of warfare with Siam's traditional enemies or rivals, Burma and Vietnam, because their rulers had been overthrown or rendered harmless by colonial occupation; and . . . he successfully sought to avoid conflict with either Britain or France. As a result of these and other factors, conditions were favorable for economic development, the extent of which is indicated by the enormous expansion of rice cultivation and the tenfold increase in exports in half a century.[6]

The leading Thai historians putting forth the revisionist interpretation of this historical period include Chatthip Nartsupha, Suthy Prasartset, Montri Chenvidyakarn, and Sompop Manarungsan. These scholars have downplayed the importance of the external constraints imposed by the treaties and inherent in Thailand's geopolitical exposure. By giving less weight to the exigencies of external policy, they have reinterpreted the domestic policies and actions of the nineteenth- and early twentieth-century governments as designed to promote the interests of the governing elite class at the expense, where necessary, of the interests of the other two main classes in the society, the Thai peasants and the nonagricultural Chinese immigrants.

At the risk of oversimplification, one can summarize this neo-Marxist challenge to the mainstream historians by drawing on Ian Brown's recent review of the debate.[7] Brown poses the issues that are key to an understanding of the policy objectives and the measures pursued by Siam in this period. "Did the Siamese administrative elite perceive either the necessity for, or the desirability of, promoting a markedly different pattern of economic change?" If the elite would have preferred a markedly different policy orientation, did it have room for maneuver? "To what extent and in what way was the administration constrained by either external or internal circumstances (including the self-interest of its own governing elite) from promoting an alternative pattern of economic change?"

> These questions have also been of central concern to the vigorous community of Thai historians . . . which has come to prominence from the early 1970s. . . . Central (to their response) is the assertion that . . . the king (frequently working through a wider royal and noble elite) controlled the major part of Siam's land, labour, and capital resources. . . . This concentration of economic power . . . meant that that class absorbed a severely disproportionate share of the kingdom's surplus product, while the cultivators . . . were reduced to bare subsistence. . . . Thus in the late nineteenth and early twentieth centuries, government expenditure was heavily concentrated on defence, internal security, and the court: only relatively small allocations were made to education or to developmental projects.
>
> Also of central importance in this analysis is the characterization of the kingdom's Chinese merchant community. It is argued that the flood of Western manufactures into Siam from the middle of the nineteenth century prevented those Chinese from establishing the industrial interests that would have provided them with a direct control over surplus production. As a result, they were forced to rely on the *sakdina* elite for access to surplus production, and in this way were drawn into a subordinate relationship with it. . . . They remained a dependent bourgeoisie, constrained from technical and organizational innovation and from the accumulation of capital. . . .
>
> The stagnation of productivity and the essential absence of diversification in agriculture is explained in part by the cultivators' impoverishment . . . [and] by the concentration of landownership in the hands of the *sakdina* elite. . . . But a particular emphasis is placed here on the failure of the government. In the early twentieth century the Siamese administration may have discussed at length a wide range of proposals to improve agricultural practices in the kingdom, but no significant action was ever taken. . . .
>
> [Regarding industry] again, particular emphasis is placed on the failure of the government. In the early twentieth century, the government elite, with the partial exception of the Crown, is seen to have disposed of its acquired surplus largely in luxurious consumption, leaving little for capital investment in industrial initiatives.[8]

Brown's study is a meticulous examination of the documentary record of this period, focusing on the technical and policy debates within the government, and the actual measures undertaken, respecting irrigation, rice technology, tin and teak development, and the promotion of domestic banking and industrial projects. He concludes that the revisionist interpretation cannot be corroborated by the empirical evidence. In the first decade of the century, the administration was clearly formulating a more promotional policy. The range of research and investment projects was sharply constrained by financial considerations (tied to foreign policy considerations). The successes and failures among the projects it did undertake can be fully explained by the economic circumstances. In the end, Brown speculates that the Siamese elite may well have been satisfied at the economic expansion and change the country was so evidently undergoing. Although there were a few dissatisfied voices, the elite as a whole appeared to have been molded by one last external intellectual influence: "the economic orthodoxy of that time, an orthodoxy that held that economies in the non-European world would secure a firmly based prosperity through strong specialization in the production and export of those (agricultural and mineral) commodities in which they had a comparative advantage . . . a final external constraint, not here on the freedom of action of the Siamese administrative elite, but on their perceptions and horizons."[9]

The two later monarchs, between Chulalongkorn and the 1932 coup, were also modernizers in the sense that they undertook further reform and development of the civil service, introduced ideas of nationalism inspired by continental European concepts, and contemplated (with no effective follow-through) political reform based on constitutional democracy. Openly criticized in their own times, their policies and the motivations of their supporting elite class have been criticized strongly by some contemporary Thai scholars, both for delaying the country's political modernization and for the foregone opportunities for more rapid economic development.[10]

The most condemnatory interpretations of the policies of the old order have been put forward by writers on the far left of the spectrum of Thai thought. These most revisionist interpretations were frankly intended to serve as points of departure for a Marxist, indeed revolutionary analysis and program for Thailand in the 1970s. Consideration of these authors' interpretation of recent economic change will be postponed until later, at which point I shall also consider the completely opposite view of a group of Thai intellectuals who hold that recent economic development and "modernization" have been excessively rapid and thereby deleterious in impact on Thai culture.

I have already noted some of the elements of the country's economic and mdernization policies in this historic period. A list of the major elements would include the following:

1. Promotion of production for export, based entirely on natural resource (agricultural and mining) commodities that were processed (milled or concen-

trated) only to the first stage that turned them into tradeable goods,

2. Reform of manpower institutions (slavery and corvée) to encourage greater numbers of scarce Thai labor to put idle cultivable land into rice production,
3. Tax incentives for land settlement and production,
4. Public-sector investment in irrigation, communications, and rail transit,
5. Encouragement of private investment in irrigation canals in the rice delta just north of Bangkok,
6. Promotion of Chinese immigration to provide nonagricultural labor,
7. Encouragement of private business and banking, largely foreign and Chinese owned and managed,
8. Strengthening of public administration,
9. Implementation of all the above within a framework of fiscal and monetary conservatism.

The remainder of this chapter will explore some aspects of these policies that have had significant impact on the development issues confronting Thailand in the most recent, post–World War II period, and on contemporary Thai policy and orientation.

The Resource Endowment: Policies of Manpower Mobilization

In retrospect, one can imagine that if the nineteenth-century Siamese had had the inclination to formulate systematic development plans they would have rationalized much of their policy package as flowing from the basic resource configuration of the country—land abundance and labor scarcity—and the need to increase the size of the labor force and extend the area of land exploitation.

For much of history, Thailand and its immediately surrounding areas were very sparsely inhabited. During the centuries of recurrent warfare and skirmishing between the rival principalities and kingdoms of the region, especially between the Thai and the Burmese (but also among the Thai), the strategic objective of these conflicts was control over populations, not territories per se. Population density was so low that there was no resource advantage to be gained by the mere extension of borders. None of the principalities was in position to settle extensive new land areas with surplus population. On the contrary, the chief spoils of war were captured populations brought back to settle inside the areas in which the rival rulers were able to exercise effective direct control. There are many communities in central and northeastern Thailand today inhabited by people whose Lao cultural identity, while no longer varying substantially from that of other Thais living in the same areas, derives from their having been resettled in Thailand as a result of warfare between the Thai and Lao kingdoms as late as the early eighteenth century.

It is no exaggeration to say that mobilization of and control over manpower was the central internal problem facing Thai statecraft for at least four centuries up to the end of the nineteenth. Drawing on early traditions of both the Tai and the Indianized Khmer, the Siamese monarchs developed a system of manpower control that integrated major cultural and material dimensions of the society—the distribution of power, the class structure, the military mobilization system, economic relationships, civil administration, religious sanction, and interpersonal relations and etiquette. It would take us beyond the scope of the present study to do justice to the complexities of this system and to its evolution over time.[11] Nevertheless, it is important to touch upon some of the salient aspects of the control system, because of its continuing impact on socioeconomic change even in the modern era.

The legitimacy and theory of absolute monarchy in Thailand long rested on two separate historical traditions. One was the Buddhist tradition under which a king derived and sustained his right to rulership through his moral authority and rectitude as demonstrated in his adherence to Buddhist principles of justice toward his subjects. The subjects, in turn, owed their loyalty to the monarch as a moral obligation in recognition of his demonstrated merit. In modern times (i.e., since King Mongkut uncovered transcriptions attributed to King Ramkhamhaeng dated to A.D. 1292) this tradition has been connected to a concept of rulership, in the earliest Tai states, based on an absence of despotic controls and on a ready access of any humble subject to the monarch himself. The second tradition was quite different, based on the adoption of Hindu concepts of the god-king and a hierarchical social system, which were drawn from Angkor following the Siamese destruction of Khmer power in the fourteenth century.

The Sakdina, Corvée, and Slavery

In their adaptation of Khmer principles of organization and governance, the Thai rulers developed what may well have been one of the most elaborate systems of manpower registration, stratification, and administration ever devised, the so-called *sakdina* (dignity marks) system.[12]

Under this system every person in the kingdom was assigned a rank and a corresponding *sakdina* number. Slaves were lowest with a *sakdina* of 5 units. Peasant freemen were assigned a *sakdina* of 25, petty officials from 100 to 400. Seven ranks of nobility were assigned *sakdina* from 400 to 30,000. Just below the king, the heir apparent had a *sakdina* of 100,000. Based largely on *sakdina* and honorific title, an elaborate edifice was created in which rank defined every individual's legal status and entitlements, social position, obligations, and behavior and etiquette, and even "a religious element, the belief that a person attained a higher status on account of his past religious merit, or [good] Karma."[13] In essence, the *sakdina* was a comprehensive system for placing the entire society within a finely delineated hierarchy that would enable the monarch to control the distribution of political power and mobilization of manpower, the ultimate power base on which all the assigned perquisites and political and economic positions rested. As Akin summarizes it, "The area being underpopulated, the labor force necessary to the performance of work and services had to be organized as efficiently as possible. The king, the peak of the society, was in theory the owner of all manpower within the kingdom. He distributed the people to be under the protection of his officials ... according to their ranks as defined by the *sakdina* system. Thus a gigantic hierarchy of officials emerged ... hierarchies of patrons and clients."[14]

The hierarchy divided into four classes—princes of the royal blood (who could be quite numerous in this polygamous society), nobility, freemen commoners, and slaves. Control of freemen and slaves by lower nobility (who doubled as military commanders and/or civil administrators), and of lower nobility by individual patrons of higher *sakdina*, set the pattern, at any time, of the distribution of political power and economic status. Within specified limits, nobility and royal patrons controlled labor time, produce, or funds of their clients, the lesser nobility, freemen and slaves. Originally developed to meet the premodern requirements of military mobilization, of consolidating and administering the emerging Thai state, and of taxation and resource mobilization for civil works, the system became a barrier to modernization and economic response to the conditions of the nineteenth century.

The individual freeman lost control over half his own labor time through the requirement that he provide his patron up to six months of corvée labor each year. Alternatively, a freeman in economic straits could (usually voluntarily) become a bondsman, or slave (or give a member of his family over to indenture), in which condition the individual lost all control over his labor.

Like the corvée, slavery originated early in Thai history. In the mid-nineteenth century slavery was still widespread but was judged to be of a "mild form." The institution had arisen from "the right of free men to sell themselves into bondage, which in most cases was exercised with the object of extricating these persons from financial difficulties."[15] As Ingram describes it, a free man could obtain security by voluntarily entering into slavery for the holder of his debt "since the owner had to provide food, clothing, and shelter without any increase in the debt owed . . . [it] appears probably that more people were attracted to some form of bondage by the security and protection it provided, than were driven to it by dire economic necessity."[16]

There were several categories of slavery in Thailand that were tantamount to different forms of bonded service.[17] Several writers on Thai slavery, both Thai and foreign, have noted the fact that the Thai term (*that*) referring to these various forms of servitude has no equivalent in Western languages and that they continue, regretfully, to use the word slavery for convenience and lacking any ready alternative. Thus Akin writes that "The necessity to use the word 'slave' for *that* is very unfortunate. The ideas associated with the word 'slave' in the Western world are quite different from the ideas associated with the word *that*." He notes that there was no slave market in Thailand; masters had no power of life and death and could be severely punished for physical maltreatment of their *that*; and he cites Bowring, who asserted that the *that* were treated better than were servants in England.[18]

In effect, the different forms of servitude arose from individual patron-client relationships that were created when a freeman applied to a patron for a loan, unable to offer any collateral except his own, or his family's, labor.

> Thai society was permeated with client and patron relationships. . . . In general the relationship . . . was interdependent. Further, it was the role of the patron to protect and help his client. When the client became destitute, the patron had to help him, and that was by lending him money. In such a society when there was no organized police force, and it was easy for a debtor to abscond, the rate of interest had to be extremely high. The best security for a loan to a man was to have the debtor or his child or his wife living in and serving in the creditor's household. Their services could be taken for the interest. . . . Thus a debtor or his wife or child would then become a *that*.[19]

There appears to be no reliable basis for estimating the proportion of the labor force that was bound by these arrangements and thereby unable to exercise free choice over their economic activity. Bowring wrote in 1857 that no less than one-third of the Thai population were *that*, but that the majority of *that* were in the category of persons who could redeem themselves by paying back their loans, and that most of the "irredeemable" slaves "absconded when they got an opportunity, and the owner had no redress."[20] Despite all the qualifications and complexities regarding the extent and nature of individual servitude in nineteenth-century Thailand, there can be little doubt that the totality of these arrangements put a significant constraint on a substantial proportion of the labor force, and thereby reduced economic efficiency under conditions of labor scarcity.

King Chulalongkorn gradually eliminated slavery through a series of decrees between 1874 and final abolishment in 1905. The provisions need not be described in detail, except to note that the process was a classic example of Thai gradualism. By setting absolute time limits on further entry into slave status and on the duration of such service for those already slaves, and by setting relatively costless manumission procedures, King Chulalongkorn achieved this major social and economic reform without polarizing the society and with little economic dislocation or serious opposition. The corvée was already declining in the mid-eighteenth century. As with slavery, the corvée was eliminated through gradual legal reform up to the end of the century.

These reforms were undertaken for a mix of motives including political tensions between the monarchy and the nobility; the state's need to shift to a more effective system of resource mobilization based on money taxes rather than labor and produce in kind; the recognition that both these institutions were anachronisms and "uncivilized" by Western standards; and a growing awareness that neither slavery nor corvée were as efficient as a labor market system based on freemen, that is, on free farmers and money wages. While it is not clear in magnitude how important was the linkage between these manpower reforms and the major economic change in Thailand in the nineteenth century, viz. the expansion of rice production, it is clear that rice expansion was the central production policy objective of the government (reflected in incentive land taxation and other measures to encourage land clearing and paddy cultivation) and that the personal freedom resulting from the reforms did increase significantly the numbers of freemen farmers and their rice output.[21]

By the middle of the nineteenth century, the *sakdina* system was in an advanced state of decay. Akin attributes the modification and then decline of the system to six factors: (1) the divisive weaknesses the system developed, which contributed to the catastrophic destruction of Ayudhya in 1767; (2) the realization by the Chakri monarchy that the threat of European colonialism necessitated domestic reform to strengthen the country's position; (3) the influx of Western ideas; (4) the opening of the country to international trade and the resulting changes in the economic relationships that had underpinned the old patron-client networks; (5) the influx of Chinese laborers from the early 1800s undermining the economic rationale for the old corvée labor system; (6) tax system changes introduced by Rama II that weakened the economic position of large numbers of officials who could then no longer maintain their status as patrons.[22] The first great wave of economic modernization thus hastened the decline of a centuries-old societal system no longer effective for coping with the nineteenth-century realities of colonial challenge, monetization, and new ideas.

Although the formal hierarchical system disappeared (except for residual titles among royal descendants), the predilection to hierarchy and to a social system in which people group themselves in patron-client networks had become deeply embedded in Thai society, the subject of extensive analysis by historians and by students of contemporary Thai bureaucratic and political behavior. (It is ironic that many Western anthropologists in the 1950s and 1960s saw Thai family and community relationships at the village level as essentially atomistic, with a far less formal and fixed structure than in most other societies. The "loosely-structured" characterization of Thai society is no longer considered accurate, a subject I shall return to below.)

Land Abundance and Expansion of Cultivation

The tax incentive policies for land settlement and cultivation were probably marginal in their impact compared with the sheer availability of land and the apparently powerful appeal of agriculture over all other occupations for the Thai. Quite unlike the situation in much of Latin America, the Indian subcontinent, or the Philippines, the bulk of the Thai peasantry, by long tradition, could settle and farm as much land as a farmer could cultivate. As Ingram describes the situation in the nineteenth century:

The freeman could take possession of uncultivated land as long as he went about it properly. In all parts of the country there was an abundance of unused lands which only needed to be cleared and cultivated. Once he had fulfilled requirements, the applicant had full rights over the land, although in theory his right remained that of a usufructuary. Nevertheless, the freeman could sell or mortgage his land. The king could take it back for public purposes, or if it went uncultivated for three years.[23]

Legislation in 1908 codified the right of people to settle as much land as they could "turn to profit." The Land Act of 1936 reaffirmed free settlement rights but put a limit of 50 rai on the amount of land that could be claimed.[24] In the nineteenth century land-tax incentives were introduced to encourage people to clear and cultivate new land.

One consequence of the free availability of land was the unimportance of land rent before 1850, perhaps because land had no exchange value.[25] Tenancy was rare in Thailand except for areas of the lower central plain rice delta close to Bangkok. Although twenty-five rai seems to have been the accepted upper limit on the size holding of the ordinary farmer prior to the 1936 legislation, average holdings are thought to have been considerably less, perhaps reflecting family size labor limitations and lack of incentive to produce surplus for exchange in a largely subsistence economy before the advent of the rice export trade. Royal land grants did create some large holdings in the lower central plain region, but these holdings did not grow, and the distribution of land remained relatively even. Once slavery and the corvée had been eliminated, the free availability of land virtually ensured the absence of landlessness.

Chinese Immigrant Manpower: Ethnic Division of Labor

To meet the shortage of labor outside agriculture, the government encouraged Chinese immigration. The number of Chinese at the time of the Bowring Treaty has been estimated at around 300,000, or 5–6 percent of Siam's total population of 5–6 million. Annual Chinese immigration rose to a peak in the 1920s, as high as 140,000. By 1950 Chinese were estimated to number around 3 million, roughly 15 percent of the population, although assimilation had long been blurring the line between ethnic Thai and Chinese, thereby reducing the meaningfulness of Chinese designation. Between their dominant position in tin mining (which began to be eroded when foreign firms introduced dredge mining starting in 1907[26]), an important minority position in rubber production (in Thailand most rubber was in the hands of small holders; in colonial Malaya the industry was dominated by large, foreign-owned plantations), and their predominance in the other nonagricultural sectors (apart from government service and the military), the Chinese made a substantial contribution to Thailand's economic development over the whole historical period.

The ethnic division of economic function arose from a rural Thai occupational preference for agriculture combined with government policy that excluded the Chinese from slavery or the corvée. The Chinese came to fill the rice milling and small commerce and manufacturing activities not manned by Thai. As will be considered below, the long-standing policy of alleviating labor scarcity and encouraging the filling of commercial and wage-labor occupations through Chinese immigration was replaced by a deliberate policy of anti-Sinicism in the 1930s with substantial effect—during the policy's course, and in its resolution in the late 1950s—on the country's politics and economic development.

The entire question of ethnicity in economic functions and in the distribution of income and economic power has played a fundamental role in the politics and economic policies of much of the Third World. In Thailand, as in virtually all the countries of Southeast Asia, economic policies in the postwar era have been affected strongly by the economic differentiations between the "overseas Chinese" minorities and the "indigenous" majorities. These differentiations, and the government policies adopted from time to time to reduce the relatively strong economic position of the Chinese, have in some countries resulted in violence and widespread social and economic instability. Thailand's experience in this respect has been especially interesting; assimilation of the Chinese has progressed farther and faster than elsewhere in the region, in one of the world's most successful "melting pot" experiences. Chinese assimilation in Thailand is one of the key social factors affecting, in easily discernible ways, the country's modern economic development.

The ethnic dimensions of Thailand's economic history have impressed virtually all social science scholarship in Thailand. The classic studies of the Thai Chinese by William G. Skinner in the 1950s remain unsurpassed and are among the leading authoritative works on Thai sociology. The historical consensus view—that it was a Thai cultural preference for agriculture that left nonagricultural functions open for the Chinese by default—is well stated by Ingram:

> The extension of riceland has been the major entrepreneurial achievement of the Thai themselves. . . they have left most other entrepreneurial functions to foreigners. The cultivation of rice is an ancient and honorable occupation to the Thai, however, and they seem to have preferred it to all others. . . . The Thai has preferred the communal life of the village, and it is not easy to break the ties of culture and tradition which have induced him to become a rice farmer. . . . This preference has probably been one of the most important determinants of the pattern of the economy which has developed in Thailand. . . . Their unwillingness to compete in other ways appears to be the overwhelmingly significant factor involved in any study of economic development in Thailand, but it simply cannot be satisfactorily analyzed by the economist.[27]

While there is no denying the importance of this ethnic economic heritage for the evolution of Thailand's recent economic development, we should make two qualifying observations at this point. First, with the economic diversification among the ethnic Thai and the emergence of a new mixed "Sino-Thai" social class, the simple Thai-Chinese dichotomy has faded rapidly as a paradigm for socioeconomic analysis in Thailand in the three decades since Skinner's work. Second, a recent paper by Constance Wilson about Bangkok in 1883 (Bangkok was already the preeminent city) shows that ethnic Thai "dominated" professional and manufacturing activities in the city. "Although the Chinese position in marketing and commerce is very strong, there is, nevertheless, a Thai presence in these fields. The Thai had not isolated themselves behind the walls of government service and agriculture. . . . This suggests that the history of Chinese economic dominance needs to be reexamined. It may not have been as complete for all periods of the nineteenth century as many authors have alleged."[28] An absence of ethnic Thai from the commercial occupations normally concentrated in urban areas, especially a primate city, would have been extraordinary in Bangkok, even as early as 1900. In that year Bangkok's population was around 500,000 (roughly 6 percent of the country's population of around 8 million); the Chinese were estimated to comprise only about 17 percent of the city's inhabitants.[29] Wilson's evidence suggests that the "cultural" preference of the Thai for agriculture may have been overstated, and that the relative decline of Thai participation in nonagricultural activities in subsequent years remains to be explained. Ingram points to conspiracy theories (secret society exclusiveness), discrimination, and clannishness,[30] but these alleged practices would pertain only to new Thai entry and would not explain the decline of dominant Thai positions demonstrated by Wilson.

Whatever the actual case may have been, and despite the earlier Chakri policies that encouraged Chinese immigration as contributing to the interests of the state, pejorative and conspiratorial views of the economic position and behavior of the Chinese commercial class came to dominate the thinking of the Thai elite in the early twentieth century. In fact the first open statement of anti-Sinicism in Thailand is found in a famous essay King Vajiravudh wrote in 1914 entitled "The Jews of the East." Vajiravudh was also a strong "modernizing" monarch, but his policies included the introduction into Thailand of some of the trappings and ethnic concepts of turn-of-the-century European nationalism.[31] Among these concepts were ideas of economic nationalism, specifically a call for the Siamese to regain control of the economy from foreigners and from the domestic Chinese whom he pictured as comparable to the image of the role of the Jews promoted by European anti-Semitism. Published under a pseudonym, his article severely criticized the Chinese for exploiting Thai hospitality.[32] Ethnic chauvinism developed into a full-blown policy in the late 1930s, despite the fact that many of the policy makers (from the Chakri monarchs to the constitutional and military powerholders of the 1930s and postwar years) had Chinese among their ancestors.[33]

Conservative Financial Policy

Right up until World War II the Thai financial system was a prime example of the classic unmanaged monetary regime. The small banking system, confined to Bangkok, served largely to finance external trade. Most transactions were settled in cash. Demand deposits amounted to only a small fraction of the money supply. With very low tariffs, no nontariff barriers to imports, and very modest (in fact, declining in the eighteenth century) domestic production of tradeable goods such as textiles, any increase in the domestic money supply arising out of an increase in export income was quickly reflected in an increase in imports. Except for fixing the exchange rate of the baht in relation to sterling, the government was completely passive with respect to the country's money supply. Although this conservatism may appear to have been partly an enforced consequence of the provisions of the Bowring (and subsequent) treaties that restricted the government's revenue-raising power, it is clear that the conservatism reached beyond the areas covered by the treaties and extended into all areas of fiscal and monetary management. Even after the treaty renegotiations in the 1920s which restored the country's full fiscal autonomy, and after the 1932 constitutional coup, financial policies remained cautious. Ingram summarizes the whole financial experience up to 1954:

> Conservative policies were initiated by the monarchy and they have been continued by the constitutional regime in spite of many changes in government. The chief aim of monetary policy has been to safeguard the international position of the baht, and the government seems to have put this aim above such national interests as economic development and stability of prices and incomes. The principal reason ... has doubtless been the very real fear of foreign intervention. The experience of other nations was not lost on Thailand, and ever since 1850 there is ample evidence that the government has deliberately pursued an ultraconservative policy in order to make certain that no nation would ever have an excuse to intervene in Thailand on the grounds of financial irresponsibility.[34]

Fiscal conservatism translated into a strong reluctance to contract external debt that might be difficult to service in years of economic hardship. Ingram cites an observer who wrote in 1891 that despite the similarities between rice plains around Bangkok and those around Rangoon, Thai rice exports had increased much less than Burmese since 1860.

> The writer concluded that the difference was to be found in the unequal provision of public works for irrigation and reclamation of land. Around Rangoon large sums were spent on such projects, while in Thailand "trade has developed by the unassisted resources of the country." This judgment is unnecessarily harsh, but comparatively the Thai government had done little. The government had borrowed no money from abroad to use in

capital improvements, nor did it have any over-all plan for the development of agriculture.[35]

Gradualism and Continuity

While it is meaningful and correct to describe past economic and social change in Thailand as comparatively gradual, conservative, and without serious disconti-nuity or opposition, it is important to emphasize the comparative aspect of this characterization. As gradual and incremental as Thai modernization appears, when compared with the scope and pace of change in Japan or in industrializing Europe (the latter marked by deep social cleavage, even violent revolution), the reforms in the organization and system of government introduced by King Chulalongkorn starting in 1873 did initiate changes that were profound in the Thai context. These changes also provoked some opposition and reaction. The evolution of the ancient *sakdina* system had left substantial power in the hands of senior nobility supported by their bureaucratic clients. As Wyatt sums it up, "In order to change Siam, Chulalongkorn first had to control his own government,"[36] an objective that took him a decade to accomplish. He also had to deal with resistance, sometimes armed, as his efforts to extend the effective reach of the central government into loosely consolidated regions of the country, essential to his policies for coping with colonial encroachment, reduced the power of re-gional and local elites. The independence of provincial powerholders was not finally ended until promulgation of the Provincial Administration Act in 1892, which established a salaried national administration. Replacement of the provin-cial militia system by a modern national army took place only in the early 1900s. It took over two decades for King Chulalongkorn to create the central institu-tional and technical capacity the state needed to extend its effective reach.

The gradualism of change in economic and other realms also sets Thailand apart from the historical discontinuities experienced by the majority of develop-ing countries as they fell under and later reemerged from colonialism after many decades if not generations of foreign rule. The Chakri monarchy did cede signifi-cant autonomy over trade and taxation policy, and did continue to accord its British financial advisers very considerable influence. But by avoiding coloniali-zation, nineteenth-century Thailand did not undergo the loss of all control over economic matters, the imposition of thoroughgoing industrial and commercial policies shaped for the benefit or the metropolitan economy's development, a long interregnum in self-government, or a struggle (whether civil or violent) to overthrow established government during which a colonial society may come to attach high honor to civil disobedience, to the flaunting of legality, and to the politics of confrontation. Difficult as it is to trace and establish causal relation-ships between the patterns of governing behavior of successive generations, in different times and under greatly altered circumstances, it does appear that this history of uninterrupted independence, and the gradualist and incrementalist tradition of public policy formation, has had important consequences for and reflections in the style and content of economic and social policy making in the modern era.

Continuity and revulsion against radical departures is evident in the very circumstances of the coup d'etat that ended the absolute monarchy on June 24, 1932, and in the policy debate that took place soon after on the economic program that should be adopted to launch the new era. Looking at the circumstances of the coup first, it is striking that although the coup is often called a revolution, it had none of the characteristics of the classic revolutions of European or Latin American history, such as prior years of widespread unrest, the mobilization of mass popular support, overthrow of the *ancien régime* by violence, or a subsequent descent into reaction. Instead, the Thai coup was conceived and developed in total secrecy over a period of seven years, by a cabal that grew to only 141 members. The events of June 24 read more like a *coup de théatre* than a revolution. None of the military participants held positions of command of troops, but the coup group, calling itself the People's Party, or the Promoters, was able to stage the appearance of a military show of force. The group seized power in less than three hours. Not one shot was fired.[37]

The Promoters were largely men who could be styled a counter-elite. They were members of the small class of civilian and military bureaucrats among whom there had been developing for several years a deep discontent with the monarch's reluctance to open up the political system and his continued allocation of senior positions to a small set of members of the royal family. The group was motivated by a mix of personal ambitions and considerations of national policy.

> Of general concern to the leaders of the 1932 Revolution was the "backwardness" of absolutism in a time of modernity and the need for adjustments. Absolutism had served the Thais ably during the past, but its foundations (had) been weakened by the establishment of necessary state bureaucracies based on rationally organized and functionally-relevant structures. The expanded modern state bureaucracy absorbed younger and new talents into its structure. These men received good education within the country and abroad. Their growing expertise and professionalism made them uneasy and frustrated with the tradition of royal prerogatives in selecting high-ranking officials based upon ascriptive criteria. Thus this modern bureaucratic organization created its own internal dynamism which eventually agitated and brought about political change.[38]

The Promoters were divided into four factions—two army, one naval, and one civilian. Although all the members agreed on the need to end monarchical absolutism, a split emerged immediately after the coup. The civilian faction led by Pridi Phanomyong and an army faction led by Plaek Phibunsongkram (better known subsequently as Field Marshal Phibun) comprised younger men who had acquired an ideological bent during their student days in France (under government scholarships) in the 1920s and who were inclined to introduce significant changes in social and economic policies. The second army faction and the naval faction comprised older and more conservative-minded men. The potentialities for conflict over the pace and direction of a new constitutional regime appear to have been unrecognized among the Promoters during the years leading up to the actual event. These potentialities would have become evident if the group, or any faction or individual among them, had seen it desirable or necessary to put a revolutionary program or rationale on paper. The contrast with the widespread and philosophical debates that preceded the classical revolutions and the fervid wordiness of twentieth-century revolutionaries is striking.

The king's ready capitulation and his acceptance of the constitution prepared by the Promoters reflected the fact that he had earlier come to the conclusion that the Thai political system needed modernization involving some widening of decision-making processes and participation. By 1931 the king had developed an agenda for reform including the gradual introduction of popular suffrage. Apparently spurred on by press criticism of the absolute monarchy's inadequacies in the face of the economic depression that had reached Thailand, and by rumors of revolutionary activity, King Prachathipok decided formally to inaugurate representative reforms by April 1932. In the event, the monarch was advised and pressured to postpone his program. The advisers (including Raymond B. Stevens, the American adviser on foreign affairs) argued that the Siamese people were not educated enough to understand representative government. The high officials and royal members of the Privy Council opposed any wider access to policy councils beyond the existing small circle.[39]

Having deliberately avoided any appeal to public opinion or any effort to develop or even test the extent of public dissatisfaction with the monarchy, the revolutionary counter-elite evidently saw the general public in the same light as did the older aristocracy—unready for and disinterested in political activity or democratic participation. Immediately after it went public with the coup itself, the group learned that it had very shallow support outside the bureaucracy. One of the leaders later recorded his wistful memory of the first revelation of the public mood:

> The fact that the people did not understand democracy and were indifferent to it was clearly shown during the inauguration of the constitutional regime at the Throne Hall on June 29, 1932. We had to round them up to attend the ceremony. Only a handful of them came and listened to the government declaration, but without the least comprehension. Had we arranged a stage play and served them with Chinese noodle soup, perhaps more people would have come.[40]

The coup leaders apparently concurred with the views of the monarch they had just moved against. On the subject of the readiness of the population to participate in the political process, King Prajadhipok wrote the following at the time of the coup:

> The question in this country is not whether we want a democracy or not, but whether a genuine democratic government is just now possible. Whether a person can cast a vote with full knowledge of the consequences of his act or not depends upon his standard of education and his age, and in view of the fact that the bulk of the people are still uneducated, it follows that if an Act of Constitution is passed in this country, such a law will have to disqualify by some method or other a large part of our population from voting. . . . Siam has done nothing toward democracy, but it is the most she could have done under existing conditions.[41]

Much of the subsequent debate (in early 1933) over the regime's initial policy declaration revolved around the question of how much, if any, of the policy should be released to the public, and whether it should be issued in full, or only bit by bit over a period of time. Even Pridi, the most articulate and radical of the leaders and the only one to produce an ideology and a program for the new regime, held paternalistic and condescending views of the public. There is no hint of the political orientation one commonly associates with modern revolution— appeal to mass mobilization, or revolutionary ideology glorifying the peasants— in Pridi's radicalism:

> We may compare our Siamese people to children. The government will have to urge them forward by means of authority applied directly or indirectly to get them to cooperate in any kind of economic endeavour. . . . If we are going to discuss the things that contribute to individual happiness, then the less we make people work the better they will like it. And we may as well let them all return to the jungle where they will have nothing at all to do. But if we are concerned here with the development of the nation then excess leisure time is undesirable because it will eventually result in the progressive invasion of our national economic system by outsiders.[42]

Prelude to Economic Policy Debate: The Pridi Program

During the entire period from the Bowring Treaty until the years just before the end of the absolute monarchy there was very little public debate in Siam on national economic objectives. This is not surprising considering how little debate, either public or within ruling circles, took place regarding the larger questions on the very nature of the Thai state and its organs of central power and policy formation. The entire modernization process that would ultimately lead to the end of royal absolutism and to the transfer of national policy making to a new elite was conceived and implemented by the monarchs themselves and their closest royal and noble confidants. While the monarchs were certainly aware of, and tolerated criticism in, the Bangkok press, newspaper readership was tiny, and there is little indication that royal policies were affected. Now and then, however, an individual among the Thai elite raised a question regarding the general thrust of economic policies. An interesting example is found in a communication to King Vajiravudh in 1915 from his brother Prince Chakrabongse, army chief of staff, following a trip the Prince had made through the northeastern region:

> I also had the opportunity to study the geographical aspects and living conditions of the people in the Northeast which I had never seen before. Some ideas then came to my mind which I think should be brought to the attention of Your Majesty. . . . The people including the Laotians who should be regarded as Thais are mostly Thais. . . . All the Thais are totally loyal to Your Majesty; they firmly love their *chao* princes and their *nai* masters, and their motherland. Besides, these people are completely obedient. . . . They would do whatever they were asked to do . . . they definitely would constitute a main supportive force for the land. . . . the people are mainly engaged in farming and raising cattle for sale. . . . All the farmlands . . . depend on rainfall.
>
> However in farming, even when the rainfalls are good producing high yields, the people would produce just enough for living only. They would not produce more because the surplus is of no use; they could not sell it due to the lack of communication link with other [regions]. . . the quantity produced [of other goods] was small, just sufficient for their own use . . . they had no cash at all. To develop [the Northeast], the important obstacle lies in the communication system. . . . Furthermore, the [Mun River] water dammed up could also be used to irrigate the farmlands.
>
> [The Northeast] has so far not been developed at all. The government, it may be said, has never invested even a single *satang* in the improvement of the farmlands or in the promotion of trade.[43]

Prince Chakrabongse's letter is revealing in its picture of economic activity in the Northeast in 1915—unaffected by the previous decades of modernization and, as it turned out subsequently, not very different from the Northeast in 1950 before the country's recent economic development got under way. It was the first time this prince of the realm had ever visited this isolated region despite its vast size and the importance of the area. His comments suggest that the national consolidation process had gone quite far in the Northeast, even in the face of economic neglect, and that much now could be accomplished that would be beneficial for the state and for the inhabitants of the area—if only the government began to do something. He believed that transportation was the key. As will be seen below, these same considerations of loyalty and consolidation, neglect, subsistence and rainfed agriculture, and transportation were still the essence of the development problems of the Northeast fifty years later. Neither these observations of the prince nor other occasional criticisms appear to have engendered sustained debate or any significant invigoration of government policy toward economic development.

One commoner individual, Tienwan, stands out as a remarkable exception to this general picture of public passivity. (A recent study of Thai radical thinkers cites only three social critic poets in the two centuries preceding King Mongkut.)[44] Tienwan was a sailor, Buddhist scholar, and lawyer who spent seventeen years in prison for his attacks on official corruption. After being pardoned by King Chulalongkorn, Tienwan started publishing a magazine in the 1890s in which he critiqued the *sakdina* system and its bureaucratic injustices and called for greater freedom and public participation in government. He disparaged the slow pace of modernization, decried the extent to which Siam was holding on to ancient traditions including slavery and polygamy, and urged the creation of a general education system. While in his own time he was certainly a radical social thinker, he did not develop a systematic ideology or program, and his call for more active industrial and agricultural promotion efforts by government appears to have envisaged the retention of a free-market economy.[45] Tienwan's ideas never reached a wide audience, and his writings sank into obscurity until their revival in the 1970s by a few modern intellectuals who acknowledged Tienwan's importance and his impact on their own thinking.[46]

Another turn-of-the-century maverick was Phraya Suriyanuwat, a prominent Western-educated diplomat. Phraya Suriyanuwat was a prolific critic of both the *sakdina* system and the nascent capitalism of the time. Drawing on European ideas of labor cooperatism, he developed a syncretic utopian socialist set of proposals for Siam. His writings and minor efforts at policy implementation caused his forced resignation. As was the case with Tienwan, he had little impact or influence, but even less posthumous attention despite his reputation as the "Father" of Thai economics.[47]

As noted above, it was only in the 1920s, among the government scholarship students in Europe, that the first *group* of intellectuals emerged and found agreement among themselves that the monarchy would have to be replaced by a constitutional regime, and by force if necessary. Once they had succeeded, it fell upon Pridi Phanomyong to draft the new government's economic program. Pridi had drafted most of the Promoters' proclamations, including a promise to draw up the country's first national economic plan. It seemed natural for the group to ask Pridi to draw up the economic program, given his position as the most articulate intellectual and perhaps the only one who had studied economics. As one of the few who had studied in Paris rather than in Great Britain, however, Pridi had absorbed the more radical atmosphere of French university life. His program included many ideas completely unacceptable to more conservative members of the group. The first debate over his program in 1933 immediately opened up factional divisions that defined Thai politics for a number of years to come. Nevertheless, it is interesting to note that the entire episode, including the plan itself, the debate over its content and handling, and the critique of the plan by (the now constitutional) King Rama VII, came to general public knowledge only in the late 1960s as a result of which Pridi (though living in exile) became a figure of inspiration for students and intellectuals.

The factional split appears to have first appeared the previous year. It was only one month after the coup, at a time when the monarchy still commanded considerable influence and deference despite the king's loss of formal power, a loss that had yet to be codified. A memoir written by one of the founders of the Promoters group records a meeting the king held in June 1932 with nine other persons of whom six were leading Promoters, in which Pridi presented the monarch with a copy of the proposed constitution he had drafted on behalf of the coup members. The king read the document on the spot and immediately raised objections, especially to language that appeared to be "following the Russian communist model." After a remarkable exchange that revealed how little these revolutionary intellectuals were given to systematic debate and formulation of policy, even with respect to a proposed foundation document for the new stage they were setting for Siamese history, two of the Promoters admitted they had not read the document. In great embarrassment they withdrew, promising to draft a new constitution adhering to the English model. "We were all stunned and slowly went out to stand in front of the palace. Phraya Song pointed at [Pridi's] face [a very insulting gesture] and said, 'You caused us disaster by not doing as told. Why do you do things beyond your assignments.' . . . Phraya Song spoke with anger. . . . This led to the irreconcilable split between Col. Phraya Song Suradet and [Pridi]."[48]

Pridi's plan is a brief document written in the first person. It mixes analysis, casual views, and policy proposals along with draft language for two pieces of enabling legislation. Many paragraphs are given over to answering criticisms Pridi encountered during the months following the coup when he was apparently airing the ideas he was putting on paper. At the core of the plan were the two proposals that the government should employ every citizen of Siam on a salary basis, and that the state should own virtually all the means of production in the country. (The limitation of employment to citizens was important in that a substantial fraction of the still ethnically distinct Chinese population held Chinese rather than Thai citizenship.) Reflecting the basic thrust of the criticism, Pridi placed at the top of every page this question: "Why do you officials with salaries and pensions oppose the granting of salaries and pensions to the people?" This leitmotif also reveals how restricted was the circle in which policy was debated.

The government would decree that "all persons between the ages of eighteen and fifty-five are to be employed in various projects according to their education, strength and abilities. . . . All employed will be entitled to receive salaries from the government or the cooperative societies."[49] The bulk of the population would be organized in cooperatives. While the coops would be set up as production units, they would perform a wide range of economic, social, and law-and-order functions for the members. Government employment would be compulsory except for the well-to-do and for those who preferred independence and could prove their ability to support themselves and educate their children. Permission would be needed, and granted, for persons wishing to engage in private professions. Existing private factory owners would have the option of exchanging their assets for government bonds. The farmers, now idle half the year, would be put to work on gardening, road building, and other government projects. People could be required by government to study arts and crafts in their spare time or to be drilled as soldiers.

Pridi expresses strong opposition to expropriation of private property, a policy he describes as part of the "social philosophy of Communism." Nevertheless and contradictively, he envisages a system where the government owns most of the physical assets (other than private homes) and enterprises in the economy: "As the Siamese people prosper, their needs will multiply. . . . When the government supplies all these things, the wages paid the people will return to the government as considerations for them, and will reestablish the internal balance of the financial system."

The salary paid would be set by law and subject to withholding deductions to pay for the cost of food, clothing, shelter, and other necessities the individual had received from the government or the cooperative society. Poverty would be eliminated at one stroke by paying every person an adequate minimum wage, even children, older people, and disabled people. On the other hand, "indolent persons shall be punished by having their salaries cut, or the hours of their employment increased."

Pridi foresees that industrial development in Siam under private enterprise would bring on industrial conflict because of the natural tendency of private enterprise to oppress the workers. There would be no conflict in his system because there would be no employer class. "The government will be the representative of the people, which is the same thing as saying that the people themselves will own everything in the nation." He also proposes to place all foreign trade in the hands of the government, and to pursue trade and industrial policies that would gradually make the economy autarchic except for the import of machinery beyond the country's capacity to produce domestically. He believes autarchy is the best policy for national strength (citing the ideas of Friedrich List as superior to Adam Smith's advocacy of trading relationships, and Germany's economic successes under policies of self-sufficiency). "The fundamental aim of the government should be the administration of all kinds of agricultural and industrial enterprises with a view to rendering this country entirely independent of all foreign nations." Such independence would be attained when the government produces all necessities and sets all prices. He then lays out rough outlines of how a national economic plan would be constructed. He appears to envisage a materials balance system that sets physical output targets and calculates physical input requirements. The plan would be launched project by project, in one part of the country at a time.

Pridi's plan cannot be critiqued by modern standards of economic development planning. It is clear that he saw his paper only as a didactic prelude, intended to clarify misconceptions and set the general direction and philosophy of economic policy. It is virtually bereft of numbers, makes no reference to any Siamese sources of fact or prior social or economic thought (Pridi cites the authority of two of his Paris professors at one point), and repeats as fact the conventional (but erroneous) wisdom of the time regarding the extent of peasant debt and loss of tenure. The paper suffers from a curious asymmetry, for example, between its passing reference to public health in one phrase and the long footnote in which Pridi details how gambling administration should be organized at the village level. The document is not without a certain casual charm that one would not likely find in a "policy paper" today.[50] Although he called himself a socialist, Pridi said he was drawing on ideas from different schools of thought. In a society with little experience of debate on concepts of economic organization that had arisen in the industrialized countries, "socialism" was an acceptable word. "Communism" by contrast had been anathema for years. When Pridi gave King Prajadhipok a briefing on the ideas he would incorporate in his economic program, "the benevolent King did not mind the fact that Pridi intended to mix some grains of socialism into the plan, and even said that he was also a socialist."[51]

Putting aside all the difficulties of vagueness, feasibility of execution, and casual naiveté, Pridi's paper contained the first set of policy proposals ever placed before and deliberately examined by the Siamese governing elite that would have set the country off in a direction radically discontinuous with the past and radical by world standards. In some respect his plan echoes a distinctly Siamese history, especially in the civil service–like ranking system into which he would place every member of the population and which looks like a twentieth century reincarnation of the ancient *sakdina* system. But in place of the free-market, free-trade, export-oriented, private-property-based economic system that had evolved since the Bowring Treaty, Pridi would have substituted a thoroughgoing command economy, a high-tariff, inward-looking import substitution policy carried to virtual autarchy, complete government ownership of all the means of production (except for a grandfathering of existing private enterprises), and a comprehensive manpower mobilization going far beyond the old corvée system. In a final paragraph, Pridi brought his paper's unreality to a utopian conclusion: "When the administration of the economic system by the government shall have brought about the final consummation of the aims set forth by the People's Party in their six-point platform, that state of prosperity and felicity which is the laudable desire of every heart and which, in classical language, is Sriaraya (utopia) will have dawned."[52]

In an attempt to counter the charge that his program was a "communist" one, he stressed his reverence for traditional values and insisted that his program would not "transform human beings into animals" or "make women common property and destroy family life." And although he denounced "social parasites," he did not propose measures against the propertied class (or even gamblers). Nevertheless, the conservatives immediately denounced the plan as Bolshevism. King Prajadhipok joined the debate and issued a closely argued and vigorous rebuttal to Pridi's paper. In his conclusion, the king wrote, "What I know for a certainty is that the proposed economic plan is identical to that of Russia's. What is not certain is who the imitator is: does Stalin imitate Luang Pradit [Pridi's title] or vice versa?"[53]

The factional splits within the People's Party now opened wide. The ideological differences between Pridi's group and the more conservative-minded among the revolutionaries heightened the personal rivalries that had existed from the start. The "policy debate" appeared to swirl around the few key terms that captured the essence of Pridi's document but remained ill-defined, partly because of the nature of Pridi's presentation and partly because the leading conservatives freely admitted that they knew nothing about economics. Thawatt points out that ideology may have been used as a cover for factional maneuvering, the conservatives knowing that Pridi would be discredited if the charge of communism could be made to stick.[54] One of the leading critics argued against issuing any policy beyond what could be realistically implemented: "According to this policy it will take another two or three hundred years to work out the details. Look at the old government. It ruled for a hundred and fifty years without any economic policy. And I fail to see that the absence of a policy was in any way detrimental."[55]

In the event, the conservatives moved quickly against Pridi and his supporters in the parliament. At a cabinet meeting that Pridi refused to attend, decrees were issued dissolving the parliament and setting up a new cabinet that excluded Pridi and his adherents. A new anticommunism law was introduced. To diffuse the public tensions these moves had caused, the conservative prime minister Phya Manopakorn urged Pridi to leave the country for a European study tour at government expense. In a complex sequence of events over the following two years, there were two coups, one between two People's Party factions, a second by a counterrevolutionary royalist group. Pridi was recalled from France. In a formal parliamentary review that cleared him of charges of being a communist, Pridi's program was aired again and for the last time. He later became minister of finance in the first Phibun cabinet at the end of 1938. Although he commanded respect and influence, in and out of office up to his second exile in 1947 (after five months as prime minister in 1946, Pridi resigned under charges of responsibility for the shooting death, under mysterious circumstances, of the young King Ananda Mahidol [Rama VIII]; his foreign policy had also led to the revival of charges that he had communist intentions for Thailand), his original economic program never resurfaced, nor did it ever have any impact on actual policy.[56]

In retrospect, the whole episode of Pridi's program is notable for the opacity of the policy debate; the readiness of the radicals to launch revolutionary social change based on a mere skeletal diagnosis of the country's problems and an almost casual set of prescriptions; the total disappearance of the whole program from Thai public life within two years (and Pridi's own disregard of his major intellectual effort and policy objective during subsequent years when his power was at its height); and the limited numbers of the bureaucratic elite in Thailand who participated in the debate. The body politic of Thailand, slender as it was, had no stomach for radical discontinuity. It also had no experience with, or institutional capacity for, the formulation of systematic economic policy or development programs. In sum, Pridi's policy proposal had no meaningful relevance to Thailand.

In fact, the new regime was more occupied with power struggles in the years between the 1932 coup and the Second World War than it was with economic policy, despite the drama surrounding the Pridi program. The economy began to recover from the deep depression of the early 1930s soon after the new regime took power, thanks to a recovery in export earnings. The new government made no significant changes in the long-standing conservative monetary and exchange rate policies that ensured strong reserve backing to the currency, automatic adjustment of the economy to the balance of trade, and annual surpluses in the government accounts. Economic policy merely sustained the economic regime inherited from the past, introducing only marginal changes.

An Episode of Economic Nationalism

It was only in 1939, after Phibun became prime minister, that fundamental departures were initiated in economic policies. As noted above, Phibun was one of the leaders among the students in Europe who began to plot the overthrow of the absolute monarchy in the mid-1920s. In contrast with Pridi's measured application of European nationalist sentiment to the issues of Thailand's future character, once the transition to a "modern" democratic constitutional monarchy had been accomplished, Phibun introduced into Thai politics and public consciousness, for the first time, a strident chauvinism.

Phibun had emerged from the turbulent postcoup politics as the first figure willing and able to use propaganda to mobilize public support for his policies and personal authority, and to apply ruthless measures (including the execution of eighteen opponents, the first such executions in more than a century[57]) to consolidate his power. He moved quickly to reduce the potential independence of the parliament and to discredit the institution of the monarchy. (After King Prajadhipok abdicated in 1935, the National Assembly invited his ten-year-old nephew Prince Ananda Mahidol, then a student in Switzerland, to succeed to the throne. Although the continuity of the monarchy was maintained, there was no monarchical presence in the country until King Ananda Mahidol's return in late

1945, and no monarchical influence until the 1960s.) In an effort to force more rapid modernization and a muscular nationalism that would strengthen the country's position in a rapidly deteriorating international environment, Phibun built up a leadership cult around his person (he had written admiringly about Hitler and Mussolini), swept away vestiges of old Siam (he changed the name of the country to Thailand to emphasize the ethnic basis of his concept of the nation-state, adopted the Western calendar, decreed a "modern" dress code, etc.), and built up the military and paramilitary forces. In his campaign to introduce a fervent and militant popular nationalism into a society that had no previous orientation or proclivities of this nature, Phibun was greatly assisted by the most prominent and prolific Thai intellectual of the period, Luang Wichit Wathakan. Although Luang Wichit's long and variegated career (spanning fine arts, play-writing, education and foreign portfolios in Phibun's wartime cabinet, and authorship of books on history, religion, and politics) directly touched economic affairs only briefly (in 1951–52 as Phibun's minister of finance and then minister of economic affairs), his impact on the broad national orientation in which economic policies were developed was greater and longer lasting than was the impact of Pridi.

Luang Wichit was the principal popularizer of the constitutional government. Convinced that Thailand needed strong authoritarian leadership, he was able to serve as a close adviser both to Phibun and subsequently to Marshal Sarit Thanarat, who ousted Phibun in a coup in 1957 and took direct control as prime minister the following year. Luang Wichit helped Phibun to formulate his nationalist policies and to create a personal leadership cult. His influence on Sarit was, if anything, stronger. In his unique position as a special assistant to the prime minister, he helped define the concepts Sarit used to legitimize his rule and to promote the authoritarian framework Sarit decreed as distinctly suitable for Thailand, a subject I shall return to below.[58]

It is interesting to pause for a moment to observe that the Promoters continued to see a direct connection between economic policy and national security. But whereas Rama IV and Rama V had opted for an open economy and for private (even largely alien and foreign) investment as the most effective policy for denying opportunities for colonial encroachment, Pridi and Phibun drew the opposite conclusion. Pridi argued that the private enterprise, open economy had caused the Thais to be "persecuted and oppressed by others in the field of economics" and that the only escape lay through imposition of a command economy.[59] Among the Promoters the conservatives argued that the radicalism of Pridi's program would provoke foreign intervention and was, therefore, too risky to adopt except piecemeal or to reveal at all.[60] Phibun's economic nationalism called for expansion of the government sector and government economic interventionism generally, emphasizing domestic aliens rather than outright foreigners. Fear of French or British intervention, still seen as a credible possibility in the early 1930s, evaporated as Japanese armed forces swept through the entire region in the early months of the war. The connection between European intervention and Thai economic policy formation finally passed away in its eighty-fifth year.

The substitution of Thailand as the country's name in place of the centuries-old Siam was a metaphor for the basic objective, the point of departure of Phibun's economic policies, that is, the reclaiming for ethnic Thai control those sectors of the economy dominated by the domestic Chinese. First initiated by King Vajiravudh, the conviction that the Chinese were exploiting the Thai had been gaining wide credence in the years before Phibun came to power. In addition to resentment against the alleged usurious practices of Chinese moneylenders and exploitative price-fixing by Chinese merchants, the image of the Chinese as undermining the country's interests was being fed by the rise of activity among them in support of China following the onset of the Sino-Japanese War in 1937. As anomalous, inapposite, and distasteful as it sounds in retrospect, Luang Wichit gave a public lecture in 1938 comparing the Siamese Chinese to the German Jews and implying that Hitler's policies (which did not at that time appear to extend as far as genocide) were possibly relevant to Siam.[61]

Phibun began immediately to promulgate a policy of economic discrimination against the Chinese. Special taxes were introduced that fell only on the Chinese. A wide range of state enterprises were established to compete with the Chinese or preempt manufacture of, or commerce in, specific commodities. In the early 1940s regulations were issued that had the effect of preventing the still largely alien Chinese from owning land. In 1949 (when Phibun was back in power after a four-year interregnum) he excluded the Chinese from rice farming and forestry and from a number of professional occupations. To complement these economic measures, the government undertook to hobble the cultural life of the minority by closing most of the Chinese-language newspapers and limiting the use of the Chinese language in Chinese schools.

With the benefit of hindsight, one can see that Phibun's effort to implant a radical, scapegoat-based, racial nationalism did not sink deep roots into a society that had no history of prejudice or discrimination sanctioned by religion or by linguistic or cultural chauvinism. The largely rural ethnic Thai held a mix of positive and negative views of the Chinese, with the negative views having only economic content and the balance not sufficiently antipathetic to predispose the Thai to respond to incitement to jingoism. The conclusions of anthropologists on this score were summarized by deYoung:

> To the peasant, the Chinese, whether peddler, miller, shopkeeper, or rice broker, is an essential link to the larger economic pattern of the country and a means of providing necessary and beneficial services. As aliens, as businessmen, and as townsmen, the Chinese of course come in for the inevitable garrulous depreciation of their rural clientele; the Thai peasant calls all Chinese peddlers *chek*, a somewhat derogatory Thai word for "Chinese," and the

villagers describe the peddler, when he is not present, as a sharp dealer who will try to cheat the village buyer whenever possible. But little of this is seen in face-to-face dealings with the peddler; in isolated villages he is a welcome visitor, for he brings not only necessary goods but news and gossip. . . . In larger villages where Chinese shop-keepers or mill owners live, they are likely to have married local Thai women, and their children are considered Thai by the villagers. . . .

The Chinese moneylender has been presented as an "unconscionable usurer" . . . bleeding the Thai peasant. . . . But incomplete information suggests that the Chinese moneylender is not any more avaricious than his Thai counterpart.[62]

Many among the Thai elite in government shared the belief that the middlemen were guilty of noncompetitive and exploitative behavior with respect to the Thai peasants, and were also well aware of the leading role played by the Chinese in commerce and industry generally. But the artificiality of Phibun's economic nationalism became clear in the late 1950s when the complete reversal of the policy (in all respects except the informal bar on Chinese advancement to senior ranks in the armed forces) by Prime Minister Sarit was unopposed and resulted in its apparent complete and immediate demise. Although Phibun's discriminatory policies were in effect for relatively few years, they did give impetus to the assimilation process. In Thailand, the differences of religion (different branches of Buddhism), race, dietary practices, and other mores between the indigenous population and the Chinese minority were much easier to bridge than has been the case in the other countries of Southeast Asia. The Chinese in Thailand readily adopted Thai names and the use of the Thai language, and in many other respects chose to continue the long-running assimilation process rather than reacting against Phibun's acculturation pressures. The ongoing assimilation of the Chinese in Thai society is a remarkable aspect of modern Thai history that has contributed profoundly to the country's economic development since the policy reversal, a subject I shall return to below.

The high tide of the new nationalism was reached quickly. The fall of France in 1940 gave Phibun the opportunity to move against Vichy-held Indochina in order to recover portions of Laos and Cambodia lost to French control between 1893 and 1907. Japanese intervention forced a settlement under which Thailand annexed the areas Phibun's forces had occupied. The following year Japan invaded Thailand after the Thai foreign minister (Phibun was away from Bangkok) rejected Japan's request to allow its armies passage through Thai territory. The invasion coincided with the attack on Pearl Harbor. When Phibun returned to Bangkok the next morning, he ordered a stop to Thai resistance in the face of the overwhelming Japanese military superiority. The following month the Phibun government concluded an alliance with Japan and declared war on the United States and Great Britain. Whatever the considerations were that moved Phibun and the Thai military to side with Japan,[63] other Thais refused to accept this policy, including Pridi (who lost his cabinet post as minister of finance) and the Thai ambassador to the United States, Seni Pramoj. Seni abroad and Pridi at home organized a Free Thai movement that rejected the government's declaration of war and developed an intelligence network in Thailand to cooperate with the Allied powers. With the war moving swiftly in Japan's favor, the Phibun government invaded Tai-speaking areas of northeastern Burma and accepted from the Japanese a reestablishment of Thai control over four northern Malay states Siam had conceded to Britain in 1909. By mid-1944, however, it was clear that the war was going against Japan and that Phibun's policies were in shambles, as was the Thai economy now suffering from Allied bombing, inflation, severe shortages, and corruption among officials. The Phibun government fell, and the stage was set for Thailand to cope with the consequences of the wartime alliance, a process in which Pridi and Seni were major players, while Phibun narrowly escaped a guilty judgment in 1946 as a war criminal (his case was set aside by the Thai supreme court partly on legal grounds, but also in response to public opinion that saw Phibun as having acted in the best interests of the country).[64]

Phibun regained the prime ministership in 1948 and held it until 1957. In the changed circumstances of the postwar years, the heady nationalism of the late 1930s and early 1940s lost its steam. The territory Phibun had acquired had to be given up. With the collapse of Japan and then nationalist China, and with the Korean War and the rise of the relationship with the United States as central to Thai security, Thailand moved into a new era heavily influenced by the U.S. relationship. A new generation of British- and American-educated technocrats began to assert increasingly powerful influence over the direction of public policy, supported by the United States and by the prestige of the new international institutions, especially the World Bank. As will be seen below, the nationalism of Phibun and Luang Wichit left a heritage that was not without benefits. Although Phibun carried his anti-Sinicism further during his second period in power, especially in the attempt to expand the state enterprise sector, the policy took an unexpected turn. Phibun and the factions struggling for dominance in the postwar years began entering into alliances with leading Chinese businessmen willing to pay for the protection that could be provided by powerful patrons, the very people who dominated the government that was pursuing the threatening policies in the first place. These accommodations had consequences of their own (which we would now categorize as rent-seeking behavior) that were unhealthy for the development of the Thai economy and polity; but as a lesser evil, this system led to the rapid disappearance of anti-Sinicist rhetoric, restored confidence within the Chinese community, and paved the way for the excision of anti-Sinicism from Thai economic policy and from the body politic as a whole. The assimilation of the Chinese or, more accurately, the emergence of the Sino-Thai as a fully domestic blend of associated cultures has been a source of dynamism for Thailand's economic development and a sociological phenomenon that has removed from Thailand the ethnic dimension that continues to trouble and cast a shadow over the future of a number of other countries of the region.

Finally, at the very margin of public policy debate were the left-wing revolutionaries. Although King Vajiravudh had attacked communism as early as 1912 (in one of his plays, entitled *The Coup D'Etat*), there was little evidence of communist presence until the late 1920s. At that time and during the 1930s, most of the adherents of formal communist organizations in Thailand were either local Chinese or Vietnamese living in northeastern Thailand. After publication of articles calling for revolutionary political and economic change, the government arrested several communists. On enactment of the Anticommunist Act of 1933, the tiny movement went underground and was relatively inactive. A Thai Communist party was formed during the war and became openly politically active in 1946. Only in the 1960s, however, did the communist movement in Thailand begin to develop even marginal support. While its subsequent armed insurgency became a problem of considerable importance in 1965 and for over fifteen years thereafter, and drew student support in the middle and late 1970s, neither the Communist Party of Thailand (CPT) nor Marxist ideology developed any direct influence over Thai economic policy.[65]

Four Major Products; Modest Promotion

Taking together the major manpower reforms, the extension of the railroad into the northern and northeastern regions, and the incentives to land settlement and the expansion of rice production, the Thai government can fairly be described as having had a policy of "promoting development" in the rice sector (which included a very substantial portion of the population) for a good fifty years. As significant as the policy measures were in the context of nineteenth-century Siam, the content and extent of promotion fell far short of what might have been done, even allowing for the constraints on public-sector investment created by treaty and strategic considerations. The first significant public-sector irrigation project was not completed until 1922, a scheme that embraced only a fraction of the flood-control-oriented program developed for the government in 1903 by a Dutch expert. During the century before World War II, very little was done to study the problems of rice production or to develop better technology. Those who focus on the half-empty part of the glass and who draw a critical judgment of the balance of economic policies over this long period have at least one strong argument for their negative conclusions, viz. the failure of these policies to put per capita income on a rising track. The continuous expansion of paddy area by the farming population must have taken place in response to an incentive of higher income. Once the corvée and slave time was transferred to increased cultivated area, however, and the farmer had achieved the potential rise in income this entailed, the absence of a flow of higher-yielding varieties or new cultivation techniques virtually locked him in, especially in the central flood plain where rice was the only feasible crop.

Thailand had three other commodities that together with rice added up to a large fraction of the country's economy, commerce, and exports—tin, teak, and rubber. The teak forests are located in the North. Exports peaked early in the nineteenth century and remained around 5 percent or less of the value of total (recorded) exports in the period after World War I. Tight government regulatory intervention came only in 1895 in response to the pattern of indiscriminate cutting that characterized forestry production at the time. Tin mining had a long history in the peninsular South, centering on the island of Phuket, now a major tourist resort. The tin was all exported, either as ore or in some periods after local smelting. Tin exports were more important than teak but were subject to wide fluctuations in world prices and demand. Government policy encouraged tin production and imposed a sliding scale of royalties that lowered the tax burden as prices declined, but the industry was prevented from exploring or developing any mining potential in the bulk of the country that lay above the province of Chumporn in the narrow neck of the peninsula. Mining in this large fraction of the country's area was reserved for government development, which by and large did not take place. Rubber production began only after World War I and became a significant export only in the mid-1930s. As was the case with rice for a much longer period, government encouragement of rubber production was important in one dimension, virtually free access to state land for potential planters, but nothing was done before the war to improve yields or raise the quality of the rubber sheet product. In the 1930s Thailand did succeed in protecting its tin and rubber sectors from cutbacks enforced on producers in other countries; by exploiting the country's position as a minor producer that could nonetheless undermine the market support measures being taken by the major exporters, the monarchy government in 1931 and the new regime in 1933 were able to negotiate Thai adherence to the tin and rubber cartels, respectively, at favorable quota levels that in effect placed no restraint on Thai producers of these two commodities.

Government efforts to encourage the development of production of nonresource-based commodities were even weaker than the policies and activities described above. For decades following the Bowring Treaty, household production of textiles and other handicrafts slowly declined as cheap imported goods reached into far corners of the country. The potential for import-substituting infant industries was virtually nil. The domestic market for manufactured goods was small and consisted of household demand for a variety of minor consumer nondurables. Up to the end of the absolute monarchy only a handful of manufacturing enterprises were established (other than rice mills). Ingram attributes this absence of a manufacturing sector to several factors besides the demand limitations—lack of entrepreneurship, skilled labor, electric power, or a capital market.[66] Most important, he cites the absence of an industrial development policy on the part of the government. Even after the treaty revisions of 1926 allowed Thailand to raise tariff levels and institute, for the first time, an infant-industry incentive structure, the government took no steps that could be interpreted as a promotional policy. "Some industries were established as a result of tariffs levied following the treaty revisions in 1926, although the government apparently did not intend to foster domestic industry when the rates were set. In fact, when domestic production [for example, of matches] began and imports declined, the principal reaction was one of concern for the lost revenue."[67]

Despite the fact that the coup Promoters swept into power determined to pursue a vigorous policy of economic development, compared with the passive laissez-faire approach of the ancien regime, they had no systematic program. The anti-Sinicism of the time led them toward the creation of a state industrial-enterprise sector. However, besides a few ventures in sugar milling, distilling, and cigarettes (in the latter two products the government bought out existing private enterprises), the government undertook very little industrial investment between 1932 and the onset of the war. The wartime shortages of many goods created some opportunities for import-substitution production, but the boost did not outlive the artificial protection. Lacking sufficient market size and supportive conditions, Thai industrial development could not duplicate the wartime expansion experience that occurred in many Latin American countries.

Summary

I have tried in this brief and selective review to capture the highlights of Thai history that are pertinent for an understanding of the country's economic system on the eve of World War II. It will be useful to summarize (with apology for omission of qualifications and disputed interpretations, and for the unavoidable disregard of detail and complexity in any effort to reduce historical experience to its essential large features) the economic inheritance Thailand's past gave to the architects of the country's modern economic development.

Starting from a largely autarkic subsistence economy, overwhelmingly agricultural and hardly penetrated by science or industry, Thailand had been slowly modernizing for nearly a century. Out of a combination of necessity and preference with only partial fiscal autonomy, and with a focus on internal political and administrative consolidation and on the need to cope with colonial encroachment, the paternalistic change processes guided by the monarchy did not give high priority to economic development or use the state as an instrument for forcing the pace of social and economic change. The main components of economic policy were (virtually) free trade, encouragement of primary exports, measures to free up scarce labor and encourage land settlement for rice production, encouragement of Chinese immigration to expand the labor supply, conservative fiscal and monetary management, maintenance of a strong external financial reserve position through trade surpluses, and minimal government intervention into the operations of the market. These policies entailed an ethnic division of economic activities, decades of low public-sector and overall investment, very modest development of human capital or improvement in public health—and overall, very little rise in per capita income.

Historical data on Thailand's population and the overall size of the economy are largely conjectural for much of this entire period. The most recent reworking of the limited information and the estimates of the handful of researchers who have tried to construct historical series is by Sompop Manarungsan. Sompop puts the population in 1850 at 5.2 million, rising to 7.3 million in 1900 and around 15.5 million at the start of World War II. The rate of population growth would have risen from around 0.5 percent per annum in the mid-nineteenth century to a peak of 2.8 percent in the years 1872–1932 (peak years of Chinese immigration), falling to around 2.0 percent at the end of the period.[68] He estimates that GDP in 1938 was 16.9 billion baht (at 1950 prices), about 30 percent higher than the GDP level (also in 1950 prices) of 5.6 billion baht in 1870. These estimates imply a per capita GDP rise over the period from 973 baht to 1,138 baht, a mere 16 percent over nearly seventy years, or an average of 0.4 percent per annum for the years 1870–1913 and zero percent thereafter. (The very low rate of increase in per capita income is to some extent a statistical artifact; Sompop has merely tied the historical series of values of several GDP sectors [for which there is no information whatsoever] to the population estimates, working backward from the [very uncertain] estimates of GDP composition in 1950.)[69] While historical exactitude on these measurements is out of the question, the essential characterization of low per capita income and slow growth is beyond doubt.

The very gradual pace of change, the limited reach of education and communication, left the largely rural population politically inert. Since the material conditions of rural life had not been subject to large-scale or rapid change, no significant alternatives or stresses had yet appeared to challenge or change the long-prevailing worldview, religious practices, village social structure, and traditions of interpersonal behavior that had given Thai rural life its widely observed tranquil stability.

There is little point in speculating what would have happened in Thai economic, social, and political history if the government had undertaken more active developmental policies over this long period. I merely observe at this point that the pursuit of a free-trade, laissez-faire economic regime that let market prices and private enterprise rule with little government intervention—that is the essence of the current prescription for underdeveloped economies—was not a sufficient condition, for nearly a full century, to impel Thailand out of the ranks of the preindustrial poor.

3

POLITICAL INSTABILITY AND
DEVELOPMENT DISARRAY: 1945–1957

Modern Thai economic development is commonly reckoned as having gotten underway after 1958 with the advent of direct rule by Marshal Sarit Thanarat. Under the Sarit regime, development became a major focus of government attention. A coherent set of policies was formulated and pursued with increasing effectiveness. An institutional framework for development planning and promotion was put in place. The political and policy leadership was strong and held to a more or less steady course. The postwar years leading up to Sarit's assumption of power present a remarkably different picture, one of policy drift, political instability, resource misallocation, and a fair degree of economic mismanagement. Nevertheless, a comprehension of the postwar period is essential for understanding the emergence of the policy reversal under Sarit and the basic thrust of economic management policy for most of the subsequent years; and the contrast between the Phibun and Sarit periods has in some respects been overdrawn.

Political Turmoil

I noted above that the National Assembly ousted the Phibun government in July 1944 in the face of deteriorating domestic economic conditions and the evident decline of Japanese fortunes. The assembly chose as prime minister one of the civilian Promoters, Khuang Aphaiwong, a decision that precipitated the deepening of the factional splits that had been developing within the Promoters between Pridi's civilian supporters (and naval backing) on one side, and Phibun and the army on the other. The prospects for civilian government based on an elected assembly appeared favorable at first, buttressed by the overriding need to develop good relations with the Allied powers in order to reestablish the country's international standing. The relationship with the United States became of immediate importance after the end of the war. The United States treated Thailand as a nonbelligerent country; when the Phibun government aligned Thailand with Japan in 1941 and declared war on the United States and Great Britain, the Department of State had accepted the refusal of the Thai ambassador, Seni Pramoj, to deliver the declaration (on the grounds that the declaration was an illegal misrepresentation of the wishes of the Thai people) as tantamount to nullification of any state of war between the two countries. Ambassador Pramoj went on to set up a Free Thai movement among Thais in the United States and Britain. Some of the Free Thai were then trained to provide the Allies with intelligence, linked with Free Thai counterparts inside Thailand who were under the leadership of Pridi.

The British government, on the other hand, took the position that Thailand had been a formal belligerent and that the Phibun government's cooperation with Japan had facilitated the Japanese invasions of Malaya, Singapore, and Burma. Accordingly, Britain pressed demands that would have compromised Thai sovereignty and imposed heavy reparations in the form of free delivery of rice to India. American support enabled the Thais to resist these demands and to obtain less onerous obligations for rice deliveries.

With Phibun and the army discredited in the immediate aftermath of the war, Pridi emerged as the preeminent civilian politician. The National Assembly chose Seni to head the first postwar government[1] in recognition of his personal standing in Washington. Elections in January 1946 gave Pridi's party a solid majority in the National Assembly. After a short-lived government under Khuang Aphaiwong, Pridi became prime minister. Unfortunately for civilian government, a series of events then transpired that created insuperable problems for Pridi and his successors.[2] Pridi's government fell, as noted earlier, under a cloud of suspicion over regicide. The short-lived civilian governments appeared unable to cope with the postwar economic disorders. The sense that the country was spinning out of control was heightened by a number of political assassinations and by the deterioration in security conditions in neighboring countries.

On November 8, 1947, a resurgent army group seized power. Calling themselves the Coup Group, the leading instigators included Phibun, Gen. Phin Chunhawan, Col. Phao Siyanon, Col. Sarit Thanarat, and General Kat Songkhram. Fearing a sharp international reaction, the Coup Group maintained the parliamentary process and installed Khuang Aphaiwong once again as prime minister. When elections in early 1948 gave Khuang's party a majority in the face of a very poor showing for the party of the Coup Group, the army forced Khuang to resign and returned Phibun to the premiership.

In his summary characterization of the first three postwar years, Wyatt noted that "No leaders of genuine mass following arose in the period save Phibun and Pridi; and the support that each commanded was qualified. . . . In neither case was there substantial mass backing. . . . We are left with the impression of a shallowly based political order involving a fragmented and fractious elite split by vague ideological orientations, attitudes toward royal authority and the economic order, and, especially, ambitions and personal interests and rivalries."[3] Although Phibun subsequently held the premiership for over nine years, this continuity did not provide the country with political stability either. Into the early 1950s Phibun had to contend with several plots and outright coup attempts designed to remove him from office by force and to restore the flagging political position of the navy. The power of the navy was finally broken in 1951 after a brief but bloody coup attempt that resulted in over 3,000 casualties. Phibun then had to cope with the rising power of the key rivals within his own faction, Phao and Sarit. Phao was the head of the Police Department, a national constabulary that he was building into a paramilitary force. As commander of the First Army, located in Bangkok, Sarit controlled the pivotal military forces bearing on Thai politics. Phibun's efforts to outmaneuver his rivals culminated in an election in early 1957. The flagrant rigging by Phibun's party, and a widely publicized timber scandal involving Phao, gave Sarit an opportunity to separate himself deftly from his two erstwhile associates, gather public support, and lead the army in a bloodless coup on September 17, 1957.

Although Sarit immediately consolidated his hold on power, he himself was obliged to travel to Washington, D.C., for extended treatment of a liver ailment, entrusting the government to Pote Sarasin, a diplomat whose primary tasks as interim prime minister were to assure the United States that Thai foreign policy would continue its pro-American orientation and to conduct early elections. To the discomfit of Sarit and his close military associates, the electorate in Bangkok denied their party a single seat, while in the country as a whole they failed to win a controlling majority of the lower house. The military attempted for a further period to rule from their parliamentary position, to demonstrate their good faith as critics of Phibun's "dirty election" of 1957 and with an eye on international opinion. When Pote Sarasin declined to continue, Gen. Thanom Kittikachorn was chosen to be the next prime minister, taking office on January 1, 1958. During Thanom's brief tenure, the government party lost ground in a by-election and was buffeted by parliamentary and press criticism. Thanom attempted to resign several times in frustration. Finally, in October 1958 Sarit, his strength recovered, returned from a rest in England, accepted Thanom's resignation, and assumed direct power. He abrogated the parliament, annulled the constitution, arrested a number of "communist sympathizers," and ushered in a new political era of dictatorial rule.[4] Sarit's accession was also a turning point for Thailand's postwar economic management.

The Policy Process: Drifting and Ineffectual

World attention to economic development of the "less developed countries," most of which were beginning to emerge from colonial status, came into focus around 1950. The attention to the economic backwardness of the underdeveloped countries followed closely on the heels of the Marshall Plan for European recovery and was propelled by the Truman administration's effort to respond to the deepening cold war as it appeared to be extending to Europe's periphery, Greece and Turkey, and beyond. The years 1949 and 1950 saw a flurry of government activity that linked Thailand into the international development system. In May 1949 Thailand was admitted to membership in the World Bank and the International Monetary Fund (IMF). Later that same year the government put a request to the U.S. Department of State for an American technical mission to survey the country's resources.[5] Diplomatic exchanges in 1949 led to the signing of agreements in late 1950 initiating the Fulbright program for financing higher education for Thais in the United States, and launching economic and military aid programs. United Nations specialized agencies such as the Food and Agriculture Organization also began programs of technical assistance. In 1950 the World Bank made its first loan to Thailand, $25.4 million for rail and port upgrading and for construction of the Chainat dam, the first component of an extensive scheme for control of the Chao Phraya River system.

The initial reviews of needs conducted by the foreign technicians found a virtually uniform weakness of trained capacities and organizational capabilities over the whole range of government departments they surveyed as they began their respective technical relationships with Thai government counterparts. One sectoral example describing the situation in 1951 will suffice here, especially pertinent given the overwhelming importance of agriculture in the Thai economy at the time:

> Seven departments of the Ministry operated field programs of an extension nature, independently and with considerable duplication and overlapping. Comparatively few of the field personnel of these various agencies had sufficient training to give useful assistance to farmers. . . . Information on land-use capabilities, soil characteristics, and plant food needs . . . is fragmentary and facilities for gathering it hardly existed. . . . Agricultural statistics, especially economic information, has been almost lacking for purposes of agricultural planning and development.[6]

Between the UN specialized agencies and the various sectoral divisions of the U.S. aid office in Bangkok (the United States Operations Mission, soon well known throughout Thailand by its acronym, USOM), virtually every piece of the government machinery that was relevant to economic development found itself surveyed, critiqued for its development orientation and capabilities, and involved in a network of assistance projects. The early capital assistance focused on rehabilitation of the war-damaged transportation system and on the initial expansion of transport, power, and other infrastructure based on the introduction of up-to-date technical standards. Technical assistance was a major element of external aid right from the start. With the access to capital funds, to overseas training opportunities, and to the supplementary local currency funds that virtually every USOM-assisted project obtained (from a "counterpart fund" financed largely from Thai government appropriations), government departments faced strong incentives to push for higher levels of activity and for expanded responsibilities. Departments also found that an aid commitment from an outside agency increased their ability to extract increased budget allocation from the government's budget bureau. It would take years of training and institution-building to effect widespread reform and strengthening of the bureaucracy, but the shift in orientation of the bureaucracy toward becoming a primary engine of development in Thailand was under way in the early 1950s.

While these early years saw aid-related activity scattered through the bureaucracy, the development policy, planning, and coordinating capabilities at the head of the bureaucracy remained woefully weak. Given the central role that foreign aid would play, it was evident that the Thai government would have to set up some administrative machinery as counterpart to the USOM (and to the UN agencies and other donor organizations as the number of countries providing development assistance grew over time), since there was no government entity in place that could perform aid-receiving and rationalizing functions. Thus, under the terms of the so-called Bilateral Agreement between Thailand and the United States that provided the legal framework for the aid relationship, the Thai government agreed "to assure efficient and practical use of all resources available . . . provide detailed information necessary to carrying out the provisions of this agreement . . . and to evaluate the effectiveness of assistance furnished or contemplated."[7] To perform these functions and to plan and administer the implementation of the U.S. aid program, the government set up the Thai Technical and Economic Committee (TTEC) in November 1950. In practice, for many years, TTEC had only minimal coordinating or planning capabilities. Its first full-time secretariat member was appointed only in 1956. As Caldwell noted, "until the late fifties USOM used to attach to its letters to TTEC draft replies which TTEC had only to approve, retype, and sign."[8] As the size and complexity of international aid to Thailand expanded, especially in the 1960s, various donors extended training and other forms of technical assistance to TTEC itself (TTEC subsequently became a department in the Prime Minister's Office and was renamed the Department of Technical and Economic Cooperation, or DTEC) to strengthen the aid administration process.

The first general "planning committee" in the government was set up under a National Economic Council, which had been established in early 1950. In fact the committee did no planning. Its work was limited to screening capital projects proposed by ministries and state enterprises and to making recommendations for the allocation of the government's limited capital budget among these projects. The committee originated no projects and rejected few, and had nothing to do with public-sector expenditures or activities that were not in the form of capital projects.[9]

Two key offices under the National Economic Council were responsible for the informational basis for economic planning, the Central Statistical Office

(CSO) and the National Income Office. When a World Bank mission surveyed the government's development management capacities in 1957, it found that the statistical office had "no single individual trained specifically for the career of statistician," and that "few if any" of 370 officials entitled statistician, in statistical units in 20 ministries and agencies, had any formal academic training in the subject.[10] The bank mission also referred to a UN expert report that described the statistical situation as "critical in the sense that after five years of UN technical assistance, the CSO was still unable 'to conduct modern censuses, sample surveys, or statistical analytical work without the assistance of outside experts.' "[11]

The state of development planning capability in 1956 was reviewed by American economist John A. Loftus soon after his arrival to serve as the economic adviser to Minister of Finance Phao Boribhandh Yuddhakich. In a memorandum to the minister, Loftus described a process of government decision making that was totally centralized in Bangkok, lacked any participation by the population or any reflection of its views, was based on superficial analysis, and culminated in no systematic judgmental mechanism.

> I have found general agreement that economic development planning in Thailand is not very far advanced. But what more forcibly strikes the newly-arrived observer . . . is that the process of development planning is undemocratic. . . . Projects do not originate in the grass roots of the provinces; the provinces are not importuning the central government to find funds to carry out programs locally conceived. Instead everything is done by a benevolent bureaucracy in Bangkok. . . .
>
> Since development schemes are formulated by Ministries, arguments about which scheme is more important become inter-Ministerial arguments, and there is no automatic mechanism for adjudicating them. . . .
>
> Projects . . . have the support and backing of the Ministries which devised them. But there is no basis on that backing on which to decide anything. The comparative importance of projects in different sectors cannot be discerned by measuring the political force that can be mustered in support of them. And the assessment of comparative utility is not subject to marginal analysis. . . .
>
> In short . . . no machinery exists for resolving these [inter-Ministerial] disputes rationally. . . . [The result is] a lot of random and uncoordinated schemes.[12]

At the time Loftus wrote these observations, the World Bank was considering how it might respond to a request the Thai government had made for a development survey mission. Since the timing or even eventuality of the proposed bank mission was uncertain, Loftus suggested that the minister authorize him, along with a small group of Thai officials (including Supharb Yossundara, Boonma Wongsawan, and Chalong Pungtrakul), to carry out a preliminary planning exercise, a first attempt to gather development project proposals from government ministries and agencies and pass them through a rough comparative screening examination. The "Economic Survey Group" found most of the ministerial proposals poorly prepared and lacking the minimal empirical basis for comparative analysis. Nevertheless, the results of the exercise were revealing of the development ideas floating around in the public sector, and served as one point of departure for the work of the World Bank survey mission, which did arrive in Bangkok in 1957.

Loftus was able to observe closely (and critique to the minister of finance) the workings of economic policy making across the board at senior levels of the Thai bureaucracy and at the political apex, the cabinet. He found a "quest for development" in the government but no "sense of proportion or priority." The government generally attempted to formulate policy and make decisions through committee processes that he judged to be grossly inadequate. Committees typically met without any agenda or prior distribution of documents. Deliberations were casual, discussions of fact "slipshod." There was seldom any staff work providing clear statements of the issues or of the options facing the decision makers. When decisions were taken they were rarely stated clearly, nor did the committees produce written records to communicate the decisions or to facilitate their implementation. He singled out the Cabinet of Ministers as wasting time on "excessive" numbers of issues that should be decided at subcabinet levels. More important, Loftus criticized the cabinet's exercise of powers to incur extensive extrabudgetary expenditures as a source of serious fiscal indiscipline.[13]

The weakness of the informational base for macroeconomic policy management was similar to that for public-sector investment management. Thailand had a dearth of the most basic information needed to assess the current state and trends of an economy. There were major inaccuracies in the trade and balance of payments data. Exports were seriously understated. In 1960 about 70 percent of the recorded current account deficit was balanced by the errors and omissions residual. The investment and other components of the national accounts rested on highly incomplete data. There was no information on the size distribution of income. Different departments in the Ministry of Agriculture issued widely differing figures on crop production. There was no reliable wholesale or consumer price information and virtually no other economic monitoring that could be collated as economic indicators. The Ministry of Industry collected a fair amount of information through its licensing and regulatory administration, but none of it was tabulated or processed in any way that would yield meaningful general information. The position was not much better in transport, communication, and other sectors. Data on public finance were especially deficient for the state enterprises. The best economic data were those compiled by the Bank of Thailand on the finance sector, but there were lags of several months in publication. At the core of the statistical weaknesses of the government was an "absence of competent professional review of the work done by the 'gathering units.' This comes down to a professional manpower weakness in the Central Statistical

Office. The Office is not, nevertheless, to be rebuked too harshly as the problem is ultimately one of funds and training facilities."[14]

The budgeting, accounting, and monitoring of Thailand's public-sector finances during this period were ill-suited for macroeconomic management or for systematic pursuit of program objectives. Many important revenue sources and expenditures were outside the budget and beyond the purview of the financial authorities. The Lottery Bureau was a major example of a public operation so loosely tied to the Ministry of Finance that it could serve as Sarit's principal source of funds and maintain hidden accounting despite wide general knowledge of the financial diversion. The accounting systems of the state enterprises were irregular and lacked transparency. There was no consolidated accounting that brought together all public-sector functions, including local government finances, to give a coherent picture of public economic activities or the flow of funds between the public and private sectors. In addition to the extrabudgetary authorizations by the cabinet criticized by Loftus, it was common practice for state enterprises to undertake expenditure obligations without prior government approval. Especially pernicious was the absence of control by the financial authorities over external borrowing by state enterprises and the ease with which some of these enterprises obtained government guarantees of debts contracted for ill-conceived investment projects. As the World Bank report noted, "not only the form of the budget but also the procedures by which it is prepared are grossly inadequate. There is no machinery for ensuring that the estimates of the different ministries bear any relation to reality, nor is the staff of the Ministry of Finance large enough or competent enough to judge whether these requests are reasonable or to determine their respective priorities."[15]

From Economic Nationalism to Bureaucratic Enterprise and Market Intervention

In sum, whatever the substance of economic policy, whatever measures the political actors were attempting to undertake, cabinet members had to work through a bureaucracy and a system that could not translate policy intent into well-defined policy tools or effective implementable programs. These weaknesses of prosecution were a blessing in disguise since much of the policy intent would have seriously compromised Thailand's development prospects if the policies had been pursued effectively for a sustained period of time.

As noted above, Thai political leadership in the second, postwar period under Prime Minister Phibun looked on private economic activity as a somewhat alien sector to control and to penetrate as a source of political (and personal) finance. If one can assume that the justifications announced by coup makers are important statements of their diagnoses of national ills and of the alternatives they will provide for the country, it is remarkable how little reference these pronouncements make to the long-term direction of economic policy. The brief pronouncements of the 1947 Coup Group criticize the ousted government for economic mismanagement and corruption and for ignoring the nation's economic hardships, but they contain nothing indicating any substance for an alternative program.[16] More revealing are the "personal notes" in which one of the leading planners of the 1947 coup, General Kat, lists the policies and acts ("38 national obstacles") of the government that caused the Coup Group to undertake forcible overthrow. Kat cites corruption, incompetence, and a number of economic problems that were being mishandled. His strongest language is applied to charges that the government was in effect selling out the economy to the local Chinese. His notes conclude with a brief reference to the Coup Group's plan to overcome the "38 obstacles." He declines to give details of the plan's secret content except to note "after building up the nation, the largest and most important task is the plan to retrieve capital from aliens."[17] Finally, it is remarkable that the 1957 coup of Marshal Sarit was accompanied by numerous pronouncements and speeches containing only occasional and vague references to economic matters despite Sarit's determination to characterize his coup as a "revolution."[18]

As suggested by General Kat's assertion that the Coup Group gave high priority to changing the structure of ownership of (nonagricultural) capital in Thailand, the second Phibun government resumed the promulgation of alien exclusion policies begun during Phibun's first period of rule. While the legislation and decrees issued under both Phibun governments were precisely worded to apply to aliens, thereby, for example, not affecting second-generation ethnic Chinese claiming Thai citizenship by right of birth in Thailand, the bulk of Thai aliens were Chinese, and the exclusionary measures were widely seen as anti-Sinic discrimination.[19]

More occupations were added to the list of those that would be closed to aliens. Regulations excluding aliens from owning land were tightened. Legislation was introduced into the National Assembly that would have forced aliens to reside in restricted areas, but it was not actually promulgated. Newspapers often carried unfounded rumors of threatened additional restrictions. In the discriminatory spirit of these policies, government officials often acted with an anti-Chinese bias in carrying out their normal duties.[20]

By the late 1950s the economic nationalism fashioned by Luang Wichit and Phibun appeared to be a spent force, and the cumulative economic impact on the Chinese appeared to have been minor. Coughlin concluded, in 1960, that the Chinese minority "has not been greatly disturbed economically" despite the impression one might gain from a catalogue of the restrictions. Coughlin cites several reasons for the "ineffectiveness" of the entire policy—the main occupations of the Chinese were not touched by the regulations; the community was responding by adopting Thai citizenship; administering officials could be bought off; regulations had loopholes that could be exploited; and enforcement generally was not rigorous.[21] In short, the wholesale forcible restructuring of the ethnic occupational distribution of the labor force that appears to have been the objective of this policy preoccupation never came about in its implementation.

The effort "to retrieve capital from aliens," however, had substantial effects on Thai politics, the role of the Thai state in commerce and industry, the ethos and economic behavior of senior levels of the bureaucracy, the relationships between the Thai elite and the Chinese business leadership, and the investment climate affecting domestic and foreign capital. With the exception, of course, of the expansion of the state's economic role, which was the core of the regime's policy, these other effects were apparently unforeseen and unintended consequences. The legislative provisions and the general atmosphere created by the educational and economic nationalist policies transformed the Chinese business community into what Riggs called "pariah entrepreneurs," that is, businessmen who were viewed as adversaries and distrusted outsiders rather than as integral participants in a society's division of labor. The evolution of this pariah condition, and of the accommodations it engendered between the entrepreneurs and the Thai elite, is one of the best-researched aspects of modern Thai sociology and political economy.[22] Describing the early accommodations as the anti-Chinese measures unfolded in the late 1940s,

> Skinner draws for us with painstaking detail [a picture] of a culturally harassed Chinese business community, surviving only by continually buying protection from the Thai elite . . . unable to secure the adoption of laws favoring their business interests or to impose effective restraints against the arbitrary exercise of power by officials. . . .
>
> Since the entrepreneurial community is, for the most part, Chinese, this means that in so far as a major goal of the [Thai] elite is to acquire wealth, it must exact tribute from the Chinese. Since the ruling elite is not politically responsible to the business community, there is no reason to think that it would want to adopt or enforce any general rules protecting the property interests of the businessman. It prefers an unrestricted hunting license to squeeze the entrepreneur, subject to the condition that he must not be destroyed lest this rich source of wealth be destroyed. . . .
>
> From an earlier stage of informal and relatively unstructured symbiosis between Chinese merchants and Siamese officials there has emerged, since the nineteen-fifties, a complex super-structure of new corporations in which Thai officials and Chinese businessmen collaborate.[23]

The collaboration was between leading Chinese businessmen and senior Thai political, military, and bureaucratic figures. It took the form of Thai officials joining the boards of directors of Chinese firms, and of Chinese businessmen (who held Thai citizenship) joining quasi-official enterprises as managers. The Thais provided favored access to government contracts, influence useful for obtaining exemption to the application of various tax and regulatory burdens that would normally fall on business transactions, and protection against harassment.[24]

In return, the officials received emoluments and shares in the equity of the enterprises. The symbiosis between the Chinese businessmen and the Thai officials and military leaders developed rapidly after Phibun's return to power. Riggs provides an analysis of the networks of these relationships based on official company registration information. He shows how extensive was the participation of both civil and military cabinet members in these arrangements, especially the most powerful among these individuals. It was also evident that over time, as the relative political power of the three main rival cliques changed, culminating in the Sarit coup of 1957, there were parallel changes in the relative business penetration of the cliques, presumably reflecting the efforts of the Chinese business groups to develop stronger bonds with the likely winners among the rival cliques of patrons.[25] While some corporations included on their boards members from only one clique, most of the boards included officials from two or all three of the cliques plus other individual cabinet members not associated with any of the political groups.

It will be recalled that the program of economic nationalism began in the 1930s with an effort to preempt and compete with Chinese business by establishing state enterprises in many lines of commerce and industry. The first industrial state enterprise created under this policy was the Siam Cotton Mill, established in 1935 by the Ministry of Defense, ostensibly for the purpose of making the military self-sufficient in the manufacture of uniforms. Other early enterprises included a paper mill, also under the Ministry of Defense, sugar mills under the Ministry of Economic Affairs, trading companies, shipping, insurance, and banking. One of the flagship enterprises was the Thai Rice Company, set up in 1941 in an effort to wrest control of the milling and trading of the country's dominant single commodity from the hands of the Chinese. Ironically, since the government had no experience in milling, the Chinese owner of the first mill acquired by the Thai Rice Company was immediately hired to be general manager of the government company, and subsequently was entrusted with the establishment of the government's Provincial Bank, itself created to provide the rice company network with financial support.[26]

These initial ventures were fully owned public companies, what now would be termed state enterprises. Some of these enterprises, like the Thai Rice Mill Company, were created through government purchase of private business assets. Others were set up to compete with private enterprise or to introduce domestic production of goods previously supplied entirely by imports. At the fullest extent in the mid-1950s, these companies numbered well over one hundred. Ownership was vested in the Ministry of Finance, but operational control was held by the respective ministries that spawned these ventures during the years when the preemption policy was running strong.[27] The creation of the state enterprises had nothing to do with socialist ideology. Thus the acquisition of private enterprises by the state was not analogous to the movements in some European and other countries to nationalize private corporations. The policy objectives of the Thai elite were equally satisfied by the creation of quasi-public or completely private enterprises, as long as a major share of the capital was in "Thai" hands.

In fact, four ownership patterns emerged during the period of economic nationalism: fully owned state enterprises, joint government–private sector enterprises (with either domestic Chinese or foreign company partners), private enterprises established by members of the different political cliques in their personal capacities, and hybrid ventures put together with ad hoc groupings. An interesting example of the latter was the Bank of Asia for Industry and Commerce established in 1939 at the bequest of Pridi, then minister of finance. The bank's founding shareholders included three close associates of Pridi, other members of the People's party, several Chinese business leaders, and Thammasat University, which provided 62 percent of the initial capital.[28]

As the original nationalist impetus and justification for state intervention into private economic activity receded, the process actually expanded in scope and in the permutations and forms employed, driven now (by the early 1950s) by the exigencies of political competition and the corrupting effects once the methods for easy and rapid access to economic rents had been demonstrated, and indeed sanctioned, as being in the purported public interest. Perhaps the most striking generalization one can make, in retrospect, is that the government of Thailand during this period, at the highest political levels and extending across and downward in the bureaucracy, plunged into the extensive practice of intervention from the political and military realms into the economic activities of the society. The characterization of Thai government policy and activity as essentially nonmarket and ascriptive is striking because of the widely accepted, and correct, perception that Thailand ranks among those developing countries that have placed greatest reliance on market forces to guide their economic development. Thus Thailand's development policy history hinges on the transition from, and substantial rejection of, a highly interventionist postwar orientation.

I have already noted some of the practices by which resource allocation, ownership of assets, and competitive advantage were determined quite apart from the operation of market forces and with little concern for economic efficiency. The majority of the state enterprises and quasi-state ventures established in this period appear to have earned losses in most years, although the accounting systems left their operations rather opaque.[29] In some cases, profits in one enterprise were generated by sales to another (both being controlled by members of the same clique) through transactions at administratively set prices.[30] In many cases the enterprises were undercapitalized, purchased defective used machinery from abroad, developed excessive overhead cost structures, hired numbers of redundant employees, or were unknowingly misled by foreign suppliers (who offered design services) into investing in excess capacity or mismatched production and storage components. Management was generally poor and inexperienced.

Once the principle had been established that political and bureaucratic competition with, and penetration of, economic activity previously left largely to the private sector was a legitimate exercise of authority on behalf of the public interest, it was a short step for the management of these enterprises to promote their operations through market manipulation and rent-seeking. For all categories of enterprise involved—state, quasi-state, private ventures of leading political and bureaucratic individuals, or penetrated Chinese firms—the political/bureaucratic board members were in position to favor their own enterprises through the granting of quotas, monopoly market positions, licenses, exclusive import agencies, mining concessions, and other dispensations from government, including the letting of contracts for construction services and equipment procurement to favored bidders despite ostensibly arms-length and transparent competitive bidding procedures.

It is important to note that, in the case of many enterprises in which the state held complete or partial equity, the government representation on the managing boards often included some senior civil servants of unimpeachable integrity. Nevertheless, once the potentialities of market intervention had been demonstrated, it was another short step into interventions designed to advance political rather than ostensive national interests, or simply to increase personal wealth. For example, it was common practice for political figures who were setting up new enterprises, or being invited to join the boards of existing private firms, to receive blocks of shares for which no investment from their personal funds was required or expected. Through control of the operations of state enterprises or of the ordinary procurement activities of government departments, political figures were able to earn lucrative rents by interposing their personal companies (often their wives' companies) as exclusive agents. In one conspicuous case, the World Bank had to arrange for the government to withdraw from project coverage certain large pieces of equipment being procured under a bank loan when neither the bank nor the Ministry of Finance was able to get the responsible state enterprise board to rescind an improperly granted bid award. Contracts for government construction projects were frequently awarded to firms that were controlled by powerful patrons of the ministry or agency making the procurement.[31]

Some of the major commodities entering into Thailand's external trade became captive to manipulation designed to create profitable market-controlling positions for individual enterprises. For example, in the mid-1950s the Thailand Jute Development Corporation (a Phin-Phao group enterprise) was given a monopsony over the purchase of domestic kenaf production and a monopoly over kenaf exports.[32] Other Soi Rajakru firms held exclusive marketing positions in livestock slaughtering in Bangkok and in livestock export. With rice production and trade the largest single economic sector of the economy, the seizure of rice control was a major objective of the government even before the war, as noted above; I shall return to this complex policy history below.

Although it is not possible to measure the quantitative extent of all these interventions taken together (e.g., their share of manufacturing output or of value-added in Thailand's GDP), there can be no doubt that the four categories of enterprises penetrated a considerable fraction of the country's monetized economic activity. Besides major agricultural commodities, political penetration and the accompanying reliance on irregular, rent-seeking, and corrupt practices reached into a sizable fraction of what was then still a minor manufacturing sector. Thus the Ministry of Defense had enterprises manufacturing textiles, shoes, bottles, batteries, paper clips, and so forth. The Ministry of Industry invested in enterprises producing paper, sugar, gunny bags, liquor, bamboo products and other items. Other nonfinancial enterprises under state or other mixed forms of political penetration were in cement, fisheries, pharmaceuticals, shipping, construction materials, and so on. Penetration of the formal financial sector was almost total (apart from the foreign-owned banks), including several of the country's leading commercial banks—the Bangkok Bank, Bank of Ayudhya, Thai Farmers Bank, Thai Military Bank, and some of the smaller banks such as Laem Thong and the Union Bank of Bangkok.

In addition, the network of changwat trading companies, which covered a large part of the country, attempted and occasionally succeeded in taking over business at the provincial level previously conducted by private traders, and in ignoring market prices. A newspaper account in 1941 conveys the flavor of these interventions:

> The operation of the Jangwat [sic] Trading Companies was diverted from the original aim of the government. Instead of giving support to the merchants, the companies caused . . . troubles as they were forced not to sell goods directly traded with the public, the company would later control the prices . . . the companies forced people to sell coconut only to their companies even though the seller was not pleased with the price set by the companies.[33]

One of the major organizations designed as a conglomerate was the War Veterans Organization. Girling's summary account distills the relationship between political penetration and commercial intervention:

> The Saha Samakki (an organization of war veterans) initiated a trading venture typical of the kind that flourished in the era of military-dominated governments following the 1947 coup. This organization, whose head in 1946 was general (later Field Marshal) Phin Chunhawan, was doing poorly in the soft drinks trade. To gain the benefit of Chinese expertise and to diversify their operations, the group worked in particular with a Chinese rice merchant and mill owner from the Northeast. An association of rice millers, formed by this businessman, received powerful military backing—for Phin was on top as a result of the 1947 coup, which indeed he had promoted. This helped enormously in the struggle for markets and the control of transportation (the railway and trucking system). In return, Phin and his military and civilian

bureaucratic colleagues were appointed members of the board of directors of the association, drawing handsome profits from the proceeds of a successful venture.[34]

One industrial enterprise in particular is worth singling out: the National Economic Development Corporation Ltd. (NEDCOL). This enterprise was set up in 1954 as a holding company with five manufacturing subsidiaries, two sugar mills, the Northeast Jute Mill, Saraburi Marble Factory, and Bangpra Paper Mill. The founders were members of the Soi Rajakru group, although their rival, General Sarit, was also given a block of shares. The roster of shareholders (they were not required to actually pay for their shares) included some of the most powerful persons in the country besides the outsider Sarit. Field Marshal Phin Chunhawan, Gen. Phao Siyanon, and Minister of Finance Gen. Pianlert Bauripanyuthakit had the three largest share allocations; other holders included General Banyat Thebhasadin, minister of industry; Gen. Siri Siriyothin, deputy minister of commerce; and Gen. Pramarn Adireksan, deputy minister of industry and of transport. Financed by bank loans and supplier credits, and saddled with inefficient management and poorly designed plant (Loftus noted that the promoters of NEDCOL had put one million dollars into the paper mill "without any real knowledge about the size and composition of the market for the mill's output."[35]), NEDCOL fell into bankruptcy within three years. Since the Ministry of Finance had guaranteed the loans involved, the government was forced to take over the company while the directors resigned without personal cost. Negotiating loan extensions and devising plans for restructuring and salvaging the factories became one of the major and most frustrating assignments given to Loftus. He succeeded in renegotiating and extending NEDCOL's debt repayment structure, but repayments had to be made by the government and were a heavy claim on the financial resources available under the country's first development plan, which began in 1961.

The NEDCOL experience stands out because of the foreign financial obligations it imposed on the Thai budget for five years and because it was the largest single industrial venture of the period. In 1962, five years after NEDCOL's financial collapse and its abandonment by its political founders, Loftus summarized its condition and how the government had handled the matter:

> While I was unable to persuade the foreign equipment suppliers to make any significant adjustment in the contractual terms of their creditorship claims, I did persuade an important creditor, the Bank of America, to convert their [$10 million] claim from the status of a demand note to that of a five-year installment contract. . . .
>
> From the financial point of view, the position today is much brighter than it was five years ago; but the brightness is largely illusory. The Company is nearly free of external debt; but almost none of this debt retirement has been effected out of net earnings (which do not exist). Debt has been liquidated

mostly at the expense of the state budget; nevertheless it has been liquidated, and that is something.

From the operational and managerial point of view, however, there is not even any illusory brightness. One factory is operating at a cash profit but not an accounting profit (that is, debt service and depreciation are being ignored). Another requires larger continuing agricultural investment than the gross profits; and indeed this particular factory this year is not even selling its output at all. (In any case, the operational rate is not only far below rated capacity but even below the "break-even point.") The paper factory has finally been "brought into production" at exorbitant cost and after incredible delay; but it too is operating far below capacity and its market prospects are uncertain.

In summary, I advocated from the beginning: (a) prompt action and prompt decision, (b) engagement of foreign management. The affairs of the Company have been administered essentially with procrastination rather than promptness; and foreign management has not been arranged or even seriously sought.[36]

Loftus was chagrined by the entire state enterprise policy and the economic wastage he observed that flowed from the disregard for ordinary good business practice. In a memorandum from 1961 addressed to M. L. Dej Snidwongse, the chairman of the Executive Committee of the National Economic Development Board (NEDB), Loftus observed that the government lacked even basic data on its own enterprises, was in no position to exercise financial or policy control over these enterprises, was allocating resources to them without applying any criteria or objectives, and was tolerating gross inefficiency in their operation:

> The first thing that is needed is a comprehensive list of state enterprises. This is not as simple as it sounds, as there is need first for an agreed definition of what is a state enterprise. . . . The list should include the most definitive evaluation possible of the government's investment in the various enterprises. . . . In many cases, no record whatever can be found of how much and when and why the government made its investment, let alone any prorating and imputation of depreciation. . . .
>
> This list should be classified according to several different breakdowns [including] whether the enterprise . . . is one that would be normally and generally conceded to be proper for a state enterprise (central banking, the large public utility organizations, etc.) or whether it would be considered likely to impinge unfavorably upon attitudes and performance in the private sector . . . what are the stated and real reasons for government participation . . . the costs of continuing government participation in comparison with the costs of disengagement. . . .
>
> It is necessary to devise a pattern of financial and other reporting to the government on the affairs of the enterprises [and] to formulate the most general criteria possible to govern the capital investment policies of the state enterprises. . . . Substantial improvement in accounting practice . . . is urgently needed and long overdue.
>
> There should also be a thorough study of business management practices in the various enterprises with a view to its early improvement. The need in this

particular is not uniform among all the enterprises (for example, the Railways and the Tobacco Monopoly seem to be reasonably well run, whereas certain other enterprises are managed with almost incredible inefficiency). . . .
Appropriations to cover the capital requirements or current deficits of certain state enterprises seem to be made in an essentially random fashion.[37]

The economic adviser often had occasion to examine and offer his views on individual state enterprises in addition to his major preoccupation with NEDCOL. One venture that roused his ire was a small oil refinery the military wanted to build at the site of a very low yielding oil field at Fang in northern Thailand. In his retrospective final report in 1962, he wrote, "I considered (and still consider) many aspects of this arrangement to have been either incompatible with the public interest or to have been based on a limited concept of what constitutes public interest. Nevertheless, the refinery project went ahead."[38]

The authors cited who have undertaken the most extensive research on the postwar evolution of the state enterprise sector, and on the parallel political penetration of the Chinese business sector, have focused on the structure of ownership and the political dynamics. There can be little doubt that the system embraced the most powerful political and military cliques and personages, large numbers of senior bureaucrats, and most of the Chinese business leaders. Skinner records that the numbers of government officials and "other members of the Thai elite" who had entered into relationships or positions with Chinese firms were in the "hundreds" by the end of 1952, several years before this process reached its peak.[39] It must be borne in mind that this projection of official capacity into policy-sanctioned positions generating private benefit came about immediately after the wartime and immediate postwar years of severe economic dislocation, during which the bureaucracy suffered a sharp loss in the real value of official salaries and as a result became widely prone to petty corruption. Furthermore, the Thai bureaucracy of the postwar years was not yet much exposed to Western education or the mores of Western and international agency bureaucracies. The behavioral traditions of the Thai bureaucracy, reaching back generations, were based on patronage systems, informal groupings that were maintained through the exchange of mutual obligations and favors between powerful individuals and lower ranking "clients." In a policy framework that encouraged the bureaucratic leadership to use its position as a base for penetrating private business, it was apparent that the mass of lower civil servants, their economic position already eroded, was readily being drawn by example and necessity into a relationship with the society as a whole that was fraught with potentially divisive consequences quite apart from its impact on economic activity.

From this summary account, one can see several economic implications. The nascent corporate industrial sector was starting its development with a raft of poor investments. The state and quasi-state enterprises were a substantial drain on the government budget. While the shareholders and board members appear to have received income from many of these enterprises even in years when the firms were making losses, the social rate of return on the resources involved was in most cases negative. Manipulation of the markets for specific commodities, transport access, and other services evolved as a logical extension of political penetration and a rent-seeking bureaucratic culture. In the face of the management weaknesses and technological errors, it is apparent that these enterprises generated little positive industrial "learning" that would serve for future investment projects. Similarly, given the high eventual failure rate among these ventures, and the fact that many of the surviving industrial state enterprises have simply stagnated into insignificance, it cannot be argued that the whole experience was justifiable as an "infant industry" phase of Thailand's development.

Corruption raised the cost of public-sector procurement and construction, imposing in effect a hidden tax to finance transfer payments to the beneficiaries. There were significant distributive effects from these transfers, from the board memberships and grants of shares, and from the use of "inside information" and political influence (for example, the timely purchase of land likely to rise in value after the location of planned new roads is decided and made known). Outright diversions of funds from public enterprises (especially the Lottery and the Tobacco Monopoly) that would otherwise flow into the government budget reached substantial proportions, with no public accounting.

I have drawn a stark picture of society in the throes of political instabilities and lacking a workable system for orderly transfer of power. The political leadership was distracted by factional struggle and looked on private economic activity as a somewhat alien sector that needed to be controlled and penetrated. Economic nationalism had opened the door to extensive intervention in market forces and to the creation of an incipient class of Chinese businessmen and Thai elite who were arranging among themselves a narrow distribution of ownership of new industrial assets and financial institutions. Public-sector investment expenditures were being made in a manner not likely to yield positive returns, and open to abuse and to uncontrolled creation of external government debt. The general direction of economic and social policy, to the extent it was not merely drifting, could hardly have been characterized as purposively designed to pursue economic development through efficient allocation of the available resources. Fortunately, there were a number of factors that limited the long-run impact of these activities and made it possible to effect a turnaround before the full potentialities of these policies could eventuate.

First, the instabilities of Thai politics stood in sharp contrast to the stability and political passivity of the society underneath the surface of Bangkok's power struggles. Much of rural Thailand was still physically isolated, barely monetized, and exposed to little intrusion from external cultures or material products. Village religious and family life was showing only marginal changes from long-established traditional practices. Changes in economic structure and technology were under way but tended to concentrate in a few areas and had not begun to suffuse the society. Although Thailand was certainly not without tensions, most scholars agree that Thai society during this period, and for long periods before, was relatively stable by international standards, although "stability" in such a broad context is not a precise concept.[40]

Second, the discriminatory policies against aliens as individuals, as noted earlier, were not implemented forcefully. Third, many of the state and quasi-state enterprises self-destructed as their technical and managerial weaknesses led them into bankruptcy. Fourth, although the industrial enterprises were large on the margin (one of only two cement companies, the only paper mill, etc.), they were marginal to the economy as a whole. (As late as 1960 the manufacturing sector accounted for 3 percent of the labor force, of which a large fraction was employed in small-scale private enterprises.) Since the industrial sector was small and shallow, these enterprises had no structure of interindustry linkage that could serve as a drag on the competitiveness of whole industrial subsectors. The oldest and largest industrial enterprise in Thailand, the Siam Cement Company, escaped politicization; it became, in time, a kind of flagship company, the outstanding industrial blue-chip in the industrialization process.

Fifth, a small group of technocrats was able to gain control over certain aspects of monetary and external economic policy soon after the war and to prepare the ground for major policy reforms. The economic policy formation process, such as it was prior to the reforms of the late 1950s, was very narrow. Decisions emerged from the interplay among the rival political cliques and the bureaucracy. Public opinion in Bangkok could not be ignored, but this opinion was informed by rumor and word-of-mouth communication and by a press that was vocal but not very independent or uncorruptible.[41] The very narrowness of the policy process, along with the limited understanding many of the political figures (especially the military) had of financial and economic complexities, gave a handful of professionals some scope for promoting a coherent alternative agenda.

The Technocratic Reaction: The Moral Purposes of Economic Liberalism

The importance of Thailand's postwar technocrats cannot be overstated. They played a central role in limiting the short-run economic damage of the policies I have described and in shaping the subsequent long-run policy thrust. They also exercised a powerful influence over the younger rising generation of Western-trained professionals who were beginning to filter back to Thailand in the mid- to late 1950s to take up junior positions in the bureaucracy. The economist who stands out among these professionals, by virtue of his international reputation and his role as mentor of the younger generation economists in particular, is Dr. Puey Ungphakorn. Born into a family of modest means, Puey won a government scholarship to study at the London School of Economics in the late 1930s. He joined the Free Thai movement in London after Ambassador Seni refused to deliver the Thai declaration of war. In early 1944 Dr. Puey, then an officer in the British Army, parachuted into Thailand with two other Free Thais to contact the resistance movement and carry out intelligence work.[42] After the war he completed his doctoral studies at the London School of Economics. Subsequently, he served in the Thai Ministry of Finance, became director of the Budget Bureau, and for twelve years governor of the Bank of Thailand. In 1970 he insisted on giving up his central bank governorship to devote full time to teaching economics and building up the economics faculty at Thammasat University. Finally he served as rector of the university until he was forced to flee the country in the wake of the repression in late 1976.[43]

Those I have loosely called professionals actually comprised three groups separated by both age and educational background. The first group was composed of a handful of people whom Dr. Puey characterized as "elders" in the mid-1950s (when Puey was around forty years of age), senior bureaucrats of intelligence, unimpeachable integrity, and devotion to the country's national interests. Among this group were M. L. Dej Snidwongse (then chairman of the NEDB Executive Committee, formerly a governor of the Bank of Thailand), Phra Boripan Yuthakit (then minister of finance), Leng Srisomwong, and Tawee Boonyaket.[44] The second group was composed of rising professionals, mostly recently graduated from immediately prewar or postwar education abroad, and mostly working in the Bank of Thailand or the Ministry of Finance. Among this group were Chalong Pungtrakul, Khunying Supharb Yossundara, Bisuthi Nimmanhaeminda, Boonma Wongsawan, and Sommai Huntrakul. The third group comprised young students of economics, public administration, and related disciplines who were returning from education abroad in the late 1950s to join the tiny initial professional staffs of the central bank, the Ministry of Finance, NEDB, the Budget Bureau, and a scattering of other positions concerned with economic policy formation.

Credit for having established the institutional basis and moral standing for a return to the tradition of monetary conservatism belongs to Prince Viwatanachai Chaiyant (known as Prince Viwat). Educated in Cambridge, Prince Viwat had been appointed the first Thai financial adviser to the Treasury after the 1932 revolution. He was the main influence behind the preservation of financial conservatism during the years leading up to the war and the principal architect of the measures Thai governments during and after the war used to counteract the wartime inflation created by the monetary expansion enforced by the Japanese military. His most important contribution was probably the creation of the Bank of Thailand and the rapid development of the institution's moral authority as the preeminent organization pursuing Thailand's national interests not only in financial but in economic matters generally. As financial adviser in the 1930s, Prince Viwat had actually opposed Pridi's desire to set up a central bank, fearing that such a money-creating institution would become a source of, rather than a bulwark against, inflation under Pridi's concept of the proper role of a reserve bank.[45] In 1942, however, Prince Viwat moved quickly to establish a central bank under Thai control in order to prevent the Japanese from creating a bank under their own control, as they had done in occupied countries.

At first, the bank had to rely on completely inexperienced staff. But through careful selection and training, Prince Viwat was able to set the new organization on a course that soon brought the bank into a position of preeminence in Thailand for its competence and its institutional "culture" of integrity. The willingness of the prince to resign, rather than implement a measure he deemed unwise for the country (as he did in 1946 when the government "compelled the Bank to sell some of its gold reserve in suspicious circumstances"[46]), set a precedent for standing by principle that was followed by his successors M. L. Dej and Kasem Sriphayak, and by Dr. Puey at various times in his career. The moral authority of the bank was buttressed by its position as the country's link with the World Bank and the IMF, which accorded the governor considerable domestic prestige and leverage, and by the general perception in Bangkok that it was mainly the Bank of Thailand that generated confidence on the part of the Western powers that Thailand's financial policies and financial condition were in supremely responsible hands.[47]

Some of the bank's scope for independent action derived from its legal status. As a state enterprise, its staff rules and salary scales were free from Civil Service Commission jurisdiction. A position with the central bank was prized over regular government employment both for greater prestige and for higher emoluments. Of major importance was the legal provision giving the bank control over the currency reserve and the Exchange Equalization Fund, a special account used to even out short-term fluctuations in the baht.

The first substantial policy consequence of the central bank's emergence was the reestablishment of the country's traditional financial orthodoxy. The bank was able to separate one whole area of economic policy—respecting inflation, the stability of the currency, and the rebuilding of the foreign exchange reserves— from the politicization that marked other areas. The buildup of the foreign exchange reserves during the 1950s served not only as a tool for maintaining an orderly foreign exchange market but also as a resource for conducting deflationary policy (as an offset to inflationary pressures from abroad and from government budgetary deficits) and as a store of value for future use.

In sum, a core of professional technocrats was able, almost from the start of the postwar period, to establish a fair degree of control over financial policy and to create an institutional basis for extending their influence into other areas of national policy. Working within a policy framework over which they had deep misgivings, rather than falling into disillusion or radical rejection, they pressed their alternative value system and prepared for an opportunity to make substantial policy reform.

Dr. Puey's reputation as the leading conceptualizer among the economic policy technocrats rests, to some extent, on the fact that he was the most articulate.

Thai politicians and military leaders often prefer to speak about sensitive issues in Delphic ambiguities, and the spoken word remains much more important than the written in policy discourse in Thailand. Dr. Puey himself was adept at the use of allusion, but he was also uncharacteristically blunt in the many speeches he gave to communicate his ideas in language the layman could understand. Thus on the subject of the proper role of government, and the hybrid enterprises:

> There must be a healthy atmosphere of fair play among all kinds of enterprises supervised and refereed by an objective and disinterested government. I believe that private business is usually not afraid of competition by public enterprises—the latter are normally not efficient enough, particularly if generals, admirals, and air marshals are persistently appointed to the top jobs. What you ought to look out for is another species of animal altogether; an influential enterprise disguised as a private concern—a sort of mongrel if you like. They are deadly, atrociously destructive of the moral as well as the economic fibre of the society.[48]

On the role of private enterprise:

> In the past eight or ten years this country has made considerable progress in economic development, although we still have a long way to go to reach a decent standard. Much of this progress has been due to the good activities in the government sector with the assistance of international bodies and foreign friends. But most of the credit must belong to the private sector, with adequate savings, good capital formation and investments and increases in productivity. . . .
> What is the meaning of all this good fortune? What is the one single most important factor for progress? My short answer is private initiative. The government can provide; but it is the individual little man and woman—perhaps mostly woman in our case—who produce. Kill the initiative, as in so many of our neighboring countries, and you can forget about the targets in your five-year development plan.
> The enemies of individual initiative (let us detect them and show them up) are monopoly, privileges and influential business.[49]

In a retrospective speech in 1969, Puey gave a concise description of Thai international economic policy:

> Thailand has, generally speaking, always followed the traditional open-door policy. . . . In its trade policy, Thailand has by successive stages reduced trade restrictions; import controls and licensing have gradually been replaced by tariffs. . . . In the sphere of international payments, exchange control has been liberalized. . . .
> Why does Thailand follow a wide open-door policy? . . .
> 1. . . the international division of labour . . . is more advantageous to us and produces more immediate results than a closed-door policy.

2. We are short of capital, technical know-how, and managerial ability. Until we can remedy these shortages it is wiser to take advantage of the assistance made available to us by the various governments, agencies and foundations.

3. We fully realize that, by leaving the economy wide open and relying on foreign assistance, we run certain risks of being exploited; in certain circumstances, we even may appear to compromise certain aspects of our sovereignty. ... We have succeeded in maintaining our independence in the past, and we hope to do so in the future. We should, therefore, avoid the inferiority complex that has been haunting other countries with a colonial past.

This prosperity was achieved in circumstances of monetary stability, and the external value of the baht was maintained throughout in accordance with the objectives of the International Monetary Fund. ... This was largely attributable to the fact that whenever domestic prices tended to press upward, we allowed imports to come in somewhat more freely. ... The open-door policy has been used as an instrument of control on the domestic economy.[50]

After listing several "weak points" in the record (regarding income distribution, the education system, agricultural productivity, etc.), Puey asserts that they "do not stem from our relations with foreign countries; they arise from our own internal regime."

While Dr. Puey was a maverick in some respects—his moral courage, his complete disinterest in personal financial advantage or political power, his outspokenness—his convictions respecting economic policy did not depart in any significant way from the canons of past Thai economic orthodoxy. However, Puey did not arrive at this orthodoxy through a mere intergenerational transfer of policy values from predecessors such as Prince Viwat. Nor did he develop his orientation through the application—separate from other social considerations—of criteria respecting economic optimization. The mainstream of development economics has always asserted the superiority of policy that is trade-oriented and that encourages private initiative and private property in the framework of a market system subject to competitive forces. Drawing a generalized lesson from the experience of South Korea, Taiwan, and Singapore in particular, some scholars have (perhaps unhappily) concluded that developing countries appear to require authoritarian government in their early stages of development in order to sustain the discipline of the optimal policy package.

Dr. Puey's argument for the superiority of the orthodox package reverses this logic, at least as it would apply to Thai realities. He sees the competitive private economy as a system that best protects a society against authoritarian power and its abuses. His concern over corruption in government was intense and colored all his thinking about economic development. In one of his lectures he attacked the view that corruption can help speed up the development process: "This is an obnoxious doctrine advocating a perverse view of development. Even if it were true that corruption speeds up development, would it not be better not to develop at all? A little less material wealth with more happiness is to be preferred."[51] His orthodoxy was not uncritical, however, for he saw that the operation of market forces, without regulation or forces and policies countervailing to the accumulation of economic power, would also lead to abuses and economic inequities.

> The issue of government versus private enterprise is a political issue as well as a question respecting individual rights. Communism and extreme socialism would advocate over-all government control, with the individuals as factors of production; whereas capitalism and liberalism emphasize private initiative with minimum interference by government. Both factions, in my opinion, are wrong and unjust: Communism ignoring individual freedom and Capitalism causing exploitation and widening the social gap. I would prefer the middle way, with government encouraging initiative, while using fiscal and monetary measures to control them. Government activities must also be extended to basic public utilities for the common benefit of the people.[52]

Pragmatism, balance, avoidance of ideological preconceptions, vigilance against the creation of opportunities for rent seeking, moderation in the weight given to material advance among the mix of a society's objectives, and a proper balance among growth, monetary stability, and equitable distribution are the themes running through Puey's didactic writings and speeches. His preference for balance and moderation (the "middle way"), and his serious questioning of the policy priority that should be given to the sheer speed of economic growth, are deeply Buddhist concepts: Puey described himself as a person brought up in a Buddhist family but who had "acquired very little faith, and much more of the ethical principle from my earliest education."[53] Also noteworthy is his remark that the faults in the country's development process should be blamed on the Thais themselves, not the outside world. This observation reflects a general inclination among Thai technocrats (and businessmen) to take the world as it is and work at extracting the benefits to be gained from the existing international system, rather than expending their energies railing against the system. Few Thais were drawn into the ranks of those who, especially in the 1970s, ascribed the disappointing growth record in the Third World to the structure of the international economic system and called for the creation of a New International Economic Order.

The younger, postwar-trained technocrats were predisposed (or "socialized") to liberal, market-oriented economics by their higher education abroad, especially the economists who studied in the United States. But this generation was only beginning to return to Thailand in the closing years of the Phibun period, filling relatively junior roles in the policy processes. The small band of "elders" and of Puey and his associates also had liberalizing predilections, but these appear to have resulted as pragmatic lessons from close-hand experience with the effects of politico-bureaucratic intervention. This can be seen in some of the specific policy conclusions they drew and then pressed into implementation under Sarit:

1. Get control over supplier credits as a source of debt financing of public sector projects.
2. Strengthen the monitoring and management systems over state enterprises.
3. Stop the extension of government into manufacturing and commerce, especially by the hybrid forms of quasi-government or quasi-private firms.
4. Repair the damage done to the investment climate.
5. Use the domestic political sensitivity to international opinion to strengthen the pressures for policy reform and higher technical standards.
6. Protect the treasury and exchange reserves.
7. Reduce opportunities for rent-seeking behavior.
8. Maintain the traditional open economy policy, to promote competition and to obtain the benefits of the international division of labor.

No account of the emergence of the Thai technocrats would be complete without reference to a group of engineers who also began to play an important role in the 1950s but whose names seldom appear in the social, political, or economic studies of modern Thailand, presumably because the scholars in the social science disciplines view the engineers as mere implementers or agents who carry out the plans and programs that have been formulated and fought over in the elevated realms of policy and power. The general literature on economic development takes little account of engineers except when it comes to problems of technology, where the engineers are accused often of choosing capital-intensive equipment or processes inappropriate to the factor endowments of developing countries. While there have been some significant examples of engineering bias (respecting technology choice and project timing and scale) and of engineering pressures on policy, to which I shall return below, the omission of the role of the engineering technocrats from the literature on Thai development is a major oversight that I can only begin briefly to correct here.

As with the leading political, military, and bureaucratic figures, the leading engineers who have had formative roles in Thai development have not been an undifferentiated class. They also have had entourages, have varied in their professionalism and integrity, and have had substantial independent impact on the allocation of resources, on the development of institutional capacities, and consequently on the efficiency of resource use. I use the term "leading" to focus on the small group of engineers returning from higher education overseas in the postwar years, who at an early age were thrown into responsible positions in public-sector infrastructure agencies and departments, and who rose quickly to senior management positions. Like the young policy technocrats, the engineers were socialized in a work ethic of professionalism and national interest. Just as in the bureaucratic departments bearing on finance and broad development policy, there was wide scope for rapid advance of newly overseas-trained technicians. Even in the State Railway of Thailand, one of the few infrastructure organizations with a long prewar history, a number of engineers and managers had to be sent to the United States for training in the early 1950s to acquire the capability to use the equipment the aid program was providing for rehabilitation of the war-damaged system.[54]

There are two particular aspects of the role of the engineering technocrats that merit attention for their importance in this period and for their continuing impact. The first concerns "absorptive capacity." This is a term used loosely to refer to the ability of a developing country to make effective use of an inflow of foreign resources. The concept is imprecise; a country with limited ability to design and construct large engineering works might still be able to "absorb" big projects installed by foreign contractors on a turnkey basis if the local capability for operation and maintenance were adequate (or strengthened with foreign assistance).

In this period Thailand had problems of absorptive capacity at both the engineering project installation and maintenance levels. The constraints on infrastructure investment varied by sector and agency. The railway organization was able to raise its absorptive capacity quickly and to qualify for a succession of World Bank loans. The Department of Highways faced greater problems of organizational capacity and was wedded to a force-account construction system. The road system had few stretches with all-weather surface and needed large-scale expansion and upgrading to be able to carry the traffic that growth in economic activity would generate. After several years of U.S. assistance, the two governments agreed that the country's need for highway development could not be met by continuing reliance on the capacity of the department. The United States would build two highways on a turnkey basis using American contractors and would help the department to develop a private engineering contracting sector in Thailand to replace the force-account system.[55] By the early 1960s the development of a private road-engineering capability was under way and the Department of Highways was in position to begin a major system expansion funded in part by World Bank loans. The investment Thailand needed to initiate in electric power generation and distribution and other areas of infrastructure also required a period of institutional and technical capacity building in which external aid played an important role.[56] Those foundation-laying projects rested on the work of a small number of Thai engineering technocrats.[57]

The second point I would draw attention to concerns the differences among these agencies. While they may all have appeared in the 1950s to be suffering from similar problems, it is clear in retrospect that different organizational "cultures" were being developed in each agency, cultures that in many cases have persisted ever since. Some of these agencies have sustained a dedication to efficiency and professionalism established by their early management. In other cases the organizations were launched with a management style and practice that tolerated, or even promoted, low professional standards, rent-seeking behavior, feather-bedding labor practices, collusion with suppliers, and other corrupt practices. The blame for the initiation of these persistent cultures can be ascribed only partly to the technocratic management in the formative years since some were penetrated or controlled by political and military individuals, as described earlier. At times, the more important among these poorly performing agencies have become serious bottlenecks in their respective sectors (e.g., in telecommunications and port operations), thereby creating numerous policy problems to which I shall return below.

The Postwar Economy

From the end of World War II through the 1950s, the Thai economy was still heavily dependent on agriculture (i.e., on the weather) and on world market prices for its chief primary commodity exports. The economy grew slowly over the period but experienced wide fluctuations from exogenous factors. The Korean War boom in 1951–53 doubled rubber and tin prices compared with their prewar levels. Droughts caused by large declines in crop production reduced aggregate economic activity by 2.0 to 2.5 percent in 1954 and 1957. Average real annual GDP growth for the decade 1950–60 was around 4.5 percent. With annual population growth probably over 3.0 percent, per capita income (also fluctuating widely from one crop year to the next) grew around 1.5 percent on average. The low rate of growth per capita reflected the overwhelming dependence on agriculture (85 percent of the labor force in 1950), the major share in agriculture of rice (two-thirds of agricultural value-added in 1950/52 was attributed to paddy production), and the fact that growth in crop output was still a function of labor force growth being applied to expanded acreage with little change in technology. In fact, rice productivity had been falling since the mid-1920s. Although higher-yielding varieties, developed during the 1950s by Thailand's first major agricultural research project, were being used by perhaps 15 percent of rice farmers by 1985, paddy yields per unit area fluctuated without a trend until a sustained rise began in the 1960/61 crop year.

Although investment expenditures rose during the 1950s, they were recovering from very low postwar levels and remained relatively low. Real gross fixed capital formation increased by an estimated 11 percent between 1950 and 1958, but the ratio of fixed capital formation to GDP in 1950 was only 7.8 percent.[58] The public sector accounted for around one-third of total fixed capital formation from 1950 to 1957. A large fraction of this investment was allocated to "economic services," including transport and communication (e.g., 47 percent in 1955–57), irrigation and other agriculture (20 percent), and electric power (7 percent). Social services including education and health received very minor allocations for fixed capital formation (3 percent in 1955–57), the major expansion in school construction starting only in the period 1958–60. The level of public investment in the economic services rose substantially during the decade[59] and is reflected in the high annual rates of growth recorded for some of the sectors involved. Construction grew at around 10.4 percent per annum, electricity and water 19.1 percent, and transport and communication 9.6 percent. Since these sectors were still small in their relative contribution to the total level of economic activity, the initial years of capital formation expenditures (especially for long-gestating projects) had a small and delayed impact on overall GDP growth. Expenditures on irrigation works in particular would take many years before yielding significant effects on agricultural production. Manufacturing was the second largest sector in 1950 (13 percent of GDP), still less than one-third the size (in terms of value-added) of agriculture. Partly for reasons explained above, investment in new manufacturing capacity during this period yielded low returns, and the sector grew by a modest average of 4.5 percent. Private foreign direct investment in Thailand before the early 1960s was insignificant, running at a level of less than $3.5 million net per year between 1955 and 1960, and unrecorded prior to 1955.[60]

Thus, despite the rising public investment in infrastructure, the reorientation of much of the bureaucracy toward development, and the proliferation of training and institution-building associated with the seemingly ubiquitous presence of foreign aid technicians, there was little change in the structure of the economy during the 1950s. It was indicative of Thailand's preindustrial condition that the only significant exceptions to this generalization were in the production and export earnings of two primary commodities, rubber and tin. Rubber output rose 24 percent in 1959 (and continued an uneven rise from this new level in subsequent years) as the expanded acreage planted during the Korean War boom came into production. Rubber export taxes were nominal compared with the tax burden on rice, but the government played almost no role otherwise in the rubber sector. The bulk of Thailand's rubber holdings were planted with unselected low-yielding trees, and unlike that in Malaysia the Thai rubber sector was not founded on plantation management or backed by strong research and extension facilities. Despite the expansion in planting and production, the future of Thai rubber was not then considered to be bright as long as its technological and institutional status remained neglected.[61]

Malaysia had embarked on a vigorous postwar program to replant its entire stock with high-yielding clones that had been developed by its Rubber Research Institute. In addition to its work on varieties, the institute's research program covered virtually every aspect of rubber cultivation, management, and processing for export. The institute was supported both by the large plantation sector (then mainly foreign owned) and by the pre- and postindependence governments, which imposed a small cess on exports to finance its work. Lacking a significant corporate presence in the rubber sector, Thailand was dependent on government initiative for modernization. The World Bank survey team viewed the absence of significant government activity along these lines as a major policy failure of omission, predicting that with proper attention Thai rubber exports earnings could rival if not exceed those of rice.[62] As noted earlier, it was only at the end

of the 1950s, when the Phibun era had come to an end, that agricultural diversification got under way—with three crops, maize, cassava, and kenaf. Tin has
remained an important source of income in the southern peninsular areas where
the mines are located. For the economy as a whole, however, tin was already
going into eclipse in the 1950s. The higher-yielding deposits were being worked
out, and production and export earnings were closely tied to the cyclical movements of international tin prices and (in the longer run) to modest improvements
in mining technology and to the inroads of competing metals.

Immediately after the war, Thailand faced two major short-run economic
problems—delivery of the rice reparations required under the peace treaties, and
restoration of its monetary system. The events surrounding these two problems
have been recounted and analyzed in depth by several authors and will only be
summarized here.[63]

From Rice Reparations to Rice Taxation

It will be recalled that the Thai government had given high priority in the prewar
years to the economic nationalist objective of wresting control over the rice
sector from private commerce. The government intervened at the milling stage in
an attempt at direct preemption of the targeted economic activities. The postwar
intervention in the rice sector had a very different genesis and resulted in greater
and longer-lasting consequences. Until the end of 1949, Thailand was required to
deliver specified, large quantities of rice for export to other countries of the
region at concessional prices. To meet these obligations, the government arro-
gated the sole right of rice export to its Rice Office. Actual handling and export
was conducted by the private traders, on license from the Rice Office. While the
mandatory quantities were gradually reduced, and the price Thailand was to
receive gradually raised, prior to the cancellation of the reparations at the end of
1949, the government was able to acquire only a portion of the domestic rice
supply entering the market; the remainder flowed into smuggled exports, drawn
by the gap between world market prices and the price at which the government
was willing to buy.

The budgetary pressure of the program led the government to attempt to
depress the domestic price of rice. The quota rents to be earned through access to
the export licenses, and the opportunities the system created for corruption in its
administration, represented unprecedented forms of government intervention into
the operation of the market for the country's premier commodity. As Ammar
Siamwalla points out, when the international control system was terminated the
government, no longer under any mandatory international requirement to intervene in the rice trade, could have returned the trade to its previous unregulated
operation. By then, however, the revenue the government was earning from the
export taxes on rice had become an important source of government finance
(e.g., 27 percent in 1949).[64] During the years 1947–55 rice exports were subject

to a large additional implicit tax imposed by the Bank of Thailand through its operation of a multiple exchange rate system. Under this regime, rice (and rubber and tin) exporters had to surrender their foreign exchange earnings to the Bank at the official rate of forty baht per pound sterling, while exporters of other commodities and merchandise could sell their foreign exchange proceeds in the free market at sixty baht per pound. The bank of Thailand earned considerable exchange profits from this tax of one-third the export value of rice. The profits more than offset the government's budget deficit[65] but were retained by the bank as the central instrument for conducting its policy of deflation and foreign exchange reserve buildup.

The export taxes (principally the so-called premium) were soon recognized as the source of a substantial political benefit, not originally foreseen; by increasing (reducing) the size of the premium as rice export price rose (fell), the government could narrow the amplitude of price fluctuations and maintain, in effect, a "cheap rice" policy for domestic consumers, meaning especially the inhabitants of Bangkok. By 1955 the intervention system was reformed with the elimination of the direct controls that had generated licensing rents (and the dropping of the special exchange rate applied to rice), but the government retained the export taxes for another three decades.

As a departure from the prewar laissez-faire, the postwar rice interventions were relatively massive in their effects, compared with the policy of industrial and commercial preemption through the instrumentality of individual corporate enterprises. The relative importance of the premium revenue declined over time as the economy and the tax base became more diversified. The distributive effects were another matter. Rice cultivation was the largest single source of income for a major fraction of the population. Although diversification of income sources and the labor force into other crops and into nonagricultural occupations was getting under way in the late 1950s, the 1970 census recorded rice farming as the principal occupation of 67 percent of the economically active population. By the 1980 census the proportion employed mainly in rice farming had fallen but was still high at 56 percent.[66] The impact of the rice export taxes on the incomes of these substantial fractions of the population could vary widely from one year to the next, depending on the size of the crop and on the movements of world prices and of the size of the premium. In addition, starting in 1965 the government recurrently operated (usually ineffective) price support schemes at times of sharp declines in paddy prices while simultaneously, and paradoxically, maintaining the export taxes that were pushing domestic prices downward below the levels that would have prevailed if it were not for the gap the taxes interposed between domestic and export prices.

The net impact of government expenditure programs on the economic position of Thai farmers became more difficult to calculate as the components of agricultural and rural policy became more numerous and complex over time. (The debate over the effects of rice taxes probably generated more economic analysis and publication than any other subject of public policy in the 1960s and 1970s, with little apparent effect on policy makers.) Nevertheless, there is no doubt that the rice export taxes introduced in the early 1950s (as a policy improvement over the postwar administrative controls) were, for many years, the largest single postwar government intervention affecting income distribution in Thailand, regressively falling on the rural sector and on farming households in the lowest income brackets, while increasing the real purchasing power of rice consumers (among whom, of course, were numerous urban and rural poor). In addition to the direct tax burden falling on the producers, the artificial depression of the returns to rice cultivation distorted the incentive structure respecting rice, resulting in large efficiency losses from depressed output. One estimate, for 1981 (before the premium was reduced to zero by the Prem government), put the total tax and efficiency costs burden on rice cultivators at 5 to 9 percent of agricultural GDP.[67]

Academic analysis and debate over the effects of the taxes on rice, mainly the export premium, began in the mid-1960s and developed into a minor growth industry of its own among Thai and foreign economists and among government officials defending premium policy. The overwhelming view among the analysts—condemning the policy on distributive and efficiency grounds—had no influence on policy until the advent of the Prem government.

Inflation and Currency

The second major economic problem inherited from the wartime dislocation was the inflation and the collapse of the prewar basis of the Thai monetary system. I noted earlier that Thailand had never had an active independent monetary or demand management system. The money supply comprised mostly currency and coins backed by and closely linked to foreign exchange reserves. Domestic monetary supply—and demand—rose and fell with export earnings. Increases in purchasing power quickly leaked outward through increases in imports unimpeded by quantitative controls or the structure of low import duties.

The wartime expansion of the money supply, the concomitant price inflation and loss of exchange reserves, and the erosion of civil servant real incomes combined to convince Prince Viwat and his successors in the Bank of Thailand that the bank had to institute a strong deflationary policy to restore the economy to its traditional stability. To rebuild the international reserves, restore the baht to stability, and restrain imports that would otherwise rise with the recovery in export earnings, the bank instituted an exchange control regime in 1946. The system was adjusted the next year to make it more workable, combining a free exchange market for most items along with the enforced surrender of export proceeds of the major commodities. Helped by the Korean War price boom and a temporary lag in import response, the policy succeeded in creating a balance of payments surplus in 1947–51 and a rapid recovery in the reserves that rose from

$150 million in 1946 to about $350 million in 1952, equivalent to fourteen months of imports.

The bank's success in restoring price stability soon after the war was temporarily set back in the wake of the Korean War boom. Government budget deficits now exceeded the bank's offsetting foreign exchange profits by a wide margin. Prince Viwat, now an adviser to the government, believed that sales of sterling reserves would serve as an alternative disinflationary instrument by appreciating the value of the baht and thereby encouraging an increase in the supply of imported goods. Government ministers pressed the reluctant bank governor, M. L. Dej, to carry out an appreciation effort, partly in response to Prince Viwat's advice, and partly for reasons of apparently naive attachment to the notion of restoring the baht to its prewar value.[68] M. L. Dej resigned rather than prosecute the policy. As he had anticipated, the flood of imports damaged the interests of influential importers who convinced the government to abandon the appreciation policy.

Soon after this episode the monetary authorities were able to push through the first significant round of postwar economic policy reform—exchange rate unification, liberalization of exchange controls, and the abandonment of the direct controls over the rice trade. Price stability was restored and the balance of payments readily improved, aided by a rising inflow of foreign aid and loans, including reparations from Japan.

In sum, while the technocrats made no meaningful progress toward dismantling the policies of economic nationalism until the advent of the Sarit government, they did succeed in recapturing control over monetary policy, removing the worst abuses of government intervention in the rice trade, and beginning to prepare the legislative and institutional ground for restoring fiscal discipline and for the gradual development of more orderly economic management.

The reestablishment of conservatism in financial policy was best illustrated by the extraordinary levels of international reserves the Bank of Thailand succeeded in maintaining. Putting aside the outsized 1952 level equal to fourteen months of imports, the reserves for the next thirteen years, 1953–65, averaged nearly eleven months, never falling below nine. In those years of fixed exchange rates under the international Bretton Woods system, an "adequate" level of reserves was essential to protect the stability of the exchange rate during periods when balance-of-payments deficits were being financed through reserve reduction. An optimal level of international liquidity for any country could never be specified in view of the many factors that entered into reserve management judgment (e.g., fluctuations in export earnings and imports, changes in domestic money supply, changes in external liabilities, investment inflows, international credit standing, etc.) and the impossibility of making precise forecasts of the net effect of these factors on reserve levels. For a developing country like Thailand, still vulnerable to wide seasonal variations in output and prices of a handful of commodities, it was considered prudent to maintain "several months" of reserves. The World Bank team described the 1958–59 level (about $300 million or nine months) as "comfortable" in light of "the necessity of maintaining" high reserves in Thailand. "Any substantial use of reserves under normal economic circumstances would, however, be ill advised in view of the ever-present possibility of crop failures or adverse shifts in export market conditions with consequent losses of export earnings."[69] The nine months coverage level in 1958–59 was actually a low point; for the succeeding five years the reserves were maintained at a level equal to a full year of imports.

Even by the rules of thumb applied to reserve management among developing countries, the conservatism of the Thai monetary authorities might appear excessive, echoing the extreme financial conservatism of the Chakri monarchs discussed earlier, conservatism that has been criticized by the revisionist historians as having sacrificed growth for the sake of stability. To our knowledge these critics have not leveled the same charge at M. L. Dej or Dr. Puey, despite the fact that capital was the factor in shortest supply, that the ratio of investment to GDP was relatively low, that most public-sector capital projects were undertaken only if foreign loans and grants were available, and that Thailand was in effect lending funds to the U.S. Treasury.

There can be no doubt that in Dr. Puey's judgment an effort to push additional public-sector investment onto a higher growth track than was already being achieved would have caused a sharp increase in the marginal capital-output ratio and large incremental leakage of public funds through corrupt practices. The Bank of Thailand's reserves policy was driven by concerns for efficiency and distributive justice that were at least as important as the orthodox considerations of financial stability. Around 1961 Dr. Puey was asked by a puzzled visiting American assistant secretary of state why the bank was lending money to the U.S. Treasury while simultaneously borrowing money from the World Bank at a higher rate. The governor responded that his apparently illogical policy was achieving two objectives. By keeping the reserves tied up, he was thwarting efforts unscrupulous leadership might make to gain access to these funds, thereby reserving these resources for the future benefit of the public. And by involving the international development agencies in major capital projects, the financial authorities could ensure that the rate of return would be reasonably positive. Feasibility analysis and project planning and implementation would be carried out in accordance with professional standards, and contracting and financial management in these projects would be transparent and reasonably free from irregularities. Economic policy in Thailand could not be understood apart from considerations of institutional capabilities and the political culture of the time.[70]

Sociopolitical Paradigms

Consideration of this period concludes with a brief excursion into the political science literature in which several writers have tried to characterize the basic elements or dynamics of the postwar years through the application of various organizing concepts or paradigms. I have attributed the economic intervention by the Thai elite to (a) the nationalist impulse to gain control of the economy; (b) the opportunistic exploitation of this intervention, once launched, by rival political cliques seeking sources of finance and the political power to be derived from control of large corporations and important economic assets and market functions; and (c) a search for alternative sources of income on the part of the senior bureaucrats in particular, following the erosion of their real purchasing power during wartime and postwar inflation. Sheer individual opportunism—or, simply put, greed—was also an important driving force. The best-documented and most publicly exposed case of personal financial aggrandizement was that of Sarit, who diverted for his own accounts a considerable portion of the public-sector (and private-sector rent-based) money flows to which he had access (after his death in 1963 his estate was estimated to be worth around $150 million[71]). Some of the prominent political families of today owe their economic position at least partly to wealth accumulated through the interventionist techniques developed during this period.

In an interpretation cast partly in cultural terms, Silcock stresses the need of the post-1932 Thai elite to find sources of income to replace the patronage and reward system formerly maintained by the monarchy. He notes that after King Chulalongkorn introduced strict accountability for public funds (especially after administrative reforms in 1892), there were two inherently conflicting value systems governing the Thai elite, one based on the king's personal distribution of prestige and financial benefits, the other based on regularized, formal bureaucratic procedures and norms. Once the system of royal salary supplements was eliminated, the inheritors of power found themselves entirely dependant on salaries and thereby unable to sustain the traditional and expected systems of patronage relationships in which they now found themselves, by appropriation, the patrons.

> The conflict between the patronage system of values and that imported by the Treasury became apparent after the 1932 revolution when the system of awarding honors was abolished and the high salary scales formerly given to princes were cut down. Positions of power were inherited by a number of Western-educated civil servants who had neither the means to acquire Western material goods nor the willingness to accept status and personal services as substitutes. Since that time many of the features of the Thai economy have resulted from a simultaneous acceptance by the Thai administrative class of two systems of value, one which expects those in power to live at a high standard and give patronage to others, and another which expects them to obey the rules relating to public funds.[72]

To the extent that the exploitation of financial sources at hand can be attributed to the commonplace search of political practitioners for money, distinguishable from political practice in Japan or the United States or elsewhere only in local detail, the Thai experience in this period was not necessarily a reflection of social or historical conditions peculiar to Thailand. Nor would be a conflict between modern Weberian bureaucratic values and preexisting ascriptive values. The conflict, however, was and remains real, and it was at the heart of the moral nature of the lessons Dr. Puey drew from the experience and his fusion of ethical and economic considerations in the formulation of economic policy.

Much of the literature on the Thai elite in this period has focused on political dynamics, on how the historical, inherited mores of the elites have been adapted to the exigencies of modern circumstances surrounding the distribution of wealth and of political power. As noted above during the discussion of the shallowness of the political base underneath the 1932 coup Promoters, and their view, no different from that of the monarchy, that the citizenry were politically passive and childlike, the Thai polity effectively comprised a small civil and military class organized into a bureaucracy. When the monarchical control was terminated, the distribution of political power was determined through struggles within this bureaucracy. As Riggs observed, "Both the People's Party and the parliamentary system proved unable to control the dynamism of intrabureaucratic conflict which broke out as the monarchical control system was dislodged." After the disruptions of the war, some of the civilian politicians attempted "to lay a new foundation for popular and constitutional government . . . but internal dissensions, increasing corruption and mismanagement, and the rising dissatisfaction of rising military officers, brought an end to their experiment. Step by step the bureaucracy reinstated its full control . . . setting in motion a pattern of intrabureaucratic politics which had become the dominant style of Siamese politics by the time the decade of the sixties had begun."[73] Another early writer on Thai politics, David Wilson, appears to ascribe the origin of this style at least partly to the political passivity of the population: "As much as the leadership of the Thai revolution might have wished things to be otherwise, it was not able to muster much popular interest outside the bureaucracy upon which to base itself. As a result, politics has become a matter of competition between bureaucratic cliques for the benefits of government."[74]

Riggs called the postmonarchical political system of Thailand a "bureaucratic polity." The extent to which political power was held by senior bureaucrats was reflected in the fact that many Thai cabinet posts, even in years when the parliamentary system was operating, were occupied by unelected senior bureaucrats. In a very real sense, the effective Thai polity was the bureaucracy for most of the period between 1932 and 1973 when extra-bureaucratic forces finally emerged as political factors. The mainstream of political writing on Thailand centered on Riggs's paradigm for many years after he first enunciated it in 1966. This literature examined the behavior of the bureaucratic elite from several angles, including the continuities with historical patron–client traditions, political tendencies from left to right, social backgrounds and intergenerational continuity, educational attainment, and other determinants of career mobility.

My own interests are limited to aspects of elite behavior that have affected the economic roles of the public sector. The weaknesses of interdepartmental coordination that Loftus decried as technical shortcomings of economic policy formulation and management domain appear in a different light when viewed as the dynamic workings of the bureaucratic polity paradigm. Norman Jacobs described a resource allocation process in which objective criteria are completely irrelevant:

> Vertical loyalty is associated with the scramble for prebends at the top level, a scramble so intense that responsibility for administering government programs, especially those involving significant prebendary grants, must be divided among the patronal decision-makers of a number of different ministries or agencies primarily on the basis of providing a fair share of the prebendary pie to all rather than on the basis of any objective criterion. Within a single ministry or agency, factionalism is rife as subpatrons struggle at the prebendary trough.[75]

Jacobs's animated characterization of life at the office was, strictly speaking, inaccurate; the distribution of resources among ministries and agencies is, in fact, extremely unequal, as one would expect from the very different financial claims inherent in the technical differences from one subject or sector to another. Nevertheless, factionalism and prebendary competition have certainly been important driving forces and have been described at length by several authors.[76]

As a parallel economic paradigm, the concept of "bureaucratic capitalism" has been used to categorize the episode of state enterprise investment and the allied bureaucratic penetration of the private corporate sector. The term is intended to distinguish the Thai state and quasi-government enterprise sector from any superficial relationship it may appear to have had with government enterprises of socialist states, where privately owned means of production were nonexistent, or from state-owned (or nationalized) enterprise sectors in mixed economies, where selected industries are reserved for the public sector on ideological grounds. In the Thai case, the individual enterprises became fiefs of their respective controlling ministries or departments, and, as I have stressed, they were not subject to systematic policy criteria or oversight controls designed to promote and protect the public interest.

In his straightforward historical account, Wyatt apparently sees no need to use any of the structural formulations of either the anthropological or political literature for an understanding of the dynamics of this period. Rather than attempting to incorporate the new factionalism and rent-seeking behavior into a model that integrates these developments with sociopolitical mores stretching far back into monarchical history, Wyatt sees the episode of economic penetration as a not very surprising exploitation by ambitious Thais, previously excluded from power

and wealth, of the new opportunities opened up to the military once the monarchical control system had ended.

> In the society of Thailand as a whole, there were roughly four institutional
> avenues of advancement: higher education, the military, the Buddhist monk-
> hood, and business. The attractions of the Buddhist monkhood were limited. . . .
> Business was virtually closed to Thai youths. . . . Entrance into universities
> was highly restricted . . . not widely accessible until the 1960s. The army, on
> the other hand, recruited officers fairly widely in the society, and none of them
> had university education. . . . By moving into politics, the military could share
> in the wealth of the society in ways that they could not otherwise. . . . The
> possibilities seemed endless, but a highly inventive and entrepreneurial Thai
> military class explored most of them.[77]

He concludes that up to the Sarit coup, "Twenty-five years had brought enormous social and economic development, but politically the kingdom seemed
stuck in 1932."

The greatest detail on the political penetration of the corporate sector in
Thailand has been gathered and analyzed by authors using a neo-Marxist framework. The analysis tends to concentrate on ownership of registered companies
and does not extend much beyond the classification of the groups involved and
their areas of economic activity, and on the phasing of these classifications over
time. Suehiro, for example, seeks to define the "dominant capital" in Thailand,
focusing on the shifting relationships and relative ownership patterns of the
traditional Thai elite (monarchy, nobility, and related institutions), the ethnic
Thai factions since 1932, the foreign companies doing business in Thailand, and
the domestic Chinese capitalists. This work is extensive and original but leads to
few conclusions on the effects for the functioning of the economy.

Another scholar writing from a political science perspective, Girling, summarizes the mainstream conception of the dynamics of this period, expressing skepticism over the applicability of some general paradigms that some authors have
applied in an attempt to fit the Thai experience to political models derived from
experience elsewhere:

> Contrary to the Marxist thesis, the Thai political superstructure is not merely a
> reflection of economic foundations. Nor are the factional struggles of the Thai
> elite simply the ideological forms (legal, political or philosophical) in which
> men become conscious of the conflict between new productive forces and
> outmoded social relations and fight it out. Contrary to pluralist assumptions,
> too, the Thai state does not represent a bargaining coalition of interest
> groups—administrative, business, professional, labor, and peasantry—nor are
> the intricate maneuvers of the elite to be seen as fulfilling a process of interest
> aggregation, and articulation. . . .
>   The development of bureaucratic-business cooperation along clique lines,
> that is, according to traditional patron–client practices was not a result of

institutional or functional collaboration, which is usually considered to be part of the process of modernization. Cooperation between wealthy Chinese "syndicates" and powerful Thai military officers and leading civilian bureaucrats . . . is merely a contemporary equivalent of the "informal" patron–client relationship between Thai kings and Chinese tax farmers more than a century before and between government officials and Chinese traders since then.[78]

Girling then attempts to explain the transition from the prewar strategy of state preemption to the postwar penetration and collaboration, noting that into the early 1950s

> the two spheres of elite control (Thai politics and Chinese business), far from merging profitably, or even maintaining a balance autonomy, perpetually grated on one another. Business was badly affected. . . . Such a situation, bordering on anarchy, threatened the very foundations of the economy, and with it the material interests of both sides. To avert this disaster, a rapprochement took place. . . . Since they could not compete with the Chinese, and dared not destroy them, they decided to join them.[79]

Although Girling provides no evidence that a deliberate desire to avoid a feared killing of the golden goose was the reason behind this transition, there can be little doubt that an extended strategy of confrontation and preemption would have led to economically and socially disastrous consequences. While that scenario never got played out, the rapprochement itself showed every promise of seriously compromising the country's development prospects if the disregard for market forces and economic efficiency had continued.

Postscript

To give a balanced account of the second Phibun period, in terms of its long-run development impact, one must return to the point made at the outset of this chapter about Thailand's entry into the postwar international movement for the development of the Third World. Whatever the balance of national interest and self-serving political motivations may have been, credit must be given to Phibun for the plunge into aid-related projects and programs that started to create the technical and institutional capabilities that are the foundation of modern economies. Within a very short period of time, the initial American and United Nations aid programs (few countries had aid programs yet operating in Thailand in the early 1950s) had launched institution-building activities that would in time alleviate the major weaknesses of planning and implementation that pervaded the ministries and agencies of significance for economic growth. The aid programs provided overseas training, assistance in organization and management, design of new budget and financial control processes, transfer of modern technology in public sector service and functions, and so on. Government functions benefiting from these programs included geological survey, meteorology, air traffic control, transport system and highway design, city planning, endemic disease control, development of university faculties, power generation and distribution system planning, primary teacher training, microwave telecommunications technology, vocational education, rice and other crop research, and so forth. Capital assistance was provided mainly by the World Bank and the U.S. aid program for public-sector infrastructure projects in irrigation, transportation, and electric power.[80]

It is ironic that many Thais (and foreign writers) credit Sarit as the man whose policies set Thailand on the road to economic development. While there is much truth in this judgment, as will be seen, there is less recognition of the fact that Sarit was able to effect this turnaround to a considerable extent by building on the institutional foundations being laid down during the Phibun years. This applies also to the capital projects undertaken by the Phibun government. The investment in transportation and electric power in particular paid off in later years, not only for the individual projects begun at the time but also for the expanded absorptive capacity to utilize the much larger volume of capital lending extended to Thailand by the international development banks during the 1960s. The Phibun years also saw research efforts in rice and maize that began to raise production and exports of these crops only in the late 1950s. Thus, Sarit began to reap the benefits of these programs and has been well regarded (in this respect) by history, while Phibun's rule was terminated before the consequences could be realized.

4

DESPOTIC PATERNALISM AND PURPOSIVE DEVELOPMENT: 1958–1972

Field Marshal Sarit Thanarat took personal power in October 1958. He closed the parliament, abrogated the constitution, and ushered in a long period of autocratic rule. After Sarit's death in December 1963, his deputy Thanom Kittikachorn took over the premiership. Thanom ruled until 1973, in effect continuing Sarit's system of autocratic governance except for an interlude of parliamentary democracy in 1969–71 (which Thanom introduced, retaining the premiership, then canceled by staging a coup against himself).

Reacting against the political instability that had prevailed since the overthrow of the absolute monarchical system, Sarit attempted to fashion a new basis of legitimacy for authoritarian rule. Whereas Phibun (with Luang Wichit as the articulate conceptualizer) had borrowed European notions of personality cult and nationalism to legitimize his authoritarianism, Sarit (again with Luang Wichit's assistance) developed a political philosophy that drew on historical Thai and Buddhist ideas. Sarit's distrust of the Western institutions of open society that Thailand had tried to adapt, on and off, since 1932 was captured succinctly in a statement made by Thanat Khoman (then ambassador to the United States) early in 1959:

> The fundamental cause of our political instability in the past lies in the sudden transplantation of alien institutions onto our own soil without proper regard to the circumstances which prevail in our homeland . . . with the result that their functioning has been haphazard and ever chaotic. If we look at our national history, we can see very well that this country works better and prospers under an authority, not a tyrannical authority, but a unifying authority around which all elements of the nation can rally. On the contrary, the dark pages of our history show that whenever such an authority is lacking and

dispersal elements had their play, the nation was plunged into one disaster after another.[1]

Sarit called the governance he was introducing a "revolution" in order to convey the idea of a sharp break with political conditions of the immediate past. He and Thanom after him ruled through a Revolutionary Council and, pending the long-delayed reestablishment of a constitutional parliament, through revolutionary decrees. The regime never abandoned the idea that "democracy" in some form should be developed in Thailand as one of the pillars of legitimation of government. However, the pronouncements of the regime did not reflect any sense of inconsistency between the immediate return to authoritarianism, based on contemporary application of traditional Thai concepts regarding power and social organization, and the assertion that this type of governance was leading to a workable democracy. Commenting on his brief interim constitution, Sarit said that "the present parliamentary system differs from normal parliamentary practice in the fact that there are no popularly elected MP's."[2] In 1965 Thanom's Revolutionary Council stated that the revolution had "abolished democratic ideas borrowed from the West and suggested that it would build a democratic system that would be appropriate to the special characteristics and realities of the Thai. It will build a democracy, a Thai way of democracy."[3] The search for a system that would provide both stability and democracy—indeed, the very use of the phrase "a Thai way of democracy"—has continued at the center of political discourse in Thailand, through alternating episodes of authoritarian, parliamentary, and "quasi-democratic" government.

In fact, Sarit's rule was more dictatorial, more harsh than was Phibun's at any time. Sarit immediately launched a crackdown on all potential opposition, jailing over a hundred people and clamping down on the press. He took a personal interest in certain types of criminal activity, especially arsonists (small merchants who burned down their premises to obtain insurance proceeds), who he ordered summarily executed in public. Ruling from a position of solid control over the military and the police, and willing to instill fear without any checks on violation of civil rights, Sarit effectively created a climate of political stability. Factional politics disappeared while disaffected elements prudently kept still. As Wyatt summed it up, "Many segments of Thai society, people who increasingly had worried that the kingdom was slipping into anarchy, welcomed such authoritarian leadership and rule, while the small following of the Democratic party, primarily urban, and the considerable rural support for the northeastern politicians, were either outraged or cast politically adrift, not to surface again for fifteen years."[4]

Drawing on traditional Thai norms respecting the relationship between powerful patrons and dependent clients, Sarit defined the role of the prime minister as that of a father who would tend to the needs of the people, and to whom the people would, in consequence, owe their loyalty and respect. Since this relationship had been the moral basis of the monarch's legitimacy (harking back to the early Thai traditions of kingship attributed to King Ramkhamhaeng in the thirteenth century), Sarit had to create a dualistic conception of legitimacy. The rebuilding of the prestige of the monarchy, as a symbol of the Thai nation and the source of all legitimacy, was one of the main objectives of his policy, and was a supportive source of his own legitimacy as the administrator of this system.

The combination of elements from Thai social and political traditions created by Luang Wichit and Sarit has been aptly termed "despotic paternalism" by Thak Chaloemtiarana. Sarit's concept of paternalism was expressed in a flurry of novel decisions respecting free medical care for the needy, reductions in utility charges and school fees, a cut in the price of a cup of coffee, instructions to the navy to deliver cheap coconuts to Bangkok, cleanliness and anti-opium campaigns, and so on. Thak noted that many of these measures were never implemented, but they did create an "atmosphere of change" and generate public enthusiasm.[5] Most important, his success at restoring a placid atmosphere and his allegiance to monarchy won him the support of the bureaucratic elite and the families of the old nobility.

Emergence of Development Policy and the Policy Technocrats

It is no exaggeration to say that the first two years of the Sarit government were pivotal to modern Thai economic development. For the first time, the pursuit of economic growth was established as one of the primary objectives of government. The shaping of economic policy was to a considerable extent put in the hands of the technocrats. The legal framework for development was strengthened. The planning and implementing institutions the technocrats needed to function effectively were created. A close relationship was established between the technocrats and the external agencies (primarily the World Bank and the U.S. aid agency), enabling the government to draw on foreign financial and technical resources, including policy advisers. Economic policy was redefined to eliminate the anti-Sinic nationalist elements, to block further growth in the state enterprise sector (except for utilities and other infrastructure), to encourage domestic and foreign private investment, and to reassert the primacy of the market system.

Because these changes in policy and in the coherence of government purpose were so marked in comparison with the preceding years, and so important for the subsequent course of the country's economic development, they have been examined by several writers seeking to explain why the changes were made. The explanations revolve around the motivations and relative roles of three parties—Sarit, the technocrats, and the external agencies.

In asserting Sarit's personal role in the evolution of development policy, it is important to recognize, as Thak demonstrates, that he took up the premiership with very few ideas about economic policy or about the broader range of policies that are implied by the term "development," beyond the rather curious idiosyncratic concerns mentioned above. As part of his effort to project a paternal image, he began to travel extensively around the country, coming away with the conclusion—fortunately, a correct insight—that transportation was a key bottleneck to Thailand's development and that road building should have high priority in the government's investment program.[6] He also apparently recognized that the country needed a set of development-promoting institutions and, as a military man, appreciated the utility of systematic planning.[7] He had come from modest circumstances in the Northeast and evinced a strong interest in rural development, reinforcing his paternalism. With respect to one policy change—the undertaking not to expand the state's manufacturing or commercial activities—Silcock speculated that Sarit was quite willing to weaken the government enterprise sector that had been the main financial base of his political rivals, because he drew his own finances and patronage (apart from the Lottery Organization) from private enterprises.[8]

Apart from these general inclinations, Sarit, as the supreme authority over public—including economic—policy, was an empty vessel. Thak cites a speech made by Sarit in 1960 that illustrates his limited perspective on development:

> You have probably seen and were annoyed with my constant interest in development [phatthana]. I have acted in matters which some of you have advised against saying that they are not the duties of the Prime Minister to spend time in overseeing the maintenance of city cleanliness, road problems, markets, river and canal problems, village welfare, public health, and activities of local government officials in the changwad and amphur. You have heard me complain about the inappropriate location of toilets and unsatisfactory sanitation. I may appear too particular. . . . I maintain that the elevation of the living conditions of the people is my ultimate task.[9]

Thak concludes that Sarit's concern for "details" reflected an "idea of development in which macroeconomic change had only a marginal place." Nevertheless, it was also evident that Sarit had a profound antipathy toward any policy agenda that smacked of "communism." His anticommunism was certainly in the mainstream of Thai thought rejecting ideologies that would nullify religion and monarchy. And Sarit had every incentive to protect the right to acquire private property as he accumulated, late in life as it turned out, considerable private wealth. While Sarit's anticommunism may have appeared to be a political tactic to justify the suppression of all opposition, the rising tide of radicalism in Laos and Vietnam in 1960–61 and the pervasive climate of threat created by the cold war were powerful external factors generating apprehension in Bangkok that reinforced the long-standing anticommunist predisposition among the public.

In this climate Sarit pursued a policy of political repression that was one of the uglier aspects of his rule. Ideas of Western liberalism that were shared by the technocrats and the social critics were suppressed. Some scholars believe that

Sarit's repression "stunted" the development of intellectualism in Thailand until the mid-1970s. In Thak's judgment, Sarit precipitated a decade in which "intellectualism in Thailand was marked by mediocrity, blandness, and orthodoxy."[10]

Thak's characterization is too harsh. The notion of intellectualism is not precise, but it would be arbitrary to define intellectual activity as comprising only social criticism and history (the main subjects in which the radical writers made original contributions). While the technocrats were generally orthodox in their ideas, it would be incorrect to grade the intellectual quality of their work as mediocre. The radical writers and social critics who were silenced, and in some deplorable cases executed, would likely have had little impact on public policy if free debate had been permitted; their boldness in reinterpreting Thai social and political dynamics was not matched by realism or coherence in programmatic proposals.[11] The policy analysis of the technocrats, on the other hand, and their continuing efforts to improve the quality of analysis and decision making involved in the intellectual-technical workings of the public sector, month in and month out, not only qualify as (applied rather than theoretical) intellectual activity, but were demonstrably effective. And when debate emerged in the early 1970s over the character of development policy—especially the failure to pay sufficient attention to distributive problems—many of the technocrats were among the leading critics, as will be seen below.

At the time, however, the technocrats were not prepared to challenge Sarit on political grounds. Like the majority of the international (non-Marxist) development professionals, the Thai technocrats believed that priority in time had to be given to accelerating the process of economic growth and establishing its institutional and policy foundations. Programs that were redistributive rather than productive should have a lesser claim on resources until the economic pie grew larger. Sarit's receptivity to their policies, and his support for the development of technocratic institutions, enabled him to forge an alliance with the bureaucracy that cleared the stage for purposive growth and enabled the leading technocrats to press their technocratic values. As much as Dr. Puey and others were also socialized to democratic values, they were prepared to work within an autocratic system. The willingness of the technocratic elite to accommodate with the military, while sustaining an expectation that development would gradually change the polity and create conditions conducive to democratic evolution, was clearly demonstrated for the first time under Sarit and would be demonstrated over again in the succeeding decades.

Most writers ascribe a substantial role to the external agencies in the policy turnaround of the late 1950s. Some authors depict these agencies as having had a determining part as independent, or indeed interventionist, actors. The bank, the U.S. aid mission, and individual Americans were involved in various ways. The bank's major contribution was the 1957–58 study team and its report (published in 1959) containing a host of recommendations that were reflected in subsequent decisions and legislation.[12] The U.S. involvement consisted of individual advisers, of whom Loftus was the principal; technical advisory reports, of which the Beitzel report on promoting foreign investment was particularly important;[13] and, according to one interpretation, conversations influential Americans held with Sarit in 1958 while he was recuperating in Washington, D.C.

These efforts to attribute a major initiating, or even dominant, role to external forces tend to exaggerate and oversimplify the influence of the outsiders. The dynamics of the policy change were more complex. Some of the recommendations adopted in 1959–60, especially relating to the planning and policy processes, had been made first during the Phibun period by earlier World Bank and U.S. reports and consultants, but to no effect (or, if adopted, without effective implementation).

More important was the report of Loftus's Economic Survey Group. As noted above, the group made the first attempt under any Thai government to rationalize the so-called capital budget. When it became clear that the World Bank was going to send a year-long mission to Thailand for a comprehensive review, the Economic Survey Group wrapped up its work in order to present the bank team with some materials and ideas as a point of departure. Although Loftus viewed the results of this exercise as technically weak, it was important for its emphasis on "basic physical public utilities" as the primary responsibility for the public sector, and for its recommendations favoring reliance on the private sector (including foreign investment) for commercial and industrial development. These recommendations foreshadowed and fed into the World Bank report and then the first development plan.[14] It is apparent that those writers who have attributed the origination of these key policies to the World Bank and the Beitzel report (or to Sarit personally) have overlooked not only the preceding Economic Survey Group but also the fact that in recommending to the government that the bank be invited to send a broad review mission, Dr. Puey would have known that any mission that institution would send out would have liberal policy proclivities.

While the technocrats had succeeded earlier in the area of monetary policy, they had lacked any independent political base from which to tackle the fiscal, public investment, and interventionist policies in which the Phibun era politics were rooted. Once Sarit turned to the economic technocrats for policy management, the latter were able to strengthen their derived authority over the mass of the bureaucracy through their unique role as the conduit to the external agencies. More important for the long run, the policy technocrats created an organizational base in the form of planning and resource allocating authorities, which gave them substantial leverage over future policy and over the bureaucracy. Thus, the policy changes at this time should be seen as resulting from a synergism among Sarit, his senior policy technocrats, and the willing facilitation of the external agencies. As Stifel, one of the closest observers of the workings of the technocrats, observed, "The senior technocrats skillfully mobilized the support of foreign aid donors in their internal political effort to make changes."[15]

The sudden expansion of technocratic authority was effected through the institutions that were created to rationalize the government's development activities. These included the Budget Bureau, established in the Prime Minister's Department; the National Economic Development Board (afterward the National Economic and Social Development Board, hereafter referred to as NESDB); the Board of Investment (BOI); and the Office of Fiscal Policy in the Ministry of Finance, all set up in 1959–60. The handful of leading technocrats held the senior positions of these organizations; the junior staff positions were filled with their younger protégés for whom "these experiences served as their technical apprenticeship and placed them strategically in the center of the expanding development-administration machinery."[16] New agencies and councils were created also for policy planning and coordination in education, electric power, research, and other areas.

In hindsight, this spate of activity may appear more definitive, more forceful, than was actually the case, and by association, the institutional role of the Americans and the World Bank may appear to have been more decisive than was the case. On the policy front it took some time before the lead agencies could bring about a reasonable degree of conformity of individual administrative actions with the general policies enunciated in the revolutionary decrees and the first plan. For example, in late 1959 the BOI extended concessions to a promoted firm planning to initiate domestic manufacture of kerosene cans and oil drums; a few months later, contrary to the policy of no new public-sector competitive investment, the Ministry of Defense entered negotiations for the construction of a refinery that would include can- and drum-making facilities. In a second instance, while the BOI was granting tax privileges to induce foreign investors to Thailand, the Ministry of Finance (without consulting the BOI) enacted a tax on remittances. In a third example, a leftover from the economic nationalism of the Phibun years, the Public Warehousing Organization (under the then Ministry of Economic Affairs, now Commerce) proposed to NESDB a project "to enable Thai retailers to compete more successfully with their non-Thai counterparts."[17] These were more in the nature of transitional inconsistencies, not intended as challenges to the policies themselves. (In the next section, I shall make a few observations on the staying power of Thai laissez-faire since Sarit.)

On the institutional front, the new policy organizations and processes were not well designed or immediately effective. Several years of training, staff buildup, and reorganization were required before NESDB in particular (and associated functions like statistics and DTEC) reached the level of competence and policy impact originally expected when the organizations were created. More generally, the entire process of turning the bureaucracy into a well-oiled engine of development took many years and to this day falls substantially short by comparison with, say, the bureaucracy in Singapore, or by the Thais' own standards. Sarit himself, driving for rapid results, and despite his unchallenged power, was dissatisfied with the continuing poor coordination and cooperation among ministries and departments four years after the policy and planning system had been installed. In 1963, hoping to improve the effectiveness of implementation of the first development plan, he pulled a number of departments from different ministries into a single Ministry of National Development. His effort to force greater coordination among the irrigation, power, cooperative, and other fiefdoms was undone in 1973 when this conglomerate ministry was disbanded and the components were mostly returned to their former locations.

The episode of the Ministry of National Development was only the most sweeping effort in a long process in which the technocrats, assisted and prodded by aid agencies, worked at improving the performance of the bureaucracy in which they assumed leading positions. The process began in the early 1950s under an aid project conducted by the Public Administration Service of Chicago. The first systematic analyses of the structure and functioning of Thai government departments were conducted under this project and led to the first reorganization along modern management lines.[18] The project sponsored the training of young officials and helped to install in 1961 the first organization and methods review staff in the Thai government, located in the Budget Bureau. These beginnings reflected an early recognition on the part of both the aid agencies and the technocrats that the Thai government was as much part of the problem as it was, hopefully, part of the solution. The weaknesses of the bureaucracy, and the difficulties these inadequacies caused in the way of practical implementation of policies and programs, drew arguably more attention, from social scientists, aid agencies, and even the policy technocrats, than did the policies themselves.

The analysis of the idiosyncrasies of Thai bureaucratic behavior and the effects of these idiosyncrasies on the government's activities relevant to economic development has been a major subject in the modern literature on Thailand. The bureaucracy as established under the reforms of King Rama V was relatively well paid and reasonably free from corruption. It was administered by members of the royal family and the nobility and was socialized in an ethic of noblesse oblige, complete loyalty to the monarchy, and unquestioned self-confidence and prestige, with more than a touch of arrogance in the relationship of provincial officials to the rural population. As noted above, after it was cut loose from the control and reward system headed by the absolute monarch, the bureaucracy became the core of the polity, and the ministries and agencies became the arena in which power, prestige, and economic rewards were won and distributed through intrabureaucratic politics. Of course, internal politics are common in bureaucracies in all countries. Bureaucratic units everywhere compete for turf and budget. The Thai bureaucracy, however, has been unusually interesting for students of government and politics because of its overwhelming importance in the history and dynamics of the society as a whole, and because its behavioral idiosyncrasies reach back generations.

It will be enough for the purposes of this study to cite some of the idiosyncrasies, relevant to the performance of developmental tasks, that have been explored in the literature on the Thai bureaucracy. Morell and Chai-ananin 1981 gave a cataloging of bureaucratic mores that they found still pervasive. They pointed to the importance of deference, distaste for open confrontation or criticism, concentration of decision making at the top, the importance of old-boy networks and factions, nepotism, overlapping responsibilities, and poor coordination. "The dominant bureaucratic values, so incongruent with legal-rational norms, prevent the bureaucracy from attaining full effectiveness in providing human resource services."19 The prominence of these problems in the 1950s and 1960s was reflected in the great attention given to training, management, and organizational strengthening in virtually all foreign aid projects of consequence.

In the postwar era of modern economic development, the workings of the bureaucracy drew the attention of scholars and development practitioners for very practical reasons. Would these idiosyncracies prove to be serious obstacles to economic growth by preventing the government from developing effective investment and service programs in essential public-sector functions? Could the bureaucracy transform itself sufficiently into a Weberian task-oriented system? As Dr. Puey's remarks cited earlier indicated, the leading technocrats favored a market-oriented economic system partly because of their skepticism over the ability of the bureaucratic institutions to operate efficiently and in the public interest, in areas of economic activity outside of the public utilities and educational and other functions the private sector could not fulfill on a large scale.

The importance of the intimate relationship between the policy and conceptual levels of development management, on the one hand, and the pragmatic, mundane translation of objectives into operational realities, on the other, cannot be exaggerated. While policy research and analysis became increasingly important and sophisticated over time, and while policy debates were often long and heated over specifics of, or glaring exceptions to, the basic thrust of the economic policy framework, there has been remarkably little debate (outside limited academic circles) on the basic orientation and economic philosophy as reformulated and stated during Sarit's tenure. There can be little doubt, as a result, that a major task of the technocrats has been to work out operational specifics and to continue to hone the bureaucratic machinery in the performance of its allotted responsibilities.

The First Development Plan: 1961–1966

The first development plan has been cited often as the formal embodiment of the Sarit reformation. Its policy content actually was skimpy. The primary objective of the plan was "to raise the standard of living." The most oft-quoted passage sets out the relative responsibilities of the public and private sectors, in effect drawing a tight line around the proper role of government to exclude its direct participation in the production of commercial goods and services:

> It is believed that in Thailand increased output will be most readily secured through the spontaneous efforts of individual citizens, fostered and assisted by Government, rather than through Government itself entering directly into the field of production. The keynote of the public development programme is, therefore, the encouragement of economic growth in the private sector, and the resources of Government will be mainly directed to projects both in the agricultural and non-agricultural sectors of the economy, which have this objective in view.

The text makes a bow in the direction of social services, but priority in the allocation of expenditures is given clearly to investment in economic infrastructure, especially water, transportation, and electric power:

> Over the next three years the construction of irrigation works, the building and improvement of roads and other means of transport, the provision of inexpensive electric power, and other physical "infrastructure" projects will claim the bulk of Government expenditure. Agricultural extension and other projects to extend technical knowledge will likewise take a high share of Government investment. The use of resources for these purposes . . . will provide means and opportunities for increased production and enable the private sector to expand on its own initiative. Government will also undertake to provide for the expansion of social services.

Much less attention has been given to the part of the plan's statement of goals that refers to "raising the standard of living" as the "primary" objective. One might be tempted to dismiss the brief disclaimer in the text, that sheer material advance is a proper objective of social policy, as a pious concession to Buddhist values. The priority given to raising the standard of living "appears to suggest a purely material goal, without regard to social, cultural, and aesthetic values. But while material well-being may be an end to itself, it is also, and more importantly, a means to a further end insofar as it enables all citizens to lead fuller, more creative and happier lives." The plan also asserts the high importance of equitable distribution: "increased output should be equitably distributed so that, to the extent possible, all citizens, and not merely a privileged few, derive benefit from it."[20] Although the plan itself neither drew out the policy implications of taking distribution into deliberate account nor allocated government investment in a manner suggesting a serious attempt at distributive programs, the two themes—distribution and the proper role of material advance among the society's objectives—reemerged relatively quickly as major policy and philosophical issues, to which I shall return below.

As an exercise in aggregate economic planning, the first plan received poor grades. It contained virtually no economic or policy analysis. Broad sectoral and overall targets were merely asserted without analytic support. The plan covered a six-year period, divided into two halves. The first half in particular was "primarily an aggregation of the perceived needs of various government agencies for infrastructure development."[21] In Silcock's view "the first half was hardly a plan at all." In his usual trenchant manner, Loftus told his Thai colleagues that the plan "hardly even pretends to be more than a 'costed' list of government programs and projects; the private sector is essentially ignored; and consequently there does not yet exist a truly 'national' development Plan."[22] For several reasons it would have been unrealistic to expect otherwise. The raw material for the investment program came up from the ministries, many of which had no planning capacity. Economic statistics were limited and unreliable. The working level of young professionals in NESDB numbered about half a dozen. And Sarit imposed a deadline that gave NESDB about four months to produce the document for cabinet approval. Nevertheless, the very process of producing a plan, the first time this had been attempted in Thai history, was an important learning experience for the planners and the bureaucracy. As Silcock records, "it brought the planning machinery to bear on the existing development ideas of the departments of the central government, allotting the available funds with a view to maximum co-ordinated achievement rather than simply curbing a wide variety of miscellaneous departmental demands."[23] Inevitably, there were shortfalls in the public sector, in terms of both the policy scope of the plan and the implementation capabilities of the bureaucracy. The expansion of public-sector "development expenditures" fell short of the targets by 15 percent because of delays in loan negotiations and in project execution, skill shortage, and other common operational problems. But despite the plan's analytic limitations, the delay in foreign-loan-financed projects, and the unanticipated costs of the government's assumptions of responsibility for NEDCOL, the pattern of public-sector development expenditures adhered fairly closely to the distribution laid out in the plan.[24]

The plan's assertions of policy that would reserve manufacturing and commercial activities for the private sector were reflected in the very limited attention given to identifying the problems of the private sector, and in the apparent absence of any consultation with the private sector in the preparation of the plan document. NESDB sought no inputs from either Thai academics or businessmen. While it might appear that the technocrats were patronizing toward, or disinterested in, the ideas of the private enterprise sector they wished to unshackle, it must be recognized that the business community at the time had neither an organizational nor an intellectual basis (nor the self-confidence) for conducting a coherent dialogue on development policy with the university-trained officials. While lessons were learned, and improvements made in the project planning cycle, the introduction of manpower planning, and NESDB's ability to plan consistency between the investment program and the macroeconomic projections and targets, the policy and planning process remained entirely an internal bureaucratic exercise.

Despite the shortfalls, the government had reason to be satisfied with the implementation of the first plan and the acceleration the economy experienced in macroeconomic performance. Growth in GDP averaged about 7 percent over the plan period, on a rising track. This exceeded the conservative expectations of NESDB (reflected in the 5 percent annual target, raised for the revised second half of the six-year period), resulting in a cumulative growth in GDP of over 50 percent in the six years compared with the target of 30 percent. The annual deficit in the balance of trade was more than offset by invisible earnings and capital inflow; international reserves rose every year. The agricultural sector grew at a 5 percent rate, well ahead of population growth. The nonagricultural sectors expanded at higher rates, initiating the decline in the relative importance of agriculture in the Thai economy that has continued ever since. The economic expansion took place within a very stable price environment. In 1967, evaluating the changes that had occurred over the first plan period, the planning board issued a paper expressing considerable satisfaction over its policy package and exuding confidence. At the same time, the evaluation identified problems that had not been adequately appreciated earlier and, in effect, attested to a learning process that would feed back into the next round of development planning. Reflecting this balance, the text concludes that

in spite of inexperience, imperfection in the planning process, project formulation and implementation and the many problems encountered, the main purposes of the Plan were accomplished and the overall development progress made was, in the words of foreign observers, an impressive record of economic achievement. This progress and the relative prosperity which came with it during this First Plan has not only given hope for a sustained growth at a higher rate in the Second Plan, but it has also lent support to the soundness of our development policies. However, many difficulties still lie ahead on the challenging journey to reach national aspiration. We must face this challenge and overcome all problems and difficulties with determination to strive for more rapid economic and social progress. The gain already made must not go to waste and there should be no room for complacency.[25]

In effect, the technocrats were proclaiming victory for the new policy framework and were turning their attention to issues and alternatives within that framework. The evaluation identified five "basic problems" of the economy, "weaknesses" that would have to be the focus of second plan policy. Four of these problems were seen as having resulted to some extent from the very rapidity of the economic progress achieved: growing inequality in the distribution of income; a "very high rate" of population growth; weaknesses in the manufacturing sector attributed to the policy of import substitution and to the absence of an effective program that could counter the emerging concentration of industry in Bangkok; and an inadequate integration among the various modes of transportation, the sector that had "developed remarkably, particularly in the field of road transport." The fifth problem was the weakness of the government's programs in agriculture, aside from the physical expansion in irrigation works. Agricultural planning, coordination research, and extension were all cited for inadequacies or ineffectiveness. Other agricultural problems noted included low utilization of irrigation water due to delays in the construction of tertiary and on-farm canals, very limited progress in rubber research and replanting, and "ineffectiveness of the forest control program" in the face of unabated and widespread illegal forest destruction. Other signs of excessive resource exploitation (e.g., fresh-water fishing was exceeding natural reproduction) were identified, along with needed corrective measures. In its sector-by-sector review of progress and shortfalls, the development board touched on several other problems worth noting, including the need to expand scientific and industrial research, then in a "preliminary" stage; among the infrastructure agencies, the administrative and staffing problems in the Telephone Organization of Thailand that stood as "major bottlenecks" in the way of expansion of telephone service; and inadequate public expenditure on education, and serious problems of educational content and quality, the supply of teachers, and the role of schools.

The board reported good progress in the mining sector, power generation and distribution, public health, and transportation. These sectors were not without problems, of course. Because doctors were reluctant to live in the provinces, the ratio of population to physicians was twenty times higher in rural areas compared with urban. The government had not yet approved introduction of family planning despite the fact that Thailand "has one of the highest rates of population growth in the world." The transportation problems of Bangkok were already "serious." "The solution in the past has been on a piece-meal basis whereby bottlenecks were removed as they occurred with little regard for long-range town planning. . . . The size and speed with which Bangkok is expanding [makes] it an urgent necessity to have far sighted and proper physical planning." In its discussion of the congestion in the port of Bangkok, the evaluation mentions, as an afterthought, that "the eventual establishment of new supplementary sea port of the east coast is necessary."

The first plan evaluation was a remarkable document, though generally ignored in the subsequent literature. The very idea of a systematic review of national development problems, and of policies and programs needed to address these problems, hardly existed in Thailand prior to the late 1950s. To be sure, the evaluation is too brief to treat any of the problems in depth, is not cast in a macroeconomic framework to explore sectoral interrelationships, and overlooks some important policy areas such as the tax system and the rice premium. Nevertheless, the paper reveals that the policy technocrats had already identified many of the key issues that have dominated the development process, and policy debate, ever since.

A Caveat on Thai Laissez-Faire

While Sarit's reversal of Thai economic policy has not since been seriously challenged, it would be misleading to characterize the commitment to a capitalist market economy as having been held by Thai policy makers without reservations, or over time without significant deviations. I noted earlier Dr. Puey's reservations over unfettered capitalism. There were many in Thailand, as in the advanced capitalist countries of the West, who were critical of market failures, of the effects of cyclical (or, in Thailand's case, externally induced) fluctuations in economic activity on the welfare of different groups. There were also concerns that private economic actors, when powerful, were prone to market manipulation and to exploitation of the relatively weak. As in the early periods of industrial development in the West, Thailand lacked countervailing pressures or regulatory structures that could serve to balance or constrain what were perceived as antisocial implications of the rising power of the entrepreneurial class. Sarit's Revolutionary Proclamation #19 had abolished the Labor Act of 1956, thereby eliminating the legal basis for trade unions. The only farmer organizations were government-promoted cooperatives designed for local marketing or credit functions and completely lacking interest representation potentialities. Political parties, when they were allowed to operate again in the late 1960s, represented factional interests, not economic or social interest group aggregations. There was no legislation aimed at economic concentration; with the industrial sector in its first decade of significant expansion, the objective of public policy was to promote the accumulation of private industrial capital, not to constrain the process.

The recognition or belief that under these institutional conditions government should selectively regulate or intervene in the operations of the private sector appeared soon after the private sector began to seize the opportunities offered by the policies enunciated in the first plan and its implementing legislation. The taxation of rice, partly as a subsidy to Bangkok consumers, has already been described. Other ad hoc interventions arose from time to time in response to new constituencies that were appearing as the economy became more diversified. As with rice, other interventions into the marketing of specific commodities were initially pressed on the Thai government by other countries that required government-to-government or other forms of regulated trade. And within the Thai government there were departments, especially in the ministries of Agriculture and Commerce, where bureaucracies with jurisdiction over specific economic functions and areas of regulation continued to hold strongly to the conviction, dating back to the 1920s, that commerce was an activity that inherently preyed on farmers and consumers. Similar suspicions have surfaced among factions in the Thai army. Vaguely defined populist ideas, most pointedly aimed at the commercial banks, have served from time to time as justifications for military assertions that major reforms—even through military assumptions of political power by force—need to be made. These ideas and interventions have been the stuff of many policy debates since, along with a final category of market interventions that in practice has been among the most important, viz. administrative actions designed to generate rents.

Macroeconomic Management

Apart from Sarit's imposition of political quietude and conformity, the primary objective of domestic policy during the Sarit–Thanom period was to put Thailand's economy on a path of continuous economic growth without sacrificing monetary stability. The technocrats did not expect the economy to grow at a very rapid rate, nor did they plan to press for a high rate through deliberate expansion of government spending that would risk the reintroduction of inflation. The target rate of growth in the first plan, a modest 5 percent per annum, was witness to these conservative expectations and intentions. In the event, the authorities had reason to be satisfied with the results. The national income accounts series then in use showed real GDP increasing by 6.5 percent in 1961–63 and 7.8 percent in 1964–66. The growth achieved appears to have been even higher than was realized at the time; the revised NESDB series now in use shows rates of 7.3 and 8.5 percent, respectively.

Although the first plan evaluation was already identifying obstacles and recognizing new policy problems, these were not serious enough to impede the first surge of the 1960s. Furthermore, it must be remembered that the conceptual framework within which economists then understood the development process focused on the expansion of a country's economic size, as defined and measured by the national accounts, and on the apparently powerful logic of simplifying models (such as the Harrod-Domar) that related aggregate growth to the volume of savings and the productivity of the investment to which those savings were applied. While this framework has subsequently been elaborated to take account of the fact that an increase in the sheer volume of investment is not in itself a *sufficient* condition for economic growth, it had the virtue for policy makers of highlighting the fact that an acceleration of investment was indeed a *necessary* condition for an acceleration in the growth of output.

Between the rising public-sector expenditures on infrastructure and the private-sector response to industrial promotion policies, the rate of gross fixed capital formation to GDP rose from the 1950–60 average of 12.1 percent, and the 1961 level of 13.2 percent, to 20.3 percent in 1966.[26] The fixed investment ratio rose further to a high of 26.7 in 1970 (a level not attained again since then). The simple one-year arithmetic relationship between the volume of investment and the following increase in GDP, the incremental capital-output ratio, ranged between 1.5 and 3.2 from 1960 to 1970. This satisfactory low ratio, although starting to rise in the late 1960s, bore out the expectations of Loftus and others that better utilization of unfinished, underutilized, and mismanaged public-sector assets could raise the return on the sunk investments of the 1950s at the cost of only modest additional investment.[27]

The rise in capital formation was financed largely from domestic savings. At the same time foreign exchange earnings and capital inflows exceeded imports. The investment expansion thus was accomplished with minor pressure on prices and with a substantial buildup in foreign exchange reserves. Wholesale prices rose by an average of 1.8 percent between 1961 and 1969. In most years the growth in the money supply was kept below the rate of growth in GDP. In addition to the rise in capital formation, two other factors contributed significantly to the economic growth of this decade, a strong export performance and rising U.S. military expenditures in Thailand related to the deepening American involvement in Thai security and in the Vietnam War. Export growth in the 1960s was still heavily dependent on the major agricultural commodities even as the agriculture sector as a whole was declining from around 40 percent of GDP in 1960 to 32 percent in 1969. Nevertheless, diversification was clearly under way, with maize, tapioca, shrimp, and other lesser commodities becoming significant export earners. The increase in U.S. military expenditures after 1965 provided a major fillip to the construction sector, which averaged 13 percent growth in 1965–69 and provided sufficient exogenous foreign exchange earnings to free Thailand from the reserves constraint that might otherwise have materialized as economic conditions turned less favorable in the closing years of the period.

A change in economic fortunes beginning in 1967 presented the government with its first episode of macroeconomic imbalance since the period of postwar stabilization. Until 1967 government revenues had grown faster than both expenditures and GDP, enabling the government to accumulate cash balances and avoid any deficit financing. Rising expenditures after 1967, especially on defense, police, and transportation (propelled by the need to counter the open insurgency the Communist Party of Thailand [CPT] had launched in August 1965), exceeded revenue growth and brought on a series of overall central government deficits that reached a peak of 4.9 percent of GDP in 1972. The balance of payments also turned unfavorable as imports continued to rise in the late 1960s in the face of a slowdown in export growth. Combined with a decline in transfers as the pace of U.S. military construction in Thailand slowed, these changes turned the surpluses of 1963–67 into current account deficits. In 1969–70 capital inflows were insufficient to finance these deficits. As a result, for the first time since 1958, Thailand experienced a decline in foreign reserves; nevertheless, the drawdown of about $170 million left the reserves at the end of 1970 at the comfortable level of $767 million, equivalent to about seven months of imports. In an international environment of price stability, the strong reserves position had enabled the Bank of Thailand to maintain the value of the baht within a small trading range of the par value (B20.8 to U.S.$1) set with the IMF in October 1963. On the other hand, a new potential threat to this stability was a sharp rise in the external debt service burden, from 9.0 percent of export earnings in 1967 to a peak of 17.7 percent in 1971. The increase in debt service payments was due entirely to private-sector borrowing, loans, and supplier credits, incident to the industrial investment boom.

It was apparent that the historic automatic correction mechanisms of the pre-war past, the swift contraction of import demand in response to a fall in commodity export earnings, were no longer operating. Although the problems were not severe, these imbalances did call for a modest demand management response by the government. Some mild demand restraint measures were introduced, including increases in 1970 in duties on imported consumer goods and in excise and other taxes. The drop in foreign exchange reserves and some slight tightening of credit to the private sector engineered by the Bank of Thailand restrained growth in the money supply. In the event, a combination of factors more powerful than the steps undertaken by the government took the steam out of the investment boom and reduced the growth in GDP in 1971–72 to a little under 5 percent a year, the slowest growth since 1959. The responsible factors were poor harvests, declining international commodity prices, and the emergence of excess capacity in the manufacturing and service sectors. The year 1973, marked by the first oil shock and the overthrow of the Thanom government, ushered in a new, third period in the country's political and economic development, which I shall take up in the next chapter.

In the face of the growth record of the Sarit–Thanom period, the moderate character of the challenges to monetary stability toward the end of the period, the relatively favorable impact of external economic events, and the strong performance of the private sector and the foreign capital and transfer payments inflows, it is almost a matter of taste whether one characterizes the performance of the government in the realm of macroeconomic policy management as effective, or merely marginal and validated by luck and self-correcting mechanisms. Ammar Siamwalla is one of the few Thai economists who explicitly posed the question of whether or not macroeconomic policy in this period was well managed. Writing in 1975, he pointed out that the circumstances of the 1960s did not require significant macroeconomic management. Once the basic decisions were made to unify the exchange rate and to let the private sector run, the economy was back on automatic pilot, so to speak. Four factors sustained relative stability and protected the authorities from being forced into making painful choices. Exports performed well, thanks to the response of Thai farmers to the opening of markets for nontraditional or "upland" crops. The balance of payments benefited from the windfall of U.S. military expenditures and from the surprising growth of tourism. (The potentiality of tourism as a source of growth for the Thai economy and as a foreign exchange earner was completely overlooked by the World Bank report of 1959. In the late 1960s tourism emerged from beyond the horizon of official policy. In 1970 tourist earnings were estimated at over B2 billion, equal to 15 percent of merchandise export earnings.)

Finally, Ammar cites evidence for the existence of a natural "fiscal drag" in Thailand. When exports were booming, government revenues (then heavily trade-dependent) rose much faster than expenditures; the expansion of purchasing power generated by the rise in exports of agricultural commodities was automatically deflated by the government's fiscal surplus. If the balance of payments moved into deficit by the time the government's budgeted expenditures had risen, in belated response to the years of fiscal surplus, a government deficit opened up that again had opposite effects on purchasing power now being depressed by the export decline. Having built up a large cushion of foreign exchange reserves, the government was not obliged to adopt any substantial policy shifts to sustain the value of the baht, combat severe inflation, restrain import growth, or achieve other structural adjustments, thanks to this combination of fortuitous circumstances and structural characteristics. Ammar concludes that "the situation before 1973 then is one which exhibits remarkable stability—a stability that owes as much to the basic economic mechanism underlying the economy as to the behavior pattern of the Thai authorities. Please note the use of the term 'behavior pattern' rather than the more purposive term 'policy'. To use the latter term would be altogether too flattering."[28]

Ammar admits that a "passive" strategy may have been optimal under the circumstances. While the government was not literally passive (witness the tax increases in 1970, the export-promoting credits of the Bank of Thailand, relaxation of bureaucratic and other inhibitions on tourists, introduction of rebates for duties paid on imports used in subsequent exports[29]), the measures undertaken were not, and did not have to be, substantial either as departures from previous policy or in their quantitative effects. Implicit in this combination of balancing trends and limitations of policy changes to the cautious and incremental is a very important point easily overlooked: with a sound basic framework in place, incrementalism ensured that the government also avoided committing major mistakes. The macroeconomic environment after the fall of the Thanon government would present much greater challenges to the formation of both short-run macroeconomic and long-run development policies.

Industrial Development

While Thai agriculture in the first half of the 1960s grew at a respectable annual rate of 5 percent, the share of manufacturing in GDP rose from 11.4 percent in 1961, the first year of the first plan, to 13.9 percent by 1966; by 1970 the share had risen to 16.0 percent. After another mere fifteen years, manufacturing value-added would surpass agriculture as a component of the Thai economy. Nevertheless, in 1967, after a bare half-decade since the establishment of the BOI and the activation of the private-sector promotional policies, NESDB was already sounding warnings about the shortcomings of the results and calling for policy adjustments. In pointing out that import-substitution consumer goods were offering "very little benefit" to consumers in quality or price, compared with imports; that manufacturing production costs had not declined despite "more than half a decade of production experience and generous tax concession"; and that the new industries were still predominantly dependent on imported raw materials and intermediates, NESDB was reflecting an early disenchantment or at least skepticism toward import substitution and the underlying infant industry rationale.[30]

In fact, import-substitution as a strategy for promoting industrial development never had unqualified support among the early policy technocrats. The 1959 World Bank report had certainly championed the private sector in its primary concern over encouraging the withdrawal of the public sector from manufacturing. But the bank's endorsement of a policy to install incentives was qualified with recommendations that the proposed new industrial promotion act should empower the authorities to grant promoted firms special tariff rates or qualitative restrictions for a maximum of five years. Special tariff benefits would be phased out in each case over a further five-year period.[31] As early as 1963, the Bank of Thailand recommended that the government promote export industries rather than build up an inefficient, high-cost import-substitution industrial structure.[32]

Despite these concerns, the apparent ineffectiveness of the incentive system and apparatus that had been established under the 1960 Industrial Investment Act (itself intended as a stronger substitute for the ineffective provisions of the industrial promotion legislation of the 1950s) led to the decision to create more powerful incentives two years later. The arrangements the World Bank had proposed for administering an import-substitution incentive system would have avoided concentrating the dispensation of benefits in a new bureaucratic entity devoted to industrial protection. In the event, the Board of Investment was set up in 1959 and was granted wide discretionary authority to grant benefits to promoted enterprises.

In the initial years of the new industrial policy the most important single authority given to the BOI was the power to guarantee that the government would not nationalize a promoted firm or undertake any new activity that would compete with such a firm. Other authorities included permission for employment of expatriates (otherwise restricted by immigration and labor laws); granting of reductions in, or exemptions from, duties on imported machinery, and from taxes on profits for periods up to eight years; and power to impose protective duties on competing imports up to 50 percent ad valorem. Although the Ministry of Commerce had powers to ban the import (or export) of virtually any commodity, under very broad authority for regulating trade in the general economic or security interest, the BOI was not given authority to impose qualitative import bans (through the Ministry of Commerce) until 1977.

Armed with these authorities the BOI began a vigorous implementation of the new policy. Private enterprise responded in kind, the individual firms probably motivated mainly by the prospect that competitors might be shut out by those suppliers who were first on the queue to preempt market positions as "promoted" domestic manufacturers. Given the small size of the domestic market, it is not surprising that the structure of this first wave of manufacturing investment was concentrated on the final assembly of consumer products. After the treaty revisions of the 1920s had given Thailand a free hand over import duties, the country had gradually developed a tariff schedule designed to accomplish the single objective of generating government revenue. As a result, the tariff structure in the 1950s had widely varying rates applying to different commodities, affecting relative domestic prices differentially without any economic rationale. The BOI's ad hoc granting of concessions in the 1960s, reflecting the initial product makeup of the promoted enterprises, skewed the tariff relationships into a pattern in which higher nominal rates were applied to consumer goods than to capital goods, raw materials, and some groups of intermediaries. This skewness became more pronounced over time, as can be seen in Table 4.1.

The table also shows the widening gap between nominal and effective rates of protection between 1964 and 1978, especially applying to consumer goods (personal vehicles are included under "transport equipment"). The additional protection above the import duty rates was provided mainly by the "business" tax. This tax was a turnover levy, a cascading point-of-sale tax only partially reduced by exemptions for taxes paid on purchase inputs for some classes of goods. Like the tariff schedule, the rate structure of the business tax reflected no general economic rationale and was highly differentiated among goods and services. While tariff rates have moved up and down from time to time, as the government has responded to fiscal deficits or swings in the balance of payments, the business tax rates have generally risen since 1966. It is apparent that the Ministry of Finance intended these latter increases partly as additional protective measures; the tax was applied to some goods only if imported, while the rates on some imported goods were set higher than the rates applied to the domestically produced counterparts.[33] Finally, to put the above discussion into international perspective, it is worth noting that comparative studies among developing countries show that prior to the 1970s Thailand had a relatively low level of protection.[34]

The promoted consumer goods generated backward linkages only where final product manufacture was based on the processing of domestic agricultural commodities such as food and beverage inputs, wood, and rubber. Of the 371 projects approved for promotional benefits in 1959–70 (projects actually implemented were usually fewer than those "approved"), 39 percent were for consumer nondurables, accounting for 43 percent of the total value of proposed investment. Intermediate goods made up 22 percent of the investment total, more than half of which was for petroleum refining. The small share of so-called capital goods shown in the BOI reporting system actually includes automobiles and other consumer durables.

Table 4.1

Rates of Protection: Nominal and Effective (%)

	1964		1978	
	Nominal	Effective	Nominal	Effective
Processed food	17.76	37.33	9.00	78.50
Beverages and tobacco	220.68	65.47	69.10	4.00
Construction and materials	26.00	21.26	12.20	91.70
Intermediate products I	5.17	6.54	14.80	16.20
Intermediate products II	26.02	54.55	19.20	55.30
Consumer nondurables	32.86	42.44	64.60	212.40
Consumer durables	27.20	21.96	57.30	495.60
Machinery[a]	21.60	17.74	21.40	58.30
Transport equipment	41.92	121.69	80.50	417.20

Source: Oey Meesok, *Political Economy*, table 3.18.
a. For 1964 "machinery" refers to wires, cables, and accessories only. Data for 1978 include tractor assembly, sewing machines, and nonelectrical machinery.

A more complete picture of the evolution of the manufacturing sector can be seen in Table 4.2, which includes the new, relatively larger-scale, and corporate enterprises going through the BOI and the remaining nonpromoted manufacturing activities. The non-BOI sector included the mass of enterprises that might be characterized as either small-scale, preexisting, producing goods and services not eligible under BOI criteria or the larger manufacturing enterprises surviving from the earlier era of bureaucratic capitalism. The preindustrial character of manufacturing in 1960 is reflected in the large share of the value-added that was generated by food and beverages and cigarettes (57 percent), and in which preeminently traditional activities such as rice milling still played an important part. Consumer products as a whole made up 77 percent of manufacturing value-added in 1960. With manufacturing overall comprising only 12.6 percent of GDP, the contribution of intermediate manufactured products to the country's total output of goods and services was a mere 2 percent, capital goods an insignificant 0.5 percent. By 1970 the composition of the manufacturing sector had changed, with capital goods rising to 9 percent and intermediate goods to 22 percent of manufactur-

Table 4.2

Structure of Manufacturing Sector (%)

	1951	1960	1970	1980
Consumer Goods	69.2	77.0	61.2	60.2
Food processing	23.7	34.2	22.0	13.7
Beverages	7.1	8.6	10.3	9.2
Tobacco	19.6	14.5	9.2	6.2
Textiles	1.1	4.9	7.9	9.2
Garments	4.2	7.9	4.9	11.3
Other	13.5	6.9	6.9	10.6
Intermediate Goods	12.7	12.4	21.9	23.4
Petroleum refining	—	—	7.5	6.7
Chemicals	9.9	7.3	6.8	6.7
Other	2.8	5.1	7.6	10.0
Capital Goods	6.9	6.0	9.2	11.3
Miscellaneous	11.3	4.8	7.7	5.1
Total Manufacturing Value-Added	100.0	100.0	100.0	100.0

Source: UN Industrial Development Organization (UNIDO), *Thailand*, table 8, p. 15.

ing value-added. But the development of backward linkages implied by these changes was not great; apart from the lumpy investment in oil refining, the share of intermediate goods had risen only 3 points; food and beverages and cigarettes still contributed about 42 percent, while final consumer goods as a whole still accounted for 61 percent of the sector.

In the face of the rapid growth in manufacturing over the decade, the employment created by this expansion was disappointing. Between 1960 and 1970 manufacturing value-added rose 2.8 times, but manufacturing employment (as recorded in the decennial censuses) rose only around 50 percent in absolute numbers, from 3.4 percent of total employment at the start of the decade to 4.1 percent at the end.[35]

Even when the industrial policy is seen as a strategy to substitute for, or reduce, imports, the record was paradoxical. The focus on the final stages of manufacture shifted the composition of imports toward raw materials and intermediates (which rose from 21 percent of merchandise imports in 1965 to 25 percent in 1970) as against consumer goods (which fell from 27 percent to 20 percent), and raised the import volume of both categories. It is difficult to know if capital goods imports would have risen slower had the incentive structure not included substantial duty exemptions on equipment imported by promoted firms, but the slow growth of manufacturing employment and the sharp increases in capital goods imports suggest that the incentive system was encouraging a capital-intensive choice of technologies in the rising modern manufacturing sector. From a macroeconomic perspective it appeared that import substitution was simultaneously import dependent and was not evolving as a structural change that would contribute to long-run strengthening of the balance of trade. While the value of consumer goods imports rose much slower than total real private consumption between 1965 and 1972 (36 percent compared with 58 percent, respectively), imports of intermediate and capital goods rose much faster than GDP in the same period (93 percent compared with 55 percent). And while there were other factors contributing to the deterioration in the balance of payments in the late 1960s besides the rapid increase in imports, the emergence of anxiety over the external balance and the volume of reserves, after well over a decade of stability and reserve buildup, contributed to the general conclusions that (a) import substitution had run its course because the domestic market, even though thriving, was still small for a large range of products, (b) for some promoted products, especially automobile assembly where economies of scale could never be achieved based on the domestic market, import substitution had resulted in high efficiency costs, and (c) the policy should shift toward the previously neglected objective of promoting manufactured exports. A World Bank report at the end of the decade summed up this conclusion:

> Thailand's industrialization is thus now at a crossroads. The current trend of import substitution is toward more electrical product and motor vehicle assembly, gradually increasing the Thai-made content in these products, and towards petrochemical industries. An alternative approach would be to move towards a less protected, more competitive industrial structure with more attention to increased efficiency in primary processing, adding emphasis on mass consumption goods, and vigorous promotions of export oriented manufacturing production.[36]

The BOI responded to these criticisms in 1970 by announcing a shift in favor of export promotion.

Besides this broadscale attack on the inward- rather than outward-looking orientation of the first decade of promoted industrialization, there were other sharp criticisms of the BOI for indiscriminate, if not counterproductive, granting of promoted status and fiscal benefits. In Ammar's 1974 summary of these criticisms he concludes that as far as the BOI was concerned, there was no policy at all:

> The main criticism . . . is that the BOI has been extremely promiscuous in giving away promotion certificates. It has never seriously asked the question:

what industry NOT to promote. . . . It has issued promotion certificates, regardless of whether they are mass consumption items (textiles) or luxury
goods consumed by relatively few people (refrigerators and air conditioners),
regardless of the minimum scale of production (motor-cars), regardless of the
actual intentions of those who asked for and got the promotion certificates
(petrochemicals), regardless of whether the industry is already firmly established and thus . . . [less] risky as in the beginning (hotels . . .) and regardless
of efficiency (fertilizers). . . . Like the bourgeois in Molière's play who one
day suddenly discovered he had been speaking prose all his life, the BOI
discovered in 1970 that it had been promoting import substitution all its life.
There is, in fact, very little evidence that the BOI was following any conscious
policy at all until then.[37]

In my earlier discussions of the beginnings of industrialization under the flag
of economic nationalism, I emphasized that implementation was never clear-cut
or thoroughgoing as a later reading of the policy might suggest. A similar ambiguity began to characterize import-substitution policy. The policy relied mainly
on fiscal protection and tax concessions. There was only minor resort to quantitative restrictions which, in the protectionism of many other developing countries,
were carried to the extreme of total bans on the import of large numbers of
competing products. In addition, trade policy even in the 1960s included several
export incentives. Exports were subject to a maximum 2 percent rate under the
business tax compared to the 5 percent rate on domestic sales. Exporters also
were eligible for a rebate of seven-eighths of the taxes (tariff plus business) they
had paid on imported materials used in an exported product. Narongchai
Akrasanee describes these incentives as ineffective for inducing new manufactured exports.[38] Much more significant was the bias against exports that was
created by the structure of the import protection system as it developed over the
1960s. Studies of the effective rates of protection, first undertaken in the early
1970s, showed that the system provided higher protection for consumer goods,
and bias against exports, including negative effective rates for some commodities. For export commodities as a whole in 1974, the average level of effective
protection was –40 percent.[39]

During the 1960s the Bank of Thailand began offering its own positive incentives in the form of concessional rediscount rates on export paper applying to
manufactured goods. Based on its own judgments as to industrial priorities, the
bank offered different concessional rates for different commodities: "Industries
using raw materials of agricultural origin and those which promote agriculture
are entitled to the highest benefit according to their degree of importance. . . .
The highest rediscount was that relating to the cement industry . . . followed by
the weaving and spinning and the gunny bag industries."[40] It is unlikely that the
Bank of Thailand concessional window for export manufactures, or a companion
rediscount window for "industry" that covered specific traded (and nontraded)
commodities, had significant impact on either manufacturing investment or ex-

ports. The credits were in the form of short maturities, they were offered in a shifting pattern that responded to short-run marketing problems of varying commodities, and the volume was seldom large in relation to credit volumes of the commercial banking system.

Finally, above and beyond the BOI's manipulation of individual tariffs, was the overriding importance of import duties as a source of government revenue and as a policy instrument for quickly and directly reducing domestic demand for imports in periods of widening external deficits. During those recurrent periods when the Ministry of Finance has resorted to raising the general level of import duties as a fiscal policy device, the general level of industrial protection also has risen as an unintended consequence. Thus, Narongchai described how trade policy went at cross purposes as the government attempted simultaneously inconsistent movements:

> Towards the end of the 1960s incentives under the industrial promotion policy were revised. Tax privileges were reduced in general cases, and more privileges were given to manufactured exports. For example, exports in effect paid only 0.125 percent of tariffs and business taxes on imported inputs. But in 1970, after the appearance of a balance of payments deficit in 1969, radical and upward changes in tariff rates were made. Obviously, an increase in tariff rates had a discriminatory effect against exports. On the other hand, the government tried to promote exports further. It was spelt out explicitly in the third development plan (1971–76) that there must be a development in manufactured exports. The industrial promotion scheme was revised in 1972 to create higher potential benefits for exports.... In the meantime tariffs were often adjusted to give protection to domestic industries ... export controls were at times used to stabilize domestic prices, resulting in a discouragement against exports.[41]

I have spelled out the ambiguity of trade and industrial policy in this period, as respects the dichotomy between inward- and outward-looking, or import- and export-promoting, orientation, partly with an eye toward the later periods right up to the present writing, during which Thailand has appeared to maintain elements of policy packages moving in opposite directions. There have been similar ambiguities in other important policy areas, such as respecting domestic rice prices, or recurrent exceptions to the general orientation of reducing government market interventions. From a later perspective it may be possible to see more clearly what role policy had in light of what the economic actors actually did and how the economy ultimately performed. Were the exceptions marginal? Were policies typically applied in a manner falling substantially short of what we might describe as thoroughgoing? Was the absence of ideological fervor behind any of the inward-looking, self-limiting policies the explanation for the tendency in so many areas for policy to gravitate toward a muddled middle ground, rather than toward any polarizing extreme? Or was the pursuit of inconsistent policies, without confronting the contradictions, the result of dithering, of an inability of the bureaucratic and political system to resolve alternative points of view, or simply a sign of strong distaste for confrontational resolution, of preference for compromise even in the face of criticism for irresolution and lack of policy clarity? If policy makers were in position to rationalize the policy packages, was the persistence of internal contradictions an indication that the policy makers were simply deficient in their understanding of the balance of effects of different policy components? All of these explanations have been put forward at different times by different observers. I shall return to these puzzles below.

The Culture of Enterprise

Microeconomic theory dealing with the production and marketing behavior of firms explicitly posits that all individual enterprises respond to market conditions with uniformly rational and maximizing decisions. While this paradigm has great explanatory power regarding firm behavior in the entire array of market economies, it has also become apparent in recent years that differences in corporate "culture" (e.g., management methods, labor–management relations, informal self-imposed constraints on competition and on the dealings among separate firms having vertical production relationships) and differences in corporate-government relationships from one country to another have had significant effects on efficiency and international competitiveness. The differences between American and Japanese firms in these respects have been the subject of intense examination.

The culture of private enterprise has been an important subject also in the literature on the developing countries of Southeast Asia. These economies can be said to have been rapidly going through a period analogous to the beginnings of capitalist accumulation in Europe, a process that cannot be understood apart from the history of the leading merchant and industrial families within the varying institutional settings of their separate countries. In Southeast Asia, ethnic Chinese entrepreneurial families are playing an analogous role in virtually all the countries of the region. The Thai case is especially interesting because of the relative speed with which the ethnicity of the business class has been fading as a category of social identity and as an issue of public policy. Elsewhere, particularly in Malaysia, Indonesia, and perhaps Vietnam, ethnicity remains a serious present or potential source of divisiveness that could deflect economic policy in directions Thailand managed to abandon.[42]

The issues of business culture go beyond mere ethnicity. Although the fading of the image of entrepreneur as "pariah" has vitiated one of the most powerful motivations for maintaining the closed family structure of enterprise ownership and management in Thailand, the transition to a "modern" corporate culture was just barely under way in the 1960s. The elements of such a transition included (a) professionalization of management and technological capability, first through the education of the founder's children in management, engineering, and accounting; (b) willingness to go outside the family in the search for senior executives rather than filling these positions with poorly qualified family members; (c) a willingness to forgo secrecy in order to obtain outside capital, thereby opening the firm to expansion beyond what might be financed through reliance only on reinvested profits; (d) ultimately, a move toward separation of ownership from management, as (with smaller families) further expansion becomes viable only if nonfamily managers are brought in to occupy the bulk of the senior positions, including top mangement. Finally, the decline of the traditional family mode of enterprise would also entail a decline in the prescriptive modes of doing business (reliance on personal networks, nonmarket favors and transactions, falsified accounting, and heavy tax evasion) as methods for gaining competitive advantage and earning profits.

In the 1960s the identification of the closed family business mode with weaknesses in the operations of corporate enterprises was recognized by the authorities only with respect to the banking sector. It would be another decade before the policy technocrats recognized the corporate culture transition as a general problem of importance for an economy increasingly dependent on internationally competitive private enterprise and devised deliberate approaches (discussed below) to encourage the assimilation of Thai business methods into international practice. The strictly technical backwardness of business management in Thailand, quite apart from these sociological context problems, was recognized at an early date, however. The widely acknowledged weaknesses in government management had captured the attention of USOM and the Thai government from the start of the U.S. aid program in 1950. After a number of ad hoc projects addressing organization and management in particular agencies and specific aspects of civil service operations, USOM financed a project starting in 1954 under which Indiana University assisted Thammasat University to establish an Institute of Public Administration, the first academic unit in Thailand that would provide a graduate degree in administration, but limited to the public sector. Loftus appears to have been one of the first to recognize that the Thai private sector's management weaknesses were serious and merited government-sponsored attention. Referring to his work in 1960 with the then two-year-old Industrial Finance Corporation of Thailand (IFCT), Loftus wrote that the experience

> gave me a fresh insight into the deficiency of the entrepreneurial function in Thailand. I had long known that the management of state enterprises could be incredibly inefficient; but I came to discover that a large number of private business promoters also were lacking in any knowledge of the fundamentals of business organization and management. This led me to certain conclusions about the imperative necessity of initiating education in business adminstration.[43]

He also suggested that IFCT could perform a useful service for "nascent" industrialists by showing applicants (for IFCT loan or equity support) why their proposals were inadequate and non-creditworthy. IFCT did take on this function, but formal education in business administration was launched in 1966 by the National Institute of Development Administration (NIDA).

Distribution: Structure of Ownership
in Banking and Industry

The withdrawal of the state from further undertakings in commerce and industry had opened the way for private interests to respond to the incentive system the government was installing and to stake out a new pattern of ownership. While the vigorous expansion of the private sector appeared to vindicate the technocratic policy package (note Dr. Puey's plaudits to the private sector for the growth it was generating, cited earlier), it was also sowing the seeds of dissatisfaction over the distribution of wealth and economic power and creating unease over some of the consequences of unrestricted laissez-faire.

The initial development of new industrial assets saw both the continued business operations of the now dominant Sisao Deves political clique, in their personal capacities, and the rise of leading Sino-Thai family economic interests. While the technocratic efforts to limit the extent of political penetration of the corporate sector occupied a lot of policy maker and donor agency attention in the 1960s, this penetration was of declining importance in the ownership structure of Thai business, even though that decline may not have been recognized at the time. Sarit, himself operating at least partly according to the new rules, held interests in nine companies that obtained promotional benefits from BOI; nine of Sarit's political associates also received BOI status.[44] One source recorded that in 1969 there were 143 government officials or family members who had seats on the boards of 347 firms.[45]

Clearly the leading officials held these memberships as prebendary positions, not as capacities in which they would make substantive contributions to management; Field Marshal Praphas Charusatien, for example, sat on forty-four boards. Their presence, however, could be utilized by the firms to advance the competitive position, or access to public-sector business, of the enterprises involved. Suehiro cites the Bank of Ayudha group as one set of enterprises where growth was accelerated by the involvement of military leaders. Nevertheless, Suehiro points out that the whole political-bureaucratic-business prebendary system was in decline over the 1960s. "But unlike the 1950's, political patronage does not seem to have acted as a crucial factor for the economic expansion of Chinese or local business groups. Rather, such factors as access to foreign capital, introduction of advanced technology, capacity to mobilize capital funds, and market conditions etc. became more and more important for the business groups."[46] Proclamation 33 in 1958 had formally eliminated the policy basis under which private enterprises sought protection from the threat of government competition or preemption. Although foreign firms initially sought political relationships as insurance, despite the fundamental change in the legal and policy environment, local entrepreneurs also found that an association with a large international joint-venture partner provided the Thai businessman with significant reinforcement to his increasing independence from the old system. The sheer expansion in the private sector, in the numbers of entrepreneurs and enterprises, gradually reduced the relative scope of the penetration system. Over the near decade and a half during which the Sarit–Thanom authoritarianism ruled without major challenge from rival cliques, the political competition that fueled the drive to acquire business clients evaporated. As Suehiro suggests, the collapse of the military government in October 1973 brought the old military-business alliance system to an end.

In the meantime, two distinct groups of entrepreneurs—one basically financial, the other industrial—were emerging as the vanguard of the economic expansion of the 1960s. The first in time consisted of a handful of Chinese merchants, rice millers, and tin and rubber interests who had been established largely before World War II. Drawing on the capital of a wide circle of Chinese business families, this handful within the community had created about a dozen commercial banks, mostly in the 1940s. The banks were initially intended to accumulate deposits that could be used by the promoters of the banks to finance their own rice and other trading activities. The traditional commodity trading of these promoters faded into relative insignificance as their banking enterprises grew in importance. The establishment of these banks was not only encouraged by the government's postwar policy of developing domestic banks to supplant the dominant position of the foreign banks, but in some cases was assisted with capital infusions from the Ministry of Finance. Prior to the 1932 coup, Thailand had had only a single domestic bank, the Siam Commercial Bank (SCB), established in 1906 with Crown capital. The first private domestic bank was set up only in 1933, by the Wang Lee family. By 1960 there were fifteen private domestic commercial banks.[47]

When economic concentration first became a political issue, in the 1970s, it was the financial rather than the industrial sector that was the target of criticism. The irony of this criticism seemed to be overlooked; the very existence and then the concentration of the Thai financial sector owed its origin to government policies that were intended, first, to wrest control of the sector from foreign hands and, second, to ensure the stability and financial viability of the domestic banking system in the interests of the general public and of the depositors. Serious problems of bank management and solvency first arose in 1959 with the collapse of the private Agriculture Bank. Preferring to avoid any threat to general confidence in the banking system, the financial authorities took over the bank, subsequently (in 1966) reestablishing it as a government-owned commercial bank, the Krung Thai Bank (currently the second largest measured by size of assets). This experience forced the Bank of Thailand to focus its attention on institutional soundness as one of the key problems of the financial sector. To give the central bank greater authority over commercial bank management, the government promulgated new legislation in 1962 that, in effect, put a lid on new entry. In practice then, the technocratic leadership adopted a policy making the banking sector a major exception to the general policy of free entry and exit that the government applied to most areas of economic activity.

The policy of no new banking licenses has remained in effect since the last license was granted in 1965. The bar to further entry has, in effect, given over to the ownership of the banks unrestricted scope for increasing their economic role and personal financial position, subject only to the limits imposed by their oligopolistic competition and their varying competence as managers and entrepreneurs.

It would turn out in the 1980s, in another ironic twist, that again in the interest of financial system stability, the Bank of Thailand would have to protect some of the weaker of these institutions, and their owner-manager families, from enforced exit due to insolvency. But in the 1950s and 1960s, with the financial sector growing faster than all other sectors of the economy (except electricity) at roughly 18 and 15 percent annually per decade, respectively, the protected status of the banks virtually guaranteed the rapid accumulation of capital on the part of the very narrow ownership. In fact, the ownership structure of the individual banks had been more diversified at their founding. Because of the importance of trust built on personal relationships in the banking business of the 1940s and 1950s (for raising initial share capital, attracting depositors, and determining creditworthiness), the founding personalities in each case tried to draw in large numbers of reputable business leaders as contributors to the initial share capital. The same practice was applied to the initial capitalization of many nonfinancial enterprises, leading to the appearance of extensive interlocking ownership relationships that reflect no meaningful management participation.

During the 1960s, however, banking ownership tended to concentrate in the hands of the main families identified with each individual institution. Four family groups in particular rose to preeminence. The largest institution was the Bangkok Bank, controlled by the Sophonpanich family. The three others were the Lamsam family (Thai Farmers Bank), Tejapaibul (Bangkok Metropolitan Bank, Thai Development Bank [later, First Bangkok City] and Bank of Asia), and Ratanarak (Bank of Ayudhya and Siam City Bank). Of the sixteen Thai commercial banks in operation in 1972, seven were controlled by these four groups. Most of the remaining banks were also family enterprises. They served as bases for these groups to invest in other types of financial enterprise (insurance, investment finance, consumer finance, etc.) and in nonfinancial activities.

The Sophonpanich family increased its proportion of the Bangkok Bank's share capital from 17 percent in 1964 to 32 percent in 1968. The Lamsam family share in the Thai Farmers Bank rose from 22 percent in 1945 to 58 percent in 1970; the Ratanarak group, Bank of Ayudhya, from 26 percent in 1964 to 43 percent in 1972; Tejapaibul, Bangkok Metropolitan Bank, from 11 percent in 1950 to 19 percent in 1972 and 44 percent in 1979. These four banks also enjoyed the fastest growth among all the banks (except one) during the 1960s. Their share of the total deposits in the commercial banking system rose from 33 percent in 1962 to 49 percent in 1972. The Bangkok Bank was the largest beneficiary by far; its deposit share rose from 19 percent to 31 percent in the same period.[48] In short, between the rapid growth of these flagship banks and the concentration of ownership within each bank (and their associated finance and nonfinancial enterprises), the major banking families became the symbol of skewed accumulation of wealth, and of economic concentration. The ranking and market shares of the private banks has not changed substantially since the 1970s, except for the relative decline of the Bangkok Metropolitan Bank. The standing of the banks in 1988 and their controlling families are shown in Table 4.3.

I need not describe the individual histories and subsequent economic fortunes of these families and associated enterprises, beyond a few general observations. The individual histories, in fact, have varied substantially. The different families have brought to the operations of their respective banking enterprises different management styles, personal idiosyncracies, and varying abilities and business acumen. Given the relatively small number of commercial banks, and the extent of concentration among the leading ones, these individual differences would have substantial consequences not only for the issue of economic concentration, but also for the efficiency and stability of Thailand's financial sector. These later problems, serious as they became, should not obscure the fact that the financial families did play their collective leading part, with apparent vigor, as fulfillers of the expectations of the policy technocrats when they (the technocrats) opted for the private sector.

The second group of entrepreneurs responding to Sarit's policy package were importers and traders who moved directly into manufacturing rather than finance. The typical pattern led from general importing, to the securing of an exclusive local dealership from the foreign supplier of specific merchandise, to the establishment of a facility to manufacture the same merchandise domestically under a joint-venture arrangement with the same supplier. As was the case with virtually all nonagricultural enterprise, these businesses began as ethnic Chinese, one-family operations. Although authority in these businesses was normally tightly held by the head of the family, many family members would have shares in the enterprise, and all the senior technical and managerial positions would be filled by family members, most often by the founder's sons—still numerous at a time when large families were the norm. Since these families also had limited technical education and (unlike the banking families) lacked direct access to capital other than their own savings, they relied on the foreign partners to provide the technology and manufacturing management, and to participate in the financing.[49] To obtain these benefits from joint ventures, the Thai side would have to accommodate to the management roles demanded by the foreign partner, accommodations that were the first steps in a continuing process of adjustment of the traditional culture and methods of family enterprise to the requirements of

Table 4.3

Domestic Commercial Banks: Controlling Families and Market Shares, 1988

Bank	Family	Share of Total Credits
Bangkok Bank	Sophonpanich	30.1
Thai Farmers	Lamsam	12.4
Krung Thai	Not applicable	12.2
Siam Commercial	Not applicable	11.1
Bank of Ayudhya	Ratanarak	6.1
Thai Military	Not applicable	5.4
First Bangkok City	Srifuengfung	3.7
Siam City	Mahadumrongkul	3.7
Bangkok Metropolitan	Tejapaibul	3.6
Bangkok Bank of Commerce		3.0
Bank of Asia	Euachukiati	2.6
Union Bank of Bangkok	Cholvicharn	1.5
Thai Danu		1.2·
Nakorn Thon	Not applicable	0.9
Laem Tong	Nandhabiwat	0.4
Foreign banks	—	2.1
		100.0

Source: Bangkok Bank.

modern technology and of larger scale industrial organization. The Thais would find that foreign corporate cultures and management practices differed from one source country to another. Generally, firms from Japan were much less inclined to share technical and management responsibility with Thai partners, to transfer knowledge about the technologies employed, or to train Thai managers to replace the expatriates, than were firms from other countries.[50]

Between import-substitution and growth of domestic demand in the expanding economy of the 1960s, the pioneer manufacturing enterprises enjoyed rapid growth and apparent high profitability, enabling them to maintain a high rate of reinvestment.[51] The leading entrepreneurial families quickly began to develop conglomerate groups of enterprises, partly vertically related to their core enterprises as input suppliers, and partly in unrelated ventures in manufacturing and other sectors. Major conglomerates launched during this period were built around such core enterprises as Siam Motors, founded by Thaworn Phornphrapa in a joint-venture with Nissan; and in textiles where Sukree Photiratanankun built up a complex of fabric and garment enterprises based on a single venture begun in 1957 and on subsequent joint ventures with Japanese capital.

The ownership structure of Thai industry prior to the advent of the import-substitution policy appears to have been very diversified. In the textiles sector, set up mainly in the 1950s, the twenty leading enterprises were established by sixteen different groups of investors.[52] Traditional industrial enterprises in rice milling, saw milling, ice manufacture, and other activities closely linked to local sources of raw materials, or to widely dispersed local demand, were inherently local small-scale operations owned and operated by individual entrepreneurs using simple technologies and very modest amounts of capital. In contrast with the financial regulatory policy that facilitated concentration, the import substitution framework appeared to be neutral with respect to impact on the ownership structure of industry. For some products, the first investors to obtain BOI privileges would be in position to preempt the market, and in some cases to block the issuance of otherwise routine operating licenses to potential new entrants. For a very capital-intensive industry like oil refining, entry was controlled by government policy and inherently limited in the number of economic operations. For the broad range of products, however, BOI's initial problem and policy objective in the 1960s was to accelerate the rate of investment, to pull in outside investors at a time when the postwar policy of state preemption or competition in manufacturing was a regime only very recently discarded. The strengthening of BOI's promotional functions was the principal objective of numerous technical assistance projects foreign donors undertook recurrently for more than two decades. In the event, the threat of loss of market shares for imported consumer goods induced a diversified range of foreign suppliers to invest in local production in joint ventures with their respective local importer-distributors. Although incomplete data from the BOI suggest that foreign capital provided only a third of the investment in promoted enterprises in the period 1959–72,[53] promoted enterprises were clearly the driving force of the manufacturing sector; the share of manufacturing value-added produced by the traditional food, beverage, and tobacco sectors fell from 49 percent in 1966 to 36 percent in 1973, while the new textile, garments, transport equipment, and other product groups rose from 31 to 42 percent. By 1973 the 558 promoted projects employed 21.5 percent of the total manufacturing work force.

The diversification of ownership in the textile sector was matched by the lack of concentration in the automotive and other sectors. What might be viewed as a more desirable social outcome than the pattern of concentration that was developing in the financial sector had less favorable implications for economic efficiency, at least in the important case of vehicle assembly. The proliferation of truck and car makes (nine foreign brands) and models limited the domestic manufacturers to very short production runs.[54] The uneconomic structure of the overcrowed automotive industry subsequently became an important issue of industrial policy.

Income Distribution: Regional Resource Endowment

The economic growth of Japan and South Korea, two countries with very limited natural resources, and the increasing importance of knowledge and human capital as sources of wealth creation under modern technological conditions, have led economists in recent years to accord only minor importance to climate and natural resources as determining factors in economic development. As recently as 1981, Todaro observed that "almost every successful example of modern economic growth has occurred in a temperate zone country" and that the under-developed state of tropical and subtropical countries was witness to "some relation to the special difficulties caused directly or indirectly by differing climatic conditions."[55] The vigorous development in the 1980s of Thailand, Malaysia, and Indonesia adds up to a major exception to, if not refutation of, the alleged importance of climate and the specific handicaps Todaro suggested, such as deterioration of soil quality under tropical heat and humidity, slow forest regeneration, poor animal health, and low levels of human physical efficiency. When it comes to natural mineral or agricultural resources, there are of course a few countries, at the margins, where geography and physical endowment have over-whelmingly determined the history of economic growth, or its absence. For the majority of countries the physical endowment plays its major role as setting the initial conditions in which the development process takes shape.

In Thailand the natural endowment and the leading primary commodities provided a favorable set of initial conditions, although not outstanding in terms of soil quality or known minerals. The pattern of agronomic and mineral endowment within the country, however, is very diverse. The peninsular concentration of tin deposits, and the superior agronomic conditions for rice in the central plain and for rubber in the peninsula, have been major factors determining an unequal spatial distribution of rural economic growth in the past. The diversification of agriculture that began in the late 1950s opened up opportunities for much wider geographic spread in the growth of income. For both political and economic reasons, several spatial configurations have at various times become subjects of development policy: the North, the Lower South, the Upper South, the Greater Bangkok Metropolitan Area, the Eastern Seaboard, and the Northeast. (In 1988 the government began promoting the concept of a development zone across the narrow neck of the southern peninsula, based on a petroleum "land bridge" transshipment scheme that could serve as an alternative or supplement to the oil transit route through the Strait of Malacca. The feasibility of this "Southern Seaboard" proposal remains to be demonstrated at this writing.)

It became apparent early on that the Northeast was Thailand's primary backward region problem. With its history of regionalist identity (the only area whose members of parliament, in the early postwar years, formed a regional bloc and saw economic and political issues in regional terms), its ethnic and linguistic differentiation, its exposure to political influence and subversion from the communist movements in Indochina, and its relative isolation from the rest of the country, the Northeast became the one entire region viewed by Bangkok as a spatially defined development problem with an overriding security rationale for its claim on resources and programs.

The endowment disadvantages of the Northeast have made it virtually inevitable that income growth would lag behind other regions. The first solid information on the resource base of the Northeast was collected in the 1950s by aid projects in soil mapping, exploratory well drilling for groundwater, and agricultural research. The soils were shown to be poor in nutrients and in physical characteristics pertinent to agriculture. Groundwater was insufficient for irrigation and, in many localities, too saline to be potable. As in other semi-arid tropical areas, agricultural research in Northeast Thailand has yet to yield substantial technological breakthroughs. Within the generally poor endowment of the region as a whole, however, there were subregional variations with some areas (e.g., suitable for irrigation) having better prospects than others (e.g., saline soil areas in the provinces along the southern border with Cambodia). Almost immediately after the new Friendship Highway connecting the Northeast with the central plain and Bangkok was opened in 1957, the southeastern portions of the region saw a boom in maize and kenaf production for export, two crops that had had no economic significance in the Northeast before. The region still had substantial forested areas that would gradually be cleared and cultivated as the local population increased and as market access improved. Thus, while the potentialities for rural income growth in the Northeast were, and have remained, much weaker than in other regions of the country, the region's prospects were certainly not zero.

The Northeast was already a major area of concentration for the U.S. aid program in the 1950s. The Friendship Highway was one link in a series of construction projects that formed the first all-weather hard-surfaced highway running from Bangkok northeastward and terminating at Nongkai on the Mekong River, nearly opposite Vientiane, the capital of Laos. While security and administrative communication were the key factors behind the choice of the Friendship Highway route, the road did induce an explosion in traffic. In contrast, there were very low economic returns to another highway project built by U.S. aid at around the same time, an east–west road (between Pitsanuloke and Lomsak) designed as a link in a roadway across the country from Burma to the Mekong.[56] From the early 1950s the Thai government and USOM also put substantial resources into Northeast health, sanitation, potable water, small-scale irrigation, and other activities.

I shall return to the problem of Thailand's lagging region repeatedly in this study. At this point I would only note, in a general policy perspective, that neither the Thai government nor the major interested donors (at this stage still the United States and the World Bank) had a coherent planning framework for rationalizing the development programs for the region. Indeed, it was many years before spatial planning respecting any region of the country yielded significant results in terms of investment location designed to achieve an integrated set of economic and social objectives. Looking back (in 1973) on the regional planning experience of the 1960s, Phisit Pakkasem (probably the first economic technocrat with spatial planning expertise) found little to praise:

The past record of national economic growth and upward change in level of aggregate income have tended to generate regional disparities in the level of economic welfare. . . . Thailand's development planning efforts in the 1960's, under the First and Second Plans, had been concerned almost exclusively with economic and social development at the national level. Any regional development implication was based on project selection at the national level rather than analysis of regional requirements. . . .

In the past, public policy makers . . . involved in national development process frequently gave lip services to some sort of regional income policy with a vague policy statement. In part this reflected the fact that regional planning was a new subfield of development planning in Thailand, was not well understood among the policy makers, and was still evolving. . . . The public development programmes and resources allocated to the Northeast have not produced much change in the structure of the regional economy. A series of ad hoc regional policy measures of short-term character, a public investment allocation pattern which was thinly scattered over a large area, and many so-called accelerated rural development programmes under the first two national Plans had proved to be ineffective either in promoting long-term regional growth or in reducing the regional income gaps.[57]

Phisit is here expressing a view that was widely held at the time, and that is still a major issue of public policy. Within an overall framework of satisfactory aggregate national growth, he considers the relative lack of momentum in the Northeast, and the persistence of a large disparity between income levels in the Northeast and elsewhere in the country, as a major policy failure. Incomes were rising in the Northeast, however, and have continued rising since, generated by a mix of economic changes within and outside the region. The most important government contribution was the construction of the road network, opening up isolated areas and reducing transport costs. The subsequent growth of crop production (especially cassava for export) was a private, market-driven response. Phisit's judgment was probably too harsh. Neither a radically different composition of public programs in the region nor an improved rationalization among the programs would likely have made much greater impact on the Northeast's economic condition during that period.

Population Policy and Demographic Transition

In the 1960s the policy technocrats and public health authorities managed a reversal of government population policy, from pronatalist to antinatalist. The pronatalist preferences of Phibun, Praphas, and Sarit stemmed from a belief that national security would be enhanced if the Thai population rose to 100 million, sooner rather than later. In 1956 Phibun actually legislated incentives to encourage larger families, but there is no indication these measures had any effect. Although the World Bank report's comments on the adverse effects of high population growth have been credited with initiating concern among government officials, the Bank of Thailand had raised the issue of demographic policy as early as 1957.

The development of Thailand's antinatal policy is interesting as an example of a major national interest issue where the determination of policy was essentially a matter of intellectual and long-run considerations. No short-run economic interests or costs were involved, especially since aid donors stood ready to finance much of the startup and program costs for many years once a policy was launched. The first development plan, which is cited by all authors as the primary evidence of World Bank influence on Thai policy, is silent on the subject of population. Although the bank had commented on the adverse effects of what was thought to be a 2 percent rate of growth in the Thai population, the first plan was written before the results of the 1960 census—revealing that the actual growth rate stood much higher, at 3.2 percent—were available to impart a sense of urgency to the technocrats and public health officials who recognized the implications.

The acceleration in Thailand's population growth began around 1950. The acceleration reflected a mortality transition, the start of a rapid decline in infant and overall mortality rates. The largest single cause was the fall in deaths due to malaria, thanks to the eradication campaign that was one of the largest aid-supported programs in the country.[58] By 1955 the crude death rate had been brought down to 18.0 per thousand population from the estimated 1948 level of 27.3. By 1960 the rate had fallen to 12.8, a decline of over 50 percent in just 12 years. Ten years later, the rate had fallen another 27 percent to 9.4 per thousand. Infectious diseases that had replaced malaria as the leading killers were also declining as a result of the expanding public health programs. Urban fertility appears to have been declining already by 1960, with rural fertility constant until the second half of the 1960s.[59]

In 1962 a program of research and seminars was begun to document the wide gap that had opened up between birth and death rates and to educate the political levels to the implications in terms of future demands on public funds for education, the pressures of the growing rural population on the remaining forest areas, and so on. In 1964 the Ministry of Health, with no publicity, undertook a pilot project to test reactions of Thai women to the availability of a family planning service. The response to this project was unexpectedly positive, with word-of-mouth information reaching women in far reaches of the country who traveled to the project site (in rural Potharam, about 80 kilometers west of Bangkok) to obtain contraceptive information and services. The success of this project helped allay fears that public promotion of family planning might provoke negative political reaction based on religious or other grounds.[60]

In 1968 NESDB created a population unit to develop a policy for cabinet consideration. Working with the Ministry of Health and the Institute of Population Studies at Chulalongkorn University, NESDB recommended to the cabinet in early 1970 that Thailand adopt an antinatal policy, introduce family planning, and undertake the necessary administrative arrangements to promote a coordinated program. One of the senior foreign experts involved in the evolution of this policy, Dr. Allan Rosenfield, observed that the cabinet resolution adopting NESDB'S recommendations was "so vaguely worded that the government's intentions remained unclear."[61] Despite the apparent skittishness at the political level, the Ministry of Health took the resolution as a full endorsement and proceeded to install a nationwide family planning program. Soon after, the third plan (1972–76) was drafted presenting a forthright statement that Thailand's high population growth rate was a serious obstacle to development. The plan announced an official target, to reduce this rate to 2.5 percent by 1976. To accomplish this, the policy called for rapid expansion of public and private family planning programs.

The general fall in fertility that was to gain momentum in the 1970s after the introduction of nationwide family planning services had already started in the late 1960s.[62] The decline resulted mainly from lowering of marital fertility, marginally reinforced by a trend toward later marriage. The reasons behind secular changes in family size preference are numerous and difficult to sort out. Some of the factors to which fertility declines have been attributed in other countries do not seem to have had substantial impact in Thailand. As Knodel, Aphichat, and Nibhon point out, the fertility revolution in Thailand, while not uniform, has been pervasive in rural and urban areas, and among couples at all levels of income and education. The growth of the education system and the parallel spread of the perception that the costs of raising children were rising while their economic value to parents was falling appear to have been important influences on married couples generally. Fertility behavior differentials due to urban/rural or other economic and social differences were apparent only in the relatively brief lags in fertility decline among such cohorts. Urbanization per se was not a major factor; the proportion of Thailand's population living in urban areas was relatively low and increased only slightly in 1960–70, from 12.5 percent to 13.2 percent. Urbanization accelerated in the 1970s, raising the proportion to only 17 percent in 1980.[63] As recently as 1988 the urban population in Thailand was a smaller fraction of the total population than in all but one of thirty-seven countries grouped together as the "lower-middle-income" by the World Bank. Thailand's 21 percent level was less than half the weighted average urbanized population for the whole group, 56 percent.[64]

Knodel and colleagues believe that the spread of communications throughout the country, and the monetization and availability of consumer goods attendant upon the penetration of the market economy through the provinces, raised the perceived "costs" of children (and created an array of alternatives to spending on children) among the rural population that was virtually as strong in its impact on family-size preference as among the urban population. They also point to the relative weakness or absence of cultural factors that have inhibited fertility decline in other societies. Buddhism says little about the subject; its focus on individual moral responsibility would naturally leave reproductive behavior decisions relatively free from communal or familial pressures. The economic and familial status of women in Thailand, set within a nuclear family context, is high and conducive to relative autonomy for a wife to determine contraceptive practice. While there can be little precision in measuring the relative influence of such cultural, educational, and economic factors in altering fertility behavior in Thailand in the 1960s and 1970s, it would be reasonable to presume that the economic and material conditions of rural life, which began to change rapidly in the 1960s, preceded and largely precipitated the change in family-size preference.

The establishment of an official antinatal stance must be recognized as one of the signal accomplishments of social policy of this period. The Thai family planning program is ranked as one of the most successful among developing countries. Nongovernmental organizations have played an important role complementary to the activities of the Ministry of Health. The educational campaigns of the Thai Population and Development Association in particular have won international recognition for innovative use of humor and economic incentives tied to contraceptive use.

In 1965 Thailand's total fertility rate (the total number of children a woman would have by the end of her childbearing years, if she followed the prevailing age-specific fertility rates) was 6.3. This was slightly higher than the 6.1 average of the thirty-seven "lower-middle-income" countries. By 1988 the Thai fertility rate had fallen to 2.5 compared to 3.9 for the same group of countries, even well below the 3.5 average for a group of seventeen "upper-middle-income" countries.[65] The demographic changes Thailand has undergone have been massive in their magnitude and effects. The accelerated growth in the size of the cohorts that comprise a population—infants and children, school attendees, labor force, longer-lived older dependents—has had enormous consequences for the spread of human settlements, the exploitation of forest and soil resources, the requirements for health and education expenditures, the scale of expansion needed in agricultural and other economic services, and as a source of pressure on the social system and culture operating through increased geographic mobility and migration, and rising density. To a considerable extent these demographic changes are the product of, and interact with, economic and technological change inherent in the modernization and development process. However, the Thai experience in this period demonstrates also the perhaps underappreciated role of public health interventions (and the malaria campaigns of the 1950s–60s in particular) as driving forces behind the population explosions with all their implications. While this study will not go deeply into the technical policy issues within the health sector, it is important to underscore the population growth-increasing, and later decreasing, interventions, as sectoral policies with profound consequences for the whole development process and for many of the subjects of economic policy proper.

The First Authoritarian Collapse:
Social and Political Finale

With great suddenness in October 1973, the fifteen years of authoritarian rule, including the ten-year regime of General Thanom Kittikachorn and his deputy General Praphat Charusatien, collapsed under student pressure. Although the circumstances were as surprising to the general public as were the events of the 1932 revolution, the popular overthrow of the Thanom–Praphas regime arose from social forces that were much more widespread than the narrowly based discontents of 1932. The very successes of the authoritarian period had created new political perspectives among a rapidly growing educated middle class. The expansion and strenghtening of the university system had produced an independent-minded student body critical of a political system from which they were excluded, a system that appeared increasingly anachronistic. With rising educational levels and media exposure, and with the influx of tourists, and foreign products and tastes (the inevitable accompaniments of an outward-looking, liberal economic orientation), the students and the middle class began to apply international perspectives and Western norms in their assessments of the directions of domestic change, or in the political realm, stagnation.

The economic changes throughout the provinces were also setting in motion changes in rural society that would quickly become more widespread and profound than had been experienced during any previous period in Thai history. I have already referred to some of these changes and the impact they were starting to have on parental value systems and the role of children. From the popular literature of the time, especially in the short-story genre, one can gain a picture of the stresses that were starting to emerge in village life. The tastes and horizons of youth in particular were altered when they came into contact with products and consumption possibilities never imagined before: the opportunity for inexpensive travel far beyond their home locality; literacy and education more advanced than that of their parents; and new occupations offering higher income. The literature tends to idealize the old ways and the presumed contentment and placidity of village life before it was touched by modern development. While one may quarrel with the accuracy of this perhaps romanticized image, the literature does capture the problems caused by the intergenerational changes in values and by the natural tendency of peasant farmers to see their own conditions, customs, and ideas in a new and depreciated light when confronted by the contrasts with the wealth, power, and sophistication emanating from Bangkok.[66]

The perception that rapid economic growth was wrenching Thai society into rapid urbanization of values and was causing deep tensions between urban and rural life was fed by the extraordinary concentration and singularity of urbanization in and around Bangkok. In 1960 the population of Bangkok (1.7 million, including Thonburi) was twenty-six times the size of Chiangmai, the country's second largest city. The next fifty-nine towns in size after Chiangmai had a population under 50,000 each, forty of which towns had less than 20,000. Bangkok's primate character, and the country's lack of any middle-sized cities, represented a singularity of urbanization unmatched in any other country in the region.[67] In 1980 Chiangmai was still the second largest city, but Bangkok's population was now fifty times larger.

In addition to its primate demographic and economic status, Bangkok was also unrivaled as the center of the country's university population, media production and exposure, political sophistication, and intellectual and artistic life, and as the focal point for the entry and catalytic effects of foreign cultural and intellectual trends. The universities in particular were affected by the worldwide attention to the problem of income maldistribution that burgeoned after 1970, while the temper of campus life was being affected by the student movements in the United States and elsewhere protesting against the Vietnam War and domestic social ills. Academic research and popular literature were contributing to awareness and concern among university students over rural problems; such concern had previously been marginal among the largely Bangkok-born student bodies.

The economic development policies of the 1960s began to be seen as misguided and narrowly focused on macroeconomic expansion. The government's concentration on infrastructure, and reliance on market forces, were criticized as being insensitive, if not conducive, to widening income disparities, continued rural poverty, and even immiseration for large numbers of farmers who were falling into indebtedness, losing their land, and becoming landless agricultural laborers or poor migrants living in Bangkok's slums. Later research would show that these problems were much less severe in magnitude than was believed at the time. Actually, the incidence of poverty was falling in the 1960s. The land frontier was indeed beginning to close, but closure was a slow process against a vaguely defined boundary. Although the land pressures were mainly confined to areas of the Central Plain and the North, the pressures were real and had had no outlets for expression of grievance.

Adding to the image of a government unresponsive to economic inequalities and injustice was the widespread resentment against corruption and against the very concept of authoritarian legitimacy. In this aspect also, the large numbers of the middle class who had been educated in the West and socialized to Western ideas of representative government brought external intellectual influence to bear on the social ferment that was taking place in the capital. Morell and Chai-anan have described the turning point at which these social forces erupted and terminated the Sarit–Thanom period:

> New groups were emerging in Thai society. Hitherto latent demands for participation were escalating exponentially. The political system of the past no longer met the needs of the present, and certainly did not promise to meet those of the future. To a large extent, the explosion of student-led unrest in

October 1973 was a direct result of frustrations and unmet aspirations associated with this large and growing gap between change in society at large and stagnation in its political institutions. The new forces, long denied access to the political system, demanded and received such access; and in the process they discredited the armed forces and the police when these groups chose to fire on masses of Thai citizens in the streets of Bangkok. At this point, royal legitimacy was withdrawn from the nation's top military leaders, who were ordered by the king to leave the country. Thailand's military returned to its barracks, at least temporarily, setting the stage for the violent polarization between the forces advocating reform and the groups reacting against them.[68]

5

DEMOCRACY AND REACTION:
ORTHODOXY IN PARTIAL ECLIPSE, 1973–1979

After Thanom dissolved his short-lived parliament in November 1971 and banned the political parties, the vanguard university students began a series of political actions in the streets. In addition to the questions people were raising regarding the directions of development policy and the frustrations over the reimposition of military control, the opposition to the Thanom regime was sharpened by the immediate prospect that Thanom and Praphas might be succeeded by the equally unpopular Lt. Col. Narong Kittikachorn, who was son to Thanom and son-in-law to Praphas. The students had the support of the middle class, who now lacked any legal and institutionalized means or forums for political participation. Despite more than a decade of vigorous economic growth and diversification, and the growing population of graduates from domestic and overseas higher education, the middle class remained unorganized. The apex student organization, the National Student Center of Thailand (NSCT), was the only remaining (legal) entity, after the political parties were banned, that was capable of openly challenging and debating government policy.[1]

The one other organization openly challenging the government was the illegal Communist Party of Thailand. The CPT was a rural-based organization. Operating on Maoist inspiration and with support from the People's Republic of China (PRC) and Vietnam, the CPT had very limited contact with the urban students at this time. In late 1972 the NSCT launched its first major effort to mobilize opposition. Preferring to attack the government only indirectly at first, the NSCT called for a ten-day boycott of Japanese imports. The choice of Japanese goods as a target reflected a widely held perception that Japan's economic presence had become excessive.[2] Although business interests involved in importing and retailing Japanese goods were not happy with the boycott, the students could count on the sympathy of Thai business organizations that had already expressed anxiety over the growing foreign, mainly Japanese, role in the domestic economy.[3] The NSCT then turned its attention to the government itself, demonstrating against the regime's refusal to install a new constitution, and its moves to extend Thanom's term in office and to designate Narong as heir to the premiership. The demonstrations gathered force, provoked by the government's arrest of several students and faculty members, culminating on October 14, 1973, in student attacks on government buildings and over 100 student deaths in clashes with the police. When the army commander refused to implement Thanom's order to deploy troops against the students, it was clear that the Thanom–Praphas–Narong triumvirate was now bereft of all power and authority. Stepping into the momentary power vacuum, the king asked the triumvirate to leave the country (a request they could not reject), announced his intention to restore constitutional government, and called on the students to desist from further disorderly actions. As Keyes sums up the denouement,

> The king was heard, and the 1973 Revolution ended. Although the king's action forced the military from then on to share power with civilian politicians, including representatives from the vocal urban middle classes, its most significant effect was to reverse the relationship between monarch and government that had existed since the 1932 Revolution. The king was now no longer a mere symbol to be manipulated by the government in power; he had become a significant center of authority in his own right.[4]

The renaissance of the palace in Thailand, albeit within the narrow legal constraints of constitutional monarchy, is analogous to the experience of no other country in the modern era except perhaps for Spain. The ability of the monarch to intervene at moments of political crisis (of which the 1973 upheaval was only the first), a role not anticipated when Sarit initiated his policy of reviving the monarchy as the symbolic and psychological center of the Thai nation, emanated from the personal characteristics of King Bhumipol. In his extensive travels around the country and into remote villages, his recurrent residence in provinces far from Bangkok, his keen interest in agriculture, especially irrigation (the king is a trained hydraulic engineer), and in rural development generally, he has come to be revered as the embodiment of the traditional Thai concept of the righteous Buddhist king. The monarch's unrivaled moral position has enabled him to grant, or withhold, legitimacy from rival contenders for power at times when constitutional process has been abrogated or threatened. In this very important respect, the political evolution of Thailand has been unique among developing countries, not easily fit into general models of Third World authoritarianism and political development.

The renaissance of the monarchy has also affected Thailand's economic development in three respects of some significance. First has been the king's direct involvement in local development projects. When the king began to initiate projects on a small scale in the 1950s and 1960s, he relied on his personal funds.

As the number of projects rose, the designation applied to these activities was changed from Royal Project to Royal Initiative, indicating that the majority of his project ideas would be included in the regular budget and programs of the responsible ministries and would be subject to normal feasibility criteria. Until the early 1980s these projects were concentrated in areas within a convenient range of the four provincial royal residences (in Chiangmai, Sakon Nakorn, Narathiwat, and Hua Hin changwats). In recent years the projects have been more widespread. The budget for new projects in the mid-1980s was running around $25 million a year, while the number of villages benefiting from Royal Initiative projects had cumulated to about 4,000, or 7 percent of the villages in the kingdom.[5] The significance of these projects, apart from their local impact, lies in the personal identification of the king with the enhancement of village life as a primary objective of economic development and his professional, hands-on involvement in these projects as a working, rather than merely symbolic, monarch.

The second aspect of interest is the special attention the king has given to projects in areas that are relatively remote from Bangkok and inhabited by ethnic minorities, especially in the mountains of the North, peopled by the Hill Tribes, and in the four southernmost changwats, where the population is largely Malay and Islamic. The king's focus on these areas can be seen as a continuation of (perhaps the last chapter in) the long historical process of consolidating the Thai state and of integrating diverse groups into the national structure. Third has been the king's role as a balancing factor, as a guarantor that at times of crisis, in a polity that has yet to achieve a well-established system for orderly transfer of power, a steady hand will be at work to help the ship of state to return to an even keel. In this role the king has reinforced the perception of Thailand as a relatively stable and conservative society, notwithstanding the events of the mid-1970s, and the violent crisis in May 1992 (of which, more below).

As an immediate consequence of the fall of the Thanom regime, however, there was an explosion of political activity over a three-year period, culminating in crisis and a right-wing reaction. After an initial year of interim government under Dr. Sanya Dharmasakti (October 1973–February 1975), a respected former president of the Supreme Court who was close to the king, parliamentary government was reinstated. The large number of the parties returned, none holding a majority, forced the successive prime ministers (M. R. Seni Pramoj again, shortly replaced by his brother and political rival M. R. Kukrit Pramoj; then Seni a second time) to form coalitions that were inherently unstable. Although the parliamentary governments successfully managed adjustments in foreign policy to take account of the U.S. withdrawal from Vietnam, they were unable to cope with the domestic issues that were fueling the protest politics that had become a daily way of life in Bangkok. In the exhilirating atmosphere of a society suddenly open, radical literature was everywhere to be seen, farmers and workers were organizing and carrying out demonstrations and strikes, and the university students appeared to be protesting on virtually every conceivable subject, with increasing stridency.

By 1975, with Communist successes in the Indochinese states threatening Thailand's security, and the university students appearing to be under growing domestic left-wing influence, a right-wing reaction developed. The middle class, along with the monarchy, threw its support to a set of strongly anticommunist organizations. An extraordinary spasm of polarization and violence resulted, causing the sudden collapse of the three-year "democracy period." As Wyatt describes it, "By 1976, political assassinations, invariably of figures on the left, were commonplace. Police harassed the electioneering of leftist parties, and even active moderates were afraid for their safety. Violence, vituperation, and incivility were now a part of public life as they never had been before in Thailand."[6] The return of Thanom from exile abroad triggered a spate of student demonstrations. In response, there was a violent assault on the campus of Thammasat University by a group of right-wing organizations backed by elements in the military and the government. On October 6, 1976, a number of students were killed in a barbarous climax on the campus. The military moved in to restore order, once again suspending the constitution and ending open political activity.

The cycle of extremism, the sharp swings of the political and civil pendulum, took another year to play out. The military first installed a civilian administration under Thanin Kraivichien. This former justice on the Supreme Court ruled with an anticommunist authoritarian fervor that exceeded even Sarit's repressive practices. It soon became apparent to the military that Thanin's political methods were counterproductive. The middle class, traumatized by the excesses of October 6 and the preceding civil disorder, were not in sympathy with an extreme reaction either. The communist insurgency showed no signs of weakening under the military's assault tactics, while the ranks of the CPT were unexpectedly being swelled by university students and intellectuals fleeing into the forests to escape the right-wing vengeance in Bangkok. The cycle finally came to an end in October 1977 when the army removed Thanin and installed General Kriangsak Chomanand as prime minister.

In the final chapter of this turbulent period, elections in 1979 again returned to the renewed parliament numerous parties from which Kriangsak was able to patch together only a shaky coalition. Lacking strong support in both the parliament and the military, the Kriangsak government was unable to cope effectively with the economic effects of the second "oil shock" that year, or with the threat to Thailand's security posed by the Vietnamese invasion of Cambodia and the positioning of Vietnamese military forces along the Thai–Cambodia border. In February 1980 military pressure was exerted once more against a prime minister, forcing Kriangsak's resignation. A new goverment was formed by General Prem Tinsulanonda, commander-in-chief of the army. Known to have the support of the king, and bearing a strong reputation for personal integrity, Prem proved to be an artful practitioner of Thai coalition politics. His accession to power helped the polity to return to the middle ground of political compromise. His accession also ushered in a new period of sustained economic management and policy, a marked contrast with the drift and shifting currents of the democracy period and its sequel.

Economic Management

Just as the turmoil of the 1973–79 period contrasted sharply with the relative political stability of the preceding era, so in the economic realm was there a sharp contrast between the stable domestic and international growth of the 1960s and the economic turmoil and unfavorable external conditions that followed. The salient external events affecting the Thai economy included OPEC's fourfold increase in oil prices in October 1973; the subsequent world inflation; international recession and simultaneous inflation (stagflation in the late 1970s and early 1980s); the withdrawal of the U.S. military from Thailand in 1976 after the end of the Vietnam War, reducing the inflow of service and transfer payments; and the fall of Cambodia to the Khmer Rouge in 1975 and the Vietnamese invasion there in 1979, causing the Thais to allocate substantial resources to defense. During the democracy period, economic management had to cope with the oil-shock inflation, recession, and stimulation of recovery, in fairly rapid sequence. From 1975 on, economic policies became unusually expansionist and interventionist. By the end of the decade, the Thai economy would slide into fiscal and monetary imbalances not experienced since the early postwar years.

A number of factors came together in the second half of the 1970s to weaken the hold of the traditional economic conservatism. The successive cabinets from Kukrit until Kriangsak's fall in February 1980 had weak holds on power and little incentive to undertake unpopular measures or demand-restraining policies. For much of this period, economic policy was dominated by individuals with strong preference for aggressive growth rather than a balance between growth and stability. The old technocratic-military alliance of the Sarit–Thanom years was not restored under the succeeding new politics of military factions and professional politicians. The departure of Dr. Puey left the technocrats without obvious or unified intellectual leadership. Macroeconomic management became secondary to security and equity as the dominant concerns of public policy.

As a broad generality, the interaction of the shifting domestic political events, and the external economic shocks and domestic fluctuations, changed the basic task of economic management. Compared with the preceding purposive concentration on development policies and programs, the successive governments, and the economic and financial authorities, were now distracted from long-term attention. For much of the period, the energies of the policy-making technocrats were absorbed in one crisis management situation after another. Abonyi and Bunyaraks summarize this retreat from a development focus:

In general, the planning environment from 1972–1976 shifted toward an atmosphere of *crisis management*. The primary focus of development planning and management moved away from long-term planning and economic management, involving the optimization of public investment, toward coping with (largely externally induced) short-term fluctuations. No effective mechanisms, however, evolved to support a development planning and management system appropriate to cope with extensive short-term fluctuations and instability in the context of long-term adjustment. In the process, the systematic project-based planning procedure imported from the World Bank eroded under an atmosphere of economic and political instability.[7]

In its annual report for 1975, the Bank of Thailand sounded an alarm over the weakened state of general economic management. It pointed out that although export promotion was already a "major official policy," the shortcomings of the special export committee were "typical of the shortcomings of the government administrative machinery which require urgent adjustments." The failure of the export committee was only one example of a general breakdown in the economic management system. It called for new working arrangements in the cabinet to increase the coherence of economic policy formation at the political level. The technocratic policy team of the 1960s, it will be recalled, was a closely knit group, the senior members of which (especially Dr. Puey) held several positions simultaneously among the "core" agencies that shared responsibilty for both long-run development and short-run economic management.

> Effective implementation of economic policies will depend on the availability of reliable and complete data. As such, it is necessary to have a sufficient number of officials who would be responsible for sorting out, collecting and carefully analyzing the relevant data. In this connection, it is noted that the previously used system for sorting out policies and operational economic plans had relied on the joint efforts of national organizations, i.e., the Ministry of Finance, the National Economic and Social Development Board, the Budget Bureau and the Bank of Thailand. Urgent consideration should be made on whether the previous system of economic management should be re-installed or abolished and replaced by a new system which should not, in any case, duplicate the work of various government agencies which are responsible for the implementation of operational plans.[8]

While the policy formulation system was going into eclipse during much of the 1970s, the country's potential capacities for economic management were reaching very substantial levels. The postwar generation of overseas-trained economists who had staffed the core agencies under Sarit now formed a network of experienced administrators. Large numbers of university graduates were filling out the ranks of the bureaucracy. By 1974 one quarter of the top 26,000 officials in the civil service (virtually all university graduates) had received some foreign training under the U.S. aid program alone, including 1,500 academic degrees.[9]

In the second half of the 1970s, some of the core agencies underwent another round of staff upgrading. After Snoh Unakul was appointed governor of the Bank of Thailand in 1975, the institution was revitalized. The bank recaptured some of the prominence and range of policy concerns projected by Dr. Puey. The programs of the 1950s and 1960s to build domestic institutional capabilities in economics, other social sciences, and public administration were now paying off in terms of the supply of professionally trained personnel, the availability of faculty to undertake policy-oriented research, and the flow of economic and social statistics. Even in the private sector, university-trained professionals began to find employment, a portent of the forthcoming end of the intellectual monopoly long held by the universities and the government.

Economic management was becoming more complex during the 1970s. The favorable external regime of stable growth was replaced by a system recurrently shocked. The international economy moved off the Bretton Woods system of stable exchange rates and presented small, open economies with the novel problem of having to make rapid structural adjustments. Although Thailand's technical resources for economic management were gathering strength during this decade, their full mobilization for policy analysis and formulation would have to await the revival of purposive and coherent planning under the Prem government. In the meantime, of course, development planning continued, producing two development plans that reflected the economic and social changes under way at the time and the evolution of thought in the mainstream.

The third development plan (1972–76) was written and launched two years before the crisis that brought down the Thanom government. In recognition of the rising importance of social problems that had not received adequate attention in the past, the plan shifted the emphasis from sheer growth to social and politically oriented programs intended to address income maldistribution and the threat to domestic stability from the related internal and external communist challenges. Antinatal population policy was incorporated for the first time. To formalize the idea of equal attention to social along with economic objectives, the names of both the plan and the planning agency were changed. The third plan was the first one to be called an "economic and social" development plan; the planning agency became the National Economic and Social Development Board. The fourth plan (1977–81) moved further toward bringing a wide range of short- and long-term problems into a single conceptual framework. It posited five objectives for the plan period:

1. Immediate acceleration of economic recovery from the mid-decade slow-down

2. Reduction of income disparities

3. Reduction of population growth, generation of increased employment opportunities, and improvement of manpower quality

4. Improved management of natural resources, and environmental rehabilitation
5. Strengthened "national security management."

While it contains a long list of projects, the plan focuses on the broader objectives and introduces "guidelines" that are recommendations for how ministries should translate objectives into program implementation. The more extended analysis and emphasis the fourth plan gave to social problems, and to the dependence of Thai development on the overexploitation of the country's natural resource base, represented important advances in the scope and depth of development planning. The plan preparation process was also an advance over earlier plans:

> The process of plan formulation shifted from a centralized, *top-down* approach involving primarily central government agencies, to one more participatory and interactive in nature. In this it reflected the changing political and social structure of Thailand. The formulation of the Fourth Plan involved participants from key sectors and professions, leading to the identification of the central development issues as perceived by the various groups making up Thai society. This broad participation was largely responsible for expanding the scope of the Plan, including such concerns as natural resources and the environment, science and technology, joint investment between the public and private sectors, distribution of social services, the role of women and children, and so on.[10]

In the event, the third and fourth plans had much less impact on government actions and successive annual budgets than did the first two plans. In designing the fourth plan, NESDB tried to build in some lasting relevance by formulating an "issue-oriented indicative" framework that could be used "for flexible response in a potentially uncertain political environment, such as the seven Cabinets of the Third Plan."[11] While one can see an evolution in the substance and process of development planning in these two documents, the distracted governments in power in this period had little interest in the plans or the planning machinery.

The Democracy Period

The governments of the democracy period left few enduring marks on development policy. This was not for lack of pressures or problems that would have justified significant new directions. The international reevaluation of postwar development, the rising concern and free discussion about growth versus distribution, and the relief over the downfall of authoritarianism created an intellectual and political climate that was open to economic change. As conservative as the third plan and the annual reports of the Bank of

Thailand were, they did recognize that the years of rapid economic growth had generated new inequalities and that public policy (while deserving kudos for overall growth) had paid insufficient attention to numbers of problems that would not resolve themselves through further benign neglect. The spate of labor agitation and of demonstrations by farmer groups, well publicized by the newly free press, raised three economic issues to a high level of political concern—rice and sugar prices, landlessness in certain areas, and wages in the modern sector.

The new labor and farm organizations, representing the interests of previously silent, lower-income groups, did not agitate for substantial changes in the society, or in the basic economic policies that were being carried forward from the previous regime. Nevertheless, their very emergence and vociferousness were startling to the middle class and the establishment. And although their demands hardly appear radical in retrospect, the more conservative elements in Thai society saw them as threatening, especially in the context of the growing CPT insurgency and the heated rhetoric of some student leaders. In the end, as I have noted, a right-wing reaction developed. The assassination of a number of the farmer protest leaders, a particularly long and bitter strike in Bangkok, and other incidents led up to the October 1976 clash at Thammasat University. The complete shutdown of the parliamentary system, the enforced collapse of the farmer and urban workers organizations, and the subsequent harrassment of academics and intellectuals temporarily closed off further evolution of political pluralism and removed all organized sources of criticism or pressure on government policy making, other than the CPT.

Dr. Puey had played a very active role during the democracy period. As rector of Thammasat, he developed a program in which student interest in rural poverty was channeled into development projects in a large irrigation scheme. As the student demonstrations became more frequent and agitated, he counseled moderation, caution, and nonviolence. Nevertheless, he was among those accused of communist complicity in the wake of October 6. His long service as Thailand's charismatic and preeminent economist came to an abrupt end when he had to flee into exile abroad. At a seminar at Georgetown University the following year, he gave his view of the major issues of the period:

1. The reevaluation of aggregate growth:

> Before 1973 I would say that we had progressed fairly well with the orthodox way of development, disregarding perhaps, to our regret, the social problems that accompanied that. We looked, together with many less-developed countries, at the gross national income and the rate of growth; we did not look inside. For this I must blame myself as one of those who had devised this kind of development.
>
> [T]he economic and social problems ... were acute. It is a problem of distribution. ... During the dictatorship, the rich got richer and the poor got poorer. During that period, perhaps in conjunction with the Vietnam war, we

had insurgencies in Thailand that gained momentum slowly. In 1963 three provinces were declared "sensitive" provinces, that is to say, they were provinces that the communist insurgents were operating in. In 1973, those three provinces became thirty-two . . . out of some seventy.

2. The initial responses to social and distributive problems:

In October 1973 we suddenly found ourselves set free. . . . Before 1973 we could not have freedom of association. Labor law was adopted and enacted towards the end of 1973, giving full freedom to negotiate and freedom to strike. The minimum wage: during the dictatorship until 1973 was about 60 cents a day which is very low by any standard. The price of rice in Thailand had been kept down by deliberate policy of favoring the urban population, etc.

[F]rom October 1973 to October 1976 we had progress . . . freedom of the press, personal freedom, academic freedom and the freedom of association. . . . We tried to solve many problems. The minimum wage went up from 60 cents per day to 80 cents to $1.00 to $1.25 in 1975. This had not been achieved without quite a lot of negotiation and, in certain cases, big rallies by the trade unions. I was then the Chairman of the Economic Advisory Council to the Prime Minister. We had been calculating this minimum wage matter and discovered two pertinent things: . . . if you take [for a man and wife] the minimum intake for food . . . shelter, clothing and medical care . . . in 1974 the minimum wage should be $1.35, not $1.25. . . . We found that on the average the wage bill that goes into the industrial product made in Thailand was only 9 percent. . . . The minimum wage could go up without endangering the economic conditions for the employers.

[T]he government found itself guaranteeing the minimum price of rice and sugar cane and other commodities. . . . The rights and the conditions of work of the farmers had been defended. . . . Measures for land reform were drafted and other kinds of reform had begun, especially the all important educational reform that we had been working at for more than two years.

3. The reaction against "instability":

All this improvement, all this partial solution of the economic and social problems was accompanied by disturbance, definitely. How else could you negotiate with reluctant employers if you did not strike? . . . [W]e were all short-sighted when we complained about the disturbances. If we don't have this kind of disturbance and this kind of negotiation, perhaps we could sit back and be quiet, but in the end it would turn into an explosion.

Ever since October 1976, strikes have not been allowed. Minimum prices for commodities have been given up. Land Reform appeared in the statue books, but no real political will exists to implement it. Education reform has just been dumped. . . . We are in the same situation that appeared before 1973.[12]

Today, with the perspective of a decade and a half since Dr. Puey's evaluation of the 1973–76 period, it is all the more striking how moderate these economic problems were, how disproportionate and exaggerated were the fears of vested interests that supported or acquiesced in the repression of pluralism, how naive were the students in thinking that they had the power to force any and all changes, and how they dissipated their support with their bombastic expression and often trivial complaints. As Dr. Puey pointed out, the increases in the minimum wage did not cause a serious escalation in production costs; probably more important than his arithmetic was the fact that the legal minimum has, at times, been below the market wage and, outside the formal sector, is widely ignored in any case. Landlessness was not at the time a serious problem except in certain localities in the North and the Central Plain; as Dr. Puey said, "The Central Plain where the land reform problem is most acute, well, not very serious like in many countries, but relatively acute, had never been touched by the government."[13]

The widespread impression that the poor were getting poorer was mistaken. Living standards had been rising, albeit unevenly, and the incidence of poverty had fallen substantially (perhaps by nearly half between 1962–63 and 1975–76, from 57 percent of the population to 31 percent, although there are obvious problems of definition and measurement of the concept of poverty). Malnutrition of a mild degree was prevalent only among young children and (as later nutrition surveys would show) appeared to result more from poor child-feeding practices than from insufficient family income. Rice policy cut several ways. The premium had subsidized the basic wage good of the urban population, raising urban welfare and the implicit real daily wage. Between conflicting political pressures to raise farmgate prices while keeping down the cost of living in Bangkok, the government launched (ineffective) rice price-raising programs while at the same time continuing to impose the price-suppressing premium and export tax. The sugar price intervention, on the other hand, developed into an effective support program that sustained domestic producer prices during years when world prices were depressed, the export subsidy costs being financed directly by the implicit tax on domestic sugar consumers.

I touch on these issues only briefly at this point to observe that the few responses of the democracy period governments to pressures for redistributive policies and programs were questionable for their economic effectiveness and for their real incidence. Nevertheless, as I will suggest in the next section, the redistributive initiatives of the democracy period were important components of the socioeconomic response Thailand was gradually constructing to deal with the CPT insurgency in rural areas.

One enduring initiative of some significance has been the Rural Employment Generation Program (REGP), initiated by the Kukrit government in 1975. Under the REGP, the central government provides a grant annually to every tambon council in the country. The tambon (a group of villages) is free to program the funds for local projects of its own choosing, the intent being to create local employment during the dry, or slack, season. Despite technical and administrative weaknesses, favoritism in contracting, and failure to achieve any real measure of rural self-government free of central control, the REGP has built much small rural infrastructure, strengthened the administrative capacity of the tambon councils, and given "the 'bottom-up' approach to rural development . . . an effective boost."[14]

A second enduring exception was the new role undertaken by the Bank of Thailand. As NESDB and the development plans receded in their impact on policy, the bank moved beyond its traditional monetary and prudential concerns in an effort to shape the course of economic development more directly.

Security and Development

Fourth Plan

An important exception to the general loss of relevance of economic planning in the 1970s was the incorporation of national security as an integral part, and major objective, of the two plans. Reflecting the expansion of the insurgency into new areas of the country during the first half of the 1970s, the fourth plan text concludes that previous economic and social programs designed to counter the appeal of the CPT were inadequate. It asserts that economic development and national security have become closely related, and that planning for the allocation of resources must now find a proper balance among conventional defense, internal security, and social and economic growth.

> Internal and External situations necessitate advanced planning for dealing with possible disturbances during the Fourth Plan period. National defence capability depends, among other things, on the economic power of the nation. As the nation must build up its own defence capabilities in order to promote self-reliance, some cutback in socioeconomic development spending may be necessary. As there is a trade-off . . . the interrelationship between the socioeconomic and the defence sectors must be explored in more detail to work out a proper balance. . . . Besides the security problems on the national level, some special attention must be given to specific problem areas of the four main regions of the nation. These problem areas are characterized by insurgency problems and economic poverty. In the past these problem areas were neglected. In future, socioeconomic development programmes must be implemented in conjunction with actions to check subversive activities.[15]

Comparing the location of internal security problems with the regional allocation of development expenditures during the previous plan period, the text notes a great disparity. For example, the northeast region in 1975 had a per capita gross regional product of about 3,000 baht, and 52.5 percent of the total population living in identified insurgency areas. The central region (excluding Bangkok) had a per capita product of about 9,400 baht, and only 9.4 percent of the insurgency area population. Nevertheless, the Northeast's per capita allocation of "development budget" expenditures under the third plan was two-thirds the allocation to the Central region, and only 30 percent of the center's per capita allocation under the "social development" budget.[16]

While the fourth plan draws no simplistic conclusions regarding matching the distribution of public-sector expenditures with the geographic distribution of insurgency activity, it does embody the technocratic agreement with the military that security warranted a larger share of government resources and that some greater targeting of public programs was warranted in areas where the CPT was making inroads. In a two-year surge, the budget allocations to the military and police forces rose from an average of 23 percent of total central government expenditures, in fiscal years 1970–77, to 26 percent in 1978 and 29 percent in 1979. The security share fell back to 24 percent in 1980 and subsequent years.[17] Most significant for macroeconomic management was the fact that the government turned to external borrowing for the first time to finance imports of military hardware. The first such loans were arranged in 1975–76 for small amounts to be financed by U.S. Foreign Military Sales (FMS) credits (on commercial terms). In 1977 the government turned to foreign commercial credits to finance the bulk of its military imports. Disbursements (of about $800 million) under these two credit sources amounted to 45 percent of total central government external loan drawings in 1978–81 (and 17 percent of total public-sector drawings taking into account external borrowing by state enterprises), contributing significantly to the growing external debt service problem.[18]

The targeting of development programs in insurgency areas was not new with the fourth plan. As noted earlier, the allocation of substantial government and aid funds to the Northeast began in the 1950s, driven by the conviction that proximity to Indochina, poverty, and regional grievance over neglect were combining to make the Northeast population potentially disaffective. It appears likely that the government's resource inputs into the Northeast, for infrastructure and for education and other social programs, exceeded the tax withdrawals from that region by a substantial margin. Needless to say, the distribution of expenditures and projects within the Northeast and other rural areas was inevitably uneven among districts and villages, as was the rate of economic and social progress. Whatever the mix of reasons (difficult to sort out) may have been behind the responsiveness of villagers in some areas to the arguments of the CPT compared with the imperviousness of people in other areas or villages, the fourth plan text reflects the conviction (gradually becoming dominant among the military also) that greater imperviousness could be created if the pertinent security and developmental activities were properly coordinated and targeted.

It would take us too far afield to discuss the history of the insurgency problem in Thailand in any detail. (The interested reader can consult an extensive literature.[19]) A few brief observations, however, may be useful in the context of the present study. Although the insurgency never approached the scale of the communist guerrilla movements in Vietnam, Cambodia, or Malaysia, it was sufficiently widespread, violent, and long-lived to pose a significant threat to domestic security. In the mid-1960s it was estimated that the CPT had 2,600 combatants (of whom 2,000 were located in the Northeast) and 10,000 village sympathizers. Armed clashes with government security forces were running about one every day. By 1970 the number of insurgents rose to 5,000–6,000 and the number of "communist-influenced" villages was put at 4,000–5,000. In the democracy period the CPT lost ground, only to enjoy one last revival when several thousand students went into the jungle to oppose the Thanin government. For a variety of reasons, the insurgency began to collapse in 1979—student disillusionment with the authoritarian rigidity of the CPT, the Vietnamese invasion of Cambodia and the revelations about the Khmer Rouge, Laos's withdrawal of sanctuary, and the withdrawal of PRC support of the CPT were among the contributing factors. The counterinsurgency programs were also important, especially as the RTG shifted emphasis (after 1976) from (the sometimes counterproductive) armed suppression to civic action, rural development, and the improvement of relationships between local officials and villagers. By 1983 the collapse of the insurgency and of the CPT was virtually complete.

The inability of the insurgency to develop wider and deeper popular backing, its failure to develop more than a relatively low-level challenge relative to the experience elsewhere in the region, ranks among the most important successes of the Thai state in the postwar era. Given the many disparate material, psychological, and military factors involved, it is unlikely that a "definitive" explanation can be formulated to impute the relative positive and negative weights of these factors to the final outcome. I have reviewed the evidence elsewhere, concluding that the government's civic action and village development programs, shaped and reshaped over more than two decades of effort, played a material role:

> The withdrawal of support from the PRC and the catastrophes in Vietnam and Cambodia may well have been major factors in the collapse of the CPT. But equal if not greater importance cannot be denied to the fact that the RTG recognized the village-level problems that the insurgency could have turned to its purposes, gradually blanketed the insurgent areas with development programs and benefits, and restaffed and retrained the cadre of district officers. The government began with strong assets in villager predispositions and attachments to the symbols of monarchy, religion, and country. Whatever it did was apparently sufficent to deny the CPT the social and economic "asset" potential (of discontent and deprivation) on which a successful insurgency could have been built.[20]

Perhaps because the centers of insurgent activity were located in remote and economically marginal areas, the internal security problem appears to have had no great impact on production, private investment, or tourism. And given the importance of civil, rather than military, expenditures in the counterinsurgency programs over the years, one could plausibly argue that the main developmental impact was to raise the priority of rural development in the allocation of public resources, providing social benefits to populations that were relatively disadvantaged because of their location, at some cost in aggregate growth if the resources had been applied to areas that would have yielded higher returns. In any case, calculations of this sort would be trivial compared with the aggregate effects on the Thai economy that would have resulted if the insurgency had not been contained.

Finally, it is worth reiterating that the insurgency, or more precisely the adherents (as distinct from the cadre), were identified as the inhabitants of specified villages and districts. Except for the students seeking an alternative to the Thanin reaction, the insurgency made no inroads in urban areas and only minor progress in the more developed agricultural changwats. It was often the case that one village was sympathetic to the insurgency while other nearby villages were hostile to it. All this reinforced the conception that poverty was location-specific, a function of geographic resource differences. Although Thai economists began from 1976 on to publish analyses of various dimensions of poverty and income distribution (size distribution, regional Gini coefficients, etc.), the dominant conception remained that rural-urban, and some regions and subregions rather than others, defined the essence of the poverty and distributional problems. Rural development policy, programmatic responses, and political debate were based on this conception. Even as the insurgency was fading in the early years of the Prem government, the villages and district-based system for differential allocation of resources was being developed to its highest level of coordination, participatory planning and execution, and monitoring and evaluation. At its apex in Bangkok, this management system commanded substantial attention from senior policy makers in NESDB, the key ministries involved, and the cabinet.

Distribution and the Bank of Thailand

It will be recalled that the prestige of the Bank of Thailand under the governorship of Dr. Puey had been enhanced by the open criticisms of government actions voiced in the bank's annual economic reports and in the governor's public speeches (especially his pithy annual address to the Thai Bankers' Association). These criticisms ventured far beyond the monetary and banking areas that were the Bank of Thailand's responsibilities, including such targets as state enterprise inefficiency, domestic monopolies, unscrupulous foreign hawking of supplier credits, and corruption in government.[21] Nevertheless, despite the fact that Dr. Puey held broad policy positions (e.g., on the board of the planning agency) in addition to the Bank of Thailand governorship, and used the bank as a platform for wide policy comment, the essential functions and focus of the bank itself as an institution remained the pursuit of monetary stability, defense of the baht, and supervision of commercial banking. In 1967 Silcock described the orientation of the Bank of Thailand in the light of its new powers under the Commercial Banking Act of 1962:

It is apparent from these changes that the main interest of the Bank of Thailand has been in ensuring adequate liquidity, increasing its power to control the money market, modifying the structure of the banks away from that of semi-political institutions furthering the interests of particular groups towards impersonal, rational agencies creating a market for various types of liquid assets. In this, though the main control has necessarily been one of curbing undesirable practices—and this has by no means ceased to be necessary—there has been some limited success in fostering new kinds of credit, particularly through rediscounts.[22]

It was not long after Silcock wrote this that the bank began to move beyond the realms of monetary stability and financial insitution oversight, and to use its authority to influence the country's development directly through incentives and administrative regulations affecting the allocation of resources.

Over the years since Dr. Puey resigned the governorship in 1970, the influence and role of the bank has varied depending on the personal strengths of succeeding governors and on their relationship with the ministers of finance. Although the expanding activism of the bank varied at times depending on these personal circumstances, the measures under consideration here have been embodied in legislation and carried forward by the central bank as an institution, less identified as personal initiatives as they would have been in previous years when the number of policy players was more limited. With the weakening of the network of technocrats in the Ministry of Finance and NESDB in the 1970s, and the accompanying politicization of economic policy making, a vacuum opened up into which the only institution capable of moving was the central bank.

The first instrument the bank used, to move into resource allocation, was the rediscount window. The bank had first provided rediscounting accommodation of export paper in the late 1950s, but limited only to rice. As the bank's concern over export promotion grew, it began in the late 1960s to add selected agricultural and industrial export products to the list of items eligible for rediscount accommodation. This selective approach reflected an effort to fine-tune the financial support that was implicit in these transactions; different discount rates were applied to different commodities based on the bank's own judgments regarding the relative importance of the commodities for the country's development. Industries using agricultural raw materials received the most concessional rediscount rates. Industries using nonagricultural raw materials were offered various rates "according to their degree of importance."[23] Other industries were added to the eligibility list from time to time under one criterion or another, for example, labor-intensive industries, in 1974.[24] Apart from the continuing accommodation provided to exporters of rice, however, the eligibility of individual commodities or industries tended to open and close frequently in response to temporary market conditions (e.g., in 1974, promissory notes of textile firms were temporarily rediscounted to help the industry get through a period of overstocking)[25] and occasionally in response to strong political pressure. Thus, the bank's accommodation was limited to provisions that strengthened the working capital position of the traders and firms involved, was never offered as an inducement to invest in the production of a commodity not already being produced and traded, and was not a form of development financing akin to long-term investment credits.

Much more significant as interventions designed to shape the sectoral allocation of finance were the measures the bank introduced in 1975 (at the behest of Boonchu Rojanasatien, Kukrit's minister of finance) to increase the amount of institutional credit being extended to the agriculture sector. The bank reported that agricultural credit at the end of 1974 amounted to only 2 percent (or B1.3 billion) of total commercial bank credit. The additional finance provided by the Bank for Agriculture and Cooperatives (BAAC), still a relatively small institution at the time, amounted to only B2.7 billion, "falling far short of total requirement." Farmers needing credit were forced to borrow from private and noninstitutional lenders at "exorbitant" rates of interest.[26] To mandate an increase in institutional credit to farmers, the Bank of Thailand would now require commercial banks to increase their agricultural loans to at least 5 percent of their total loans outstanding at the end of 1974. The term "farmers" was defined as farmer groups and cooperatives, excluding commercial firms and agro-industries. To the extent any commercial bank was unable to reach the 5 percent target, it would have to deposit the shortfall with the BAAC, which could then relend these funds to farmers.[27] In successive years the Bank of Thailand has adjusted the calculation and the definition of the target, raising the mandated percentage up to 13 by 1979, of which 2 percent could be in the form of loans to "agribusiness."

In a third allocative policy, the bank in 1975 instituted a requirement that new commercial bank branches would have to extend loans to "local enterprises" equal to at least 60 percent of the deposits each branch received from within its own district (amphur). (Until this requirement was put into effect, bank branches in the provinces generally employed only a fraction of their deposits for making local loans. In effect, the branches served to transfer rural deposits to their headquarters for urban and industrial lending.) One-third of the local loans should be extended to farmers. Any shortfall from these targets would have to be deposited with the Bank of Thailand, as a penalty, in a non-interest-bearing account.

Fourth, the bank began to offer concessional rediscounting to commercial banks for a portion of the financing the latter were willing to extend in connection with government schemes to support the farmgate price of paddy.[28] Finally, the bank provided concessional accommodation to the BAAC, which, together with the compulsory commercial bank deposits (which earned below-market rates of interest) and external loans on aid terms, provided the large expansion in resources flowing into the BAAC in the latter half of the 1970s.

By 1980 the staff of the BOT began internally to question the effectiveness and desirability of these credit allocation policies. However, credit allocation was not openly questioned by any of its governors until 1990 when Governor Chavalit Thanachanan, discussing a program of wide-ranging policy reform the bank was introducing as a financial "modernization" program, announced that it was considering removing the requirements to extend agricultural credit in order to allow the commercial banks to enhance their "efficiency in resource allocation."[29] How did it happen that such an anomalous policy was adopted, strengthened, and sustained for over a decade and a half, during a period of rapid industrial growth and of entry of powerful industrial and financial business interests into the political system, and despite the collapse of farmer's organizations?

The policy was initiated during the democracy period. Radical academic criticism of the direction of Thai development had singled out the commercial banks as primary culprits behind a number of the society's economic and social ills. The banks were criticized for profiteering, insider lending, exploiting farmers, and extending very little credit to agriculture.[30] In the general atmosphere of concern over the course of income distribution and the skewed accumulation of new wealth, there were many bureaucrats who were sympathetic to radical calls for reevaluating the policy framework following the overthrow of the Thanom regime. The commercial banks expressed little opposition to the allocation requirement when it was introduced. They have characterized their adherence since as an example of their willingness to support socially progressive policies of the government.[31] In the face of recurrent populist statements of military figures that ironically have echoed the views of the radical critics, one might interpret the muted response of the banks as a prudent accommodation designed to avoid feeding latent antibank populism in the army.

In sum, the economic technocrats agreed with the right and the left that financial policies should be geared to correct an imbalance against agriculture. The policy has survived well beyond the democracy period because of the sensitivity of all political actors in Thailand to the importance of avoiding any appearance of being opposed to the interests of farmers. The policy has been under criticism for several years, mostly in technical studies that have gone relatively unnoticed in Thailand, as a moderate distortion ("financial repression") in the operations of the financial sector.

In a related response to the concerns over the role and economic power of the commercial banks—and of the leading families controlling these banks— the Bank of Thailand introduced in 1979 amendments to the Commercial Banking Act that were aimed at putting some constraints on the concentration of ownership and on the expansion of bank holdings in nonfinancial corporations. Shares held by any individual were not to exceed 5 percent of the total shares outstanding. The banks were required to increase the numbers of shareholders to at least 250 (with further criteria that would bring their total shareholdings to a majority, but with each holder having a small fraction). The banks were prohibited from extending loans to their own directors or to companies in which the directors have an interest. The banks also were enjoined from holding more than 10 percent of the shares of other companies, or from holding any shares of other banks.[32] These rules proved difficult to implement, some for technical reasons and some because legal evasions were easily devised. The collapse of the stock exchange in 1979 made open market divestiture of shares (of banks' own equity or holdings of other corporate equity) temporarily infeasible. In the 1980s, some deconcentration of ownership of individual banks did take place in the formal sense that the banks raised capital by floating stock for public trading in the SET; but for separation of controlling ownership from actual management—which is occurring in some of the banks—the dilution of family shareholding proportions has been irrelevant. In any case, the policy of weakening the control of the banking families was put on ice during most of the 1980s when the problem of concentration was overtaken by the prudential problems of bank solvency. From a political point of view, the issue has receded almost entirely, resurfacing now and then in the remarks of one military figure or another and as the subject of an occasional academic paper or book, but no longer (for the present) a subject of public debate or even apparent interest. Given this indifference, none of the political parties, during periods when they have not been part of a cabinet coalition, have attacked the government for failure to pursue banking deconcentration, a policy stance that would jeopardize the financial contributions that some banks have provided to parties seeking funds to defray the costs of election campaigns.

The upshot is that the central bank has been under no pressure to push the implementation of the deconcentration provisions of the law. From an economic point of view, it is not at all clear that divestiture would eliminate or lessen the undesirable consequences normally attributed to excessive concentration of market power, or indeed that these consequences were even present as general characteristics of the Thai commercial banking sector. Insider lending without adequate collateral has resulted in weak loan portfolios in some family-controlled banks. Other family-controlled banks have made it a practice of applying uniform criteria even to insider lending. In any case, control can continue to be exercised by the same management, even with smaller proportionate shareholdings, as long as ownership and management are not separated. It would be difficult to demonstrate the existence of oligopoly profits in the banking sector. Several members of the group would have become insolvent if it were not for the rescue operations of the central bank, while the level of profitability of the banking sector in many years has been below that of other, nonfinancial sectors.

As far as competition and market power are concerned, a recent close study of the Thai financial system reached conclusions contrary to the common view that the banking sector is highly concentrated and that the top five banks exercise monopoly power through "a strong grip on the market."[33] First, as measured by size of assets, the degree of concentration among commercial banks in Thailand increased between 1960 and 1980, then declined through 1988. While the banking sector is concentrated (the top five banks held 69 percent of total commercial bank assets in 1988, Bangkok Bank alone holding 28 percent), the degree of concentration relative to other developing countries may or may not be high depending on the measures used. Second, the study found that "little firm evidence is available substantiating monopolistic abuses" and that "the magnitude of any associated inefficiency does not seem high compared to the situation in some other developing countries." The large banks possessed size advantages over the smaller banks in the provision of some services, but disadvantages in other services. The small banks were "unable to point to notable examples" of significant abuses by the large banks. Most important, "although large banks may attempt to tie in other services to those for which they have a comparative advantage, there does not appear to be collusion among the large banks in shutting out smaller banks from business. Furthermore, competition among the large banks helps limit margins on most lines of business."

The policies of the monetary authorities toward concentration in the private commercial banking sector have moved in opposite directions at once, curiously reminiscent of the government's maintenance of contradictory policies over long periods of time in several other important areas of economic management (e.g., trade and rice prices). On the one hand, in the interests of efficiency and diversification, the government legislated divestiture requirements and limits on bank investments in other corporations, and used moral suasion to press for professionalization of management.[34] On the other hand, the single most important factor contributing to the concentration of ownership, and to whatever oligopolistic consequences this may have had, has been the financial authorities' own long-standing policy of allowing no new entrants into the commercial banking field. In effect, the authorities put bank solvency and prudential management ahead of competition, with the distributive implications falling out as a consequence to be ameliorated (inadequately, as seen above) through administrative, nonmarket solutions.

The efficiency consequences do not seem to have been substantial, taking a broad view of the banking sector's record in expanding its branch system, accumulating deposits, and intermediating with the sectors seeking finance. Still, it is likely that increased competition from foreign banks in particular (there has been a severe constraint on the right of the existing foreign banks to open new branches, aside from the bar on new entry) would have pressured the system to correct some of its major operating inefficiencies. Chief among these have been reliance on collateral and size (or personal knowledge) of borrower rather than project evaluation as the basis for loan decisions; use of overdraft facilities rather than term loans even when credit is to be used for investment rather than for trading or working capital; outdated customer service procedures and backroom operations, and the costs of insider lending for ill-conceived projects. Although political and technocratic sentiment on new entry appeared to be moving toward liberalization by the end of the 1980s, the policy remains in place as of this writing.[35]

The Industry–Trade Policy Regime

In chapter 4 I noted that Thailand had a relatively low level of tariff protection prior to 1970 compared with other developing countries. At the same time, import duties remained the largest single source of government tax revenue through the 1970s even though they had come down from 34 percent in 1961 to 30 percent in 1971 and 24–25 percent in 1976–79. Set mainly for revenue-raising purposes, tariff rates in the 1960s ranged between 15 and 30 percent. In the late 1960s, the Ministry of Finance began increasing the rates on finished consumer goods. In 1974 the rates were lowered again as a counterinflationary measure. Over the rest of the decade, tariffs were raised sharply as protectionist policy became more aggressive. (The counterinflationary tariff reductions of 1974 brought the average effective rate of protection [ERP] down from 87 percent to 19 percent. By 1978 the average ERP had been raised back to 70 percent).

In 1977 the BOI was authorized by law to impose tariff surcharges on imports of goods manufactured by promoted firms. The BOI's new authority created a third track for tariff increases, independent of the Fiscal Policy Office (in the Ministry of Finance), which had the responsibility for general tariff adjustment and of the interministerial Tariff Committee (chaired by the Ministry of Finance), which dealt with individual requests from the private sector for protection. Other instruments for protecting domestic producers were under the authority of yet additional agencies, each working independently under separate legislative mandates. The Ministry of Commerce administered import licensing, giving it the power to impose quantitative restrictions. The Ministry of Industry had the authority to issue domestic content regulations, that is, requirements that manufacturers of specified products buy fixed proportions of their inputs from local suppliers.[36] The Ministry of Industry could also limit new entry and capacity expansion if it judged that there was a danger of "excessive competition."

The workings of this system on the protective structure, by the end of decade, are summarized by Bhattacharya and Brimble:

> (a) extremely high and variable nominal rates on many finished products (For example: automobiles—150%, many textile products and garments—100%, leather products—100%, alcoholic beverages—100%, electrical goods—up to 100%, many processed foods—80%); (b) the proliferation of product-specific exemptions, largely on inputs into the highly protected sectors . . . and BOI surcharges on the outputs of BOI promoted companies; and (c) the increased use of quantitative restrictions, price controls, and domestic content requirements to provide protection to domestic industries. . . . The overall average (effective rates of protection) rose more than two-fold from 1971–1980, with consumer goods and transport equipment accounting for much of the increase, and there was a substantial increase in the dispersion of the rates.[37]

The doubling of the average effective rate of protection (ERP) appears to have shifted Thailand's degree of tariff protection relative to other countries of the region. In the mid-1970s tariff protection in Thailand appeared to be higher than in Malaysia and Taiwan, but lower than in Korea, Indonesia, and the Philippines (apart from Thailand's extraordinarily high ERP for automobiles).[38] By the early 1980s Thailand's unweighted average nominal tariff rate of 34 percent had risen above Korea (22 percent) and the Philippines (29 percent). A World Bank study found that during the 1970s Thailand had moved "from a country with relatively low protection to a country with medium-to-high protection levels, marking a rather significant reversal in Thailand's trade policy."[39]

Despite the rush to intervention and protection in the last few years of the 1970s, there were mitigating factors that limited the potential long-run effects of this policy shift. The most important, of course, was the fact that the general thrust of these policies (not every aspect, to be sure) was soon reversed, in the early years of the 1980s, under the Prem government. There were perhaps only four or five years in which this thickening policy framework was shifting the incentive structure affecting investment decisions. Second, the overwhelming importance of final consumer goods among the industries securing protection, the often lamented sparseness of backward linkages to intermediate, basic, and capital goods manufacturing, also meant that the system had not yet saddled the economy with uncompetitive domestic production of inputs. (From 1970 to 1980 the share of consumer goods in total manufacturing value-added declined only marginally from 66.6 percent to 64.3 percent.) The one outstanding exception was the motor vehicle assembly industry, which long predated the late 1970s' protectionist surge.

Third, in practice the application of the nontariff measures did not add up to a major source of distortion, with the exception of the automobile industry.[40] Fourth, extensive smuggling and irregularities in administration meant that the protective umbrella was full of holes. Fifth, since state enterprises played a relatively minor role in the manufacturing sector, Thailand was free of the kind of powerful pressures within government itself that were forcing specific subsector protection measures onto the economic authorities of Indonesia, the Philippines, and other governments pursuing state direct investment in manufacturing. Sixth, and perhaps most important for setting the Thai import-substitution experience apart from that of many other developing countries, was the continuity of policy (since the NEDCOL experience) to refrain from direct government investment of budget resources into manufacturing and to avoid intervention in the banking system to direct the allocation of finance into industry in general, or into specific manufacturing lines that would require protection.

The extent of other distortions that were building up over the 1970s was similarly moderate in practice, especially when compared with the effects of similar measures being implemented in other developing countries. For example, the BOI was frequently criticized for promoting capital-intensive enterprise. This bias apparently stemmed from BOI administrative practice favoring large clients rather than from a distortionary impact on the technology choice of the firms that were "promoted." According to an IMF study, Thailand had a lower rate of capital subsidy, for regular or for promoted firms, than Indonesia, Malaysia, the Philippines, and Singapore.[41]

The fact that industrial promotion policy was to a considerable extent driven by, and (as in the 1974 tariff reduction) subordinated to, the macroeconomic objective of reducing the chronic trade deficit, meant that the government was pursuing export promotion simultaneously with its import-substitution efforts. Both orientations had become integral to Thai industrial and trade policies since the 1960s. The creation of a manufacturing incentive structure (and implementing institutional arrangements like the process managed by the BOI) had been recommended by Loftus and by the World Bank study in 1959,[42] with cautionary qualifications about the span of time allowed for infant industries to get established behind protective barriers. While criticism of import-substitution industrialization had developed in the economic literature by the late 1960s,[43] based on distortions and efficiency costs experienced by countries pursuing these policies in a thoroughgoing manner, the call for export-orientation arose in Thailand from the traditional concern to avoid external deficits and their financial consequences.

The central bank's annual drumbeat for export promotion was matched by measures the bank undertook to provide accommodating export credit. In the 1960s about 36 percent of the credit extended through rediscounting accommodated agricultural (mainly rice) exports. Industrial exports received only 7 percent. During the 1970s the share of exports rose to 74 percent, nearly two-thirds of which was allocated to manufactures.[44] In addition, the government introduced a system of tax rebates and import duty refunds designed to relieve manufacturers of the costs these taxes imposed on industrial exports. Different departments of government also began offering services to facilitate and promote exports.

On balance, however, it was clear by the late 1970s that the network of interventions and programs had a strong anti-export bias. The programmatic measures to assist exporters were functioning poorly, while the rebate system in its actual operation generated only insignificant offset to the tax burden on exports. I noted above the Bank of Thailand's observations on the nonfunctioning of the export promotion coordinating machinery. NESDB gives a full indictment of the export promotion efforts as of 1977:

> The development of basic infrastructural facilities for promoting exports has not been impressive so far. Though major facilities such as deep sea ports and export processing zones have been given hign priority status, actual implementation has been slow. The necessary marketing information and services provided by Thai commercial attaches stationed in foreign countries are still

very limited. In addition, no financial institution has been established to serve exporters. . . .

The provision of export incentives in the form of tax concessions and rebates is still very limited and ineffectively organized. In applying for a refund on tax paid on imports of materials used as inputs in the production of export products, exporters have to encounter considerable bureaucratic red-tape and cumbersome procedures. Moreover, the existing tax system is not adequately geared towards the promotion of exports. . . .

So far, research on marketing has been conducted on a very limited scale. . . . The lack of standardization has also created frequent problems on the export of low quality products. This problem is not only attributed to the system of inspection and licensing but also to the lack of quality standardization.

Cumbersome procedures increase the cost of exporting . . . in terms of time and money. . . . The lack of effective coordination among [the many regulatory] agencies has caused considerable delays.[45]

While few manufactured exports were subject to export duties, effective rates of protection were lowest for export products (though raised from –40 percent in 1974 to a positive 40 percent in 1978) compared with other categories of manufactures (import competing goods and nontradables).[46]

Finally, it is important to note that the administration of this complex of contradictory policies was poorly coordinated. Year-to-year changes in rates and regulations emanating from different agencies were largely ad hoc, piling on further complexities rather than moving toward economic coherence and administrative simplicity. The key agencies administering the policy structure (Fiscal Policy Office, BOI, the Tariff Committee) had weak capability for analyzing the potential effects of alternative decisions.

By the late 1970s the incentive structure and promotional system had resulted in the development of numerous enterprises that appeared to lack any realistic prospect of being able to operate profitably without continuing, substantial protection. The motor vehicle assembly firms were the most conspicuous, operating well below capacity levels, which, even if realized, would not enable them to achieve the economies of scale required for international competitiveness. In addition, the accumulation of ad hoc tariff increases, without the application of general criteria or standard rates, had produced a patchwork of (partially) administered price relationships among imported final goods and intermediates within individual industry sectors. While the analysts recognized the distortions this produced in the incentive structure for investment, the producers and users within these industries (the electrical goods sector was a major case in point) were at odds over the differential benefits among them.[47]

The technocrats were aware of the inconsistencies between the import-substitution and export promotion policy structures no later than 1974 when the first studies of industrial policy by Narongchai Akrasanee were published.[48] In 1977 NESDB still stated explicitly that both policy directions would continue to be pursued in order to strengthen the balance of payments.[49] Other aspects of industrial promotion policy were also coming under criticism, including the loss of tax revenue forgiven under BOI incentives (estimated at 3 percent of total tax revenue in 1980[50]); the interest rate subsidies offered by the Bank of Thailand through the discount facility for selected sectors or products (in effect, financed by cross-subsidy from all other borrowers); the price burden imposed on consumers of protected products; and the distorting effects of selected price controls introduced to benefit particular producers.

In retrospect, it is striking that the incentive structure built up during the 1970s appeared to have little discernible impact on the aggregate performance of Thai industry. With motor vehicles again the major exception, the rapid development of manufactures in the 1970s was consistent with Thailand's comparative advantages in agricultural inputs and in labor-intensive production. The expansion of manufactured exports demonstrated competitiveness, aggressive marketing, and the ability to attract foreign direct investment. The share of manufactures in total exports rose from 6 percent in 1970 to 32 percent in 1980 (Table 5.1). Textiles, garments, precious stones, and integrated circuits led the way, rising from 22 percent of manufactured exports in 1970 to 28 percent in 1980. And by 1980 exports took substantial shares of the output of several industry subsectors (e.g., processed food, 38 percent; textiles, 14 percent; leather products, 32 percent; rubber and plastic, 85 percent; machinery [including circuits], 33 percent). Thus, the recognition of need for trade regime reform stemmed from an anticipation of the *potential* structural impact on the economy, rather than from a present necessity to undo a large-scale accumulation of unccompetitive industries.

An Economic Chronology

Let us now take a closer look at economic events and the course of macroeconomic policy management in this period. The opening shock was a sharp drop (around 9 percent) in rice production in 1972. Responding to high world prices in 1972–73, Thai rice exports shot up. Apparently caught by surprise, the government found itself with unexpectedly tight domestic supplies and rising retail rice prices. In mid-year 1973 rice exports were banned altogether. This extraordinary episode contributed to the decline in public confidence that was weakening the Thanom government. The general world inflation in 1972–73, greatly augmented by the oil price increase in 1973, added to the pressures on domestic prices of traded goods across the board. The result was an inflationary spike for the two years 1973–74, of 15 percent and 24 percent, respectively. Real GDP grew 9.4 percent in 1973 as agricultural production recovered and as many promoted companies came on stream, especially in the textiles sector.

In an attempt to dampen the inflation, the financial authorities raised commercial bank reserve requirements and the "basic" rate applied to commercial bank borrowing from the Bank of Thailand, increased the rice premium and reduced

Table 5.1

Distribution of Goods Exports (percent of value)

Sector	1960	1970	1980
Agriculture	84.38	67.50	46.93
Fishery	0.41	2.49	4.16
Forestry	1.33	1.48	0.05
Mining	6.69	13.93	11.58
Manufacturing	2.44	6.10	32.33
Others	4.74	8.50	4.95
Total	100.00	100.00	100.00

Source: Bank of Thailand.

import duties to lower domestic prices of rice and imported goods, and imposed controlled prices on fuel products in order to block the full passage of the oil price increase through to domestic consumers. At the same time, Ammar's fiscal drag was still at work. The boom in commodity export products raised government revenues faster than the bureaucracy was able to raise its expenditure level. The upshot was domestic stagflation in 1974. The easing of the inflation in 1974 and the continued strength in the level of foreign exchange reserves meant that there were no significant constraints on the government's shift to an expansionary budget policy in October 1974 (the start of the 1975 fiscal year). The central bank also shifted gears in mid-1974, easing credit in an effort to promote recovery in economic activity. Relative price stability was restored by 1975 and maintained until 1979.

The upshot for the first half of the decade was an average rate of growth in GDP of 6.4 percent, down nearly one quarter from the 8.4 percent average growth in 1960–70. The slowdown of 1973–74 turned out to be a relatively moderate and temporary drag on economic growth (Table 5.2), with the oil price tax on the economy and the poor crop yields of 1974 offset by the boom in export commodity prices and the quick resurgence of domestic and export demand for manufactured goods.

The government acted with commendable alacrity in this episode, using the fiscal and monetary instruments available; but it is apparent that the ability of the authorities to implement counterbalancing demand management policies was not really tested. The external factors that were generating the inflationary strains eased off quickly, while the commodity price boom associated with the oil price rise compensated for the balance of payments effect of the oil shock. International reserves at the end of 1975 were at a comfortable five months' import level. Between the rise in export earnings and the absence of a need for expanding short-term external debt, the debt service ratio fell from 14.0 percent in 1973 to 10.2 percent in 1974. The fiscal surplus in fact overshot the government's

Table 5.2

Real Growth Rates, 1970–79 (percent per annum)

	1970–75	1976	1977	1978	1979
GDP	6.4	9.3	7.3	11.7	6.7
Agriculture	5.1	6.1	–0.6	14.7	–2.0
Industry	7.3	15.7	14.7	11.5	10.1
Manufacturing	9.8	15.5	13.3	9.8	9.8
Tertiary	6.8	9.3	7.3	11.7	6.7

Source: NESDB.

intentions; public-sector capital expenditures would have been significantly higher in 1974 if it were not for the unexpected delays enforced by the need to renegotiate contracts to take account of the unplanned escalation in domestic prices. While the demand-constraining actions certainly took the steam out of the inflation in nontraded goods and services, they also contributed to the recession.

The Bank of Thailand concluded that Thailand could have done better, avoiding or at least moderating the stagnation of 1974, if the government had had the administrative capability to implement the projected capital expenditures in a timely fashion. The bank noted in effect that economic management now required "delicate" handling, flexibility, and good coordination. Somewhat unrealistically, the bank called on the same government machinery that had produced a deflationary "fiscal drag" in 1974 to design and execute a budget in 1975 (including an extra mid-year budget if necessary) that would stimulate the economy, but short of the magnitude that would bring about "excessive" demand.[51] The bank also recommended that controlled prices of food, oil, and fertilizer should be eased, but only gradually as inflation eased, and taking into account the income effects on the poor. Finally, the bank suggested that it be empowered to exercise "selective credit control," and that the government undertake measures to help farmers and to promote development in depressed areas. The suggestions included price supports for some agricultural commodities; various steps to expand the volume (and subsidy element) of farm lending by the BAAC; regional development planning; interest rate and tax incentives for investment in lagging regions; transport system improvements (including "revamping" the monopoly privileges held by the state enterprise, the Express Transport Organization); planning for a new deep-sea port; incentives to raise the level of private investment; family planning promotion and educational reform; and a "comprehensive development policy which clearly sets out investments according to their priority."[52]

The policy discussion in the 1974 annual report was remarkable in two respects. It was a sign that the Bank of Thailand was reasserting a wider role in economic policy after several years of confining itself to monetary and demand management issues. And it reflected the fact that even the citadel of economic orthodoxy in Thailand endorsed the idea that it was proper for the government to intervene more extensively in the economy. In effect, the bank was arguing that the relatively slower advance in the economic position of lagging regions and classes of farmers amounted to major market failures; the society's social welfare objectives required that these failures be corrected by government action.

As the Bank of Thailand's view indicated, the second half of the decade began with a sense of satisfaction over the macroeconomic situation. The economy had adjusted quickly to the first oil shock and its consequences. Exports were diversifying and growing rapidly. Real oil prices were falling. World Bank officials looked on Thailand as a strong member country that could and should take on a greatly enlarged flow of World Bank loan funds. Thailand's excellent credit rating also gave it ready access to the international capital market which was now awash with petro dollars needing to be "recycled." In this framework of an apparently restored set of favorable conditions, public-sector expenditures grew rapidly and the private sector responded with an investment boom. Real GDP growth recovered sharply, averaging 8.3 percent between 1975 and 1978. There were several problems developing, however, that threatened the sustainability of this recovery.

The adjustment to the first oil shock had been incomplete, especially with respect to energy prices. The remaining distortions were now compounded by other macroeconomic effects of the growth of excess demand. In hindsight it became obvious, after the second oil shock in 1979, that the expansionary policies of 1975–78 had brought the economy to a position of considerable vulnerability, contrasting sharply with the traditional conservatism of Thai economic management. The second oil shock was not foreseen, needless to say. If it had not occurred, the expectation of the Thai economic authorities that the unfolding situation was manageable without heroic measures might well have proved correct. In 1978 a World Bank team proposed that the government should embark on an even more expansionist strategy in order to achieve a higher rate of growth in rural income. The report asserted that an aggressive program was within Thailand's resource mobilization capabilities.

> A development strategy based on continued expansion of agriculture through more intensive use of land, accelerated growth of incomes in the poorest areas, a balanced and better dispersal of industrial growth based on domestic as well as foreign markets, and more equal access to economic and social services should enable Thailand to aim at an aggregate growth rate of at least 8% a year in the 1980s, or a per capita income growth of close to 6% per year, significantly faster than in the 1960s and 1970s. More importantly, incomes of poor farmers in the North and Northeast should be able to grow substantially.... The opportunity cost of unskilled labor should begin to rise by the late 1980s and unskilled workers throughout the economy could expect to benefit from a significant increase in real wages.

The development strategy proposed above requires an increase in the level of public spending as well as a reorientation of government policy and programs. . . .

A high growth rate of agriculture and manufactured exports should also help to alleviate the emerging problem in Thailand's balance of payments. A substantial current account deficit through the late 1970s and the early 1980s, averaging about $1.7 billion in current prices equivalent to 4.5% of GDP, may be difficult to avoid. But continued growth of agriculture, increasing importance of manufacturing exports and an increasingly diversified structure of exports should allow the country to remain highly creditworthy for substantial borrowing from both private and official sources. The size of the balance of payments deficit should begin to decline by the second half of the 1980s to about 3% of GDP and the country's debt service ratio should not present a problem at any time.[53]

The fourth development plan, written in 1976, and the annual reports of the Bank of Thailand for 1976–78, had a similar view of the basic orientation economic policy should take and of the feasibility of containing the macroeconomic pressures that a more expansionary public program would generate. The fourth plan projected that the savings-investment gap would decline between 1977 and 1981 and that the current account deficit, as a consequence, would fall to 1.5 percent of GDP by 1981. As events unfolded, the bank grew increasingly concerned, but certainly not alarmed, that demand was rising too rapidly.

The position as of 1977 was described by the bank as follows:

In order to stimulate recovery in business and investment conditions which had been extremely stagnant in 1974 and 1975, various trade, fiscal and monetary measures were introduced by the authorities throughout the past four years following the energy crisis in 1973 when the price of crude oil more than tripled. . . . Fiscal policy aimed at maintaining a large budget deficit for several consecutive years. As for monetary policy . . . stimulative measures were undertaken in line with fiscal policy.

During 1977, the level of export earnings remained high. . . . Import of raw materials . . . also went up at a high rate along with import of capital goods, petroleum and other products. On the other hand, the agriculture sector . . . was affected by a severe drought . . . [which] reduced the volume of export. . . . The balance of trade and payments deficits widened rapidly . . . [and] is expected to deteriorate further during 1978 owing to the downturn in exports and the continuing rise in imports resulting from planned investment outlays.[54]

The Bank of Thailand concluded that several problems needed to be "urgently tackled" in 1978. To help offset the effects of the drought on farm incomes, paddy prices should be supported at a "high" level and agricultural credit expanded. As for the balance of payments, the bank opined that the 1977 deficit was not a "major" problem considering the "sufficiently high" level of international reserves. However, in the face of a likely flattening of export earnings in

1978, another sizable deficit would imply that the economy would be expanding "at a rate which exceeds the financial resources and the production capacity of the country." It was time to shift from expansion to a "more restrictive approach" including a slowdown in government expenditures, a temporarily restrained monetary policy, and a broad energy program of conservation and more rapid development of domestic energy sources. Finally, on inflation, the bank put part of the blame (besides the rise in prices of traded goods) on profiteering and market imperfections, but concluded that increases in productivity would provide the fundamental corrective especially as (in the following three to five years) large-scale projects in natural gas, cement, and other products came into production. This would enable the government to turn its attention to "fundamental adjustments" regarding agriculture, rural incomes, urban employment, income distribution, and setting up a social security system.[55]

In 1978 the economic expansion reached full tilt with real GDP rising 11.7 percent. Exports rose 17 percent, spearheaded by a growing diversification of products and markets. Tapioca pellets, an animal feed with a growing market in the European Economic Community (EEC), became the largest single foreign exchange earner. Light manufactures (especially transistors, textiles, gems, and canned pineapple) were emerging as important exchange earners. Further diversification came from tourism (up over 60 percent in one year) and from remittances of Thais working in the Middle East. Imports also continued to rise as did the overall deficit. While both the Bank of Thailand and the government did move in the direction of less expansionary policies, the measures undertaken were not strong enough to have a significant dampening effect. The government's cash deficit registered a small increase, and state enterprise capital expenditures (which were on a track relatively independent from fiscal policy) rose as these organizations increased their foreign borrowing. Commercial bank credit to the private sector increased nearly 30 percent in 1978 despite several actions of the central bank to raise interest rates and reduce liquidity. The bank itself, somewhat inconsistently, continued to expand credit availability to the sectors it defined as "high priority," namely, agriculture (including both agribusiness and poorer and landless farmers), small exporters, and small manufactures.

The weaknesses in the armory of instruments for short-run countercycle management were especially evident in the bank's frustration over the continued rise in domestic prices. Measured against the price stability objective (which was one of the two primary policy objectives of the Bank of Thailand, the other being defense of the exchange rate without resort to quantitative restrictions on payments or capital movements), the aggregate demand management measures had proved inadequate. The consumer price index rose 8.4 percent in 1978 compared with 7.2 percent in 1977, indicating a continuing acceleration of the inflation. Apart from the failure of the aggregate demand measures, several steps the government had undertaken for other policy purposes had undermined the price stabilization effort, such as increases in import duties designed to reduce import demand, and an inflation adjustment in civil service salaries. Finally, international reserves actually rose 6 percent, thanks to drawings from the IMF and increasing inflows from foreign loans.

The bank concluded that the external imbalances would persist for another two or three years. In the meantime, the government must press ahead, but more vigorously, with the package of measures in hand. These included speeding up the large (capacity enhancing) investment projects, promoting exports, reducing nonessential and nonproductive imports, energy conservation, and so on. For the first time, the bank identified the investment-savings gap as the heart of the imbalances problems. It noted that Thailand's savings rate was considerably lower than that of South Korea, Taiwan, and other ASEAN countries, and called for a variety of measures to reduce public and private consumption. Continuing its expanded interest in nonfinancial development matters, the bank expressed agreement with government price-support programs (for rice, soybeans, groundnuts, cotton, and rubber) and with the government's intention to set up buffer stocks to supplement the minimum price efforts, and offered to cooperate in the financial aspects of implementing these policies.[56]

All optimism that Thailand could simply grow its way out of the structural imbalances emerging in the late 1970s vanished during 1979. In three OPEC increases between December 1978 and November 1979, world oil prices rose 80 percent. Thailand depended on petroleum imports for 90 percent of its commercial energy. The cost of petroleum product imports rose from 3.5 percent of GDP in 1978 to 5.7 percent in 1980. Unlike the situation following the (proportionately much greater, i.e., fourfold) increase in oil prices in 1973–74, the second round was followed by severe contractionary policies in the OECD countries and no commodity price boom. It became clear that the mildly countercyclical measures were quite inadequate against the pressures that were generating domestic inflation and rapidly growing imports, both now reinforced by the impact of the energy cost increases. Early in 1980, in its annual report for the preceding year, the central bank introduced for the first time the notion that the growth of the economy would have to be deliberately slowed in order to tackle fundamental structural adjustment.

Even in the normally pacifying public language of the Bank of Thailand, the 1979 report makes striking reading and contains strong explicit criticism of government inattention. It warns that the balance-of-payments problem will be more severe in 1980 "unless appropriate remedial actions are taken in good time." The capital goods imports scheduled for the natural gas and cement projects have now become part of the short-run import problem (rather than merely part of the medium-term import-substitution solution). The government still has no strategy for energy conservation or development of alternative sources despite the wide acceptance in the country that such measures are urgent needs. The government must exercise more effective control over foreign borrowing. At bottom, the bank ascribes the whole spectrum of economic instabilities that have been developing since 1973 to structural, rather than marginal, problems. Although the bank for several years had been recommending stronger government action in several policy areas, including energy, taxation, and the investment-savings balance, it was now saying that these problems were no longer transitional or in the realm of fine-tuning, but called for major policy overhaul.

In the areas of economic management under the responsibility of the Bank of Thailand, 1979 was also a particularly difficult year. The stock exchange experienced a sharp speculative rise beginning in late 1978, followed by a collapse of 40 percent in market capitalization in early 1979. The collapse was triggered by the failure (partly due to fraud) of one large finance company. Numerous other finance companies were affected by these developments, necessitating bank intervention in the interest of restoring public confidence. The bank also had to cope with sharp swings in the liquidity of the banking system, due in part to the extraordinarily high runup in world interest rates and some resulting bouts of capital flight. These episodes underscored the inflexibility of the authorities given to the Bank of Thailand (under the then-existing usury legislation) for upward adjustment of domestic interest rates.

Orthodoxy in Partial Eclipse

Looking at the 1970s in perspective, it is clear that the credit expansion introduced by the central bank in mid-1974 and the fiscal pump-priming of the government's budget for the 1975 fiscal year (starting in October 1974) mark the beginning of a period in which economic management departed substantially from the norms of the past. Fiscal and monetary conservatism were replaced by aggressive expansion of domestic demand. Limited government intervention in the operations of domestic markets (rice the major exception) gave way to widening intervention in the financial system, in the industrial incentive structure, and in the markets for individual commodities. Distributive objectives, relatively neglected in the 1960s, were now linked with growth in an unbalanced domination over stability. The economic management system was unraveling at a time when the demands on economic policy were becoming increasingly complex.

The apparent overall success of these policies can be seen in the summary measures of growth shown in Table 5.2. Despite two years of crops poor enough to contract the agriculture sector, the growth of the economy as a whole was exceptionally strong. Weather was still a powerful and recurrently unfavorable factor, and the land frontier was closing. Nevertheless, agriculture still contributed substantially to growth over a several-year period, thanks to the spread of irrigated double-cropping and the expanding cultivation (primarily for export) of higher value crops (see Table 5.3).

The rapid growth of the manufacturing sector was also fueled by export demand. Manufactured exports as a proportion of total manufacturing output rose from 14 percent in 1975 to 20 percent in 1980.[57] Textiles and garments were

Table 5.3

Crop Diversification (average percent of value-added)

	1960–65	1966–70	1971–75	1976–79
Rice[a]	49.1	47.6	44.0	36.7
Rubber	7.5	5.3	4.6	5.7
Maize	3.3	5.9	7.3	5.0
Sugarcane	2.0	2.2	5.2	5.7
Cassava	2.8	2.4	4.1	7.4
Other	35.1	36.5	34.8	39.5
Total crops value-added	100.0[b]	100.0[b]	100.0	100.0

Source: NESDB.

a. Paddy
b. Errors of addition due to rounding.

a leading category of exports even at a time of rising import restrictions in developed country markets. Thailand's ability to gain increased market shares was based on low-wage cost competitiveness and the fact that the country was starting from a very low base.[58] Many of the leading export growth products were labor-intensive, with wages comprising a large fraction of total production costs.[59] It was also noteworthy that much of the output of these growth commodities was produced by the small end of the manufacturing sector, that is, by so-called small and medium enterprises (SMEs) defined as those employing 50 workers or less. The BOI's focus on larger scale enterprises left the SME sector substantially excluded from the promotional benefit system. The low-end enterprises were also excluded from access to the Industrial Finance Corporation of Thailand's (IFCT) long-term project financing and were more dependent on high-cost credit from the informal financial sector. Nevertheless, the SMEs were reported to be more export-oriented than large enterprises employing 200 or more workers (SMEs exported 27 percent of their sales compared with 15 percent for the latter). In the late 1970s, the SMEs were recorded as producing 27 percent of manufacturing value-added.[60]

The advance of the manufacturing sector over agriculture as the leading source of economic growth is mirrored in the changing composition of Thai exports (Table 5.1). Agricultural exports have contributed a declining share since 1960. The shift in relative contribution was especially marked in the 1970s when agriculture fell from 68 percent to 47 percent of the value of merchandise exports while manufacturing rose from a 6 percent share to 32 percent. (Comparisons of relative output and export shares in Thailand can be affected strongly by swings in the terms of trade, mainly influenced [apart from oil] by movements of key agricultural commodity prices. Thus agricultural export volume grew slower than value in the first half of the 1970s and faster in the second half.)

Many of the elements of the economic surge of this period were solidly based, reflecting fundamental economic strengths. The crude birth rate fell from an estimated average of 40.6 per thousand in 1965–69 to 30.1 in 1980. Annual population growth is estimated to have fallen from 3.1 percent in 1970 to 2.2 percent in 1980. The economic infrastructure and supporting institutional capacities were in significant measure well developed to support the economy's growth.[61] The market positions of the growth exports continued to expand over the 1980s. Thailand's touristic attractions were gaining wide recognition. Investor confidence recovered quickly from the destabilizing political events of 1976. The financial system was expanding rapidly, both in the geographic spread of bank branches and in the growth of finance companies providing forms of credit not offered by the commercial banks. The stock exchange was set up in 1975 to give the corporate sector institutionalized access to private savings. Various indices of the state of human capital and welfare showed significant progress. The first studies of the course of poverty over time suggested that the incidence had been halved between 1962–63 and 1975–76, from 57 percent to 31 percent. Real GDP nearly doubled from 1970 to 1980. Although the population had grown from 36.4 million in 1970 to 46.7 million in 1980, per capita GDP had risen a little over 50 percent.

In contrast with these strengths, a number of sectoral and aggregate weaknesses were also developing in the later 1970s, aggravated by the very strength of the economic expansion. Between 1977 and 1980 the share of central government expenditures in total expenditures on GDP rose from 17.0 to 18.9 percent. Domestic resource mobilization did not keep pace with this expansion. Central government revenue remained virtually flat as a share of GDP, averaging 15.2 percent. In contrast to the 1960s, when taxes were rising as a percent of GDP, the elasticity of the tax structure as a whole (partly due to problems in administration and enforcement) was around unity during the 1970s. (By middle-income country standards Thailand's tax effort was below average.)[62] Both revenues and expenditures were adversely affected by the government's policy of allowing domestic energy prices to rise much slower than the increases in the costs of imported crude and refined products. By 1978 domestic fuel product prices had only been doubled compared with 1970, while import prices had risen sixfold. To prevent domestic prices from fully reflecting import costs, the government at various times lowered fuel taxes and maintained refinery margins through provision of subsidies. Although the government began in 1979 a more vigorous policy of narrowing these price gaps, the delay in passing energy cost increases through to the domestic economy saddled the Prem government with a serious adjustment problem (both as to energy price levels and as to the distorted relationships among different fuels) and added substantially to the fiscal deficit.[63]

As a result, the government's current account surplus as a percentage of GDP fell between 1977 and 1980, from an average of 2.4 percent in 1970–77 to 0.6 percent in 1980. The government's overall deficit, after taking into account investment expenditures, rose from an average of 2.0 percent of GDP in 1970–77 to 4.3 percent in 1980. The fiscal performance of the state enterprises also deteriorated in this same period. As state enterprise investment shot up, the proportion financed by internal savings (operating surpluses) fell in an uneven decline (which had begun in 1972) from an average of 58 percent in 1966–71 to a low of 17 percent in 1980. When the government and state enterprise deficits are taken together (as shown in Table 5.4), the total public-sector deficit climbed from an average of 3.2 percent of GDP in 1970–77 to 8.0 percent in 1980.[64]

The central government and the state enterprises turned increasingly to debt financing to meet their growing deficit requirements. In earlier periods, the public sector had been able to draw on net private savings large enough to limit public recourse to external borrowing to relatively low levels. In the latter half of the 1970s net private savings fell to a zero average, as the monetary authorities allowed real domestic interest rates to turn sharply negative by holding nominal rates well below the rate of inflation. For the economy as a whole, the upshot was a sharp rise in the overall resource deficit. These relationships are shown in summary form in Table 5.5. When the net outflows of factor income (including the rising external interest payments) are added to complete the accounting of the external balances, the table shows an increase in the average current account deficit from 1.6 percent of GDP in 1970–74 to 5.0 percent in 1975–79. In 1980 the current account deficit peaked at 8.6 percent. The acceleration in foreign borrowing (external debt increased 40 percent in 1978 and 47 percent in both 1979 and 1980) took place during a period of unusually high international interest rates. The external debt service ratio (payments on public and private debt with a maturity longer than one year, as a proportion of exports) rose from an average of 10.3 percent in 1974–77 to 15.8 percent in 1978, diminishing slightly to 14.4 percent in 1979–80.

In a nutshell, one sees an economy where government has opted for high growth, confident that the macroeconomic imbalance consequences will be readily manageable. The government embarked on an expansionary monetary and fiscal course, along with increasing price, interest rate, and credit interventions and controls. Private investment and domestic demand responded vigorously, and the economy moved to a fast growth track. Within a very short period of time, demand growth caused an acceleration in imports that outpaced export earnings. The excess of imports over exports reflected the basic weakness of the monetary and fiscal policies affecting public and private savings; the result was an excess of total absorption that had to be financed through a substantial rise in external debt. The expansionary path was supported, at least up to 1978, by analysts of the World Bank, and external financing was facilitated by both the World Bank's proffering of higher levels of lending and by the creditworthiness

Table 5.4

Public Sector Summary Accounts (percent of GDP)

Fiscal years	1970–77	1977	1978	1979	1980
General Government					
Current surplus	2.4	1.9	1.8	1.0	0.6
(Revenue)	(15.1)	(14.7)	(15.2)	(15.0)	(15.7)
(Expenditure)	(12.7)	(12.8)	(13.4)	(14.0)	(15.1)
Investment	4.4	4.6	4.5	4.0	4.9
Deficit	−2.0	−2.7	−2.8	−3.0	−4.3
State Enterprises					
Operating surplus	0.7	0.9	1.0	0.9	0.8
Investment	1.9	2.5	3.5	2.9	4.4
Deficit	−1.2	−1.6	−2.5	−2.1	−3.7
Total Public Sector					
Current surplus	3.1	2.8	2.7	1.8	1.3
Investment	6.3	7.1	8.1	6.9	9.3
Deficit	−3.2	−4.3	−5.4	−5.1	−8.0

Source: World Bank, *Managing Public Resources,* table 4.3.

that enabled Thailand to borrow commercially at favorable interest rates. Given the lack of tight control by the monetary authorities over state enterprise borrowing, and of a systematic financial planning framework, the resulting imbalances were able to develop rapidly before the authorities gained a full appreciation of the emerging economic position and its implications. The traditional antipathy toward inflation and external deficits appeared to inform monetary and fiscal policy. But in fact the government essentially tinkered with the problems, applying selected price controls against the former, and selected import controls against the latter, rather than addressing the underlying problem of excess demand.

Finally, before proceeding to examine the policy reforms of the Prem period and the ensuing economic record of the most recent decade, I will attempt to put the 1970s into perspective. Just how seriously did economic policy, in its actual implementation, pull the economy away from the orthodoxy of the past? How serious were the distortions and imbalances that resulted from the combination of intervention and expansionism?

I have already noted the factors that limited the extent to which import-substitution protectionism determined the actual course of investment and the underlying competitiveness of the emerging industrial sector. I will now bring

Table 5.5

Savings-Investment Balances (percent of GDP)

	Averages		
	1965–69	1970–74	1975–79
Public savings	4.5	3.1	2.4
Public investment	7.2	6.1	7.0
Net	−2.7	−3.0	−4.6
Private savings	17.3	19.3	19.1
Private investment	14.7	15.9	19.1
Net	2.6	3.4	0.0
Total savings	22.5	22.3	21.5
Total investment	23.6	22.0	26.1
Overall balance	−1.1	0.3	−4.6
Current account deficit	−1.3	−1.6	−5.0

Source: Bank of Thailand.

together from the economic literature on Thailand the conclusions of a number of policy studies, including some that compare the Thai experience in this period with other countries that are broadly comparable. It is important to note, as an aside, that even the most determined supporters of minimal government intervention into the workings of the market recognize the merits of government actions of certain kinds. For example, governments set and maintain ground rules (e.g., respecting private property, the legal status of contracts, the procedures for dispute resolution) that are essential for the predictability and confidence on which an efficient economic system rests. Markets are also subject to "failures" that warrant intervention, such as the distortions arising from the exercise of monopoly power, or macroeconomic outcomes the polity views as socially undesirable, such as wide inequalities in wealth and income. Nevertheless, there is an enormous weight of theory and post-war experience that supports the overall superiority of market to nonmarket economic systems, and that presumes that economies are likely to grow faster, and resource allocation and use is likely to be more efficient, the fewer the distortions introduced into the operations of markets by the actions of government.

For a number of years the World Bank has used complex techniques for calculating measures of distortion of prices for individual (or classes of) products and production inputs, and of distortions of financial prices (interest and exchange rates), to arrive at "shadow prices" for use in the economic analysis of projects. The shadow price represents the price that would prevail domestically if international prices were allowed to affect local ones undisturbed by government interventions. The degree of adjustment required to compensate for these distortions is conveniently represented by a conversion factor, the ratio of the shadow price to the domestic price. In the absence of any distortion, the shadow and domestic prices would be the same, and the value of the ratio would 1.0. Values less than 1.0 indicate that domestic prices are being distorted above market levels, with lower values indicating greater distortion.

In a nine-country comparison of two conversion factors, one for wage rates (a labor cost factor, or LCF) and one for traded goods (or standard conversion factor, SCF), Thailand had the least distortion of the group (Table 5.6). Sadiq Ahmed developed conversion factors for eight products and average prices for 1976–1980. In addition to the SCF and LCF, these included consumption, intermediate and capital goods, construction, electricity, transportation, and rice. All the values were below 1.0 except for rice (1.11), for which domestic prices were suppressed below border prices by the premium and export taxes. Capital goods showed the highest rate of distortion (0.84), consumption goods the least (0.95). However, when the consumption goods category was disaggregated to separate imported and exported consumption goods, the import factor (0.77) turned out (not surprisingly, given what has been seen of the tariff structure) to reflect the highest distortion of any category. If imported vehicles are excluded from capital goods, the distortion in this category drops (the conversion factor rises to 0.87). Under further product disaggregation, the two product groups with highest outlying distortion were textiles and textile products (0.75) and motor vehicles and parts (0.73).[65]

Ahmed concludes that the general level of price distortion in Thailand is low, because most of the values calculated are close to 1.0, and that the price structure is relatively undistorted because there is "relatively little dispersion" among the conversion factors. He attributes these results to (a) efficiency and competitiveness in the domestic marketing systems; (b) limited government use of quantitative restrictions on trade, the most important being cassava export quotas mandated by the feed import quota system of the EEC, and the ban on imports of fully assembled cars or those components designated for domestic sourcing; (c) the minor nature of distortions arising from other nonprice interventions; (d) retail price controls that were very limited in number and duration; (e) net export subsidies that were nil; (f) the efficient labor market and market-determined wages.

In another comparative study the World Bank ranked thirty-one developing countries according to the degree of distortion in 1970–80 caused by government policies affecting the exchange rate, manufacturing protection, agricultural pro-

Table 5.6

Shadow Price Conversion Factors

Country	SCF	LCF
Turkey (1980)	0.59	0.39
Morocco (1979)	0.60	0.51
Ghana (1975)	0.75	NA
Tanzania (1974)	0.77	0.45
Ivory Coast (1977)	0.83	0.83
Malaysia (1976)	0.85	0.42
Colombia (1979)	0.90	0.58
Philippines (1976)	0.91	NA
Thailand (1981)	0.92	0.92

Source: Ahmed, *Shadow Prices,* table 4.

SCF = standard conversion factor
LCF = labor cost factor

tection or taxation, the prices of labor and capital, electric power rates, and general inflation. With "low" distortion for all the factors except for manufacturing protection (medium) and power rates (high), Thailand was ranked second lowest distorting country of the group.[66]

Another World Bank staff study in 1990 ranked forty-eight developing countries according to degree of overall price distortion. Thailand was the sixth lowest of the group, while the degree of dispersal of price distortions from the overall country index was narrower than Thailand's in only three other countries.[67] Giovannini and de Melo measured distortions in interest and exchange rates in twenty-five developing countries; the distortions are measured by implicit tax revenue arising from the difference (the saving to government) between foreign and domestic costs of borrowing that results from "a combination of international capital controls and requirements for domestic financial institutions (often public) to hold government debt at less than market interest rates."[68] The data cover varying periods between 1972 and 1987 for the different countries, 1976 and 1986 in the case of Thailand. As measured by the average difference between foreign and (artificially repressed) domestic costs of borrowing by the government, Thailand had the third lowest implicit tax rate.

I have touched on the central bank's administrative and allocative interventions (prudential and ownership issues aside) in the financial sector. These have included interest rate ceilings, interest rate differentials for preferred borrowers and economic purposes, directed credit allocation in favor of agriculture and rural areas, and "moral suasion" to get commercial banks to reduce their lending for activities undergoing speculative or excessive expansion. I noted the sharp increase in Bank of Thailand intervention in the second half of the 1970s. In a comparative study of ten developing countries, Hanson and Neal observed that even in the relatively interventionist period (1975–80) the Thai monetary authorities were constrained in their scope for preventing increases in the domestic interest rates in line with increases in corresponding international rates. As with many aspects of economic management, the objective of maintaining the stability of the baht dominated other considerations and, in effect, set limits on the room for actions that could have destabilizing results for the currency. Excessively repressed deposit rates would induce savers to shift funds outside the country, reducing exchange reserves. Interest ceilings that created a large spread between rates in Bangkok and elsewhere could force the banks to lower deposit rates and place their own funds outside. Borrowers could also profit from arbitrage rather than investing domestically. These movements have been possible because the financial system has been open, de facto, and the baht freely convertible, despite the existence of a formal control system on capital movements (substantially eliminated finally in 1990). While there were differences among the various rates (general loans, overdrafts, discounted bills, etc.), real interest rates generally were repressed to significantly negative values only during the two inflation episodes of the 1970s. Compared with other developing countries, the Thai performance was "quite respectable, as measured by the frequency of positive real rates." Taking into account interest rate management and the Bank of Thailand's credit allocation policies, they conclude that "[i]n comparison to most developing countries, Thailand's financial sector is quite advanced, open and deep. Market forces, in particular, international market forces, govern the financial sector to a much greater degree than most countries at Thailand's income level. Correspondingly, the Thai government plays a relatively less important role, although it is far from a passive player."[69]

The bank's regulations for raising the allocation of formal credit to the agriculture sector, and the below-market interest rates charged by the BAAC (and paid by the BAAC on the deposits it receives from the commercial banks unable to meet the Bank of Thailand's agricultural lending targets) are major interventions that have attracted criticism from analysts (but not from Thai politicians). The sources of potential distortion include (a) discriminatory costs imposed on the smaller commercial banks that have few branches outside the Bangkok urban region; (b) cross-subsidy costs imposed on nonagricultural borrowers to compensate banks for the higher costs of agricultural loans (which are constrained by the interest ceilings); (c) denial of access to higher-risk borrowers who would be willing to pay above-ceiling rates and who are thereby forced into the informal credit market with its much higher rates; (d) the opportunity costs of funds the commercial banks are required to deposit with BAAC, which they could presumably lend to alternative, higher-return users. Finally there is the direct lending by the Bank of Thailand itself for agricultural uses, through its discount windows, at subsidized rates. The effort to fine-tune central bank assistance to the agriculture sector actually reached what may have been its peak in 1985–89 during the governorship of Kamchorn Sathirakul, a period in which technocratic opinion inside the bank and elsewhere was shifting in favor of reduced intervention of this type.

The shift of resources into the BAAC has been of major benefit to the agricultural sector. Although the BAAC has been open to occasional political criticism for not lending significant amounts to the poorest strata of small farmers, it has successfully resisted pressures to expose itself to decapitalization from delinquent loans and has developed techniques that enabled it to replace a large volume of high-interest informal rural credit. In 1990 formal institutional credit was estimated to be reaching nearly 60 percent of agricultural families, compared with 15–20 percent prior to 1975. About 80 percent of the agricultural borrowers utilizing institutional credit in 1990 were being served by the BAAC.[70]

The presumed distortions arising from the agricultural intermediation policies of the Bank of Thailand and BAAC were examined recently by a World Bank mission. Although their study concludes that the administered allocations are unnecessary and generate economic costs, they found these costs either small or uncertain.[71] In another recent study of Thai financial policy, Easterly and Honohan reach similar conclusions:

> While there [are] a number of selective credit measures favoring agriculture, agribusiness and commodity exports, these are either relatively small in their scope, or tend to be only partially enforced, and so only distort the allocation of credit slightly. A number of quasi-fiscal requirements add about 1.5 percentage points to gross banking spreads. . . . The interest rate ceilings on bank loans have probably lowered the cost for some non-prime borrowers, but may have increased rates for others and excluded some high-risk borrowers.[72]

Finally, unlike the experience of many developing countries, the Thai authorities, even in the 1970s, made relatively little effort to shape the size or content of industrial investment through the manipulation of credit allocation.[73]

In sum, I believe it would be a fair characterization to describe the economic management policies of the later 1970s as unusually dirigist and expansionist compared with prior (and subsequent) Thai practice, but only moderately interventionist and unbalanced by international (developing country) standards. What emerges as the most striking feature of the subsequent turnaround was the speed with which the reversal of economic policy was adopted and the fact that the reversal was undertaken as a preventive act. It was recognized that continued pursuit of the policies of the late 1970s might well bring the economy to a position—of indebtedness, damage to creditworthiness, fiscal and monetary indiscipline, price distortions, and resource misallocations—that would be far more difficult and damaging than would be the pain of anticipatory medicine. In the event, the Prem government's implementation of structural adjustment was not free of delays, flaws, and even major challenges. But the pursuit of structural adjustment, especially to bring the basic macroeconomic relationships back into balance, was not challenged in principle.

6

STRUCTURAL ADJUSTMENT, QUASI-DEMOCRACY, AND THE BIRTH OF THE FIFTH TIGER

Prime Minister Prem Tinsulanonda governed continuously for eight years (March 1980–July 1988), the longest parliamentary premiership in Thai history. During this period there were two unsuccessful military coups, three elections, and five cabinets. The two coups were conducted by members of an army faction known as the Young Turks. This faction had emerged in the late 1970s as a group of power brokers, throwing their support in succession to General Kriangsak, in the coup that unhorsed Thanin in 1977, and then to General Prem against Kriangsak in 1980. In April 1981 they mounted the so-called April Fool's Coup against the Prem government. Although the coup was ostensibly aimed at parliament, and not Prem, the prime minister opposed the Young Turks, left Bangkok (where the group had seized commanding positions), and fled to Korat where he marshaled the support of military units that had not joined the coup. The coup collapsed within four days, primarily because the king and queen had demonstrated strong support for Prem. Some of the same Young Turk officers (having been pardoned and reinstated in typical Thai leniency toward establishment sedition) attempted another coup in September 1985, this time with the support of (now retired) Kriangsak. This last attempt had almost no military support, no army units of consequence. It collapsed in a day (causing a handful of civilian casualties), apparently a victim of ineptitude and double-crossing, and again clearly a bid that lacked any palace support.

These coup attempts were only the most dramatic manifestations of the factional power struggles that have been endemic in the Thai army. The factions consisted mainly of officers who had formed personal bonds as classmates in the same graduating classes in the military academy. Although it is customary for

Thai coup makers to issue justifying statements that include references to economic mismanagement on the part of the targeted government, the economic significance of these coups, and of the factional power struggles within the army, has in fact been slight. One of the main criticisms leveled against military officers who mount coups, or who threaten to resort to forcible overthrow, is that such actions would undermine the country's foreign image and reduce the inflow of foreign capital.

As described by a recent study of the Thai military, the ideas of the Young Turks concerning national problems had no clear framework. Their political thought was "simple, unstructured, and pragmatic," their solutions "seemingly conventional." They believed national security was threatened by corruption, government inefficiency, nepotism in the bureaucracy, and rural poverty. They sought incorruptible leadership, nondemocratic if necessary. A rival group of older officers, known as the Democratic Soldiers, supported democratization in Thailand, but also defined their objectives in generalities that "raised more questions than answers." In fact, the various military factions share a common outlook that is essentially nonideological. They lay claim to a preeminent responsibility, and extra-constitutional authority, to bring about "true democracy and safeguard the nation's interests," and to provide "appropriate" leadership for these purposes if necessary. In their unsuccessful efforts in 1983 to sustain the power of the Thai Senate, in which the military held a large bloc of appointed positions, the Democratic Soldiers argued that "the present constitution, the party, and electoral laws were all instruments of robbery and exploitation . . . chains enslaving the people." Through the 1980s, the vague populism discussed previously in connection with the role of the banking sector remained inchoate. Military thinking on political reform was "still in a very formative stage, incoherent, and inconsistent."[1] Despite their radical-sounding pronouncements, no military group has formulated a program of alternative economic policies, or been seriously involved in economic matters (regarding which they usually defer to the technocrats), except for an occasional venture into rural development or expression of personal opinion on a topical issue. Perhaps most important as an influence on military thinking, especially in the wake of the disappearance of the insurgency, is the fact that military incomes are supplemented by a miscellany of relationships with commercial activities that are thriving within the existing economic system.

Of much greater significance was the reestablishment of the old alliance between the bureaucracy, especially the economic policy technocrats, and the senior military. While I shall focus here on the formal government policy machinery, it is important to note that some of the leading military personalities have made it a practice to gather a group of technocrats to serve, in informal personal capacity, as informants and advisers on civil affairs. In the early years of the decade, the technocrats were flourishing again, working in a policy process that was reshaped and strengthened.

The objectives of economic policy became sharply focused and more vigorously pursued under Prem. Although the cohesion of his successive cabinets was often threatened by the rivalries among the coalition parties, and between individuals and factions within some of the parties, Prem was able to sustain painful adjustment policies through some of the most difficult years the economy had faced in the postwar period. In mid-decade, the economy experienced its slowest growth since 1957–58 and an episode of severe business distress and shakeout. While politicians and technocrats alike accepted the necessity of imposing rigid fiscal discipline on the public sector, the struggle over the composition of public investment within these constraints revealed that the technocratic community was now as deeply divided over development objectives as it was unified over the overall framework of conservative macroeconomic policies and the broad limits on the economic role of the state.

As Prem's political position weakened in 1987–88, macroeconomic health was finally restored and Thailand entered a period of double-digit growth. Domestic and foreign economists, business circles, and financial journals began to hail Thailand as the fifth "Asian Tiger" (the first four tigers being South Korea, Taiwan, Hong Kong, and Singapore) or the next newly industrializing country (NIC). Following elections in July 1988, Prem (who had never actually stood for elections but had been given the premiership by the major parties, themselves unable to produce a member of parliament or other alternative personage acceptable to the military) announced that he would not accept the premiership again. Chatichai Choonhavan was chosen instead from among the parliamentarians, ushering in the first all-civilian, all-elected cabinet in Thai history. The move from Prem to Chatichai, from an unelected military figure with a cabinet containing several key unelected ministers, to a full-scale parliamentary-based government, appeared to substantiate the growing conviction that Thailand's "quasi-democracy" was indeed moving toward the real thing. The conventional wisdom about the course of Thai political development appeared increasingly valid—that the military coup was becoming more unacceptable, more unlikely, with each passing month of parliamentary government.

The Chatichai administration began with an immediate move by several powerful ministers to cut the power of the bureaucracy. Motivated partly by the desire to remove the constraints the Prem policy process (especially the role played by NESDB) had imposed on the economic ambitions of leading businessmen-cum-politicians, the advent of full parliamentary rule suddenly broke the hold of the technocrats on economic policy formation. The central issue of economic policy then became whether parliamentary democracy would be able to sustain the economic policy framework, or whether the unhorsing of the technocrats would open the way to narrow pursuit of business interests, of the particular politicians and their clients, at the expense of the public interest and the economy as a whole.

Looking over the decade as a whole, one can see a striking replay of the theme of change amid continuity that has figured so strongly in Thai historiography and anthropology. Depending on whether one took a broad, long view or concentrated on current imperfections, it was possible to reach two apparently inconsistent judgments about the state of both political and socioeconomic affairs, one stressing stability and progress, the other stressing inadequate resolution of structural problems. The two views were well summarized by Neher, writing in early 1988 about half a year before the end of Prem's administration. In the "conventional" view,

> the capacity of the government to cope is high, the future is bright for all segments of the nation, democracy is flourishing (at least compared to other developing nations), and the remarkable stability of the kingdom is constant. Those agreeing with this interpretation note the consistent and rapid economic growth, the manageable foreign debt, the end of communist insurgency, and the extraordinary fact that no successful military coup d'etat has taken place in ten years. . . .
>
> A contrary view has emerged among some Thai scholars and politicians who are raising fundamental questions about the Thai political system. . . . King Bhumibol Adulyadej pronounced that Thailand's brand of democracy was not working well because it was patterned after foreign models. He said that what Thailand really needs is a government that could make a concerted effort to help people. . . . [General Chavalit, army commander-in-chief] was particularly scathing in his criticism of political parties, which he referred to as business concerns run by merchants. . . .
>
> [Chai-anan] wrote that Thai political parties have not gone far in performing even the minimum functions of mobilizing support from people at the grass roots. He criticized parties as reflecting elite self-interests. . . .
>
> Thus, on the one hand, politics in Thailand is viewed as successful, pragmatic, balanced among the principal forces, stable and capable of coping with the needs of the people. On the other hand, Thai politics is portrayed as self serving, corrupt, cumbersome, inappropriate for the kingdom, and ultimately unable to solve the fundamental problems of poverty, too rapid urbanization, and inequitable economic development. Both positions can easily be substantiated by a selective use of the evidence.[2]

For the two and a half years of the Chatichai government (July 1988– February 1991), the combination of extraordinarily rapid economic growth and of increasingly blatant factional scrapping over the spoils accessible to certain cabinet portfolios in particular lent further credence to both these interpretations. On the one hand, the basic economic policy framework was undisturbed, Thailand was perhaps the fastest growing economy in the world, the whole labor market was starting to tighten and raise real wages, and foreign investment was flooding in. The persistent ASEAN effort to force Vietnamese withdrawal from Cambodia finally paid off (other factors were also at work, of course, such as the decline of the cold war and the reduction of Soviet economic aid to Vietnam).

Thailand emerged, in the eyes of many Thai political and military (and academic) figures, as the dominant subregional power, now in position to conduct a more active and independent foreign policy that would forge new relationships between Thailand and its economically lagging neighbors—Laos, Cambodia, Vietnam, and Burma (Myanmar). Unlike the earlier episode of Thai regional activism at the start of World War II, during which the government seized upon opportunities created by Japan's military penetration of Southeast Asia, the geopolitical concepts being floated in the late 1980s had no irredentist content and were largely economic in nature. They envisaged mutual economic relationships replacing the conflicts of the past, with Thailand's role as a center of communications, finance, trade, and technical assistance flowing naturally from the preeminent economic strength the country now enjoyed, in stark contrast to the economic shambles of the Indochinese states, which were now ready to move away from years of command mismanagement.

On the other hand, the fractious Chatichai cabinet appeared increasingly fixed on extracting personal and factional benefits from political office. The prime minister and some of his aides and cabinet colleagues became caught up in disputes and incidents involving leading military figures, which had little if any policy substance beyond questions (not unimportant in themselves) of prestige and political weight. Between inattention to substantive issues other than those of direct interest to coalition members, the widely discussed corruption (believed to be of unprecedented and unseemly magnitudes) involved in the selection of companies to carry out some very large investment projects, and the prime minister's efforts to exploit the factional rivalries within the military, the Chatichai government lost the support of the press and the middle class. When the coup that was "increasingly unlikely" finally occurred in February 1991, it appeared to have wide public support. Kukrit Pramoj said the military had "legitimate reasons" for carrying out a coup. The general reaction was to view the overthrow as a "new-style" coup, acceptable if the military kept its promise (as it did, with qualifications) to turn the government over to civilians. At a meeting within hours of the coup, "senior technocrats" expressed the commonly heard ambivalence of the middle class: "While some were disappointed the government had not been removed democratically, the bureaucrats were pleased to be rid of interference by self-interested politicians within Chatichai's administration."[3]

Apparently there was wide agreement (not universal, of course) that the parliamentary system in Thailand was still sufficiently flawed to justify the resort to *force majeur* as the only way out of an impasse that stood in the way of further democratic progress.

This was not a simple return to authoritarian rule, another period of military stewardship in which power would be held by the military to "protect" the nation from "disorder." Within days the coup perpetrators announced their intention of holding elections to restore parliamentary government under a suitably reconfigured constitution. In the interim, the country would be governed by an appointed cabinet. The cabinet that was formed, under Anand Panyarachun (a retired ambassador then in his second career as a senior business executive and president of the Association of Thai Industries), gathered together the most professional and experienced technocratic group Thailand had ever had to fill in ministerial positions. In what was intended to be a period no longer than fourteen months, the technocratic-military alliance, uneasy as it might be on one issue or another, was restored for a third time with the technocrats now having more thoroughgoing control of economic policy than they had possessed at any previous time in the postwar era.

The new cabinet came into office making it clear that they intended to take full advantage of their authority to complete the unfinished agenda of structural reforms, some of which dated back to the adjustment policy agenda of the early Prem years. The legitimacy of this government, in the eyes of the public so it appeared, and in the eyes of the technocratic members, rested on the belief in Thailand and abroad that Anand was an independent who had surrounded himself with like-minded professionals, that this cabinet would do everything it could to ensure the restoration of parliamentary rule, and that in the meantime the country would be actively governed by ministers whose competence and probity compared very favorably with that of the discredited members of the usurped government.

These rapid turns of the wheel appeared to be further demonstrations of the underlying pragmatism of the Thai polity and of its ability to return to its central long-run policy tendencies, at least as far as economic affairs are concerned. It remains to be seen what political configuration emerges, if and when Thailand will evolve a stable system for orderly transfer of power, and what implications that will have for the role of the bureaucracy and the inclusion of contending economic interests in the future formulation of economic policy.

In sum, it was still possible to argue plausibly that Thailand was marked by outstanding economic performance and policy stability, and that the society was continuing to grope toward the rule of law and parliament; or, that economic development had failed to produce substantial interest group aggregations and stable institutional arrangements for orderly granting and removing of power by democratic process, thereby leaving the military as the self-appointed power brokers, a role still not fundamentally challenged by the middle class, the bureaucracy, or the passive farmers and nonagricultural workers.

A New Technocratic Policy Structure

Thailand was one of many developing countries hard hit by the second oil shock, in 1979, and by the subsequent stagflation of the industrial economies, which entailed extraordinary gyrations in world interest rates and exchange rates. Although the Kriangsak government had begun to cope with the economic difficulties by raising fuel prices and government revenues, and by exercising some monetary restraint, these measures were inadequate in the face of the pressures from outside and from the domestic overheating that had been building since 1975. Under the Prem government the pace of policy reform quickened, leading up to the formulation of a full-fledged structural adjustment program that formed the macroeconomic core of the fifth plan (1981–86) which came into effect in October 1981. The program was spelled out in its fullest details under the two so-called structural adjustment loans (SAL I and SAL II) the government obtained from the World Bank, the first in March 1982 for $150 million and the second in April 1983 for $175.5 million, and in "standby" agreements with the IMF in 1981, 1983, and 1985.

It took over a year for the Prem government to develop the coherence of adjustment policy reflected in the fifth plan and the World Bank and IMF understandings. In the prime minister's first coalition cabinet (so-called Prem I), economic policy authority was held by Boonchu Rojanasatien, deputy prime minister for economic affairs. Trained as an accountant, Boonchu had risen to become executive vice president of the Bangkok Bank before entering politics with the Social Action party (SAP). In 1975 he was minister of finance in the Kukrit government, then returned to the Bangkok Bank as its president. Boonchu had an expansionist predisposition to economic management, most vividly expressed in his proposals for developing a "Thai Inc." analogue to the close government–business relationship expressed in the notion of "Japan Inc."[4]

While adjustment measures were put into effect under Prem I (lifting of price controls, reduction of some import duties, additional fuel price increases, etc.), and while the economic agencies were designing the program that would be promulgated in the fifth plan, fiscal policy in 1980 continued on an expansionary track. Boonchu's term as economic czar was terminated suddenly in March 1981 when the SAP resigned from the government in a sharp dispute with its coalition partner, the Chart Thai party, over alleged SAP improprieties in connection with the purchase of oil from Saudi Arabia. The annual report of the Bank of Thailand for 1980 described the macroeconomic outcome of Prem I as follows:

> The immediate problem now confronting the Thai economy is economic instability that continues from last year. Of major concern are the problems of budget deficit, high cost of living and the rising trend in expenditures on consumption and investment. As government revenue maintained its normal trend, the resultant cash deficit surpassed previous records, imposing a greater financing burden on the financial system. This problem is expected to recur this year [i.e., FY 1981, which began in October 1980] on an aggravated scale, in light of high budgetary appropriations and indications that government revenue may fall short of budgetary targets.
>
> The severe inflation of 1980 will persist into this year. . . . The current account deficit . . . will continue further in line with price increases for oil and

other imports. A sizable growth in import volume is also forecast for 1981 in light of the domestic economic revival.[5]

The bank noted that the Prem II government was "now urgently mapping out corrective measures aimed at accelerating revenue collection and cutting down expenditure."

It will be recalled that in 1975 the central bank had lamented the disarray into which the economic policy machinery had fallen. I also noted that during the 1970s the country's social science and policy research capabilities were continuing to strengthen even as the interest of government in mobilizing these intellectual resources declined. Under the Prem II government there was a vigorous effort to correct these shortcomings. The architects of the reform recognized that the processes through which the adjustment policies would be developed and then stewarded were as important as the policies themselves. The fall of the Kriangsak government in February 1980 had resulted, to a considerable extent, from the severe public reaction to both the scope of the electricity, oil, and gas price increases Kriangsak announced and the fact that the increases were imposed with no prior public or parliamentary discussion.[6] If anything, as will be seen, the exposure and porosity of economic decision making in the 1980s would open the Thai policy processes to criticism for vacillation and indecision.

Rather than replacing Boonchu with another czar, Prem oversaw the creation of a system of committees and collegiate relationships in which the decision processes were once again regularized, professional, and more widely consultative. As the policy system evolved, the lines between policy and implementation blurred. The apex committees and agencies took on the dual functions of brokering and defining policy and of monitoring and encouraging the implementation activities of the relevant line organizations, even trouble-shooting as policies ran into day-to-day snags.

At the apex of the system was the Council of Economic Ministers, a committee of the cabinet, designed to serve as a more streamlined decision-making body. Thus, while the Prem II and Prem III cabinets comprised forty and forty-one members, respectively, the Council of Economic Ministers numbered around twenty. Interministerial committees were established to oversee key areas of economic and social policy, including a National Economic Policy Steering Committee to oversee the structural adjustment program, and the Eastern Seaboard Development Committee. The Export Development and the Debt Policy committees were revitalized. Building on the earlier unsuccessful attempt by Boonchu to set up a government–business coordinating mechanism, Prem II established a Joint Public Private Sector Consultative Committee (JPPCC) to formalize systematic dialogue between government officials and the apex commercial and industrial organizations of the private sector. Over the course of the Prem years various ad hoc groups were set up to promote specific areas of economic policy and activity that were accorded high priority under the changing economic circumstances, such as the planning of the elaborate celebrations in 1987–88 in honor of His Majesty's sixtieth birthday and of the expansion of tourism generated by the Visit Thailand Year in 1987, and the investment-promotion presentations in industrial countries, with the prime minister heading the delegations.

NESDB played a key role as coordinator and analytic center for this policy formation and monitoring structure. As secretariat for the Council of Economic Ministers and for the Eastern Seaboard (ESB), state enterprise and rural development committees, and the JPPCC, the planning agency set the agendas and screened or prepared the issues papers to ensure that committee meetings were able to deal with issues in an orderly and informed manner. While NESDB had only a consultative role regarding monetary, financial system, taxation, and other policy areas under the jurisdiction of the Ministry of Finance and the Bank of Thailand (its involvement in these areas depended more on informal relationships among staff and between agency seniors than on formal responsibilities or committee memberships), the planning agency was the one organization where the largest array of economic and social development issues came together. Between these secretarial functions, the responsibility for drafting the national development plans, and NESDB's role as coordinator of the preparation work for projects submitted for World Bank, Japanese, and other external loan financing, NESDB was in position to become a stronger center of policy influence and power than at any previous time in its history.

While the efficacy of this policy system flowed to a considerable extent from its structure, the authority that accrued to the bureaucrats who administered the system was derivative, based on the role played by the prime minister. The position of Snoh Unakul as secretary-general of NESDB, and as senior civil servant directing its secretarial functions, was enhanced by his frequent participation in professional and public forums to discuss development issues and to explain the objectives of the fifth and sixth development plans. Although there were now large numbers of participants in development policy formation, and many academic and business economists with wide reputations, Snoh came to symbolize the revival of technocratic power by virtue of his position, seniority, and international recognition.

At bottom, however, the authority of the secretary-general derived from the prime minister's frequent demonstrations of confidence in the secretary-general's views. It was Prem's practice in the weekly meeting of the full cabinet to turn to the secretary-general (who, like all the civil servants present, sat against the wall rather than at the cabinet table) for his opinion and then, more often than not, agree with it and adopt it as the cabinet's conclusion. The derivative nature of NESDB's authority became evident immediately after Prem's retirement. Some members of the Chatichai cabinet called for Snoh's removal within days of taking office. Although Chatichai rebuffed their efforts,

Snoh retired to the private sector a few months later. Major decisions tended to be made privately among the ministers, greatly reducing NESDB's role in, and access to, the political levels of decision making. In the Chatichai cabinet meetings, decisions on large projects were often made peremptorily without benefit of NESDB review and without advanced circulation of documentation.

Despite the prominence of NESDB during the Prem years and the strengthening of rationalized decision making compared with the 1970s, the system was still prone to vacillation. Absent a cabinet economic czar, it often took months of negotiation and maneuvering before final decisions were made. Consensus over economic policies was relatively easy to attain among the technocrats, the advisers to the prime minister (especially the economic adviser Virabongsa Ramangkura), and the nonparty members of the cabinet (Finance Minister Sommai Huntrakul, Meechai Ruchupan and Sulee Mahasantana, ministers without portfolio, and Suthee Singhasaneh, deputy finance minister, then finance minister in 1986, suceeding Sommai). But consensus on public-sector capital projects was often difficult to reach. The political parties and their respective cabinet members voiced few ideas and showed little interest in general economic policy matters outside their own portfolios. However, they did show intense interest in capital projects involving large-scale contracts, equipment procurement, exclusive licenses, and so on. As political rivals became associated with competing business interests attempting to capture these projects, the decision process appeared to lose coherence. Since foreign aid and foreign contractors were often involved, foreign embassies also intervened, bringing the Ministry of Foreign Affairs into decisions normally outside its jurisdiction.

The weakness of the Prem cabinet in its handling of these projects, and the prime minister's reluctance to impose firm decisions (opening him up to criticism for irresolution), stemmed from the fact that no single party was able to obtain a parliamentary majority from the Thai electorate.[7] To maintain unity in the fragile coalition cabinets, opponents of any project sponsored by a rival party (or faction of a party) would avoid up-or-down decision confrontations, preferring to delay or to give equivocal support, hoping to submerge a project in confusion or frustration. Open opposition to a rival's project would invite retaliation against one's own projects. Sometimes projects that appeared dubious from the start would, nonetheless, appear to get serious consideration over many months and in many cabinet meetings, and would go through formal bidding and negotiations processes, before the cabinet found itself in a position where there was no alternative for the opponents but formal rejection.[8] The prime minister was similarly constrained from forcing confrontations that might shatter the coalition.

By the mid-1980s, despite the improvements in the economic policy formation process installed by the Prem government, and despite the relative clarity in policy objectives that had been restored by the promulgation of the fifth plan, the remaining weaknesses in cabinet decision making were sparking renewed debate on the structural weaknesses of the political system as a whole. Some suggested that the cabinet needed to restore a position equivalent to Boonchu's. This role might be accorded to the minister of finance, or alternatively to the secretary-general of an NESDB given ministerial status. Others pointed to the intellectual weakness of the political parties and their devotion to narrow self-interest; the parties were in effect abdicating the role of representing the public interest, or wide interest groups, thereby shutting the general public out of the decision processes altogether. The decision processes were further insulated from public involvement by the general lack of transparency in government operations, and the absence of hearings or other mechanisms for public consultation.[9] It is worth noting that the fifth and sixth development plans were prepared in a process that included many open seminars and drew heavily on input from the academic community. Although these activities were much more consultative than the processes of preparing the earlier plans, the content of the plans was not subject to parliamentary review or any other process that could be construed as eliciting consultation with the population at large.

The most important of these extended decision processes concerned the Eastern Seaboard program, which will be discussed below. At this point I would make only two further observations regarding the decision process problem. First, the process might be viewed paradoxically as an efficient, perhaps even socially optimizing, method of dealing with large-scale resource allocation decisions. In retrospect, the outcome in virtually every instance was the defeat (or fading away) of bad projects. White elephants, technologically inappropriate, excessively scaled projects, often entailing magnified costs and corrupt under-the-table payments, have generally been scuttled through these processes. While the losers in these cases may have keenly regretted the lost opportunities, they could not fault the system for not having granted them ample scope to promote their interests or their viewpoint. Second, it was not a problem peculiar to the Prem administration. The succeeding Chatichai cabinet had similar project rivalries and vacillation.[10] Lacking the disinterested leadership of a General Prem or strong technical and analytic inputs from the bureaucracy, the Chatichai cabinet reached decisions that in some cases would have yielded projects with apparent substantial defects or scope for abuses. The coup against the Chatichai government threw these projects back into the hands of the technocratic interim cabinet for review and renegotiation.

The Fifth Plan (1981–86)

The fifth plan was a milestone document. It was prepared with the benefit of wide bureaucratic, academic, and professional sounding. In contrast to the limited relevance of the third and fourth plans, the fifth set out a statement of the country's conditions and principal problems, as understood by the revitalized technocratic leadership, and defined the policy priorities that were to be taken seriously by an administration with a restored sense of purpose, and by a prime minister who relied heavily on professionalism and who would provide the continuity the economic policies needed to achieve their expected results. To create a framework within which annual programs would remain consistent with policy objectives, even as circumstances might change, the document was put forward as a "policy plan" with directions that would be translated into ministerial operational plans. For all the qualifications I will note that delayed or blunted the implementation of the policies and programs laid out in the fifth plan, there can be no doubt that it had the most pervasive impact on the public sector and on the economy as a whole of all Thailand's postwar development plans.

The fifth plan reflects the increasing complexity of the Thai economy and the opportunity the Prem government was giving to the bureaucracy once again to range over the entire process of socioeconomic change the country was experiencing, to analyze the major problems of the time as they saw them, to define the near-term policies and programs for the public sector, and to give guidance and respect to the role of the business community. As is often the case in the prosecution of public policy, the consistency among a diverse set of objectives turns out to be more apparent than real, especially when the available resources fall short and choices must be made among the objectives. The very scope of the plan, and its accommodation of the salient concerns of bureaucratic groups who had divergent notions of social priorities, laid the basis for conflict as the plan became overtaken by events.

To elucidate the course of policy under the fifth plan, it is convenient to group its objectives under two headings, economic equity and social and rural development, and growth and structural adjustment. The related concerns over distribution and social stability in rural areas carried over from the 1970s and were addressed in more systematic and effective programs that drew on the experience of the previous decade. Social services were to be greatly expanded in the provinces, especially the primary health care system. In an effort to tackle the poverty problem directly, the plan identified 246 districts and subdistricts that contained the bulk of the population living below the poverty line and that would be targeted for special assistance. The population program would attempt to reduce the growth rate from the 2.1 percent reached by the end of the fourth plan (1981) to 1.5 percent by 1986. The plan reiterated the need to correct the urban-rural and other structural imbalances that had been criticized in previous plans. It was the first plan, however, to address (albeit briefly) the question of economic concentration and to state that it was government policy to dilute the ownership of the nation's financial institutions and large industries.

Considerable progress was made in the social program areas during the fifth plan period. The prime minister himself gave every appearance of being more interested in rural development than in other aspects of economic policy and programs where his personal attention was often focused by virtue of the cabinet's agenda and his role as chairman of the JPPCC, ESB, and other committees. Nevertheless, the distributional and rural development aspects of the plan were overshadowed first by the severity of the macroeconomic adjustment process, and second, as the economy accelerated once again, by the preoccupation with graduation to NIC status. The suggestions in the fifth plan for measures to reduce the concentration of wealth were not acted upon, nor were they repeated in the sixth plan, which is silent altogether on the subject of concentration of wealth apart from the traditional spatial and sectoral (rural-urban) perspectives.

To convey in a nutshell the growth and economic restructuring objectives of the plan, Snoh in his public addresses described the plan's strategy as "Growth Plus Four," that is, growth with stabilization, diversification, decentralization, and cooperation. The "target" for overall growth was 6.6 percent, soon informally lowered to 5 or 6 percent, per annum. While overall growth targets had little operational significance, they were important as a symbol that the government expected the economy to grow more slowly in this period than it had in all previous plan periods. This lowering of sights was a realistic representation of the domestic and international constraints at the time, and a sign that the focus of policy would be on structural problems and on the restoration of economic stability.

As far as stabilization (or structural adjustment, in World Bank lingo) was concerned, "One of the major reasons for accepting a lower target was our keen awareness of the need to maintain a sound financial position. This awareness somehow seems to be in line with the long tradition of prudence and conservatism in the Thai financial and economic management system." Diversification of the country's economic structure was already serving as a stabilizing factor against the effects of external fluctuations. Services were turning out to be an economic sector in which Thailand had strong comparative advantages. Thailand was now the largest food exporter among the developing countries, the fifth largest food exporter in the world. Industrial diversification into intermediate goods was beginning, and the gas-based petrochemical investment program would create new industrial capabilities. All of these diversified lines would be advanced under the plan. Diversification might mean that Thailand would miss the "crest" of booms that other countries with more focused and managed investment programs might enjoy, "but in the slump the Thai economy will continue to float and will not sink the way some other countries do either." In other words, some growth might be deliberately foregone in the interests of stability and some reduction of risk exposure.

Decentralization referred to the oft-cited need to deflect growth and industrial investment that was otherwise concentrating excessively in the greater Bangkok area. While the plan contained provisions for improving the infrastructure of regional cities and smaller provincial towns, the focus of decentralization was on the Eastern Seaboard as a "strong alternative to Bangkok as an urban-industrial location," the only location that offered a realistic potentiality for such a complex some distance from the capital.

Growth with cooperation referred to the JPPCC, the workable Thai version of "Japan Inc.":

> Prior to the Fifth Plan period, the atmosphere of public/private sector relationships was not good. There was a prevailing sense of distrust, and elements of arrogance on both sides. The public sector regarded the private sector as selfish entrepreneurs and thinking only of their personal profits with little sense of social responsibility. The private sector, on the other hand, suspected Government officials of being extremely inefficient, corrupt and bureaucratic. . . . The two points of view were rarely reconciled as there was no formal mechanism to bring about more fruitful dialogues.[11]

The JPPCC was set up as a mechanism to help overcome the simplistic prejudices on both sides. The private sector was represented by the Thai Chamber of Commerce, the Thai Bankers Association, and the Association of Thai Industries. Occasional meetings were held with the foreign chambers of commerce. The JPPCC met monthly, chaired by the prime minister. For the first time, the private sector had a forum with the most senior officials of the government in which the business community could give its views on everything from policy to red tape affecting their interests. It was understood that the JPPCC was not to be used for lobbying related to the interests of any individual company. Only matters of general public or business interest would be discussed. The meetings were open to the press, and the government side was under pressure, between the press and the prime minister, to respond. Though cynics pointed to the public relations benefits for the prime minister and for the business personalities involved, the process did result in many changes, in administrative practices in particular, that improved the business climate. Once the JPPCC was firmly established, the participants decided to extend the model into the provinces, beginning with the major regional cities. Eventually, the majority of the changwats organized local joint committees in which the provincial business communities could meet regularly with the governor and his staff to discuss business problems and local development. The institutional future of these arrangements remains to be seen. Not grounded in law, their continuity depends on the personalities and politics of government–business relations.

To present its views in well-argued fashion, the private sector side of the JPPCC had to develop a professional capability for open policy discussion. It was hoped that this experience, and the whole arrangement based on organizations, issues, and transparency, rather than inside dealings and the pursuit of individual commercial advantage, would promote the "maturation" of the Thai business sector and contribute to the reduction of particularistic or corrupt relationships between business and officialdom. The advent of the

Chatichai business cabinet, however, rendered the JPPCC dormant. The policy and regulatory framework that is the natural subject of interest to the private sector across the board receded into the background as the rivalries among a handful of individual businessmen and groups, then having captured the very mechanisms designed to regulate them and dispense public resources, took center stage.[12] The further evolution of institutionalized relationships between government and business organizations was put on hold as the individual businessmen/politicians and government leadership became one and the same.

Structural Adjustment

Structural adjustment is a loose term of art. It came into common usage in the early 1980s to describe programs of broad macro- and microeconomic policy change among developing countries that would be assisted by World Bank loans. The structural adjustment loan (SAL) would be extended in conjunction with complementary assistance from the IMF. The SAL was a loan form that enabled the bank to address the borrower's general economic management. In contrast with the normal project-oriented lending of the bank, the SAL would provide "program" funds, that is, balance-of-payments support similar to the general import availability of drawings from the fund. While SAL funds would normally be disbursed in tranches over a twelve- to eighteen-month period, the World Bank generally expected that the adjustment process would take three to five years, during which it would provide financial and technical support.[13] The basic objective was to help reorient the borrower's economic policy framework in order to put long-term growth back onto a sustainable track. The world economic environment had become much less favorable for the developing countries in the 1970s, compared with the 1950s and 1960s, two decades of favorable world growth in which the developing countries overall (but with substantial variation among them) experienced rates of economic growth that outpaced the historic experience of the industrialized nations. The developing countries as a group had accumulated fiscal, monetary, investment, and other policies that had resulted in two fundamental problems that were threatening long-run growth prospects: (a) excess financial absorption, leading to unsustainable external debt burdens and domestic inflation, and (b) economic incentive systems that were creating production structures at once noncompetitive internationally and insufficiently flexible to adjust to the increasing rapidity of changing external economic conditions.

With the adjustment problems occupying center stage in the 1980s, a large literature has grown up that analyzes the differences between those developing countries where growth (and poverty alleviation and other dimensions of the growth process) has been severely reduced and adjustment has been an extended (and still incomplete) process, and those countries where the process has been successful and growth has revived. While it would not be relevant here to go into this literature at any length, I shall draw on it briefly below to help put the Thai experience into international perspective.

The Thai structural adjustment program was a comprehensive and ambitious attempt to restore economic stability, to reduce the distortions and inefficiencies that had accumulated during the 1970s, especially as a result of government policies, and to enhance the competitiveness and flexibility of an economy committed to a development pattern of interaction with the world economy. As summarized by the Bank of Thailand,

> Monetary and fiscal discipline would be strictly pursued through cuts in un-necessary expenditures, control of the money supply and credit expansion, mobilization of savings in both the government and private sectors; restructur-ing of the tax system, increased efficiency in tax collection and operations of government enterprises; stimulation of private savings through improved sta-bility and efficiency of the financial institutions as well as establishment of new financial institutions. In addition, higher overall productivity and higher export capacity would be achieved through economic restructuring to ensure more efficient resource allocation, reduced dependency on imported energy and raw materials.[14]

While it will be convenient to lay out the program as crystallized in the fifth plan and in the SALs and IMF "standbys," the adoption of structural adjustment measures—of the concept of a broad adjustment program—began in 1980, preceding these formal embodiments and understandings. In addition to the seminars mentioned above, and a number of research studies commissioned to explore alternatives where the optimal course of policy adjustment was not self-evident, the early measures taken included (a) liberalization of restrictions on agricultural commodity exports; (b) devaluation of the baht in May and September 1981, amounting to nearly 10 percent; (c) passage of export tax drawback legislation; (d) increases in energy prices; and (e) increases in government revenues and state enterprise tariffs.[15] The government then negotiated a two-year standby agreement with the IMF, beginning in June 1981. As is the usual practice in the adjustment programs of developing countries, the World Bank's loans were designed to facilitate long-run and structural changes, while the fund's resources were linked to very short-run fiscal and monetary adjustments aimed at stabilization and reduction of the country's external imbalances. Although a country's negotiations with the two institutions move on separate tracks, the content of the agreements must form a consistent macroeconomic program. The bank normally will not proceed if a fund agreement is called for but not successfully reached. Under the 1981 standby, the Thai government undertook to meet a number of fiscal, financial, and pricing targets. A shortfall in the revenue target for 1982 caused the government to exceed the standby's ceilings on the volume of credit extended to it by the central bank. Consequently the fund and the government renegotiated the short-term target framework in a new fourteen-month standby starting in November 1982.

The IMF resources available to Thailand were substantially larger than the funds provided by the SALs, a not unusual relationship. The 1981 standby provided a line of credit of Special Drawing Rights (SDR) 814 million ($936 million), of which Thailand drew SDR 345 million ($398 million) before the agreement was renegotiated. Thailand also drew funds from IMF's "compensatory financing" window (credits to help finance short-term losses of foreign exchange earnings due to cyclical declines in export earnings) that brought the country's total IMF drawings in 1981 to $610 million. The 1982–83 standby provided a line of SDR 271.5 million, all of which was drawn. The importance of the relationship with the IMF extends beyond the mere size of the resources the fund can make available. For a developing country like Thailand that has maintained a reputation for conservative monetary management and has been able to borrow freely in international capital markets, continuing policy endorsements by the fund are seen by the monetary authorities as important contributions to the country's credit-worthiness. While the World Bank SALs contained components that were relevant to the achievement of the standby quantitative targets, SALs do not have the direct relationship with the creditworthiness that goes with standing at the IMF. As will be seen below, the maintainance of Thailand's standing with the fund became a critical factor in the government's response to the most difficult economic policy challenges the Prem administration had to face, in 1985–86.

In a final point of comparison between the World Bank and IMF roles, it is interesting to note that the relationship with the IMF has always been given little public attention in Thailand compared with the World Bank's relatively high profile. To some extent this is a natural result of the much wider scope of bank activities in terms of sectors and the numbers of public-sector agencies involved as borrowers or implementing organizations. Furthermore, in most years the relationship with the IMF was confined to annual consultations (and occasional technical assistance), which were given no publicity. Little publicity was accorded to the occasional drawings from the fund or to the negotiation and existence of standby agreements. Even within the small circle of economic technocrats, the IMF negotiations were restricted to the Ministry of Finance and the central bank. Few officials in other agencies, let alone the general public, were privy to the substance of the agreements. As a consequence of this low profile and the absence of conflict between the government and the IMF, the fund never became a scapegoat for the Prem administration when it undertook unpopular economic measures, or a target of attack for the government's critics and political opponents.

The timing of the early policy adjustment actions was noteworthy. Since the government had embarked with some vigor on the adjustment program prior to its formalization in the first SAL, the World Bank acceded to the government's request that it dispense with its normal practice of imposing "conditionality," that is, prior initiation of reforms before any loan funds are released, and/or the release of funds over a period of time in "tranches," or segments, conditioned upon the government meeting a series of timed performance objectives. The government argued that conditioning would expose the authorities to attack for having submitted to World Bank interventionist pressure. The bank saw benefits to both sides in this avoidance of conditionality: "The prior initiation of these reforms reduced the vulnerability of the governments concerned (Thailand and Turkey) to opposition charges of yielding under duress to Bank imposed prescriptions, and for the Bank it demonstrated not only commitment to the reform process, but also the capacity to carry it out. Countries which placed the greatest reliance on commitments to future actions ... experienced greater delays in implementation."[16]

In developing the SAL program, the World Bank was replaying for the first time the broad role it undertook when it diagnosed the development problems of Thailand in 1957–58. While there were no resident missions comparable to the Ellsworth team, a number of short-term missions wrote a series of reports, starting in 1980, that examined the economy from various perspectives and fed into the work on the SALs themselves. The conclusions of these reports and the development of the SAL content drew on much greater Thai professional input than was the case with the Ellsworth report.

The program was divided into five policy areas—agriculture, industry, energy, fiscal, and institutional development. (Since SAL II carried forward the content of SAL I, the two may conveniently be treated as a single program.) In agriculture, recognizing that the closing of the land frontier was at hand and that further export and income growth in this sector would now depend on productivity, the program focused on farmer incentives and land tenure. Objectives included a land-use reclassification program, accelerated issuance of certificates establishing land-use rights, reductions in export taxes on major agricultural commodities, elimination of rice-holding requirements by exporters, and other rationalizations of rice distribution and pricing policies. The industrial policy objectives aimed at export promotion, and the investment incentive structure included tariff reform, restructuring reforms in eight specific subsectors (electrical goods, automobiles, textiles, etc.), reforms of the Board of Investment incentive structure, export promotion measures, and reevaluation of the large-scale industrial projects on the drawing boards (e.g., associated with the Eastern Seaboard) in which the government was playing a significant promotional role.

The energy-sector objectives included the rationalization of the structure of energy product prices and the promotion of conservation. The fiscal policy measures were especially ambitious, including tax increases and reforms; tax administration improvements; local taxation development; state enterprise tariff increases, efficiency reforms, and subsidy reductions; and development of an expenditure control program within the framework of an overall fiscal policy for the public sector. The institutional development program aimed to improve public-sector resource management efficiency and the government's policy analysis and implementation capabilities. Specifically, it was intended to strengthen the government's planning, budgeting, accounting, and auditing systems; develop a plan for civil service reform; and create a new, independent development research institute. In most of these areas the SALs provided for studies to clarify alternatives for further policy and program adjustments.

The government's implementation of the SAL and standby programs, and the movement of the macroeconomic indices toward the various targets, was monitored regularly by the economic authorities and recorded and evaluated as the programs evolved over the duration of the Prem administration. As noted, implementation of the adjustment program got off to a fast start. Most notable was the reduction in inflation, brought down from 20 percent in 1980 to 5 percent in 1981. Inflationary expectations appeared to have decreased quickly, presumably because the stabilizing policies of the government could be seen as a return to long-term monetary conservatism. The weakness of domestic investment caused imports to fall in 1982, resulting in a sharper contraction of the current account deficit (from 7.1 percent of GDP in 1981 to 3.2 percent in 1982) than had been planned.

It was clear, however, that the first SAL program had been overtaken by unfavorable external economic changes and that the macro framework of the adjustment process as outlined in the fifth plan would have to be stretched out. The major failure was the rise in the fiscal deficit to over 5 percent of GDP in 1982 compared with the target 2.5–3.0 percent. The deficit increase resulted from the very success in import and domestic demand restraint, which cut into the government's revenue base. This was one of the early indications that the sequencing and timing of the adjustment process contained inconsistencies and other problems of implementation not well understood at the outset. While the consensus of economic opinion, after nearly a decade of adjustment experience, on the policy objectives and content of structural programs is strong, few robust conclusions have been drawn about optimal sequencing.[17] The Thai case is interesting in this respect (as discussed below) because it turned out to be perhaps the most gradual example of successful adjustment in the 1980s. In sum, although the first-year outcomes were mixed and necessitated a revision in the quantitative program, the World Bank was satisfied that the initial progress (including the installation of the new policy apparatus) justified proceeding immediately with SAL II (again with immediate disbursement without tranching).

It was inevitable that a program containing so many elements would experience shortfalls and would be affected by unforeseeable external economic, and domestic political, circumstances. The external environment deteriorated again in mid-decade, then turned powerfully favorable in the late 1980s. The government's political strength and cohesion was highest during the Prem II and Prem III cabinets (January 1981–April 1983), then began to weaken (as did the policy consensus among the technocrats) during Prem IV (May 1983–August 1986). A better perspective on the course of Thai policy over the entire experience can be gained by examining the major components and their final outcomes.

Institutional Development

A case can be made that the most important contribution the loans made to the structural adjustment process in Thailand was in the area of institutional development rather than in the funds provided or the specific policy adjustments incorporated in the loan agreements. As noted, policy responses were being initiated from the start of the Prem government. The necessity for the measures under the SALs was well understood by the Thai authorities; they would likely have been initiated in any case. The overriding macroeconomic targets that were the standard stuff of IMF standbys would have driven much of the SAL policy content required to shift the trends of the major economic magnitudes, even if the World Bank had not been involved.

The major contribution of the SALs was to help the policy apparatus, chiefly NESDB, the Budget Bureau, and the Ministry of Finance, to organize the policy concerns within a rationalizing framework and to create the institutional arrangements for implementing and monitoring the program. The prestige of the bank, the technical contributions of bank staff, and the international vote of confidence that was implied in a satisfactory structural adjustment relationship with the bank strengthened the hands of the "core" agencies of the government that were shepherding the adjustment process. This strengthening applied only to the ability of the core agencies to gain the cooperation of other agencies within the bureaucracy and the concurrence of the cabinet. Outside the bureaucracy, public explanation that the government was undertaking a particular step under obligation to the World Bank would have weakened rather than strengthened the government's position. While some of the institutional studies and measures were not carried out, noteworthy provisions that were implemented included the establishment of the structural adjustment secretariat staffed by NESDB and the Ministry of Finance, and the creation in 1984 of the country's first independent policy research organization, the Thailand Development Research Institute.

Judged by the accomplishments of the refurbished policy apparatus during the structural adjustment period, the overall purposes of the refurbishment were achieved. However, when significant policy differences emerged within this apparatus, the speed and harmony of the decision process were (not surprisingly) impaired and the scope for lobbying by extra-bureaucratic forces greatly increased. Quite apart from the larger political problem in Thailand of how the competing interest groups of a now complex socioeconomic system were going to increase their effective participation in governmental decision making, it was clear that the "permanent" institutions of macroeconomic policy management were still not firmly established compared with their counterparts in, say, Japan, Britain, or the United States. At the political level (that is, the role of these institutions in relation to whatever political configuration happens to prevail in the parliament and cabinet), the sudden eclipse of NESDB, the central bank, and Prem's committee structures when the Chatichai government came to power, followed by the technocratic revival after Chatichai's fall, demonstrated again the susceptibility of these bureaucratic institutions to the transience at the level of the political institutions.

Even if the basic interface between the policy apparatus and the political level were finally fixed, however, the viability of the policy apparatus is still threatened by other problems. The very success of the long-run technocratic policy of building up the private sector has weakened the bureaucracy by drawing away some of the best talent. The salary differentials between government and the private sector have become substantial at all levels of skill and experience. In addition to the private sector's financial advantage, government has lost the monopoly it once had on prestige and international exposure. While the private sector's competitive advantages are not total (e.g., the loose concepts of conflict of interest in Thailand give wide scope to bureaucrats to engage in business activities on the side), they have drawn middle- and senior-level professionals out of the core agencies, especially NESDB and the Ministry of Finance. The Bank of Thailand is better positioned to resist brain drain but has also been affected. At various times over its history, NESDB has had to rebuild its capacity by resorting to staff training programs (largely graduate training in economics) financed with assistance from external aid agencies. In short, the institutional refurbishing of the policy agencies overseeing the structural adjustment process succeeded in its short-term objectives, but the long-term institutional arrangements remain fluid, dependent on transient political conditions and on the personal strengths and leadership qualities of the key managers.

When the World Bank's evaluators reviewed the results of the SALs as of 1986, they looked at the agencies and processes that had been addressed, not at the overall effectiveness of the policy apparatus. In this narrower framework, the evaluation concluded that the institutional results were mixed, at best. To some extent this was because the bank had unrealistic expectations on the extent of institutional change they would be able to facilitate within the short time frame of the SALs. In some areas (e.g., civil service reform) the studies required to lay out proposed changes were still incomplete when the SAL relationship terminated. Some consultant recommendations were rejected as unrealistic. More fundamental, however, was the bank's expectation that the SAL would be an effective instrument for reforming some of the traditional problems of policy formulation and interministerial coordination that have long roots in Thai bureaucratic history and in the government's legislative foundations.

It will be recalled that the Ellsworth mission had given considerable attention to the institutional arrangements and capacities for development policy formation in the late 1950s. After a twenty-year lapse, the bank returned to this subject in 1979. A development management mission reviewed the policy scene that year and prepared a paper that laid the basis for the SALs' institutional content. Apparently, Thailand was the only country for which the bank had ever prepared such a paper, and the resulting emphasis on institutional development in the Thai SALs was unusual.[18]

It is unlikely that the bank's relatively deep involvement in institutional development in Thailand reflects a deliberate choice by its senior management. Nevertheless, it is ironic that the bank (Asia regional) management concerned with Thailand saw greater need for World Bank work on institutional reform there, as a "prerequisite to continued expansion and poverty alleviation," than did bank management concerned with any other developing country, despite the fact that Thailand's bureaucratic institutions had presided over one of the strongest long-term growth performances among all the bank's member countries.

By setting unrealistic goals respecting the speed with which reforms (respecting program budgeting, accounting, investment programming, project appraisal procedures, performance auditing, etc.) would be designed and implemented, including policy and management reforms in bureaucratic entities beyond the core agencies (i.e., in entities concerned with agriculture, industry, and energy), the SALs' institutional program, when judged by these particulars, headed for almost inevitable "mixed results." The mixed results conclusion refers both to the technical assistance activities provided by the bank in each of the specific institutional areas and to the implementation efforts of the Thai government. Regarding the bank's own activities, this disappointment should be seen in the context of the bank's own recognition that technical assistance for institutional development has been perhaps the weakest area of the World Bank's operations in most countries.[19] The bank's Evaluation Division ultimately concluded that the institutional development components of SALs in all countries achieved limited results, that institutional development takes much longer than envisaged in the SALs, and that the structural adjustment loan did not turn out to be an instrument well suited to institutional reform and any associated technical assistance.[20]

Agriculture

The looseness of the term "structural adjustment" is illustrated by the agricultural components of the Thai SAL. Since the basic objective of structural adjustment has been to increase an economy's flexibility and adaptability, in order to sustain growth in the face of adverse changes, virtually any source of rigidity or growth inhibition might be a pertinent SAL target in any given situation. Relevant factors could include such things as population and environmental pollution, long-run determinants of an economy's scope for adjustment compared with factors such as trade or exchange rate policy that have more direct and immediate impact on fiscal and balance-of-payment deficits.[21] The agricultural marketing and pricing objectives of the SAL fell into the category of factors likely to have immediate effects on production and export flexibility. The duties and premiums that for over three decades reduced farmgate (and domestic retail) rice prices, and the returns to rice production, compared with most other agricultural commodities, were to be eliminated. Duties and restrictions on a few other agricultural commodities were also to be reduced or eliminated. Some of these objectives were achieved quickly (e.g., elimination of the rubber cess and of the rice price support program; authorization of private slaughterhouses for beef and hog products intended primarily for export) and represented important liberalization of policies that had long distorted the incentive structure and/or marketing systems for the commodities involved.

The elimination of the rice export duties and of the premium had to await the arrival of a period of low rice prices in late 1985 and early 1986, when removal of these taxes would raise farmgate prices while consumer prices were in a trough. The delay in accomplishing removal of these long-contested levies has been a source of frustration to the technocrats who wanted to take advantage of the structural adjustment momentum to eliminate these burdens on the rice farmers. While the premium was reduced to zero, the authority to impose the premium remained on the books. When the zero premium was finally achieved, there remained some apprehension that the decision would be undone in the next cyclical rise in prices. As it turned out, the policy was not tested for the next year and a half, during which domestic rice prices moved within a narrow range. Prices then shot up in late 1987 and early 1988. Average retail rice prices in Bangkok in 1988 were around 50 percent above the year before and rose another 10 percent in 1989. There was no reaction among Bangkok consumers. After generating more policy debate, and more economic analysis, than any other issue for some decades, the premium that had been justified as essential for protecting rice consumers disappeared without their apparent concern. The explanation, as Ammar has pointed out, probably lies in the declining importance of (non-glutinous) rice in the Thai diet. He notes that domestic rice consumption fell by as much as 20 percent between 1976–78 and 1984–86. Rice undoubtedly remains the core of the Thai diet but has shrunk as a proportion of food expenditures.[22]

The land-use measures under the SAL attempted to tackle complex issues of classification and tenure that could be addressed only over relatively long periods of time and that would have much less direct effect on production. The SAL focused on lands designated as forest under the full ownership or legal jurisdiction of the government (either the Royal Forestry Department or the Land Development Department). These so-called reserved or prereserved areas occupy about half of the country's total land area. As of 1985, around 44 million rai, or 32 percent of the "forest" area had, in fact, been cleared and settled illegally by an estimated one million farmers.[23] Lacking legal tenure, these farmers could not use their holdings as collateral for institutional credit and were not eligible for many agricultural services. It was assumed that a program to legalize the status of these holdings would make a substantial contribution toward raising the level of technology, input use, and productivity of the large land area involved.[24] The program called for an accelerated survey of the "forest" area, reclassification of the lands according to their appropriate future use, and legitimization of existing occupation.

Although the certification process was accelerated under the SAL, the land-use rights issued by the forestry department fell short of the level of ownership required to serve as collateral and consequently did not affect credit eligibility. While the limited research in Thailand on the relationship between tenure and farmer adoption of more productive cultivation methods (using higher levels of inputs purchased with institutional credit) appears to show that secure ownership does lead to higher productivity, research elsewhere suggests that the link between ownership and productivity is tenuous in the absence of access to credit.[25] In any case, the forestry department, which had jurisdiction over the forest reserve areas, did not have authority (or capacity) to provide the newly legitimized farmers with agricultural production services. The extension and other service divisions of the ministry would obtain access to these farmers, and the responsibility to provide services, if and when the newly titled areas were "degazetted," that is, reclassified as suitable for agriculture and removed from the category of "forest" domain. The de-gazetting process has proven to be much more difficult than the SAL program envisaged and stands as one illustration of the complexities of land policy that led the World Bank evaluation to the guarded conclusion that the SAL had been a "useful forum" for raising basic issues, had helped accelerate the "initial stages" of land reform, but would have indeterminable impact on agricultural production.[26]

Energy

Energy policy was an important component of the structural adjustment program. After a decade of inadequate efforts to increase national energy efficiency and develop domestic supplies, and after a huge rise in the energy import bill, the fifth plan launched a comprehensive effort aimed at production, conservation, and price reform. Unfortunately little was achieved in conservation. The subject was not accorded high priority by the Thai government until the late 1980s and was not effectively pursued by the World Bank under the SAL or other policy research efforts in Thailand in this sector. Conservation proved to be a subject of partial and minor interest to several departments and agencies and was not championed by NESDB or any other coordinating mechanism in position to generate bureaucratic or political focus. The low efficiency and large losses generated in the transport sector, especially by the traffic congestion in Bangkok, have been hostage to a wider set of urban development problems that continue to defy solution.

The government's record on energy pricing was considerably better at the start of the adjustment period but lagged in mid-decade when the government hesitated to adjust local fuel prices again after the 1984 devaluation. By 1988 however, domestic fuel price levels were in line with real import costs, the distortions in the structure of fuel prices had been largely removed, and a serious effort at electricity conservation began to be formulated.[27] The administrative arrangements for coordinating and formulating energy pricing had also been strengthened, especially with the establishment in 1986 of the National Energy Policy Office. Most important, for immediate effect on the balance of payments, substantial domestic energy sources had been developed (mainly natural gas and lignite, with further development of residual hydroelectric potential now blocked by local opposition to dam construction).

Export Promotion

Soon after the 1984 devaluation, manufacturing exports began to rise very rapidly, from an average of about 12 percent annually in 1982–84 to over 35 percent on average in 1985–87. By correcting the antiexport bias of the exchange rate (which developed as the baht, linked with the dollar, appreciated in the early 1980s in relation to the yen and European currencies), the devaluation was a major factor restoring the competitiveness of Thai exports. However, the extraordinary growth in manufacturing exports since 1985 cannot be attributed solely to the 1984 devaluation, even as reinforced by further de facto devaluation in 1985 as the (now trade-weighted) baht rode down with the depreciating dollar. The export promotion focus of the adjustment program reflected a recognition that besides a realistic exchange rate, a number of conditions affecting export performance needed to be strengthened. These conditions were mainly institutional in nature. It is not surprising that Thai policy makers focused on institutional impediments. As has been seen, the import-substituting industries (auto excepted) had developed behind an incentive structure that was only mildly protective by developing country standards. For most of the postwar era there had been relatively little antiexport bias in the exchange rate. The artificially depressed domestic price of rice over most of this period, subsidizing the basic wage-good, had enabled the manufacturing sector to enjoy a wage-bill even lower than the already low real level that would have prevailed if consumer rice prices had been market-determined. While the need to promote manufacturing exports had been recognized in the late 1960s, and repeatedly called for by the Bank of Thailand, the overall export performance and the position of the balance of payments and external reserves in most years was normally satisfactory (or readily correctable). Some of the early industrial sectors, especially textiles, had in fact shifted into exports under the old policy regime. In short, no previous Thai government had been under the kind of severe and sustained economic pressure that now brought the technocrats to the conclusion that a thoroughgoing shift to an export orientation could no longer be delayed, and that given the broad market orientation of past economic policy, an export orientation of institutional factors would be central to a successful policy.

At the firm level, an important constraint was believed to be restrictive provisions in agreements with foreign firms that prevented the Thai enterprises from exporting to third countries. The prevalence of export restrictions was analyzed by Mingsarn Santikarn in 1981, using information in agreements filed with the Bank of Thailand as of 1973. Mingsarn found that of 184 technology transfer agreements (not all were associated with joint ventures), nearly half had provisions restricting or prohibiting the Thai firm from exporting the products involved. The restrictions were most common in the electrical appliance, chemical, and petrochemical industries, but were also found among agreements covering manufacture of pharmaceuticals and other products.[28]

Mingsarn also presents evidence suggesting that joint ventures were more fixed on import-substitution than were wholly domestic ventures in the same industries, even at a time (1973) when the joint ventures and the domestic firms were operating below capacity.[29]

Prior to the advent of the Prem government, the export restrictions in technology and joint venture agreements were not seen as a problem serious enough to warrant government action. Although the government was aware of these covenants, it feared (especially in the aftermath of the Vietnam War) that a high-profile push to revoke the constraints would damage the general investment climate. However, bureaucratic concern over export growth combined with pressures from some industrial firms to persuade Prime Minister Prem to voice his government's dissatisfaction over these provisions, during a trip to Japan.[30] Following the wave of Japanese, Taiwanese, and other investment in the later 1980s seeking export "platforms," the restrictive covenant problem appears to have subsided.

More important than the question of firm-level restrictions, in the judgment of the policy technocrats, was the weakness of management orientation toward export marketing. With a few exceptions (such as textiles, preserved food products, and automotive parts), exports were a minor fraction of industry sales. Even among the exceptions the degree of export orientation among firms producing similar products varied substantially, reflecting differences in management objectives more than differences in product mix.[31]

The architects of structural adjustment concluded that the economic policy measures aimed at industrial cost-competitiveness would have to be complemented by the introduction of an export "campaign" mentality in the relevant agencies of the government, in place of the lip service that had characterized past efforts to promote industrial exports, and the relatively marginal incentives offered by the BOI and the central bank. Through its emphasis on exports in the JPPCC, the government elicited from the private sector a litany of administrative obstacles that made the processing of export paper a management nightmare. In one joint study conducted by the JPPCC, the entire run of administrative requirements for a commodity export, with steps numbering in the hundreds, was diagrammed in a printout several meters long. With NESDB providing a continuous drum-beating, the reduction of obstacles and red tape was complemented by the development of various government services designed to assist the private sector to penetrate foreign markets, improve product quality standards and packaging, participate in foreign trade fairs, and mount domestic trade fairs. Eligibility for BOI incentives was liberalized so that foreign investors proposing to produce largely for export would no longer be required to have any portion of such a new venture held by Thai partners.

The essential purpose of the policy reforms and programmatic measures bearing on Thailand's export performance was to increase the economic flexibility that had been the key to past export-led growth, and that appeared increasingly vital at a time when major export markets were threatened by rising protectionism. The purpose of the structural adjustments should be seen not in terms of the specific policy configurations as they were formulated to respond to the particular circumstances of the early 1980s, but rather as the reestablishment of flexible adjustment capability as the organizing principle of Thai economic philosophy.

The role of sheer flexibility in Thailand's export performance, taking agricultural commodities, manufactures, and all other components together, has been demonstrated neatly by Dapice and Flatters.[32] Seeking to explain in 1988 why Thai exports had grown so quickly over the past twenty years, they point out, first, that this growth shows no correlation with the general movement of income in Thailand's major export markets. While real GDP growth in the OECD countries fell from an average of 4.5 percent in 1966–73 to 2.8 percent in 1984–88, the volume of Thai exports experienced accelerating growth from 6.6 percent in 1966–73 to 16.1 percent in 1984–88. Second, changes in the geographic mix of Thai exports showed no correlation with relative income growth rates among the different markets. Third, while improvements in exchange rate competitiveness contributed to export growth, the relationship over time (between movements in the real exchange rate and growth in exports) was neither systematic nor strong enough to provide more than a partial explanation of export performance. They conclude that much of the explanation lies in the economy's ability over this period to increase its market shares as part of a structural shift involving the leading export-oriented economies of the region, Japan and the Asian NICs. As the rising domestic costs and shifting industrial structures changed the structure of comparative advantage of the latter countries, Thailand (and Malaysia and Indonesia) benefited by moving along behind, in what should be seen as a long-run pattern of change in regional economic relationships (the so-called flying geese pattern involving Japan, South Korea, Taiwan, Hong Kong, and Singapore, and the other ASEAN countries). The pace of this regional change accelerated dramatically after the yen revaluation and the subsequent shift of industrial location from Japan and the NICs to Thailand and other lower-cost economies of the region. In the end, Thailand's long-run export performance in manufactures must be attributed to the economic factors (such as trainable and low-cost labor) and policy framework (affecting especially foreign investment and the flexibility of domestic factors of production) that enabled the economy to articulate with these regional changes.

The Prem government's promotion of international tourism probably should be ranked as the single most important export policy success. Of all the economic programs undertaken in the 1980s, tourism promotion may well have been the most far-reaching in terms of social and environmental impact, and certainly one of the most important in terms of multiplier effects on such activities as construction, land transactions, public investment in airport facilities, and handicrafts and recreation services. Despite its economic importance (gross foreign exchange earnings from tourism in 1980 were estimated to be second only to rice), the development of Thailand's tourist industry was not a major subject in the fifth plan, and was ignored altogether in the SAL. The World Bank has given cursory attention to tourism in Thailand generally in its sectoral work and overall economic surveys. Insofar as the 1980s are concerned, this recurrent neglect presumably reflects the fact that the Bank ceased all lending for tourism in the late 1970s in response to criticism that tourism was an activity that facilitated colonial-type relationships between the rich visitors from the industrial countries and the poor citizens of the Third-World touristic enclaves.

Although arrivals and earnings were growing over 10 percent a year (except for a dip in 1983), the government decided in 1985 to make an extraordinary effort in the belief that tourism might be the one sector—in the midst of the general gloomy prospects in the mid-decade recession—that could generate large increases in foreign exchange earnings if properly promoted. The economic managers proceeded to organize the public- and private-sector components (the hotel industry, tourism companies, the Tourism Authority, Thai Airways, the Airport Authority, and so on), and to oversee the development of an integrated program of international promotion, and domestic investment in accommodations and services, built around the "Visit Thailand Year" of 1987. The result was a rise in tourism earnings from around $1 billion in 1985 to nearly $2 billion in 1987 and over $3 billion (roughly 15 percent of goods and services receipts) in 1988.[33]

Thailand's comparative advantages in tourism had already been demonstrated in the sector's growth during the 1970s. It is unlikely, however, that the explosive growth since 1987 would have occurred if it were not for the international promotional campaigns, or that the tourism infrastructure would have been able to handle the inrush if the industry had not been organized to prepare for such an eventuality.

Prior to this expansion, tourism had been fairly confined to Bangkok, a few southern seaboard beach areas, and the environs of Chiangmai. Short itineraries to a few provincial historic sites generated relatively little tourist expenditure in these localities. As the tourist density rose in the popular areas, the tourists and the industry sought out a wider range of locations, including previously untouched or lightly populated beaches, islands, and mountainous regions. In the competition for tourist business, many provinces that had been neglected by the industry began to revive and/or promote traditional local handicrafts, festivals, and historic archaeological sites. In some areas, conversion of farmland to golf courses catering to foreign clientele created conspicuous touristic enclaves.

Despite the rapid spread of tourism, its major contribution to the country's foreign exchange earnings and thus to the objectives of the structural adjustment program, and its multiplier effects on employment and income through all the allied services, the industry remains surprisingly unstudied and its economic impact not well understood. The problems attributed wholly or in part to tourism's rapid growth, by contrast, have probably received wider media coverage and been subject to more heated debate than have the diseconomies generated by economic activity in any other sector, with the possible exception of deforestation. Given the prominence of prostitution, environmental degradation, and the perception of deleterious cultural impact among the problems associated with tourism, it is not surprising that the few serious studies have been more anthropological than economic.[34] I shall return to these issues below.

Three Frustrations

In some important areas, the adjustment objectives were achieved only partially, or totally frustrated, due to a combination of adverse external economic circumstances and weakening government resolve. The three outstanding cases were tariff reform, industrial restructuring, and state enterprise privatization.

Between the rate changes made from time to time by the Ministry of Finance for revenue purposes, the ad hoc concessions granted by the Tariff Commission, and the protectionist concessions granted by the BOI, the import tariff schedule had developed into a jungle of rates lacking any rational economic structure. NESDB proposed that the Tariff Commission prepare a comprehensive reform program, arguing that an ad hoc approach would simply perpetuate the complexity and anomalies of the schedule. The proposal was incorporated in the SAL but the Ministry of Finance neglected to carry out the planned studies and program preparation work. Some partial reductions and adjustments of the schedule were introduced under SAL I, however, designed to move toward a narrowing of the range of tariff rates (i.e., toward "neutrality" of tariff impact on relative prices).

Unfortunately this work was partially undone in 1985 when the government raised import duties again for revenue purposes. There was little further progress until late in 1990 when tariffs on machinery were reduced to a uniform 5 percent. Further important reforms were put into effect in 1991 by the interim government, including sharp reductions in the tariffs on fully assembled automobiles and on computers. As of this writing, broad reduction of rates and neutrality were still unattained.

The reformers were forced to fall back on a second-best approach also contained in the SALs. This involved an industry-by-industry attack on industrial restructuring, in which tariff reform was one component, along with domestic content requirements and other protective and promotive regulations. Automotive, electrical goods, and other product areas were specified for studies that would lay out a restructuring plan for each sector. While the studies were performed, the restructuring programs foundered in every case. Whereas in Korea the government has been able to enforce a sector-by-sector approach that has led to the graduation (or failure) of infant industries, the same approach in Thailand focused industry opposition, which might otherwise have been diffused by across-the-board measures. The first minister of industry who presided over the sector reviews and negotiations was not in sympathy with the objectives of liberalization; in the automotive case, he urged that protection (in the form of a rise in the domestic content requirement from 45 percent to 100 percent) be strengthened. The reformers considered it the main accomplishment of the industrial restructuring exercise when the automotive negotiations concluded with an agreement to let the domestic content level remain unchanged. The succeeding minister was too distracted by crises in other matters under his responsibility to provide the political attention needed to push the sector exercises further along. The upshot was a government unwillingness to force restructuring in the absence of compromises acceptable to the industries, although additions to the protective structure were warded off.

While some progress was made toward putting the state enterprises' financial condition in order, little was achieved in management reform of the major poorly administered agencies. Privatization was not a significant subject under the SALs but was turned into a central restructuring issue subsequently by NESDB. It warrants a closer look.

It will be recalled that the policy adopted in the late 1950s to restrict further development of the state enterprise sector applied to industrial and commercial enterprises, not to public infrastructure. As in many nonsocialist industrial countries, the provision of electric power, telecommunications, rail and bus systems, port operation, and urban water remained largely in the hands of state enterprise monopolies. The domestic and international airlines were also state enterprises. In some areas, the state sector has been expanded in scope. In 1975 Bangkok's fleet of decrepit buses operated by twenty-four private companies began to be taken over by a new metropolitan public enterprise. Substitution of the Bangkok

Metropolitan Transit Authority (BMTA) for private ownership became unavoidable when the Kukrit government refused to allow fare increases despite the jump in fuel costs. The largest new state enterprises (and state minority equity participation) were set up in the petroleum and natural gas sector.

The industrial and commercial organizations comprised the majority of the roughly seventy state enterprises. Although many of these were seldom profitable, the state enterprise sector as a whole earned net revenues for the government prior to the first oil shock. The unwillingness or inability of successive governments in the 1970s to allow major state enterprises providing public services to recover rising costs through tariff adjustments caused a deterioration in their financial condition. Forced to turn to external borrowing to finance their capital expenditure requirements, the enterprise sector, as noted earlier, contributed substantially to the overall growth in Thailand's foreign debt, amounting to around half the outstanding external debt in 1984.[35] The emergence of the state enterprise sector as a major factor in the macroeconomic storm that was gathering around the end of the 1970s coincided with general international reevaluation of public ownership and a movement toward privatization of state enterprises in developing and developed countries alike.

While Thai opinion on privatization was affected by this international trend, the need to reconsider the future of the state enterprises in Thailand arose in the early 1980s directly from two principal domestic concerns—finance and efficiency. Privatization appeared as a possible solution to the search for new capital sources that could reduce the accumulation of debt. In one form or another, privatization also offered ways to introduce competition into the markets for the services provided by the state enterprises. Although monitoring and supervision had improved over the years since Loftus complained that the enterprise sector was almost out of control, the continuing inadequacy of financial oversight reappeared as a serious problem as the general fiscal condition of the public sector deteriorated. The problem was characterized precisely by Phisit Pakkasem in 1984:

> Thai state enterprises are not subject to budget overview or review. In fact they contribute to national budget revenue and their operating losses are often financed through a number of extra-budgetary means. Moreover, despite the fact that these state enterprises submit their annual investment and operational plans to NESDB in terms of current operations and investments, there are no functioning means for ensuring follow-up in many of these areas, so that in practice many of these state enterprises enjoy virtually complete de facto autonomy, with the important exception of price-setting. The mechanism for enforcement and control [is] not very strong and data necessary for monitoring are not available centrally.[36]

The state enterprises were a heterogeneous mix. While some form of private participation began to be considered in electric power and domestic air service

for financial reasons (the relevant state enterprises being among the more efficiently managed), privatization was proposed in other areas (especially other
transport and telecommunications) on the grounds that private firms would be
more efficient and that the state enterprises in question should be subject to
competitive pressure. Phisit gives a catalogue of the management weaknesses of
these enterprises:

> For a variety of reasons, the performance of many Thai state enterprises has
> fallen short of expectations, especially in the utility and transport fields. They
> need to incorporate some private management disciplines . . . particularly the
> senses of business mindedness, competition, efficiency and by relaxing some
> of the government controls or interference in the internal management. Their
> operational problems include overmanning, inexperienced management and
> widespread practices of deputation as well as secondment of civil servants and
> military officers to the top posts . . . frequent changes of top management, lack
> of development or business mindedness . . . irregular and costly supplies, inflexi-
> ble price controls, poor maintenance of capital equipment, under-utilization of
> installed capacity . . . and political interference as well as control by various
> agencies of government.[37]

The most urgent reform—bringing state enterprise external borrowing under
tighter control of the monetary authorities—was accomplished in the early
1980s. Reforms in state enterprise oversight, financing, and management were
incorporated in the structural adjustment program and in the fifth plan. These
included (a) installation of a new management information system for the joint
use of the four oversight agencies, NESDB, the Ministry of Finance, the Budget
Bureau, and the Office of the Auditor General; (b) establishment of a central
coordinating and supervising unit; (c) introduction of corporate planning and
performance evaluation; and (d) substantial increases in tariffs to enable enterprises to move toward financial self-sufficiency. If any of the "essential" public
utilities failed to improve efficiency, the government would bring in private
management and sell portions of the equity to the general public. If other state
enterprises failed to meet the operating guidelines within a reasonable period of
time, the government would consider liquidation or privatization.[38]

The record of the government's accomplishments under this program was
mixed. By the start of the sixth plan in 1987, the monitoring and oversight
system had been improved; the majority of the enterprises were earning profits,
while the growth of total losses among the unprofitable enterprises (mainly the
BMTA and the State Railways) was at least contained; some rate reforms had
been accomplished, but the position was still not satisfactory; arrears in payments of bills owed by some agencies for services acquired from others had
accumulated to an enormous sum (6.5 billion baht), shifting the cash flow problems of the debtor enterprises to the creditor organizations; some of the serious
management problems cited by Phisit remained unresolved; and corporate plan-

ning had been adopted but was not yet fulfilling expectations. To pursue the policy further, the sixth plan set up tighter financial guidelines and again called for the establishment of a central monitoring agency.[39]

The effort of the core agencies, led by NESDB, to promote privatization is worth a close look for what it reveals about the policy and decision-making processes. The fate of the state industrial and commercial enterprises is most easily summarized. They were largely allowed to continue operating, fading into insignificance as the private sector grew up around them. Even in the early 1980s under the Prem administration, when the combination of financial pressures and political strength behind structural adjustment added up to the most favorable conditions for state enterprise reform since the NEDCOL disaster, the government was able to liquidate only three organizations, the Bangkok Jute Mill, the Gunny Bag Factory, and the Wire Diffusion Company, the first two of which Loftus had recommended selling or liquidating more that two decades earlier. Divestiture was accomplished in only a single case, the small maritime shipping enterprise.

State enterprise reform policy focused on the more important utility and infrastructure agencies. Nevertheless, although liquidation or divestiture were never seriously contemplated as measures applicable to these agencies, the government was able to carry through very few innovations among the more partial and paralleling forms embraced by the term "privatization." In various instances the proposed privatization steps took the form of public offerings of minority fractions of equity; leasing some selected facilities to private operation, while retaining ownership and supervision in the hands of the state enterprise involved; or inviting private investment to construct a new facility (e.g., overhead rail transit in Bangkok) that would be incremental to existing state enterprise assets and operations.

Two kinds of problems arose to frustrate privatization in these forms. First was the opposition of vested interests that viewed even these incremental ideas as threats. The most vocal opponents were the state enterprise unions. In occasional demonstrations in the streets of Bangkok (including a march past NESDB's office, with banners citing NESDB and the World Bank as the privatization villains), the unions voiced their fear that private ownership or management would lead to a loss of the wage, health, work safety, and other benefits that are provided by state enterprises but might erode under private control, which in many instances fails to follow the mandates of laws governing the workplace. It was also generally believed in Bangkok that less obvious motivations were behind union resistance; at times, union demonstrations were alleged to be inspired by one or another of the groups in opposition to the Prem government.[40] More direct in some cases was the joint opposition of both unions and management of a state enterprise. Whatever the politics may have been, the union opposition arose even in cases where the form of possible privatization was still undefined.[41]

The Prem government became increasingly sensitive to open demonstrations and threats of work disruption by the state enterprise unions. It also was hobbled by opposition to privatization on the part of enterprise managements and the bureaucratic interests in the ministries that had these organizations under their jurisdiction and fiefdom. At bottom, the privatization program lacked a political base because the state enterprises were not subject to a unitary set of political supervisors representing the public interest. It was possible to strengthen centralized control by the monetary authorities over external borrowing, but much more difficult to translate a general privatization objective into measures affecting specific enterprises under separate ministerial control, in cabinets where the power and patronage to be drawn from these enterprises were distributed among rival parties in unsteady coalition. Thus the divergences between state enterprise interests and public interests, arising out of the inefficiencies and market power of some of the most conspicuously ill-performing organizations, were not mirrored by a parallel divergence of interests between the enterprise and the political levels that were the actual decision makers (decision blockers) in each case. Particularly discouraging to the proponents of privatization was the inability of the Ministry of Finance to get cabinet acceptance of a privatization plan the ministry had developed for an enterprise under its own jurisdiction, the Tobacco Monopoly. The monopoly proved able to muster political support sufficient to counter its own controlling minister.

The second problem was the reaction of privatization proponents themselves against a number of schemes that would have transferred monopoly rents from a state enterprise into private hands, or created new opportunities for such private rents, under the flag of privatization. The most blatant and potentially most economically damaging of these schemes was a contract in which the Port Authority of Thailand (in 1987) granted to a private company exclusive rights to operate all the cranes in the Port of Bangkok for eighteen months. All shippers were obliged to pay fees to the company, and ships with onboard cranes were enjoined from using them rather than the port cranes. Facing higher loading and off-loading charges and the likelihood of congestion in the port and delayed turn-around, the shippers announced they would impose surcharges. With the prospect that the f.o.b. costs of all exports moving through the port of Bangkok would be raised if the surcharges came into effect, the contract quickly became a hotly contested issue to be resolved by the Economic Ministers. Seeking to blunt NESDB's call for cancellation of the contract, the minister of communications defended the arrangement as an example of privatization. The issue was settled in a compromise that left the company to operate the port cranes while giving the shippers several alternatives (e.g., the right to set up their own river ports outside PAT jurisdiction) that enabled them to avoid imposing the surcharges.

In another case, NESDB found itself opposing the plan of the same ministry to "privatize" three highway projects. The roads would be built by private engineering firms on public right-of-way, and would by operated as private toll roads. This proposal was rejected by the Economic Ministers, with NESDB arguing that it was poor policy to grant private monopolies for toll road operation between points where vehicle operators had no alternative option. The fact that NESDB was opposing a purported privatization served to obscure further the whole subject and to cast doubt on the direction of the government's policies in this regard.

The privatization that was accomplished consisted mainly of incremental projects, new services that were add-ons to those already being provided by the state enterprise in question. Examples included franchises for private urban minibuses, cellular phone systems in Bangkok, and a private feeder-route airline. Privatization on the margin, so to speak, generated much less opposition than privatization, in any form, that would encroach on existing assets or activities. While opposition to private preemption of opportunities for extension of state enterprise operations on new ground was not nil, it was easily managed through artful compromise. In an interesting example involving the future operation of the wharves under construction at the new port at Laem Chabang, an accommodation was reached after a short strike that had paralyzed exports. The government had decided to lease all four wharves for private operation; the union demanded that all four should be operated by the PAT. The cabinet then adjusted the decision, giving responsibility for two of the wharves to the PAT and two to private companies, an arrangement that would allow for a test of the relative efficiency of the public and private organizations.[42]

In sum, Thai governments through the 1980s, from the thrust of structural adjustment through the specious schemes of the later years, failed to make much use of privatization as an instrument for coping with the more serious cases of state enterprise inefficiency and unprofitability. With the potential exceptions of telecommunications and port services, where neither privatization nor other reform instruments have yet been developed to disarm the resistance to fundamental overhaul, the failure of privatization has not had serious consequences for the performance of the Thai economy. The relatively tight boundary drawn around the state enterprise sector in the 1950s, and the fact that some major state enterprises, like the electric power agencies, have been well managed, have kept the efficiency costs of aggregate public ownership relatively modest compared with the costs imposed on the economies of many other countries (e.g., Chile, or the Eastern European countries) where state enterprise sectors have been very large or dominant. The Thai solution thus far (although falling short of the government's objectives) has turned on allowing the industrial and commercial enterprises largely to fade (now under the added general pressure of financial performance criteria), on privatizing on the margin where public utility services are growing, and in both sectors avoiding the political price that would have to be paid if privatization (or liquidation) were forced through direct confrontation. Finally, the examples of the efficient organizations among the Thai state enterprises serve as further evidence of the general finding in the economic literature "that private ownership has efficiency advantages in competitive conditions, but [that the evidence] does not show either public or private ownership to be generally superior when market power is present."[43] In this light, the limitation to privatization on the margin in the case of the efficient enterprises exercising natural monopolies or substantial market power should not be misinterpreted as a policy failure.

The Eastern Seaboard

It will be recalled that, in 1975, the Bank of Thailand called attention to the need for a deep-sea port along the Eastern Seaboard of the Gulf of Thailand. The need for a deep-sea port on this coast, somewhere south of Bangkok, appeared to be a long-run necessity. At some point the Bangkok port (Klong Toey) would become a bottleneck to the country's foreign trade, if not its growth overall. Given Thailand's configuration, only the peninsular South could avoid channelling its trade through a port (or ports) located around the head of the Gulf. Besides the question of limits to the cargo-handling capacity of the Bangkok port (and the private piers and bulk-loading facilities on the Chao Phraya River), no river port in the Bangkok vicinity could accommodate deep-draft ocean-going vessels. All traffic through Bangkok had to be transshipped from lighters, either via Singapore or via Thailand's Ko Sichang Island, south of Bangkok in the gulf.

The movement of virtually all nonpeninsular trade through Bangkok, over several generations, was also a major factor contributing to Bangkok's emergence as the one primate city where the bulk of the industrial sector would locate and where the bulk of Thailand's economies and costs of urban agglomeration would be sited. As industrial land would become scarce and urbanization diseconomies (like traffic congestion) would begin to outweigh the advantages of concentration, it was inevitable that industry and urbanization would spread beyond Bangkok.

These considerations pointed to the necessity, and inevitability, of urban-cum-industrial development in other locations, tied to new port capacity. In fact, a first study for an Eastern Seaboard port had been carried out in 1968. The fourth plan includes a brief reference to the need for improving commercial use of Sattahip port and an intention to begin development of a new port at Laem Chabang.[44]

The Thanin government set up a committee in 1976 to study Laem Chabang, but nothing came of it. Construction of a pipeline began in 1979 to convey natural gas from the off-shore field in the gulf to a separation plant that would be located south of Sattahip. The government began to consider heavy industry projects that might be tied to the forthcoming power source, including soda ash, iron and steel, and petrochemicals. Associated development of rail and industrial estate facilities was also under study by the government agencies involved.

Early in the new Prem administration, in response to a suggestion by the deputy minister of agriculture, Dr. Anat Arbhabhirama, the prime minister called for a master plan for Eastern Seaboard development that would bring all the elements together in an integrated concept. Anat assembled a group of professionals, many of whom became key players in subsequent events, and a general scheme was drawn up and accepted. The group recommended the establishment of special planning and implementation arrangements, and the carrying out of a comprehensive feasibility study. As a result, an interministerial Eastern Seaboard Development Committee was set up under the chairmanship of the prime minister. NESDB would serve as secretariat to the new committee, and within NESDB exclusive responsibility would be assigned to a new division, the Center for Integrated Plan of Operations (CIPO), reporting directly to the NESDB secretary-general. One of CIPO's initial tasks was the launching of the overall feasibility study, conducted by external consultants.

The Eastern Seaboard (ESB) program became one of the central development programs of the entire postwar era and will no doubt have large-scale effects on the country's future. Because the development of ESB was planned and launched during the structural adjustment period—more precisely, because the timing of the required financing commitments (in 1985–86) turned out to coincide with the moment of maximum apprehension over the economy's near-term financial condition—it became the subject of the most intense policy conflict of the Prem period. The ESB program became a microcosm in which many of the social and economic issues that would shape the country for some years to come were involved and debated.

From the original grand conception of the consultants' first report[45] through the reexaminations and actual realization of the ESB program to date, there have been many revisions, canceled components, delays, cost reductions, and substantial investments accomplished, most of the details of which need not be described. In its first and largest configuration the program proposed three components—light export industries centered at a new port at Laem Chabang; the tourism complex to the south at Pattaya; and a heavy (polluting) petrochemical and basic industrial area further to the south, centered at a new port at Map Ta Phut. The capital cost of the program would be $4.5 billion, of which twenty percent would be for infrastructure and about two-thirds for heavy industry. Construction would stretch until the year 2001, but around 90 percent would be completed by 1991. The peak years of construction and capital outlays would be 1982–86. The capital requirements for both the private- and public-sector components would amount to substantial fractions of domestic private equity and credit resources and of the public sector's financial availabilities, and would entail heavy external borrowing.[46]

The planned size of the overall program began to recede as the government undertook closer studies of the components. The soda ash and iron and steel projects were early casualties of these reevaluations. Some of the elements got off to an early start, such as the rail line and the petrochemical units. The time required for planning much of the public infrastructure, and for developing the financial arrangements for the chemical fertilizer plant, delayed the critical decisions on these components until 1985. By that time, the economy had taken a bad turn and the clouded short-term prospects provided a background against which all the questions that had been only peripheral reservations up to that point came to the fore.

Although the complex was conceived as an integrated whole, the degree of technical and economic interdependence among the parts varied. The petrochemical complex in particular developed rapidly along a separate track under the general authority of the ESB Committee. Unlike the cumbersome arrangements required to mobilize and coordinate the many agencies and potential investment sources involved in the port, fertilizer, and other related projects, the petrochemical players were relatively few in number and tightly coordinated.[47] The leading organizations, the Petroleum Authority of Thailand (PTT) and the National Petrochemical Corporation (NPC), assembled a team of outstanding professional and technical competence that proceeded to put the plan into operation with relatively few setbacks. In detailed feasibility studies the size of the plan was reduced by half. Upstream construction costs turned out substantially lower than the estimates, as the depressed international construction industry came in with unexpectedly low bids. The petrochemical complex had the advantage of virtual certitude as to its economic feasibility; although the Thai gas fields could never be the basis of export industries competitive with Middle East suppliers, the complex would be justifiable for import-substitution, and most likely would be operating at full capacity fairly soon based on projections of domestic demand growth. These expectations have in fact been realized.

The rest of the ESB program (the tourist complex aside, which leads an independent economic life) appeared to be a very different story, vulnerable because of its essentially demand-leading character, the disparity of interests among its more numerous participants, and the fact that it appeared postponable, if necessary. This vulnerability became evident in early 1985 when the ESB Committee decided to cut the overall program by 4.3 percent, to stretch out some of the projects, and to drop the soda ash and steel projects. Over the course of that year, as we have already noted, the deteriorating economic position brought intense pressure to bear on the size and content of public-sector investment. The large expenditures planned for the ESB program became the prime target.

Critical views regarding the ESB program had been developing among some of the technocrats before these events forced the confrontation, but had not surfaced for several reasons. First, the organizational arrangements for developing the ESB investment program had in effect excluded the potential critics. Because the program was handled completely within CIPO, it was protected from the project screening and adversarial scrutiny procedures that other NESDB sectoral and technical planning offices would normally have conducted.

Second, these arrangements sanctified the scheme as a major personal initiative of the prime minister, strongly advocated by the secretary-general of NESDB, and supported by many of the most powerful figures in the government. Many of its top supporters had formidable reputations as intellectuals and administrators. Third, the program was being developed within a planning framework that drew heavily on prestigious consulting engineering firms. The petrochemical components and the fertilizer project had the blessing and planned financial participation of the International Finance Corporation, the World Bank's private-sector investment arm.

The review process see-sawed back and forth with announcements of cabinet decisions approving loans for ESB projects followed by contrary announcements of implementation freezes and further review. The publicity, rumors, and "disinformation" surrounding this argumentation and politicking gave the impression that the Thai decision process was baffling if not chaotic. In the event, the review process occupied about one year, from September 1985 to October 1986. The delay itself was a significant accomplishment in the eyes of those most concerned to restrain public-sector expenditure and external borrowing in order to preserve the integrity of the relationship with the IMF (which had raised the question of ESB project viability in the discussions over the standby) and to prevent a worsening of the key accounting ratios. The major casualty of the final cabinet decision was the National Fertilizer Corporation (NFC) project. By deciding not to expand the government equity portion or to offer any government guarantees on loan financing NFC might obtain, the cabinet left NFC dependent on rounding up additional private equity and loan financing without further help from the government. Although the government appeared to support the efforts of successive chairmen of NFC (appointed by the government) to obtain this financing, and to resolve the numerous problems bedeviling the involvement of Japanese (OECF) concessional loans, events and the government's firm stand against raising its own financial stake conspired to frustrate the project.[48] While the fertilizer project was never actually canceled, and while there have been recurrent press stories about individuals calling for its revival or possible new foreign interest, the project has been dormant if not moribund ever since. By not formally dropping the project, the cabinet avoided a formal, public repudiation that could have embarrassed those who had been the most forceful champions.

One of the most significant aspects of the government's abandonment of NFC was its implicit reaffirmation of the long-standing policies respecting private investment and the industrial sector. At an early stage in the development of the fertilizer project, the government had persuaded a number of the commercial banks to agree to take up portions of the NFC equity. As it became evident that the total equity requirements were not being mobilized, the Ministry of Finance attempted to obtain increased equity commitments from the banks. The Bangkok Bank voiced some reservations about the project (the bank also had the Metro group, the major fertilizer importer/mixer, as one of its important clients) and was prepared to be much less accommodating than was the Thai Farmers Bank (which, in contrast, had interests with firms that would have participated in engineering aspects of the project). Although the absence of a common interest within the banking sector in effect scuttled the project, the government did not attempt, finally, to force the commercial banks to comply with the government's resource allocation priorities. A decision that the government would provide the necessary equity would have made the government a majority shareholder and turned NFC into a state enterprise, while, incidentally, forcing the IFC to withdraw.

The World Bank had only a minor part in the debate. Having withdrawn from financing any of the ESB components as early as 1981, the bank had no direct entree as financier. Until 1985 the bank had complimented NESDB and CIPO on the systematic planning, the extensive use of foreign consultants in feasibility studies, and the caution with which they were approaching the large-scale industrial components. In the changed economic environment of 1985, the World Bank staff in Bangkok thought it would be prudent to cancel (or postpone for several years) the two new ports and to increase the capacity of Bangkok and Sattahip ports instead. The publication of a memo to NESDB to this effect in late 1985 drew press criticism that the bank was interfering in Thai internal affairs.[49] It was ironic that the bank was charged with intervention at a time when its involvement with Thai policy questions was probably at an all-time low. The cancellation of negotiations for a SAL III had removed the bank from further discussion of economic policy issues. Project loan activity had virtually collapsed compared with the hectic pace of the late 1970s and early 1980s; only two loans were signed in 1985, none in 1986. In another irony, World Bank staff found themselves at odds with the IFC. Having committed itself to equity participation in the fertilizer project, the IFC management rejected suggestions from bank staff, and from some analysts within IFC, that the finance corporation consider withdrawing based on the project's deteriorating economic prospects. (Questions of face and of meeting IFC funding targets were said to have been involved.) IFC withdrawal would probably have brought on the cancellation of the fertilizer project, but IFC persistence was not sufficient to save it.

I should digress for a moment to point out that the deterioration in the relationship with the World Bank was mainly due to causes outside the ESB controversy. First, World Bank practice shifts to the borrower the entire exchange risk attached to the value of outstanding loans. The yen revaluation raised the dollar value of Thailand's debt to the bank and brought home to the Thai authorities the bank's rigid policy in this respect. This was the first occasion in which the interests of the World Bank as an institution diverged from those of the Thai government. Second, the relationship was further strained when Thailand turned to the commercial market for credits it could obtain on terms better that those offered by the bank. Third, under the general pressure from senior management to meet high lending targets, the bank staff began to see NESDB as the principal agency responsible for the decline in Thai projects. In earlier years the bank had supported NESDB for its project quality review and coordinating role. Now the review process appeared to be blocking loan preparation work. To circumvent NESDB, bank staff began to work directly with the operating ministries. For NESDB, the bank had turned into a loose cannon, intervening in the development of the government's investment program and undermining the relationship between NESDB and the ministries. Under changing circumstances, the relationship recovered in the later 1980s.

The special administrative arrangements for ESB showed strengths and weaknesses similar to those experienced in other developing countries where agencies outside, or insulated from, the regular bureaucracy have been created (often at the behest of aid donors) to carry out a complex program that appeared beyond the capability of existing governmental machinery. The arrangements worked well as long as the financial underpinnings appeared strong. The performance of the various agencies and departments was not uniformly effective, but the centralization of the planning in CIPO, the forcefulness of CIPO's leadership, and the coordination and political drive from the ESB ministerial committee brought the complex of studies, legal preparations, financial (including major aid) commitments, and implementing activities to an advanced state before the financial crisis struck. Under financial pressure, the weaknesses of the system were exposed and became part of the policy debate over how best to proceed. On the positive side, the independence of CIPO from the rest of the NESDB bureaucracy facilitated the rapid development of the ESB planning and implementation processes. On the negative side, questionable planning assumptions—some going to the heart of the projected rates of return and the time profiles of potential utilization of infrastructure components—that might have been corrected earlier if open to normal examination procedures now surfaced all at once, complicating the policy dialogue and weakening the credibility of the advocates. Personal rivalries and resentments that stemmed from the relatively insulated position CIPO had enjoyed as an ad hoc solution to the normal coordination problems of the bureaucracy further complicated the review process.

Officials inside NESDB and elsewhere in the government, and observers in the aid agency community, were concerned about the effects the ESB debate might have on the integrity of the development planning system that had been central to the performance of the Prem administration. It was argued that the incorporation of the ESB secretariat inside NESDB had compromised the role of the agency as an independent arbiter of the planning process. On the other hand, similar program-focused arrangements incorporated within NESDB had been made for the coordination of rural development, and for the secretariat functions serving the JPPCC and the Royal Initiative projects. In these cases, NESDB's coordination and executive functions were still approved (by some of those criticizing the CIPO arrangements) as effective measures that had enhanced, not compromised, NESDB's role. One might conclude from this that no general principle of public administration was really at issue here. The role of NESDB in policy management (as distinct from policy planning) in the Prem government was strongly approved, and disapproved, at various times depending on the issues under contention and on the policy preferences and interests of the approvers and disapprovers.

The CIPO/NESDB communication problems were at the program and project levels of development management. But the crisis also revealed fissures among the economic technocrats and lapses of coordination among the economic agencies that would not have surfaced or caused problems of policy management if financial stability had not appeared to be facing such a threat. A principal failure revolved around the core of the macroeconomic problem. As has been seen, the relationship with the IMF was fundamental to the program for restoring the external balances and sustaining the country's creditworthiness. Critical as the IMF targets were to the management of short-term economic policy, the Bank of Thailand and the Ministry of Finance did not include NESDB (or any other agency) in the analytic preparation of the standby, nor were the exchanges with the IMF coordinated, or even shared, with NESDB. The IMF relationship had long been considered the exclusive preserve of the Bank of Thailand and a few officials in the Ministry of Finance. As long as the IMF relationship consisted of little more than annual visitations and exchange of information, the narrowness of the relationship presented no problem. On the understandings between the Thai monetary authorities and the IMF, the coordination between the IMF and World Bank staffs was greater than that between those authorities and the NESDB. While this hiatus was closed in late 1985 when the economic technocrats were forced to join issue on the threat to the standby, the intense negotiation entailed some unusually adversarial meetings. An unfortunate consequence of some of these confrontations, and of the maneuvering behind the scenes, was some loss of confidence on both sides among the inner core of the cadre that had been first brought together under Dr. Puey as the second postwar generation of economists. In fact, as the ESB controversy played itself out, an unpleasant undercurrent of accusations began to surface alleging conflicts of interest among a wide circle of public- and private-sector participants. The conspiratorial tone that began to surround the issues was reinforced by the irritation many of the participants felt over the actual and alleged lobbying by outside players, especially Japanese official and commercial interests.

There is an interesting sidelight to the Japanese role in ESB that illustrates the Thai government's intent to seek diversification in the pattern of foreign investment. While the government had made no effort to mask its exhortations to Japanese officials and business to increase their investment in Thailand and the ESB in particular, Thai officials quickly shifted their ground in the 1980s when Japanese companies began to flood in. Facing a queue of foreign firms interested in the petrochemical and other industrial opportunities, the ESB Committee reverted to the traditional Thai policy of seeking a balance among foreign economic interests. They adopted a screening procedure under which firms from countries already represented in the area would have lower priority for successive projects. In effect, the system discriminated in favor of European and American firms, much to the chagrin of the Japanese (who were providing the bulk of the aid financing for ESB infrastructure). It is also worth noting that the process was transparent and was not exploited by its technocratic managers for its under-the-table potentialities.

On substantive issues, those who thought that the primary objective of economic development at that stage should be the reduction of poverty saw the ESB program as a mistake. It would yoke the government for the first time to the promotion of heavy industry. Although the ESB advocates foresaw large-scale employment creation effects in the long run, many of the projects planned for the first few years would be highly capital-intensive. In the now heated competition for resources, ESB would "crowd out" substantial investment that would otherwise follow Thailand's pattern of comparative advantages in agriculture and in labor-intensive manufacturing. The proponents of ESB were sacrificing the rural poor in their pursuit of industrialization. The funds should be allocated instead to activities that were agricultural, labor-intensive, and export-crop oriented. The critics also saw an element of heedless devotion to bigness, a determination to promote engineering objectives regardless of economic and social considerations.

In response, the advocates argued that the mutual exclusivity between industrial and rural development was overdrawn and misleading. The light industries complex planned for Laem Chabang would provide a new stimulation for the Northeast as a hinterland for agroindustrial inputs. Further, industrialization was an inevitable characteristic of economic development and would be a more powerful generator of income growth than agriculture. There was an unrealistic, one might say romantic, element in the extent to which some of the partisans of rural development appeared to oppose allocation of resources to nonagricultural sectors in favor of a strategy that appeared to stress welfare rather than growth.

Paradoxically, the fertilizer project was the most controversial component in the agriculture versus industry context, but the sides appeared to reverse themselves. The ESB advocates argued that Thailand's dependence on imported fertilizers was an important factor explaining the very low levels of fertilizer application. Consequently, this dependence was constraining the growth of agricultural productivity, a drag on farm incomes. The fertilizer importers were supplying farmers with inappropriate mixtures and were failing to educate farmers on effective application. Local production of the proper mixtures would correct this weakness. Those opposed to NFC, including the partisans of agriculture, argued that this was a very costly way to solve the mixture problem. More fundamentally, the NFC project admittedly had only a marginally acceptable rate of return which could quickly be rendered negative, depending on movements of international prices for petroleum and fertilizer away from the levels that had been used in the studies of the project's feasibility. Who would bear the cost in such an event? If the prices of imported fertilizer dropped below the levels that would allow the NFC to operate at a profit, the government would be pressured to protect NFC (in which the government would be a shareholder) by denying farmers access to the cheaper imports. On the up side, it would be unrealistic to presume that NFC would not raise its prices when international fertilizer prices were rising or that the government would intervene to hold prices down. Thus, it could not be presumed that farmers would be better off with domestic production.

Critics also stressed the macroeconomic implications. The ESB program was a major component of total planned public-sector expenditure. The OECD countries' economic recovery of 1983–84 was faltering in 1985. At its annual meeting in September 1985, the World Bank reported that global economic prospects were deteriorating; nonfuel commodity prices were at their lowest level in more than ten years and were still heading downward; the industrial countries were continuing their contractionary fiscal policies, and the outlook for developing countries was worsening. Forecasts of the short-term prospects for the Thai economy, especially the external debt service ratio, were turning increasingly gloomy.[50] Therefore, the ESB program should be delayed or stretched out as part of a general demand retrenchment. The proponents of staying the course argued that timing was indeed important, but ESB was a long-run structural program that should not be derailed as part of a countercyclical adjustment policy. World economic conditions would certainly turn more favorable again. Thailand needed to be ready to exploit the next round of opportunities. It would be a mistake to ignore the momentum ESB had generated and to cancel four years worth of preparation in order to ease the way through a short-term transitional problem.

As the debate heated up in the first half of 1986, the repeated recalculations of projected rates of return on the fertilizer project, ports, and other components became weapons of argument rather than analytic tools for clarifying policy options. This was because the rates of return were originally projected to be only marginally positive for several components (compared with the conventionally accepted floors of 10–12 percent for Thailand) and could easily be lowered through the floor by moderate changes in the price or other key assumptions that go into such analyses. The favorable assumptions and outcomes of some of the justifying analyses were not "robust." For example, early in 1986 the evaluation division of the Bureau of the Budget reassessed the ESB projects for which the Industrial Estate Authority of Thailand (IEAT) would be financially responsible, Map Ta Phut port and the Map Ta Phut and Lam Chaebang industrial estates. The bureau concluded that (a) the three projects together would yield an unacceptably low 7.2 percent return, (b) the potential financial burden for IEAT should be alleviated by shifting capital costs to the Ministry of Finance, and (c) to sustain IEAT's financial position, the authority should be allowed to raise its projected charges to user projects like the fertilizer and petrochemical plants. As economic conditions worsened, the more pessimistic project arithmetic grew increasingly credible.

The demise of the fertilizer project was foreshadowed in May 1986 when the prime minister's economic adviser, Virabongsa Ramangkura, for the first time publicly expressed his opposition. He highlighted the fact that the recent yen revaluation had undermined the project's financial viability by raising the (baht and U.S. dollar-denominated) size of the planned Japanese aid loan from its original $85 million to $120 million, with further escalation likely.[51]

In a sense, the ESB program was a striking exception to the general direction of the structural adjustment. The macro program aimed at a retreat from the interventionism, resource allocation fine tuning, and public-sector expansion that had brought the economy to the vulnerability of the late 1970s. The role of the public sector in ESB would be unprecedented for the scope of its resource allocation and spatial planning. The feasibility of the entire complex would rest on the willingness of private investors to be drawn to the new industrial locations, or on the ability of the government to ensure that such private decisions eventuated. In perspective, however, it is clear that just as the shift toward intervention and investment allocation tuning in the 1970s had been quite moderate by international standards, so the demand-leading aspects of ESB were not, in the event, substantial departures toward a Korean or more dirigist model of development. No special incentive structure was even proposed to ensure that private investment would locate at ESB and thereby vindicate the program.[52] Major components were delayed in the interests of macroeconomic discipline. Several industrial components were dropped, including potential white elephants. Despite all the pressures and commitments behind the fertilizer project, the government refrained from forcing a solution to the financing problem; it resorted neither to establishing NFC as a state enterprise nor to compelling the private-sector parties to meet the capital requirements.

Within two or three years, the entire debate was overtaken by an investment and trade boom that was beyond anyone's expectations in 1985–86 and that appeared likely to generate ESB-located investment and traffic, in the early 1990s, in excess of what the advocates projected as illustrative justification. It remains to be seen if and when domestic production of chemical fertilizers will reemerge as an economically feasible industrial investment project. The proponents' confidence that ESB would develop as a major industrial alternative to the greater Bangkok area seems well on the way to vindication. On the other hand, the collapse of the standby, which might have been precipitated if the program had not been delayed, would have jeopardized the return to a sustainable monetary position in 1986, and would have undermined the confidence on which the investment inflow and extraordinary growth since 1987 has rested. In sum, between the force of economic argument, the delays and political maneuvers, and subsequent turn of events, the balance of actions taken and deferred on ESB appears in retrospect to have been sound.

The struggle over ESB took place at a time when coalition politicking was weakening the policy processes put in place in the early 1980s. The relative clarity of direction within the government, and the regular application of orthodox policy and project analysis criteria to cabinet decision making, were giving way to more complex and adversarial processes in which incommensurable political and economic considerations came into play. At the technocratic levels, the debates were largely conducted in the realm of substance, by colleagues well schooled and articulate. The single most important independent variable in these debates was the short-term course of the economy, over which honest men could disagree. In the climactic cabinet meetings, little ministerial debate was devoted to either macroeconomic or project substance. The major (spoken) considerations included the effects that yes or no decisions might have on relations with the Japanese government, and on the confidence of foreign investors in a government that was dithering or that was drawing back from earlier intentions.

Prime Minister Prem was normally a laconic and austere figure who played his cards close to the chest. His normal practice was to close cabinet meetings by stating what in his view had been agreed, although there was seldom any actual voting or hammering out of agreed statements; the official, formal records of decisions were normally not made public. Thus, the reporting of cabinet decisions by the media frequently varied from one newspaper to another depending on which minister (or spokesman or other source) each paper had access to, or chose to rely on. Prem's own statements to the press were frequently equivocal. All of these common features of government communication that normally leave wide scope for Bangkok's lively traffic in rumors were heightened during the ESB controversy.

With benefit of hindsight, however, one may conclude that (a) the broad guidelines of government policy respecting the roles and relationships between the public and private sectors prevailed, (b) the arguments for macroeconomic discipline prevailed, and (c) the arguments based on politics, diplomatic assumptions, and government "image" did not prevail and, in the event, proved erroneous. Any greater inflow of foreign investment than what occurred in 1987–90, not long after this year-long display of vacillation, would have been undesirable, perhaps infeasible; the fate of NFC was apparently irrelevant to the confidence of Japanese and other investors. As far as the Japanese government was concerned, any problems of loss of face were apparently resolved in late 1986 when the eminent economist Saburo Okita moderated his earlier strong public support for the whole of ESB by pointing to the need for the Thai government to take account of the troubling economic outlook. The active role the Japanese government took during the ESB debate stands out as an exception, presumably, to Japan's long-standing aid policies of non-intervention, i.e. of adopting a "passive attitude" toward the selection of projects for which the aid will be used, "adhering to the principle that aid should basically be carried out in response to and in line with requests" from the governments being assisted. (This description is drawn from *Japan's ODA 1987*, Japanese Ministry of Foreign Affairs, Tokyo, 1988, p.15. This publication asserts that Japanese aid in the future should move away from passivity toward a more active dialogue with recipients regarding aid use.) Strictly speaking, the pressures from the Japanese government were aimed at sustaining projects already selected, and publicly identified as earmarked for Japanese aid, the selections having been made by Thailand. Japanese sensitivities over possible cancellation arose after choices had been made, elaborate planning undertaken, and potential Japanese contractors identified, all well publicized in Thailand and Japan.

I conclude this discussion of the ESB controversy with the observation that it was played out with no participation by the general public. ESB would command the largest allocation of public-sector resources among all investment programs of the Prem administration. It would have profound effects on the country's industrial structure, and on the future location of population. It raised questions regarding compatibility with the existing tourist industry, which was of major economic importance for the eastern littoral. The crowding-out effects would deny resources that could be allocated to other areas and to potentially substantial numbers in the labor force. Besides the issues I have identified that aroused intense controversy among the technocrats (vested interests aside), there was a potential issue of national defense. The Eastern Seaboard was more vulnerable to a Vietnamese incursion than any location in the country of major economic significance. (A large Vietnamese army was then located along the Thai-Cambodian border and no resolution to the Cambodian issue was in sight.) Despite the importance of these issues, the ESB debate in 1985–86 took place almost entirely within the bureaucracy and the cabinet. There was no participation by public opinion, no placing of the issues before the parliament or any parliamentary oversight committee, no public hearings. The controversy was covered extensively in the local press and was the subject of frequent comment in editorials and by columnists. Although the pressures brought to bear on the decision-making process by outside forces were successful and unsuccessful elements in the decision process, as were related domestic interests of course, the Thai body politic was a nonparticipating observer. This nonparticipation stands as salient testimony to the "quasi" nature of Thai democracy at the time.

Gradualism in Macroeconomic Adjustment

The reader will recall that the Prem administration inherited from the 1970s a set of interacting macroeconomic problems resulting from inadequate adjustment to the effects of the first oil shock. These included government budget deficits, growing external deficits financed by rising foreign debt, and a reemergence of inflation. These problems were aggravated by the second oil shock's impact on the import bill, the industrial country recession with its depressing effects on commodity prices and world trade, and the sharp rise in international interest rates applying to the increments in Thailand's external debt. To reduce the excessive domestic absorption, that is, the excess of investment over domestic savings, the government had to induce a reduction in overall economic activity and an increase in mainly public-sector savings. The instruments to bring about these changes included reductions in public-sector current and investment expenditures, increases in government and state enterprise revenue, increases in real interest rates and constraints on credit growth, and measures to promote exports and restrain imports.

Within the overall determination to reinstall a conservative fiscal and monetary regime and to pursue painful retrenchment as long as it would take, there were frequent problems, indeed struggles, over timing and program specifics, some of which have been detailed above. In addition, external economic conditions (trade volume and agricultural commodity prices) developed less favorably than had been anticipated. The government's fiscal deficit proved particularly difficult to bring down. On the expenditure side, the government maintained tight control over current outlays (e.g., government employment growth was held to 2 percent a year) and set restrictive ceilings on public-sector borrowing. On the revenue side however, annual receipts fell short of the budget targets by 10 percent on average every year in 1981–86 due to the recession in economic activity and to the tax reductions that were part of the adjustment program. Revenues finally recovered substantially (to 104 percent of target) in the economic resurgence in 1987.

The closure of the investment-savings gap and the associated current account deficit was not achieved until 1986–87. By the time economic recovery (starting in late 1986) reopened the resource gap (to levels lower than those reached in 1980–85), the debt service ratio was down by nearly half from its 1985 peak and the financing of the gap presented no problem. Investment as a proportion of GDP had had to be cut from over 26 percent in 1980–81 to a low of 21.8 percent in 1986. GDP growth dipped in 1982, recovered in the next two years, then fell sharply to 3.5 percent in 1985 before starting to recover in late 1986. Inflation was brought down quickly to manageable levels by 1982, returning as a moderate problem at the end of the decade as the economy heated up under the pressure of double-digit growth.

As can be seen from Tables 6.1 and 6.2 showing the movements of these magnitudes over the decade, initial progress toward reduction of the basic fiscal and external balances was followed by slippage in 1983–85. The slippage resulted from a temporary easing of fiscal and monetary policies as the government sought to overcome what was judged an excessively severe fall in economic growth in 1982. The government then faced what appeared to be the emergence of an external imbalance (presented to the prime minister as potentially dragging Thailand down to the position of the Philippines, the one ASEAN

Table 6.1

Growth and Basic Balances

	1980	1981	1982	1983	1984	1985	1986	1987	1988	1989	1990b
GDP real growth (%)	4.8	6.3	4.1	7.3	7.1	3.5	4.9	9.5	13.2	12.2	10.0
Gross domestic investment as % of GDP	26.4	26.3	23.1	25.9	24.9	24.0	21.8	23.9	28.8	31.1	36.8
Gross national savings as % of GDP	20.0	18.9	20.3	18.7	19.8	20.0	22.4	23.4	26.1	27.8	30.3
Central government balance as % of GDP	-4.3	-3.2a	-5.8a	-4.3	-3.9	-5.4	-4.8	-2.3	1.0	-0.2	5.2
Current account deficit as % of GDP	-6.5	-7.4	-2.8	-7.3	-5.1	-4.0	0.6	-0.5	-2.7	-3.3	8.7
Inflation—annual % change in CPI	19.7	12.7	5.2	3.8	0.1	2.4	1.9	2.5	3.8	5.4	6.0

Sources: NESDB; Bank of Thailand.

a. Fiscal years.
b. Estimated.

Table 6.2

Trade, Debt, and Foreign Exchange

	1980	1981	1982	1983	1984	1985	1986	1987	1988	1989	1990
Indices (1985 = 100)											
Exports:											
Volume	68.1	75.9	85.3	77.1	93.1	100.0	117.4	140.9	175.1	217.6	241.1
Value	68.9	79.1	82.6	75.8	90.1	100.0	120.7	155.1	208.7	267.0	305.0
Imports:											
Volume	94.8	92.2	81.6	104.0	106.2	100.0	103.5	132.5	184.3	222.4	269.5
Value	75.1	86.3	78.3	94.2	97.6	100.0	96.1	133.1	204.3	263.9	337.3
Terms of trade	127.7	117.4	100.9	108.5	105.9	100.0	110.7	109.6	107.6	103.4	101.3
Debt service ratio (% of export earnings)	14.5	14.4	16.0	19.1	21.5	25.3	25.4	18.9	13.4	13.5	12.3
Official reserves—months of imports	4	3.5	4	3	3	3.5	5	5	4	5	4.5
Exchange rate (B/U.S.$ annual average)	20.5	21.8	23.0	23.0	23.6	27.2	26.3	25.8	25.3	25.7	25.6

Sources: NESBD; Bank of Thailand; World Bank; Debt Service Ratio.

country with a severe debt crisis) calling for a renewed and more sustained adjustment effort. Development of a new set of quantitative targets was triggered when the government failed to hold public borrowing below the 1985 ceilings set under the IMF performance criteria. As a result, the standby was extended until the end of 1987, based on a set of new criteria. The revised program called for a two-year adjustment in 1986–87 in which (among other things) the central government deficit would be brought down to less than 3.5 percent of GDP.

The most difficult year of the entire adjustment process was 1985. The devaluation of November 1984 proved costly to the commercial banks and large firms that had been caught with foreign-denominated debt. The tight government budgets, revenue increase measures, and cuts in public-sector capital outlays had contributed to several years of slow GDP growth, culminating in the trough of 1985, without bringing the adjustment process to a foreseeable end. The continuing discipline required to meet the standby targets caused both the vacillations and struggles over the capital budget and ESB program, and a rising chorus of complaint in the business community that the government was in danger of creating conditions that could lead to social unrest. It is interesting to note that the IMF concurred with proposed timing of the 1986–87 adjustment program. The fund agreed with the government's judgment that the slippage had been due partly to circumstances beyond Thailand's control and that some further stretching was justifiable in the interests of avoiding too much pressure on the rate of economic growth. In the event, the final perseverance of the government through 1986, combined with the favorable turns in external economic conditions, brought the standby to a successful conclusion. While important components of the structural adjustment program still lagged and were still being put in place in 1990 and 1991, the restoration of macroeconomic balance and the strengthening of the economy's flexibility were achieved by 1987, laying the basis for the surge in economic growth of the most recent years and the return to a high order of economic confidence.

Abstracting from the month-by-month pulling and hauling, the indecision and temporizing that often characterize Thai policy making, one may gain additional perspective on the Thai structural adjustment experience through some international comparison. There is a consensus on the lessons to be drawn from developing country experience respecting policies that will help create an economy able to avoid or mitigate macroeconomic crises in the face of unfavorable shocks, and to return relatively quickly to a sustainable growth track. While every economy has many unique features, not least of which is unique politics, there are strong commonalities of policy among the countries that have avoided deep crises, effected substantial structural adjustments, and resumed financially sustainable economic expansion. And there are obverse commonalities among the countries that have experienced severe crises and have not adjusted well or resumed a satisfactory rate of growth. These lessons have been summarized recently by W. Max Corden in a paper drawing on a World Bank research project studying the macroeconomic policies and growth record of seventeen developing countries since the mid-1960s, including Thailand.[53]

Corden outlines the course of events experienced by a large number of developing countries from the mid-1970s to the early 1980s. The path toward economic destabilization begins with a domestic public spending boom. The widening gap between public-sector savings and investment is financed by foreign borrowing. The heavy borrowing takes place at a time when world interest rates are rising sharply, causing a steep increase in debt service obligations in relation to export earnings. The boom pumps up domestic demand, which causes imports to rise and inflation in the prices of nontradables. The second oil shock adds substantially to the import bill (except, of course, in the case of oil-exporting countries). If the nominal exchange rate is fixed, as it was to the dollar in the Thai case, the real exchange rate appreciates, with adverse effects on the trade balance. Just how severe is the upshot depends on the actual magnitudes, their timing, and the effects of expectations, that is, how high is the inflation; how damaging the external deterioration has been to the country's reserves, debt service capability, and access to external finance; the impact on investor confidence; and so on. The country's ability to restore economic balance, and the time required to do so, depends partly on external circumstances, but mainly on the domestic credibility of its adjustment program, how efficient (or distorted) was the pattern of investment in the years leading up to the crisis, and on the government's ability to sustain demand-reducing and politically unpopular measures.

On the spending booms that initiated these experiences, Corden notes that even "cautious Thailand" indulged in a "modest" public investment expansion. When the second oil shock made adjustment a necessity, Thailand proceeded with its "characteristic" gradualism. Slow adjustment was possible because the country's creditworthiness sustained private capital inflow and strong support from official lenders. The real exchange rate had appreciated "mildly" but was depreciated in 1984–85.

> Thailand thus suffered a considerable external shock, and yet it was able to get over it without a crisis comparable to that of so many other countries, and without a severe recession. Initial conditions—a relatively low debt-GDP ratio and a tradition of fairly conservative management—helped, as did the underlying high growth rate. And even though the policy response was rather slow, it was credible on the basis of previous experience. Arguably, it was a stabilizing policy, which might be favorable for long term growth. On the other hand, Thailand may have run undue risks by delaying full adjustment for some time but was rescued by the 1986 oil price decline. . . .
>
> The current success for Thailand seems to make a case for gradualism in adjustment policies, but such gradualism may be appropriate only in circumstances such as Thailand's—when there is no crisis situation, when distortions do exist but are not as major as in so many other countries, and when there is a tradition of firm conservative financial management. One should not advocate

such gradual macroeconomic adjustment for some other countries (particularly Argentina and Brazil) because their authorities lack credibility. That is, people would not believe that the proclaimed path of adjustment would be followed consistently. One should also distinguish gradualism in a planned adjustment program from slowness in making a decision to adjust adequately over a period. Provided there is no credibility problem and new borrowing remains possible, a case for gradualism can be made.[54]

The distinction Corden draws between deciding to adjust and the speed with which the adjustment is carried out goes to the heart of the Thai experience. The decision was taken in the first year of the Prem government and communicated to the Thai public and the foreign community as the economic framework of the fifth plan. The gradualism as events unfolded extended beyond the government's original expectations and intent, partly forced by external events, and partly a characteristic consequence of Thai political behavior that seeks accommodaton and the avoidance of outcomes that create palpable big winners and big losers. Thus, if one follows closely the course of decision making respecting some of the key elements of the structural adjustment, the timing appears (a) slower than it should have been based on economic criteria, (b) appropriate for waiting until bureaucratic and/or political feasibility had been reached, and (c) adequate for avoiding seriously damaging consequences and for capturing the intended benefits. In short, it is a decision process neither brisk nor disciplined, but effective in final outcome and sustained within the general parameters and objectives of the overall policy framework. Since briskness of decision making is probably the exception rather than the rule, especially in countries not burdened with "hard" authoritarian systems, the main lesson to draw from Corden's comparison would seem to be this: The pain in adjustment processes can be minimized by following a regimen of preventive economic health policies that avoid crisis to begin with. The Thai preference for staying within manageable limits, in economic as well as other dimensions in life, as it was applied to coping with the adjustment problems of the 1980s, was expressed well by Chaiyawat Wibulswasdi (then director of economic research at the Bank of Thailand):

The conduct of stabilization policies in Thailand could be said to follow the following principles: balance, flexibility, and caution. The policies aimed to balance growth and stability objectives to the extent possible and keep the degree of trade-off [to a] minimum. The policies were then flexibly implemented, allowing appropriate shift in the stance of policies from restrictive to accommodating when the economic environments and the nature of problems changed. Lastly, when dealing with problems of accumulated nature (such as debt), or with uncertain situations (such as international financial environment), the policies remain rather cautious.[55]

7

THE FIFTH TIGER AT ITS BIRTH

In this chapter I attempt to round out the picture of the Thai economy on the threshold of joining the select company of the four Asian Tigers, or newly industrializing countries. (It is pertinent to record that the Thais, recognizing and wanting to symbolize the differences in economic character between themselves and the established NICs, began to search for an alternative sobriquet soon after it became fashionable to hail the country's impending NIC-dom. Two suggestions that got media attention were NIC–Thai Style, and NIASE, or newly industrializing and service economy.) To complement the coverage of macroeconomic adjustment in the previous chapter, I will discuss some of the additional structural and policy outcomes of the 1980s that have brought the Thai economy to its present state, and also review some of the development issues that confront the policy makers of the 1990s. The role of the state in addressing these issues is likely to be affected profoundly by the violent and astonishing political events of 1992, with their democratic denouement. Finally, I examine briefly the social changes that have accompanied economic development and the questions the Thais have put to themselves as they contemplate the benefits and costs to life in Thailand.

The structural adjustment agenda of the 1980s was a logical set of reforms, refinements, and institutional advances, building on the basic economic framework defined under Sarit. Important parts of that agenda remained to be implemented when Prime Minister Prem departed from the political scene. The reforms up to that time made possible the rapid economic recovery and growth of the Chatichai years. But the Chatichai government took limited advantage of the political scope for completing the adjustment package that three successive boom years might have afforded. Despite the announced determination to push the privatization of state enterprises, little progress was made, as noted earlier, and the approach of granting concessions and exclusive franchises for projects of enormous size threw the idea of privatization into at least temporary disrepute. Import tariffs on capital goods and machinery were reduced and rationalized, but the rest of the tariff reform remained undone along with the replacement of the cascade business tax by a value-added tax (VAT). To Chatichai's credit, his government succeeded in passing the long-delayed social security legislation (a matter that preceded and had no part in the adjustment program).

The economic boom of the late 1980s meant that the Chatichai government was under none of the pressures for policy reform that figured so largely during the Prem years. I have also noted that this government in effect suspended the policy apparatus and processes that it inherited, leaving the economic technocrats with only marginal influence. The technocrats in NESDB and other agencies were supplanted by Chatichai's team of personal advisers, most of whom were relatively young academics with no previous direct government experience. While this group was imaginative and intelligent, the penchant of some of its members to bypass the responsible bureaucrats, or even to push them aside in unceremonious displays of authority deriving directly from the prime minister, created resentment among the technocrats involved and was disruptive to the policy process. This style of operation differed sharply from the working methods of Prem's economic advisers. The latter were also from outside the bureaucracy but maintained close relations with the Council of Economic Ministers and with NESDB and the other core policy agencies. (Chatichai's advisers were also the architects of his government's negotiating positions with the United States over the economic issues, which, in the latter 1980s, were the source of friction between the two governments. In the area of intellectual property rights in particular, with its potentiality for U.S. retaliatory acts against Thai exports to the U.S. market, the U.S. side saw the advisers as the source of the [in the U.S. view] inflexibility of the Thai side.)

The technocratic Anand government installed after the 1991 coup picked up (in addition to Anand's own initiatives) important remaining parts of the Prem government's agenda. These further policy reforms had been researched and designed during the Prem years, although needing some revision in detail to take account of changed economic circumstances and of the politics of 1991. Furthermore, economic policy under the Anand government was put in the hands of many of the same individuals who, at one time or another, had made up the economic team of Prime Minister Prem. Thus, the content of economic policy, and the direction of its further changes in the early 1990s, carried forward the policy orientation and objectives of the Prem years with substantial continuity, despite the sharp discontinuities—of politics, and in the decision processes—in the two succeeding governments. From an economic policy perspective, the Chatichai government represented mainly a pause, characterized by preoccupation with political games, selected large projects, and the pursuit of economic rents.

The interim Anand government reinstated the technocratic apparatus and its leading personalities, reactivated cabinet attention to the business of economic policy, and promulgated an extraordinary amount of legislation and liberalizing deregulation. The interim administration was to govern while a restructuring of the political system took place, a process in which the military would have a dominating role through their majority representation on the appointed constituent assembly charged with drafting a new constitution. The junta allowed its installed prime minister to carry out the elections as promised, in March 1992. The elections were hotly contested by eleven parties. Although the traditional vote-buying in rural areas was widespread, the election was seen as otherwise free of fraud.

A provision of the new constitution had carried forward the stipulation of previous constitutions allowing the parties forming a government to select an individual who was not a member of parliament to serve as prime minister (in the expected event that, absent a majority for any one party, a compromise candidate would have to be selected by a coalition of wary parties), and to choose a mixed cabinet comprising elected MPs and his personal appointees of people who were not MPs. The coup leaders had succeeded in riding over the objections many politicians and academics had raised against this provision in the last stages of adopting the new constitution in late 1992. During all the debate and politicking, Gen. Suchinda Kraprayoon, the leading officer in the coup group, repeatedly denied any interest in the premiership. In the event, a coalition of parties offered the job to Suchinda, who readily accepted. It appeared to be a return to business as usual; the coalition included some of the very politicians the general had denounced and ousted in his coup one year before.

It became clear immediately that the same Bangkok public that had acquiesced in, if not applauded, Suchinda's recent coup, was now deeply disappointed over the return of unelected military to power and felt betrayed by the political personalities who had engineered this outcome. Calls for Suchinda to resign culminated in massive demonstrations in May 1992. Chamlong Srimuang and other opposition leaders stepped in to inspire and direct what was apparently a large-scale and spontaneous reaction against the latest turn in military political manipulation and civilian political connivance.

The events following were important enough to describe in some detail. As the first few days of still orderly demonstrations subsided, behind-the-scenes negotiations began that, in retrospect, might have resulted in a compromise in which Suchinda would have agreed to a face-saving withdrawal. Before such a resolution had time to play out, Chamlong decided to force the issue by calling for renewed demonstrations and a mass march on Government House, the offices of the prime minister. Suchinda called in military units to prevent the march. In the face of the undeterred crowd the troops opened fire, killing scores, if not hundreds; the numbers remain in dispute, and several hundred people are said to be still unaccounted for. The ensuing crisis was resolved only after the king appeared in an extraordinary televised meeting with Suchinda and Chamlong, who were seen in silent and deferential posture. The king called on the two to settle the issues peacefully. In effect, Suchinda had no alternative but to resign.

Once again Anand was called in to head an interim government, this time to run an election within three months. The electorate faced choices among parties that were identified as falling into two camps—those headed by the politicians who had joined Suchinda's cabinet and supported his right to remain premier, and those "prodemocracy" opposition parties that had called for Suchinda's resignation. The prodemocracy parties won a majority and formed a government headed by Chuan Leekpai.

It is tempting to conclude that these events, perhaps because of their lamentable aspects, have propelled the Thai polity firmly in the direction of democratic politics based on law and civilian government. In addition to the reasons that gave rise to the wide belief that the peaceful transition to the Chatichai government signaled the end of power transfer by coup in Thailand, there were some unprecedented aspects of this latest crisis that reflected a further sharp rise in the assertiveness, and democratic preferences, of the middle class, and further decline in the military's political acumen and credibility.

While Suchinda and his military associates went so far as to supplant the civil functions of the police and then fire on peaceful demonstrators, their room for the exercise of power was clearly constrained. They blocked the upcountry flow of news for several days on the television (the media was entirely government-owned), but made no move to interfere with the newspapers, some of which ran thundering editorials denouncing the military's acts. Videocassettes of the military's violence, taken from foreign television broadcasts and made by amateur observers and participants, circulated throughout the country. The demonstrations in Bangkok were then reinforced by numerous demonstrations in provincial capitals. During his first interim government, Anand had succeeded in removing senior military officers from controlling positions in transport and communications state enterprises. Now the slaughter and disappearances substantially discredited the military, as had their violence against the students in 1973. But, most remarkably, in the eyes of Thai public opinion, the demonstrators of 1992 were perceived as comprising the middle class, not radicalized students. One of the most striking sights was the large number of well-dressed adults who were sporting cellular phones and using them to help maintain coordination among the demonstrators. After the press began to observe that businessmen were well represented in the streets but that the leading banking and manufacturing associations had remained silent, these organizations broke their traditional political reticence and joined the call for Suchinda's resignation and for political reform.

The appointment of Chuan as prime minister appeared to cap these events with the installation of a government elected by due process, no longer beholden to the military, and headed by a man of impeccable reputation who had risen from humble origins through a parliamentary career. Chuan's selection of re-

spected banking professionals to hold three of the most important cabinet positions (two deputy prime ministerships and the finance portfolio) promised both a
continuity with the conservative fiscal management of the past and a departure in
the replacement of discredited rent-seeking politician-cum-businessmen with the
professionally educated business technocrats, representatives of the new industrial and commercial elite that had been nurtured by the Prem government. I shall
return below to a reconsideration of this putative turning point in the character of
the Thai polity, and of its implications for economic policy making.

Emergent Tiger

At the end of the decade Thai technocrats and business leaders could take satisfaction in the restoration of economic strength and the extraordinary growth
surge the country was experiencing. The population growth rate was down to
around 1.5 percent. The crude death rate of 7 per thousand was about average for
middle-income countries, but the crude birth rate of 22 per thousand was among
the lowest for all developing countries. At around 55 million persons (about the
size of Turkey or France), the population was now three times larger that it was
at the end of World War II, and more than double its size in 1960. The GDP in
1989 reached about $70 billion, more than $1,250 per capita. The economy grew
an estimated 12 percent in 1989 and another 10 percent in 1990. (In 1989 GNP
per capita in India was $340, Indonesia $500, Mexico $2,010, Malaysia $2,160,
Korea $4,400, Japan $23,810.[1])

Manufacturing continued to outpace agriculture, resulting in an acceleration
in the long-term decline of agriculture, especially the traditional crops, as a
proportion of GDP. By 1989 the contribution of agriculture had fallen from 23.2
percent in 1980 to 15.2 percent, while manufacturing had risen from 15.9 percent
to 25.4 percent. Exports and expenditure on capital formation were the driving
forces, especially in the late 1980s. While real consumption expenditures rose 38
percent in 1985–89, investment in fixed capital rose 68 percent (in 1987–89).
The value of exports of goods and services averaged 25 percent growth per year
in 1985–89. The composition of manufacturing and of exports was marked by
increasing diversification. The change in the composition of exports was especially marked as a reflection of the role of external demand as a source of change
in the structure of domestic production. In 1965 primary commodities made up
no less than 95 percent of Thai merchandise exports. By 1985 the share of
primary commodities had fallen to about 50 percent. In the next four years, the
surge in manufactures reduced the primary commodity share to about 31 percent.

So far, so good. A country that has (a) managed above-average growth and
relative price stability over a long period of time, (b) been changing its structure
to reduce the relative shares of products and economic activities of lower factor
productivity, (c) recently experienced a four-year expansion in economic size
totaling over 40 percent, and (d) reconfirmed a long-run market- and trade-

oriented development strategy, supported by policies reinforcing the flexibility of domestic factor and product markets and keeping market distortions and interventions to relatively minor magnitudes, would appear to have done well by international standards. If anything, the surge in growth caused both surprise and even dismay in Bangkok at some of the immediate effects: a speculative run-up in land prices, 6 percent annual inflation in 1990, and pressure on infrastructure facilities with insufficient capacity in the face of the demand surge. While the threat to macroeconomic balance in 1990 was not serious (the spike in oil prices caused by the Persian Gulf crisis was temporary; the current account deficit of 7.5 percent of GDP in 1990 was offset by private capital inflows, and external reserves were at a comfortable level of five months of imports; the government enjoyed a third year of fiscal surplus and was able to prepay and to reduce public debt), the monetary authorities undertook countercyclical measures to restrain demand and reduce land and stock market speculation.[2] In a step that brought considerable publicity to the concept of continued liberalization of economic policy, Prime Minister Chatichai announced in May 1990, with unaccustomed fanfare (for the normally obscure subject of Thai-IMF relations), that Thailand was moving to formal adherence to Article 8 status with the IMF, the status shared by the developed country members of the fund. To comply with Article 8 requirements, the Bank of Thailand immediately launched a program of liberalization and elimination of controls over foreign exchange transactions and capital movements.

The basic economic characteristics of Thailand's postwar growth and structural change resemble those of the Asian super-performers, Taiwan and South Korea, in many respects. At the risk of oversimplication, one can cite some of the key factors explored in the extensive literature on Taiwanese and Korean development. Their growth has been export-led, with merchandise exports substantially outpacing growth in GDP and income per capita. The reliance on export growth developed as a shift from initial periods of "inner-oriented trade strategies, quantitative controls over imports, and slow growth."[3] The export growth was achieved within policy frameworks that included realistic exchange rates; import regimes that did not hobble export competitiveness; the provision by the state of transport and communications infrastructure necessary for exporting; restraints on the government's regulation of imports; early use of credit and other subsidies and privileges for exporters, followed by a shift toward "reasonable" uniformity of the incentive system; only exceptional reliance (more so in Korea than in Taiwan) on government interventions to "pick the winners" among potential export commodities; and relatively efficient labor markets. Other policies also contributed to the growth of both tradables and nontradables, including the development of human capital; the maintenance of strong balance-of-payments positions that allowed governments to avoid recurrent "stop-go" macroeconomic management; and a move over time toward financial liberalization and positive real interest rates. Kreuger hypothesizes that because outward orientation makes the costs of big mistakes highly and quickly visible, the export-based economic regimes of the Asian NICs enabled them to avoid "the huge mistakes in policy that seem to have enormous costs in terms of foregone output and growth in many other developing countries." The NICs have made mistakes but have had the flexibility to reverse course. In addition, a "virtuous policy circle" may have operated as success reinforced the apparently effective policy directions; for example, the inefficiencies of government trade, allocation, and other interventions become increasingly glaring as the industrial and financial structure grows more complex and articulated with changing external markets.

Although there have been important differences among the NICs (and Japan), for example, in the role and treatment of agriculture, the broad "East Asian" policy model does capture the common highlights that contrast with the inner-oriented and highly interventionist model that has characterized (until quite recently) a large number of the generally slower-growing developing countries in South Asia and other parts of the world.

The Thai model might be characterized as a laggard NIC. Due to such factors as Thailand's much greater size and the scope remaining into the early 1980s for vent-for-surplus expansion in tropical agricultural exports, industrialization got under way later. Instead of starting out with import substitution and moving toward liberalization, Thailand began with a relatively liberal policy regime from the mid-1950s, became more interventionist and protectionist in the 1970s, then developed a strong export orientation in the 1980s that thus far has run parallel with the import-substitution incentive system only now being partially dismantled. Financial dirigism for industrial and export development has been much less extensive in Thailand, and in practice, if not formally, the government has begun to move away from the mandatory provisions favoring agricultural lending. The automotive promotion policies were a mistake in terms of their efficiency costs, but not "huge" in their overall economic impact. The only other modern "picked winners" were beyond reasonable doubt—tourism and natural gas-based industries. Parts of the communications and transportation systems appear to have been less well managed in Thailand, with their weaknesses recurring in spurts but not severely hampering economic growth. Thailand's domestic savings and investment rates have generally been lower than in the NICs, and the inflow of concessional funds in earlier decades was much lower in Thailand, in relation to total resource availability, than was the case in Taiwan and Korea. Finally, the NICs moved faster than Thailand into knowledge- and skill-based industries, on an earlier path of industrial evolution, human capital formation, and a general rise in wage rates and income levels.

Thailand's development is likely to continue along a path that differs from the East Asian model in significant ways. The product composition of manufacturing and exports is likely to continue to differ substantially, partly because of Thailand's strong comparative advantage in processed foods (which are classified as manufactured exports), partly because of the continuing shift of manufacturing from the NICs and Japan to Thailand (and other ASEAN countries). Tourism is of much greater importance in Thailand. Nevertheless, in broad policy outlines Thailand has been another example, or variant, of the East Asian model, a strong exporter aimed at becoming another "super-exporter."

Will Thailand be able to continue along this route, and will the outcomes bring about, on balance, continuing improvement in economic productivity and social welfare? The remainder of this chapter considers the major issues of sustainability of growth, and of social impact, that have been debated in recent years. They range from questions of economic and environmental feasibility, to questions of social changes and imbalances that could react back upon the economic growth process and that have raised, in the minds of many Thais, fundamental concerns about the future of Thai culture and society. Is Thailand becoming the next Asian Tiger by wise and considered choice, or has it merely grasped the development tiger by the tail to be pulled away ineluctably from a way of life that was simpler but had many strengths? Is economic growth merely conjuring up a new set of material problems and unresolved weaknesses in the political order?

Export Pessimism

As one might expect in a country that has hitched its economic growth to an export engine, the feasibility of this policy has been questioned now and then as one Thai economist or another has been afflicted with export pessimism. I noted earlier that Thailand was not affected materially by the trade-inhibiting developments of the 1980s. As a small and flexible supplier, its manufactures of labor-intensive, foot-loose products found niches in increasingly diversified markets, while the manufactures based on Thailand's tropical agricultural products were exploiting the country's traditional comparative advantage. Quite apart from the bilateral trade disputes with the United States in the latter 1980s, the broad possibility that the 1990s might see the development of two trading blocs—the EEC (and its associated developing countries, mainly African and Caribbean) and a North American group (extending to less developed Latin American countries)—has caused disquiet in Thailand as in the rest of Southeast and East Asia. As a trade-oriented region, these Asian countries could face loss of export markets due to trade diversion effects, if not exclusionary discrimination, if the two blocs develop in a rival and inward-looking fashion. Although trial balloons have been floated (especially by Malaysia) suggesting that the Asian countries create a defensive trade grouping of their own, the position of most of the putative members, including Thailand and Japan, has been to eschew formation of a third bloc in favor of pressing the two emerging blocs to maintain and indeed further liberalize the existing global trading system. The ASEAN countries have agreed to move toward meaningful internal liberalization of trade in the 1990s, partly as a means of preserving the mutual security benefits of ASEAN cohesiveness, in a post–cold war environment, and partly to create a stronger subregional economic system in which Vietnam, Cambodia, Laos, and eventually Myanmar can be peacefully integrated. But any such ASEAN arrangements are certain to be outward-oriented, that is, aimed at creating a large market area, growing faster than any other developing country area, and thereby will be more attractive to foreign investment and external trade expansion.

Any fundamental change in the world trading system that would discriminate against Asian exports to the EEC and North America would pose serious obstacles to the export-based growth of the Asian economies. At this writing, these threats are still problematical and in the realm of economic diplomacy surrounding the Uruguay Round of multilateral trade negotiations. And the occasional expressions in Bangkok of export pessimism, along with calls for Thailand to consider a more domestically oriented development strategy, have yet to be adumbrated in any specific policy alternatives beyond intra-ASEAN preferences. In any case, as the occasional pessimist regretted the export dependence of the latest surge in economic growth, the business sector appeared to be increasing its export orientation and diversity. As the growth of manufactured exports accelerated in 1986, it was observed that many new entrants and small operators were participating, and that quality upgrading (e.g., of garments) was diversifying the product mix and raising the value-added content. Perhaps more important, exporters were increasingly showing the aggressive pricing and marketing tactics that have long been attributed to the Asian NICs in partial explanation of their export performance. Exporters were shipping to buyers in new Latin American and African markets even when payment remained uncertain, taking risks in markets where they had no previous experience, in order to gain entry and establish a foothold. Among banking observers, the heightened aggressiveness in the business community was seen as a further outward-looking response to the concern over protectionism, a rejection of inward-looking defensive retreat.[4]

Environment and Natural Resources

It is in the area of environment and natural resources that questions of sustainability of growth have been most sharply focused. Given the resource-intensive, resource-depleting character of Thailand's economic development for well over a century, are the environmental limits and breakdowns now being experienced signs that the very nature of the country's economic activities will render growth of this speed and character unsustainable? Most of the issues raised by these signs of environmental stress have technical aspects I will not pursue, such as whether or not fast-growing eucalyptus trees are appropriate for degraded soils in the Northeast, how to dispose of toxic waste, or how to replace chemical fertilizers with organic stimulants that will not cause downstream run-off damage.[5] These issues will be examined from a general policy perspective.

Thailand's environmental problems fall into three broad categories differentiated by their socioeconomic character and their politics. First, there have been conflicts pitting cultural, conservationist, and wildlife values against "development" projects. Conservationist groups have lobbied against commercial or infrastructure projects that would intrude on undeveloped areas valued for wilderness and species habitat. In recent years, conservation for the sake of wilderness preservation has been a concern of small groups of middle- and upper-class Thais, but has received increasing publicity and support from the press. While some of the objectives of these groups would be consonant with economic activities, especially the preservation of the integrity of environments that draw tourism, other concerns are not, such as their opposition to the blatant local traffic in endangered species, a brisk trade that violates unenforced regulation. The conservationists draw support from royal interest and from international environmental organizations. Although the government has conservationist activities to its credit, such as the establishment of many national parks, the government has generally been either the active despoiler or the lax protector of the environment in the eyes of the conservationists.

The potential political importance of conservationist values was first demonstrated in a notorious case in 1973 in which some ranking military officers used government equipment for a hunting expedition in a wildlife preserve. Press criticism and student agitation aroused public opinion in an incident that contributed to the fall of the Thanom–Praphas government. The perpetrators were seen as corrupt individuals rather than as representatives of government per se.[6]

The second category, issues of the "tragedy of the commons," is of much greater economic importance. In these issues, the pursuit of individual (or individual corporate or group) economic interest generates diseconomies that fall on that individual only slightly, but that are borne by the community as a whole; the diseconomies resulting from each individual's actions cumulate to the eventual detriment of the entire community. Unless such individuals can be made to bear the cost of their own environment-degrading acts, or can be constrained by law, the sum of the individual acts, initially individually beneficial, becomes destructive for all. Primary examples of diffused tragedies of the commons are the general deforestation and the extraordinary congestion and automotive air pollution in Bangkok.

Thailand is arguably a society that has particular difficulty dealing with tragedies of the commons. For one thing, the society is very tolerant of individual economic choice and life-style (lax by the standards of societies that impose manifold strictures on individual behavior in the name of social harmony). The Thai attitude toward intervening in the individual's economic behavior is expressed in the folk injunction not to break someone else's rice bowl. For another, during most of the country's history of land abundance and, in effect, unhindered settlement, resource depletion and environmental degradation appeared to be a positive-sum game: nobody else's rice bowl was being broken.

The third category of environmental issues comprises local conflicts of interest over resource use, or over environmental damage caused by one group that impinges directly on the welfare of another. Rice bowls are being broken, and both the owners and the breakers are clearly identifiable. In numerous cases, different commercial activities have been clashing over competition for local resources, and over the effects of effluents and other incompatibilities. Examples have included disputes between small-scale and large commercial fishing interests, and between tourism enterprises and local industrial plants. The central government almost invariably gets drawn into these disputes. While these problems have not raised general economic policy issues, they have focused attention on the fact that conflicts of local interests can no longer be elided through the safety valve of further expansion against a distant land frontier, and that Thailand has lacked effective and regularized processes for environmental dispute resolution at the local level.

There have also been a rash of village protests against neighborhood projects that intrude, or threaten to intrude, on village economic welfare and, in many cases, survival. Some of the intrusions originate from private upstream activities, such as salt mining in the Northeast that causes salinity in downstream farmland. Most widespread have been disputes with the Royal Forestry Department over land (commonly designated "degraded forest") that villagers have been using, without legal title, and that the department wants to reclaim for (often commercial) reforestation. Most of these protests, numbering in the hundreds over the past few years, appear to have been spontaneous and locally organized. They have been drawing support and organizational advice from Bangkok-based nongovernmental organizations that see these confrontations as reflections of the need for village "empowerment" against outside forces. Contrasted with the traditional passivity and deference of villagers toward district and provincial officials, the village demonstrations represent a remarkable change toward assertiveness, confrontation, and political participation from the ground up.[7]

Prior to the 1980s, deforestation was the only aspect of Thailand's resource-dependent development that was recognized as a problem of environmental degradation. The conversion of public forest lands to private squatter agriculture was a massive, nationwide phenomenon. Since the exploitation of additional land was the only option available for the bulk of the increasing rural labor force, there was no realistic possibility for the government to have more than marginal effect on this settlement process, even if it had become an objective of national policy before the 1980s. In fact there have been times when the government has cleared extensive forested areas in the deliberate pursuit of public policy objectives that were at variance with environmental conservation, but arguably more urgent at the time. In the mid-1970s in particular, the Thai army cleared swaths of virgin forest adjacent to highways that had been rendered unsafe by armed insurgents operating from the forest cover. The government similarly promoted clearance by landless settlers in order to secure areas the insurgents had been using as refuges. The annual forest destruction between 1976 and 1978 from this settlement was the highest Thailand has ever experienced.[8] Given the country's resource endowment in the 1950s and the incontestable need for infrastructure that would open up access to resources and markets, it was inevitable that the government's development programs would accelerate what would only later be reinterpreted as resource and natural environment degradation. Even into the early 1980s (and despite the establishment of a watch-dog agency, the National Environmental Board, in 1975), the prevention of environmental destruction as a general issue of national policy was not accorded high priority by the Thai government, the World Bank or other aid agencies, or Thai public opinion, nor were environmental problems well understood.

The fifth plan called attention to problems of mining and hillside erosion, saline water intrusion, water pollution damage to agriculture and marine life, and the environmental damage caused by the construction of dams and reservoirs, in addition to deforestation and watershed destruction, but the entire subject was given little emphasis.[9] Environmental consciousness developed very rapidly thereafter, however, as scientific and economic studies, the media, and numerous seminars drew attention to the increasingly better-understood problems of both urban and rural environments. Natural resources and the environment appears as a discrete subject of development policy for the first time in the sixth plan. By then (1987) the list of environmental problems had expanded to include waste discharge into the Chao Phraya River, air pollution, decline of marine resources through over-fishing and degradation of natural habitat, river siltation, coral reef destruction, introduction of toxic wastes into the food chain, and the reduction of coastal mangrove forests. The brief reference to actions taken under previous plans is limited to studies and the beginnings of project-level consideration of local environmental impact.

While some of these problems reflect the early environmental diseconomies of industrialization, the plan recognizes that the environmental problems have arisen mainly from the resource-intensive character of past Thai development, and that "the hope for natural resources to play a similar role to that of the past is not likely to be realized." The magnitude of the problems is reflected in the fact, noted in the plan, that the proportion of the labor force employed for all or part of the year in extractive occupations (agriculture, mining, and quarrying) was still high at 70 percent in 1984, compared with 79 percent during the first plan period. The implication is that programs to limit the further expansion of economic activities causing the major nonurban environmental degradation problems could reduce opportunities for income growth of large numbers of Thais in the short run, even if the controls might be justified on long-run income maintenance grounds or on the need to protect others from incurring the costs.

The conflicts and inequities inherent in the policy reversal—from long-standing encouragement (or at least toleration) of forest clearance and settlement by land-hungry small farmers, to removal and relocation of settled communities (who lack legal land title) in order to clear areas for reforestation—became evident in 1991. It was estimated by the Royal Forestry Department (RFD) that more than ten million Thais were now living and farming in areas legally designated as forest under RFD jurisdiction. Supporting the position of the RFD that much of this "degraded forest" land should be reforested to restore its watershed and other natural environmental functions, the Thai army began to implement its own Project for Agricultural Land Distribution to Poor People Living in Degraded Forest, in effect a resettlement scheme. Before it was suspended, the project created intense controversy among small farmers (who have resisted on the grounds that the resettlement areas were smaller and/or inferior), environmentalists (who otherwise find the interests of the poor and the environment to be in harmony), commercial farming enterprises (which obtain large holdings from the RFD for reforestation as eucalyptus plantations), and the army (which has resorted to intimidation and forced removal).[10] Scientific and bureaucratic opinion has also been divided over the effects of eucalyptus plantations on soils and water tables compared with the economic benefits for a domestic pulp and paper industry. While a policy of evicting large numbers of farmers from deforested areas is not likely to succeed (or to be adopted), the pressures for further illegal clearance and settlement may be coming to an end. As Ammar Siamwalla has pointed out, "A shift to a manufacturing base will ease the pressure on the forest cover after four decades of continual land expansion. It is expected that the absolute size of the (permanent) agricultural labor force will shrink sometime during the 1990s. This will lower the demand for land."[11]

The first critical mass of research into environmental problems was performed by TDRI only in 1990.[12] TDRI proposed that Thailand adopt market-based mechanisms to control pollution, drawing on the experience of some developed countries. Some of these ideas were incorporated in the Anand government's landmark environmental legislation in 1991 and may well provide feasible alternatives to the traditional but problematical reliance on administrative regulation. While it might reasonably be argued that Thai governments until now have not had the factual and analytic basis for formulating effective legislation and policies to cope with these problems, it is also true that past governments, including the Prem administration, have failed to implement laws already on the books dealing with relatively unequivocal degradation sources.

Air quality tests in Bangkok between 1983 and 1989 confirm what any casual pedestrian would attest: substantial increases in pollutants. The lowest reported average blood lead levels are three times as great as levels in the United States and Western Europe. Measured levels of particulate matter and carbon monoxide are well above the standards set by the National Environmental Board.[13] The chief source of this pollution is automobile emissions. Major culprits have been the public bus system and poorly functioning mufflers, especially on Bangkok's army of motorcycles. Although these emissions violated standing regulations (and although the buses belong to a state enterprise), no serious effort had been made to reduce these health hazards until the Anand government introduced unleaded gasoline.

The Prem government can take credit for encouraging the research that explored these problems for the first time and for formulating the first broad environmental programs. Most fundamental, however, was the recognition that the long-heralded disappearance of the land frontier had finally arrived in the 1980s, and that the land pressure, natural resource depletion, and environmental diseconomies were combining to alter the factor proportions and comparative advantages on which growth had rested in the past. The sixth plan does not state this generalization explicitly, but its emphasis on efficiency of resource use, land conservation, and the promotion of science and technology (which first appeared as a separate subject of development policy in the fifth plan) stem from the logic of changing factor endowment and the rising marginal costs of land and water as productive inputs. Explicit in the sixth plan is the recognition that resource and environment degradation could become serious threats to growth, and that the government's determination and capability to cope with these problems was not adequate.

Environmental problems in Thailand, like elsewhere, are very heterogeneous. While the effort to bring them together within an embracing conceptual framework has served as a powerful organizing principle, and has led in Thailand, as elsewhere, to the creation of a central environmental agency in the government, the individual problems vary in scientific character and economic locus, and are scattered through the government in terms of agency responsibility. In this respect, and in recognition of the local character of many environmental disputes, the sixth plan initiated an effort to cope with these disputes through decentralized processes that would incorporate environment dimensions into the administrative system for rural development.[14] For most of the problems, I noted that Thailand lacked regulatory criteria, experience, or even a legislative basis. (As far as deforestation was concerned, the ample accumulation of law, regulation, and overlapping jurisdictions has been part of the problem. In addition, corruption within the Forestry Department and among local officials responsible for controlling illegal logging has been endemic.) While the attention given to environmental problems in the 1980s appeared to be setting the stage for future actions, enforcement authorities remained weak and the volume of government expenditures allocated to environmental protection was relatively low (0.24 percent of GDP) compared with that of other countries (e.g., 0.38 percent in Indonesia, 0.40 percent in Korea, and an average of 1.28 percent in OECD countries).[15]

Despite the accomplishments of the Prem government, the environmental record was "mixed," taking account of the many sins of omission, and of the numerous projects where conflicts between environmental and development policy considerations were unresolved. In fact, in one of the most conspicuous project disputes, the Prem administration was cast as the environmental antagonist. The project had been developed by the Electricity Generating Authority of

Thailand (EGAT) and called for construction of a hydroelectric dam in Kanchanaburi Province. Student and provincial opposition forced the government to shelve the project in 1982. When the government tried to revive the Nam Choan project in 1986, the reaction among Kanchanaburi residents, students, environmental groups, and the media was even stronger yet. The objections ranged from feared effects on local climate, soil fertility, and fisheries, to concern over the dam's safety, since it would be sited on a geologic fault line. In a broad mobilization of national public opinion, the opposition to the project appeared to be developing into a potential challenge to the stability of the government. Once again, in 1988, the project was shelved.

After decades of environment-intensive development, the conflicts over the uses and abuses of water, agricultural land, forests, beaches, marine areas, and other environmental contexts have been emerging as a prime source of interest group formation and of political contention. It is noteworthy as an indication of the essentially factional nature of formal Thai politics that the political parties have not taken up the environment as a defining issue. In the Nam Choan case the political parties played no role, coming out in opposition to the dam only when it was clear that the general public was opposed.[16] While the environmental issues have been generating some of the first middle-class and village "political" activity since the 1970s and are likely to grow as a field of conflict among private interest groups and between the public and the bureaucracy, there is no sign yet of these forces developing into a European-style "green" movement.

The rising technocratic concern over environmental degradation found a window of opportunity under Anand. In a burst of activity, the government launched a raft of projects, regulations, and legislation affecting sewage treatment, mining, antipollution incentives, and other environmental issues. The Anand cabinet apparently viewed its environmental initiatives as the centerpiece of its administration. Whether or not this technocratic perception of priorities has a lasting effect on the politics of the environment, and on the implementation of the laws now in place, remains to be seen.[17]

Fairness and Balance: Absolutes and Relatives

Inequalities in income, wealth, market power, and access to economic infrastructure and social services were recognized from the first development plan as major problems. Each plan has presumed that economic development would lessen these maldistributions and has included programs addressing aspects of economic inequality among the Thai population. The concentration of nonagricultural activity in the Bangkok area, the inequalities in regional agricultural resource endowment, and the concentration of tourism at favored locations have been among the important structural factors that have built geographic and urban-rural imbalances into Thailand's development process, imbalances not easily reshaped or compensated for by public policy. Development has reduced the extent of absolute poverty. But the impact on distribution is uncertain in important respects, partly because the basic data appear to contain large-scale inaccuracies or ambiguities.

The analyses of these imbalances have examined different dimensions—the distribution of income; the distribution of educational, health, and other human service facilities by region; health and nutritional status; sectoral distribution of the labor force and relative productivity in agriculture versus industry; and so on. When the rural and urban divisions are further broken down into regions and subregions, there are relative lags, even within the rural economy, of the Northeast and some northern and southern subregions. Finally, there is the problem touched on earlier of concentration of income and economic power at the very top, focused on the largest commercial banks in particular.

Looking at the absolutes first, by the usual measures of change in the material conditions of life, and in the measurable health and educational status of the population, economic development has brought substantial improvement. Life expectancy at birth was up from forty-nine years in 1960 to sixty-five in 1988. Infant mortality was down from 88 per thousand live births in 1965 to 30 in 1988. Before the 1980s, improvement in the nutritional status of preschool children appeared to be lagging in Thailand compared with other developing countries, especially considering the historically satisfactory caloric supply position of the country. During the 1980s, village-based nutritional programs of the Ministry of Public Health, designed to improve nutritional surveillance and child-feeding practices and to supplement the food supply of poor households with underweight infants, brought about substantial reductions in preschool malnutrition.[18] The leading causes of death changed over the past twenty years, from those associated with poverty and unsanitary rural living conditions (diarrheal disease, tuberculosis, and pneumonia) to ills associated with higher-income societies (accidents, heart disease, and cancer). Medical and health-care services have become relatively strong by developing country standards, and even by international standards, in the quality of medical and public health education and in research and service capabilities in some medical specialties. The shift of priorities from urban-based curative services to provincial, district, and village-based primary health care became evident in the 1980s in the proliferation of service facilities and entry-points, increases in provincial medical and paramedical personnel, and the changed allocations in the health budget. Concentration of private medical providers in Bangkok has been inevitable, of course, but the programs of the health ministry have gone far to raise the standards and accessibility of provincial services and of village health infrastructure, which was still weak in the early 1980s. For example, the proportion of the population having access to safe drinking water was raised from only 33 percent in 1982 to 71 percent in 1987 and was programmed to reach 95 percent in 1991.[19] Of particular interest have been the ministry's programs in potable water and village sanitation, and in subsidized and prepaid systems for low-income households.

The health system is not without problems, the exploration of which would go beyond the scope of this study. Most immediately relevant are the essential conclusions that health status has improved greatly, both absolutely and relative to the general improvement experienced in developing countries in recent decades; that allocation of public resources for control of vector-borne and other endemic diseases, and for the extension of a primary health care system throughout the country, has brought substantial health benefits to the rural population; and that the policy planning and program implementation capabilities of the health ministry are recognized as strong compared with those of other developing countries and with those of other ministries in the Thai government. In the 1990s, AIDS is likely to be the major new health threat.

The other major factor in the creation of human capital for an economy (and for the socioeconomic mobility and empowerment of the individual) is education. While Thailand has invested substantially in education, in both public and private funded facilities, the educational attainment of the population can be said to be less satisfactory than the health status attainment, viewed from the perspectives of economic and labor force needs and of equality of access and accomplishment. Adult literacy rose from 68 percent in 1960 to 91 percent in 1985, the highest rate among the ASEAN countries, but educational attainment is relatively low by developed country standards, reflecting the limitations on past educational availability for present-day adults. Current enrollment of school-age population, however, is near 100 percent at the primary level. The primary system has started to contract as declining fertility has reduced the size of primary-age cohorts. Enrollment differentiations by gender and region have narrowed over time, the regional differences noted in many contexts also appearing in educational enrollment and attainment, drop-out ratios, and other measures. In general, "current enrollment ratios compare favorably with countries at similar levels of per capita income. The one exception is enrollment in lower and upper academic secondary schools where Thailand lags behind the Asian NICs at comparable or lower per capita incomes."[20]

Between the expansion in enrollment and improvements in the quality of education at all levels, the educational efforts of the postwar period are producing large-scale intergenerational increases in the country's human capital endowment. These increases result from the expansion in the educational system, the increase in demand for schooling, and the enforcement of the requirements for compulsory primary attendance. The enrollment ratios and the higher completion ratios for younger cohorts compared with older population point to a continuing rise in the levels of educational attainment of higher future proportions of the labor force. Apprenticeship in the informal sector has traditionally been an important source of vocational training, probably more important than the formal vocational system. In the modern sector, on-the-job training has also become an important source of labor force upgrading. It is commonly observed that foreign investors consider Thai workers highly trainable and well adapted to workplace discipline in modern-sector employment.

While the educational and skill-training systems have obviously been suffi-cient to meet the labor force needs generated by the country's growth over a long period, there have been difficult issues of structure, fees, curriculum, and differ-ential access that would take this study beyond its terms of reference. I would only note (a) the relative lag in secondary education mentioned above, which has been cited as a potential drag on the ability of the economy to continue on the industrial restructuring path of the Asian NICs; (b) the need to adjust the second-ary curriculum, shifting from its current university preparation orientation to a terminal concept better suited to labor market requirements; c) the limited num-ber of engineers produced by Thai universities in relation to the needs of the industrial sector, and the constraints that insufficient scientific and technological capability may place on future economic growth; and (d) the distributive im-plications of two features of the higher educational system working in opposite directions: while the growth in (lower-middle- and middle-class) enrollment in the country's open and regional universities is already beginning to erode the dominance in business and government of graduates from the country's two elite universities, the common practice among upper-middle-class and wealthy families of sending their children to elite preparatory schools, and then to English-language universities abroad, is creating an educational differential along income lines.

Primary health care and adult education were among a group of sectoral programs that were launched within the rural development program framework created by the Prem administration. The other sector programs covered agricul-ture and local public works. The rural development program was designed as a multifaceted microlevel effort to correct specific deficiencies and alleviate the effects of poverty. Conceived as a direct response to poverty conditions at the village level, the program was administered through an elaborate provincial and district system that was supposed to promote decentralization of responsibility. Planning and educational activities were introduced with the intention of raising the level of villagers' understanding of local conditions, and of promoting self-help efforts where community action might be effective against local social and economic problems. Based on a survey of local conditions, 12,562 villages (about 23 percent of the total number of villages) in 288 districts were designated as poverty areas eligible for incremental resources and projects. The regional distribution of the target localities reflected the geographic pattern of poverty, with 60 percent in the Northeast, 29 percent in the North, 11 percent in the South, and none in the Center.

The program showered the target villages with projects—potable water, household sanitation, village dispensaries, literacy and other adult education, community fish ponds and small irrigation facilities, local roads, veterinary ser-vices, community revolving funds for livestock purchase, soil improvement, dis-tribution of fruit trees, community high-nutrient food plots, timber bridge replacement, electrification, and so on. An elaborate monitoring and evaluation system was set up to track the course of the program for the National Rural Development Committee. As the village deficits declined year by year, villages would "graduate" from poverty status and lose eligibility for specific program components that had been incremental to the normal level of government resource allocation and services.

By the end of the decade, the concept of defining poverty status by village had lost its legitimacy. Residents of districts excluded from the program (and their members of parliament) objected that the targeting system ignored the poverty remaining in some of their villages. In many districts and villages excluded on the grounds of generally higher socioeconomic status, there were still deficits in some of the program subjects; denial of access to incremental resources to erase these selected deficits was criticized as unfair. In response to the political pressure, the program was opened up for nationwide eligibility.

As can be seen from the partial listing above of the program's contents, some of the activities would (at least potentially) raise the standard of living of all households in a village (e.g., improved access to main roads; health facilities; fish ponds) while others might affect relative economic position among households. Some of the activities would bear directly on measurable income; others would improve living conditions in ways not captured by household income surveys. And while some of the activities (e.g., the nutrition programs for underweight infants) favored the relatively poor within a village, other activities increased within-village income differences because of the differential abilities among households to exploit the services offered. It was not uncommon for some components to create differentials and community resentments that did not exist beforehand, even as the activities raised the living standards of the majority of inhabitants. Examples of such unintended inequitable consequences were the revolving funds for financing household construction of sanitation and other health facilities; in some villages that had achieved a high percentage of household coverage, the majority were no longer interested in operating the funds despite the fact that a few disadvantaged households remained without the financial means to build the facilities in question.

The loss of political legitimacy of the target village approach was a reflection of the increasing complexity of income and living standard differentiation in recent years. The regional differentiations have remained, probably permanent features of the structure of income in Thailand because of the geographic differences in resource endowment and transport costs to the major urban and export markets. But within regions, towns, and villages, economic complexity and labor force differentiation have been creating local size-distribution differences in income that have reduced the accuracy of the long-standing area-based definitions of poverty and the effectiveness of area-based interventions for poverty alleviation.

The deprivations in the life of the poor—in nutrition, health, life expectancy, education, housing quality, electrification, and so on—add up to a set of meager personal and material circumstances that commonly define the notion of poverty. But if policy makers are to have a quantitative basis for comparison over time and among countries, it is useful to define some level of income (or expenditure) that can serve as a single indicator of poverty status. Thus, poverty "lines" have been developed in many countries, defined as the minimum annual household income (or expenditure) level a family needs to meet its "basic" consumption requirements. There are many conceptual and statistical difficulties in drawing such lines, or comparing across countries and over time.[21] Nevertheless, if attention is paid to consistency of definition over time and to correction for price changes, the poverty lines give a rough measure of the numbers of people living at substandard levels and the progress, or lack of it, toward poverty reduction.

The incidence of poverty in Thailand in selected years, as calculated by several researchers, is shown in Table 7.1. Keeping in mind the arbitrary (if reasonable) character of any definition that assigns poverty status to households below a precise level of annual income (and nonpoverty status to all those above), the researchers who have calculated these lines (using moderately different definitions) have come up with numbers that tell essentially the same story. Between 1963 and 1981 the percentage of the population in poverty status fell by more than half. As one might expect, the percentage in poverty in urban areas was lower than that in rural; the proportion in Bangkok City was much lower than in the rest of the country; in 1988 the Northeast was home to about one-third Thailand's population, but almost 60 percent of the country's population below the poverty line.

Since poverty is concentrated among agricultural households, the proportion under the poverty line can swing sharply up and down over short periods of time, depending on the movements in the prices of a few main crops. This can be seen from the 28 percent rise in the poverty proportion, from 23 percent of the population in 1981 to 29.5 percent in 1986, with the incidence falling back in 1988 to about the same level of 1981. Rural household incomes in 1981 and 1988 were boosted by above-trend crop prices, and depressed by below-trend prices in 1988.[22] While the premium and export tax imposed on rice for most of the 1962–88 period reduced the incomes of most rice farmers below what they would have been in most years without the tax buffer between farm-gate and export prices, these taxes also moderated the annual swings in rice prices and the attendant swings in income. The reduction of the rice export taxes to zero has increased the exposure of rice-dependent farm households to swings in annual income. For the farm sector as a whole, however, diversification of income sources is likely to be reducing the amplitude of short-term income fluctuations, while for the total population the declining proportion of income dependence on agriculture should be reducing the exposure of the above-line households to cyclical descent into the poverty category, as defined.

Translating the proportions in Table 7.1 into absolute numbers, there would have been about 16 million people under the poverty line in 1962 out of the total

Table 7.1

Poverty Incidence (% of population below poverty line)

	1962	1975/76	1981	1986	1988
O. Meesook et al.					
Whole kingdom	57.0	33.0	24.0		
Urban	38	22	16		
Rural	61	37	26		
Northeast	74	46	36		
Hutaserance and Jitsuchon					
Whole kingdom		30.0	23.0	29.5	22.8
M. Krongkaew et al.					
Whole kingdom			23.0		21.2
Municipal			7.5		6.1
Sanitary districts			13.5		12.2
Village			27.3		26.3
Bangkok			3.7		2.7
Northeast			35.9		34.6
Municipal			18.0		18.7
Village			37.9		36.8

Sources: Oey Meesook et al., *The Political Economy*, table 3.25; Hutaserance and Jitsuchon, *Thailand's Income Distribution*, cited in Medhi et al., *Priority Issues*; (1988 figure by M. Krongkaew using same methodology); Medhi et. al., *Priority Issues*, tables 2.3 and 2.10.

population of 28 million. After two decades, the population had risen to 47.7 million and the numbers below the line had fallen (as of 1981) to about 11 million. Those in poverty rose in 1986 to around 15.5 million, then fell back in 1988 to over 11 million, or roughly the same level as in 1981, but now out of a total population of 54.5 million. Given the high growth of GDP in 1989–90 and the continued strength of agricultural prices,[23] it is likely that the absolute numbers and proportion of population below the poverty line has fallen, perhaps sharply, since 1988. Since the households below the poverty line are headed to a large extent by farmers and laborers who have no more than elementary education,[24] the extent of further declines in the poverty numbers will depend (agriculture prices aside) on the speed with which the nonagricultural economy is growing, generating employment and drawing younger family members away from the small and marginal landholdings that lock in the income potentialities of those dependent on these minimal assets.

Although we do not observe this directly from the socioeconomic surveys, it is likely that a large fraction of households accounting for the figure of 11 million below the poverty line in 1981 were the same households below the line in 1988, for the landholding (or landlessness) and educational characteristics noted. On the other hand, I would reiterate that much of this population resided in the "poverty villages" in the rural development program, benefiting from improvements in their "basic human needs" condition in ways that do not get recorded as imputed income.

The varying rates of economic growth stemming from the regional and sectoral imbalances are reflected in the measures of income distribution that have been drawn from the seven household surveys conducted by the National Statistical Office between 1962–63 and 1988. After reviewing the work of earlier analysts, Medhi concluded that income inequality had increased over this twenty-five-year period. While the trend is consistent among the various studies, there are differences among them in terms of income shares as distributed among five income quintiles from the poorest 20 percent of households to the richest 20 percent, and in the overall (Gini coefficient) measure of income concentration. Medhi's most recent work, based on the 1988 household survey, shows some reduction in overall inequality compared with 1986, as measured by a decline in the Gini coefficient and by a modest shift in income shares from the top to the second quintile.[25] Nevertheless, the inequality remained substantial. The poorest 20 percent of the population earned a 4.5 percent share of total household income; the top quintile, 54.9 percent. Shares of this order would place Thailand's distribution roughly comparable to Malaysia's, more equal than Brazil, and less equal than Indonesia.

The changes in distribution have arisen from the interaction of three factors: resource endowments, changes in economic structure, and the effects of government policies. I am not in a position to lay out a precise picture relating these factors to the course of income distribution over time, but the general outlines can be suggested. The reader is familiar already with the regional variations in agronomic conditions that were the primary determinants of income differentials for the many decades during which primary commodity production comprised the bulk of Thai economic activity. On the regional scale, the most favored agricultural areas were also those that enjoyed the earliest and lowest cost transport connections with Bangkok, thereby gaining advantages (measured in decades) in the accumulation of assets. Advances in agricultural technology for the rainfed and semi-arid areas have been limited compared with research results applicable to well-rained and irrigated areas. Irrigation potential is very unevenly distributed. I would add to this picture by noting that local income differentiation was a feature of the village economy before national integration or the reach of government had become important economic forces.

Village history studies in the Northeast have shown how differentiation—primarily in ownership of quality land and in numbers of buffalo—arose among Laotian migrants settling abundant virgin land, partly because those who arrived first settled on the locations with the best soil and water conditions, and partly through the accidents of misfortune and the unequal distribution of normal variations of individual ability and motivation. As regional economic development opened up new opportunities for these villages, the better-positioned families were better able to exploit them.[26] In short, within the agriculture sector there are agronomic and self-reinforcing factors that have been working to widen "natural" disparities, which one may characterize as "initial conditions."

The net impact of government policies on income distribution is much less clear despite the considerable literature on this subject. For one thing, no account has been taken of the (admittedly undeterminable) income opportunities the lowest deciles have gained from migration to the newly cleared lands made accessible by government road building. The distributional impact of rice taxation is one of the most intensely studied subjects in the economic literature on Thailand. While farm households that were net rice sellers have been unambiguously taxed, the beneficiaries of the implicit retail price subsidies have included (in addition to all households unambiguously enjoying incomes higher than that of rice farmers) the even poorer near-landless rice growers who are net buyers of rice, the landless agricultural laborers who are also poor buyers and low-income urban workers. In the case of the urban workers, however, it has been argued that the price of rice has been the major factor determining the supply price of labor. If urban wages were, in fact, influenced by retail rice prices, during the years when the rice taxes were being imposed, then at least some of implicit subsidy was being transferred to (higher-income) employers.[27] Despite these uncertainties over the incidence of the implicit subsidy, Medhi and others are convinced that the net impact of rice taxation has been to worsen the distribution of income overall.[28]

While rice taxation (now eliminated) was a large fiscal extraction from the agricultural sector (estimated at 5–9 percent of agricultural value-added in 1981),[29] calculations of the resource flows into and out of agriculture as a result of government taxation and expenditure programs, while not complete, show a net positive flow into this sector in virtually every year between 1964 and 1982.[30] Further research would be needed to reach definitive conclusions about the net impact of government policies and programs, but on the basis of the work done thus far there is no prima facie case for putting Thailand into the category of countries that have financed modern industrial development through large net transfers of a surplus out of the agricultural sector. Ronald Findlay has cited Thailand as a rare exception to the general experience of developing countries that have "drained substantial fractions" of peasant income to finance public expenditures of "dubious social value." "The experience of peasant agriculture and the state in Africa and parts of Southeast Asia such as Burma and the Philippines is, if anything, even more dismal than with the *estancias* and plantations of Latin America during the *Belle Epoque*. Only the case of Thailand offers encouragement, with a healthy expansion of peasant exports that is taxed in the interests of urban manufacturing and service sectors but in a manner that still permits the 'goose' to go on laying its 'golden eggs'."[31]

Like most analysts of poverty in Thailand, I have stressed the structure of production and the distribution of physical assets (especially lands and their associated climates) as determinants of income levels and differentiation. Government policies to alleviate poverty have been based on the same framework. Over time, however, the characteristics of households per se, especially the distribution of human capital through acquisition of more years of education, an enhanced capacity to acquire and apply improved agricultural technologies, and a wider range of nonagricultural skills, are becoming increasingly important factors affecting income at the individual household level. The rise of off-farm income, the seasonal and long-term migration of younger family members into nonagricultural employment, and the growth in the demand for nonagricultural labor, which has probably accelerated in the past five years, have been weakening the old close correlation between location and the distribution of household income.

The extension of the public health and education systems throughout the provinces has been fundamental for opening up access for lower-income households to improve their human capital status. However, the sequence of the spread of these services in the 1960s and 1970s was uneven. By the mid-1970s there was a gradient in the availability of human services as one moved away from Bangkok, with the poorest provinces having the lowest levels of government expenditure per capita and the lowest proportions of primary and secondary school enrollment, among other measures.[32] Higher dropout rates, fewer secondary schools, and poorer quality of instruction have contributed to the differential investment in human capital, reinforcing the household income differentials arising from the production gradient running parallel along location lines. According to one estimate for 1972–73, government expenditure on education, transportation, and health and welfare was distributed among households roughly proportional to income levels. Households in the highest income class received ten times the average level of expenditures benefiting the lowest income households.[33] While the elimination of the taxes on rice and the beginning of tariff reform have been recently reducing the regressivity of the tax system, the overall conclusion one may draw from the diverse aspects of government policies affecting income distribution points to several decades in which these policies probably reinforced the structural forces that were working to increase inequalities, even as these same policies were working to promote development across the board and the general long-run rise in incomes at all levels.

As Chalongphob has pointed out, households in the lower deciles can narrow the distribution only to the extent they are able to gain entry and integrate their labor into the relatively faster-growing sectors of the economy. This is especially the case for those still substantially dependent on the export crops that appear to offer little scope for secular increases in production value per household—rice, maize, sugarcane, and cassava. To achieve liberation from the historical structural constraints on income, the relatively poor need to be better served by the systems and institutions that help to create human capital and facilitate intersectoral mobility:

> Changes in the structure of production require a parallel change in the structure of employment to minimize income disparities. Clearly, some of the problems arise from lags in adjustment; for example, migration in the case of the seasonal problem and the problem of employment structure imbalance, and changes in wages for different types of educated workers in the case of open educated unemployment and skill shortages. However, there are also factors working against adjustments in the form of market rigidities, market failures, or bureaucratic structures. The lack of information for seasonal migration is one example. Labour market segmentation may also work against appropriate adjustments in wages. The complex and bureaucratic nature of the education system may also lead to slow adjustments on the supply side of education. Finally, policies on land, and rigidities in the land market can make migration from agriculture more difficult.[34]

Even if the adjustment processes work well, there will remain, for many years to come, large numbers of farmers whose income growth will lag behind the rest of the economy. These are farmers more or less locked into the four main crops, unable to diversify, and facing technical constraints on increases in their productivity. After a few years, cassava cultivation absorbs the meager nutrient content of Northeast soils, leaving these initially low fertile areas virtually barren. Even aside from the cassava-depleted soils, it is difficult to foresee an agronomic basis throughout the region (minor irrigation projects excepted) for more than marginal and slow increases in agriculture-based income.[35] For much of the Central Plain the design of the irrigation system precludes diversification out of rice.

> The existing system . . . does not allow total (or even partial) control over the water level on each individual farm. Thus in areas where second-cropping is practiced, not only can each farmer not choose what crops he can grow, but there is even little choice as to what variety of rice he can grow. The lockstep nature of most farm activities in a locality has in its turn created severe labor constraints.[36]

Noting the pressure the government was under in the mid-1980s to help producers of the four main crops to diversify, Ammar posed the question: "In its supply of support services, for example: credit, irrigation, research and extension, it has theoretically the tools to shift the production structure . . . [but] is the government structure itself free enough to induce these shifts? Our answer is mostly in the negative. In some cases (research and extension) it is the procedural rigidity that holds up the needed changes."[37]

In the face of the differences in initial conditions respecting the potentialities for growth in productivity, the economic geography that has focused industrial development in the Bangkok area, the virtually unavoidable reinforcing patterns of distribution of human capital formation, and the inequalities in flexibility within the agriculture sector, one can conclude that an increase in income inequality has been an inevitable consequence of Thailand's economic development thus far. While the widening in distribution could have been reduced if the government had pursued less regressive tax policies, promoted the development of provincial urban centers more vigorously, and so on, it is unlikely that a major shift could have been affected to bring the rates of regional growth within a narrow range of each other. Resource transfers of the magnitude necessary to accomplish this would have been very costly to overall growth. Radical redistribution that would have crippled general income growth was never contemplated.

Given the changes in income distribution since the early 1960s, Thailand appears to be an illustration of the "inverted-U" hypothesis first suggested by Simon Kuznets in 1955. Based on a comparison of a cross section of countries, Kuznets observed that income inequality was greater among developing than among developed countries, and that inequality was on average lower among the poorest developing countries than among the relatively less poor ones. The inverted-U hypothesis posits that inequality of distribution increases as average income rises, then diminishes as income levels rise further at higher stages of economic development. While subsequent cross-sectional country studies have confirmed and updated Kuznets' observations, they have not confirmed the more controversial causal connection that some have drawn from these observations, that is, that the inverted U describes a general and strong relationship, even a historical necessity, between rising income and rising inequality (before structural changes and advanced country redistributive policies reverse the relationship).[38]

I do not believe the Thai case would support the thesis that the rise in GDP per capita itself provides any meaningful explanation of the rising inequality except in the sense that, without a generous rise in income, those households that have been better positioned to participate in growth would have had less opportunity to create the income differentials they have. As I see it, the explanation lies in the initial conditions, the geographic and agronomic configuration in relation to population location, and the impact of these factors on the patterns of technological change and of household accumulation of human capital. Government action appears to have reinforced these factors, but not consistently by any means, and not with the forcefulness of governments elsewhere given to policies of pervasive intervention. Because the Thai experience has been characterized by relatively moderate interventionism and relatively wide reliance on market forces, Thailand should provide an interesting case for future comparative studies of income distribution, especially if the factors cited here can be incorporated into a model that could be applied elsewhere.

Thai social critics have faulted the economic managers for failing to intervene in ways that might have contained the growth in income inequality. The critics have tended to ignore (apart from the rice problem) the regressivity of the tax structure. Instead they have echoed Dr. Puey, arguing that public expenditure programs have been designed to maximize growth at the cost of more even distribution, and that government "benign neglect" of market outcomes has worked to the advantage of the more rapacious. The technocrats could make a better defense than they have, regarding the argument that the incidence of poverty could have been lowered more and faster if public programs had allocated more resources directly to the poor and to the factors determining their income status. One can never be sure of what might have happened under moderately different policy regimes, although the relatively slow development of access to secondary education could probably be cited as partly responsible for foregone income growth of an important fraction of the labor force. But if, in fact, the allocation of resources had been determined in a thoroughgoing way by calculations of expected alternative economic returns to competing investments, the economic planners would have denied the Northeast much of the investment that has been made in that region's infrastructure, in favor of higher allocations to other parts of the country possessing superior resources and offering higher returns to scarce capital. As has been the case with poorly endowed regions in many other countries, such as the American Appalachia or southern Italy, the substantial public resource flows into these areas have been driven by political and social considerations, not simply dismal or indifferent economics.

Structural Imbalances: Urban and Rural

One of the primary distortions in Thailand's pattern of development has been the extreme concentration of the country's urbanization in the Bangkok Metropolitan Region (BMR), comprising Bangkok Municipality and five surrounding provinces. Despite the momentum to the country's economic development that has derived from the economics of this concentration and from Bangkok's social and economic dynamism, there appears to be a consensus that the diseconomies and social ills attributable to this concentration are cumulating into a major threat to future social and economic conditions. This view has been expressed succinctly by Medhi:

> Although the present [1987] growth of Bangkok in terms of population at 2.9% per year represents a decline from the 1970s, it is still much higher than the country's average population growth rate. By the year 2000, the BMR's

population would be 11.5 million. Under the present course of development, this rate of growth for Bangkok may create enormous social costs associated with congested living conditions, traffic problems, environmental pollution and social tensions unless drastic measures are taken to change this pattern of urbanization. Other core cities must be promoted to relieve the burden of Bangkok.[39]

The regional cities and most provincial capitals have progressed in terms of infrastructure, amenities, transport access, and health and educational facilities, and in many respects have healthier and more pleasant living environments than Bangkok. However, none has yet developed economies of location offering competition to Bangkok substantial enough to serve as a large rival for urban migration. It is unlikely that the programs for regional city development can do more than incrementally strengthen their relative economic and population drawing power. Nevertheless, it is difficult to avoid the conclusion that the large-scale inefficiencies and diseconomies arising from Bangkok's transportation and land-use configuration could have been significantly ameliorated, and that the present critical position results from one of the major policy failures of the postwar era.

Bangkok has a reputation for perhaps the most congested traffic of any city in the world. It has suffered severe subsidence and flooding, and heavy pressure on inadequate housing, piped water, and other infrastructure. The private and public costs of time lost in traffic, excess fuel consumption and vehicle operating costs, and expenditures to cope with flooding are substantial. Since the late 1950s, the government has undertaken several comprehensive planning exercises as frameworks for coping with Bangkok's relentlessly growing problems, but neither the central government nor the city administration has been willing or able to enforce zoning, building, or traffic regulations that would impinge in a significant way on builders, commerce, or drivers. When NESDB unveiled some well-researched proposals developed for the sixth plan to discourage personal automobile entry into the city core (e.g., installation of a toll system), they were shouted down in the introductory meeting without serious consideration and abandoned by the government.

I have already noted some of the problems that have contributed to this situation, such as the parlous financial condition of the public transport system due to the low level of bus fares. It is beyond the scope of this study to examine the problems of Bangkok urbanization at length. What is pertinent to this study is the extent to which these problems can be attributed to institutional and planning failures rather than sheer resource shortages or the workings of market forces and of investment and consumer choice. This point was admitted by NESDB in its BMR study.

Bangkok's road network has developed over the years with little planning and control. As a result, the network lacks structural coherence and, quite apart from capacity problems, serves traffic needs very inefficiently. In particular:

there is no attempt to provide a hierarchy which concentrates through traffic on primary or secondary roads and local traffic on distributor and secondary access roads. . . . The development of access roads is almost completely unplanned and often leads to local congestion. . . . The poor and incomplete design of the network creates needless traffic and concentrates traffic on main roads. . . .

The failings of the BMR transport system are as much due to *institutional deficiencies* as to lack of material resources. The main institutional problems in the transport sector are: lack of agreed policies and plans; prolonged decision making; complex and inflexible procedures; gap between project and financial planning; land acquisition difficulties; and lack of suitably trained and experienced staff.[40]

The development of Bangkok across the board has suffered from similar institutional weaknesses:

Public administration in Bangkok suffers from many problems that inhibit efficient management. These include: the existence of a multiplicity of organizations with overlapping and divided responsibilities; poor coordination of public investment; and a lack of clarity in the decision process. Fragmented decision making results in a disjointed pattern of investment in urban services, implying a failure to realize potential economies.[41]

Bangkok's "fragmented" decision processes stem from the city's anomalous legal status. Although Bangkok has a municipal administration that is autonomous in some respects, headed by a governor who is an elected official, the governor, and the entire administration, are under the jurisdiction of the Ministry of Interior. The city has an administering structure with limited accountability to an electorate and limited autonomy from the national government. The restricted powers of the municipality are best illustrated by its marginal role in the planning and implementation of capital projects for the city's transport system. The shift from an appointed to an elected governor did result in discernible improvement in some of the city's services. But the governor's authority is limited and subject to the politics of relationships with the Ministry of Interior and the political party holding that portfolio.

Bangkok's immensity belies the extent to which Thailand has become urbanized. Thailand's urban residents in 1988 made up 21 percent of the total population. This is unusually low compared with the average level of 56 percent for the thirty-seven countries the World Bank classifies as lower middle income, or even the average level of 35 percent in the forty-two poorest countries.[42] Compared with the fifteen developing countries having a population over 30 million (in 1983), Thailand was fourth in GDP per capita but twelfth in terms of urbanization. The fact that nearly 70 percent of Thai urbanites lived in the one largest city compared with an average (largest-city population) of 27 percent for these countries as a group has given rise to the impression that Thailand is urbanizing like other developing countries, whereas in fact Thailand is one of the least urbanized of the group.[43] The concentration of income and economic activity in Bangkok is all the more striking seen against the still predominantly rural pattern of human settlement. The BMR (which includes some minor agricultural areas) accounted (in 1987) for about half of Thailand's GDP. Three-fourths of manufacturing value-added and two-thirds of banking and trade value-added were attributed to the BMR in the national accounts. In 1987 about 54 percent of all registered manufacturing establishments (excluding rice mills) were located in the BMR. While there was a clear trend of manufacturing decentralization away from the city to the surrounding provinces of the metropolitan region, and even of more rapid growth of manufacturing establishments in other parts of the country compared with Bangkok Municipality, the distribution was still highly skewed.[44]

These differences in regional production allocation are reflected in regional income differentials. As shown in Table 7.2, per capita income in Bangkok in 1981 was double that of the second-ranking region, the Center, and more than three times average income levels in the poorest region, the Northeast. By 1988 the differentials had widened as growth in the BMR continued to outpace other regions. In short periods these relationships can change moderately, affected by wide swings in important regional crops (reflected in the 1986–88 growth spurts in the North and Northeast and the agriculture spurt in 1988–89). There are also some changwats within regions (e.g., in southern tourist areas) that have per capita incomes multiples higher than the averages.

The widest imbalance in the Thai economy, pushing Thailand off the scale, so to speak, comes out of comparisons of labor force structure and sectoral value-added. According to the labor force surveys, the share of employment in the agriculture sector has been declining but remains at anomalously high levels for an economy with Thailand's sectoral structure. Thus in 1971, 79 percent of the labor force was recorded as agricultural, producing about 24 percent of GDP. By 1986 agricultural employment had fallen to 66 percent and agricultural value-added had dropped to 16.5 percent of GDP. These numbers imply that labor productivity in Thai agriculture is extraordinarily low by international standards and would be a basis for expecting Thailand to have extraordinary inequality between urban and rural incomes. In one recent comparison of 1985 data for eleven Asian countries, Thailand's nonagricultural GDP per capita was twelve times that in agriculture, an "outlier" figure compared with the other countries that had nonagriculture productivity ratios of 5.8 or less.[45] In another such comparison (using different measurement sources and concepts), Thailand's outlier status appears less extreme but still marked in the anomalously low relative productivity of agriculture and high productivity of industry and services (measured by employment/GDP share ratios) compared with Malaysia, Indonesia, Philippines, Korea, and Taiwan.[46] These differences would be narrowed somewhat if account were taken of the relatively severe decline in Thailand's agriculture terms of trade in the early 1980s, but the essential disparities would still be

Table 7.2
Relative Per Capita Income Ratios

	1981	1988	Annual Growth	
			1981–88	1986–88
Region				
Bangkok	100	100	6.1	8.9
Central	50	42	3.2	5.7
North	42	38	4.6	12.8
South	44	37	3.5	9.0
Northeast	29	25	3.6	13.2
Agriculture	100	100	3.4	14.9
Nonagriculture	230	224	3.0	4.1

Source: Based on National Statistics Office, Socio-Economic Surveys, from Medhi et al., *Priority Issues*, table 2.9.

large. However, it also turns out that the definitions and methods of measurement of labor force and of employment in Thailand appear to have overstated the size of the labor force, exaggerated the extent of rural unemployment, and overstated the relative size of agricultural employment. These measurement problems arise from the highly seasonal rhythms of work in the agriculture sector, which are only partially captured by the annual schedule of recurrent labor force field surveys.

Sectoral measurement of labor force distribution requires that an individual be counted as assigned to one sector or another, but in the seasonal movements many workers shift between agricultural and nonagricultural employment over the course of the year. Nonfarm income forms an important fraction of total annual income in many parts of the rural economy even among those not migrating, and much of the nonfarm income is nonagricultural. The decision to enumerate the (predominantly male) heads of farm household as employed but not "at work" during the off-season, while their wives and other family members are classified as "inactive labor force," exaggerates either agricultural employment or unemployment, depending on the meanings attached to "work" in rural settings. The net impact of the many technicalities of definition is to yield data that show large swings in labor force participation rates and in seasonal employment among females in rural areas. Measurement of income or productivity at the household level by sector is also ambiguous because rural households in many parts of the country, especially in the Northeast, typically have young family members who are working in an urban sector, who remit income regularly, and who consider themselves to be rural people who have only temporarily moved out of agriculture. In fact, the multisectoral character of Thai rural households has been high for years and is rising as development proceeds. In 1987 nonagricultural income amounted to about 59 percent of total farm family income, up from 44 percent in 1976.

The technical problems of employment measurement in Thailand[47] are important for the large-scale misimpressions they have created respecting the magnitude of the perceived rural-urban dualism and income differentials of the Thai economy. As the farm household income data show, the labor force survey data overlook the complexities of rural time-allocation among agricultural, industrial, and commercial or service activities and mistakenly allocate all the latter to the agriculture sector.

While some of the analysts working these numbers have proposed reductions in the agricultural proportion of the labor force, there is at present no reliable basis for developing an accurate picture. There are several policy issues that have been colored by what one may take to be a large magnitude statistical error. First, despite the fact that three-fourths of manufacturing value-added derives from the BMR and that some of the service sectors show similar urban concentration, the nonagricultural sectors have also achieved wide provincial penetration. Second, to the extent that a family's cultural identity and sense of place within society are shaped by the nature and location of their work, the polarization of Thai society between agricultural and nonagricultural spheres may be significantly less than literature and casual observation have led people to believe. Third, the programs for off-season rural employment generation, initiated in the "democracy period," may have outlived their usefulness. In the growth spurt of the past few years the labor market has become tight and wages for unskilled labor in rural areas, and in the off-season, have been rising. Fourth, while decentralization of industry away from Bangkok continues to be an economically justifiable policy objective, it no longer appears justifiable to consider fiscal or other concessions for provincial location for employment generation or equity purposes.

Finally, a revision of the presumed employment and sectoral structure of the economy in the directions suggested also implies that Thailand might be on a path of structural change that is less dissimilar from Taiwanese and Korean experience in some respects than has been assumed so far. The World Bank has pointed out that a revised employment structure putting agriculture at 50 percent of the labor force, at the existing structure of production of GDP, would place Thailand about where Taiwan was in 1965 and Korea in 1970.[48] It also implies that the Thai labor force is already undergoing a substantial adjustment, following along with the changes in the structure of demand for labor. All studies of the Thai labor market have attested to its relative (if imperfect) efficiency.

As recently as 1986, just before the resurgence in economic activity, Thai policy planners were convinced that open unemployment was about to become a major economic and social problem. While the downward course of fertility since the mid-1970s would translate into declining growth in the labor force sometime in the 1990s, the near-term prospect was for a worsening of the employment situation. Open unemployment had always been low, thanks to the man–land ratio and the growth in the absorption of university graduates by the public sector. The sixth plan foresaw an end to these historic relationships:

> It is projected that 0.8 million people will enter the labour market each year during the Sixth Plan period while government employment declines, agricultural employment becomes more restricted and nonagricultural employment rises more slowly. All this points to increasing unemployment, which is expected to grow from 389,700 or 1.5 percent of the labour force in 1984 to 800,000 or 2.5 percent, during the final period of the Sixth Plan. In particular the number of educated unemployed will be critically high, rising from 117,400 in 1984 to about 240,000 in 1991.[49]

It is not at all clear that unemployment has worsened in this period or that the continued rise in open municipal unemployment projected by TDRI through the course of the seventh plan period (i.e., to 6.5 percent in 1996) is in fact taking place.[50] These expectations date from 1986 and have been overtaken by the unexpectedly high GDP growth since then. With nonagricultural employment rising an average of 7.1 percent a year in 1987–89, and total employment 3.6 percent,[51] recent job creation has probably exceeded labor force growth (which is estimated at 2.75 percent). Rising wages for many skill categories and widespread business complaints about shortages of engineers, managers, and other professionals in the late 1980s indicate that the feared rise in open unemployment among the politically important vocational and university educated has not arisen. The job placement service administered by the Department of Labor reported sharp increases in both the numbers of placed workers and in vacancies in 1990, with unfilled jobs running three to four times the number of monthly placements.[52]

Corporate Concentration and Modernization

Concentration in the commercial banking sector has been the subject of economic analysis, as discussed earlier, and does not appear to have restricted competition except for the open agreements respecting interest offered on deposits. Greater competition in this sector awaits a decision by the monetary authorities to open the system to new licensees, including new foreign banks. Aside from the benefits (for efficiency, and for achieving the Bank of Thailand's ambition to make Bangkok an international banking center rivaling Hong Kong and Singapore[53]) that might be expected to flow from opening this sector to new entry, the decision to grant new foreign licenses is a negotiating point that is likely to be resolved in the context of the Uruguay Round trade bargaining.

The literature on corporate ownership and concentration in Thailand has a limited scope. To my knowledge, the work done to date focuses almost entirely on identifying the changing ownership of major corporate entities. The most extensive work by Suehiro lays out selected corporate histories, factors in the direct investment of Japanese and non-Japanese enterprises, tracks the changing fortunes of leading business individuals and family groups, and attempts to aggregate the numbers on holdings in order to delineate the interlocking relationships and the relative size of the leading financial and industrial barons and groups. Interesting as this literature is, it appears to have had little impact, probably because it lacked discernible policy relevance for the 1980s. It did not attempt to measure the extent of concentration by sector or product group, whether such concentration was increasing or decreasing and what dynamics were at work that should, or might, be the subject of public policy. It did not explore whether the concentration of ownership was itself a source of market power that had been exercised in ways that might be detrimental to economic efficiency or free entry.

There have been no studies of the practical consequences of ownership relations and interlocking directorates, for example, in the extent to which individual firms within a group operate as independent entities making market-determined choices, or whether they tend to be constrained to intragroup purchases regardless of price or quality considerations. Further, I have noted elsewhere that many of the larger blue-chip enterprises and conglomerates maintain arms-length relationships with the government and with politics, leaving rent-seeking and nonmarket manipulation to a minority of political businessmen. Entry and exit in commerce and industry have been free except for some cases of exclusivity granted by the Ministry of Industry. Even in these cases the direction of policy is toward reducing these monopoly positions. The strong growth of the economy has fostered entry of new firms and the rise of "new" wealth among a class of previously obscure entrepreneurs. The ability of interests in the commercial banking sector to exploit their market power through veiled insider dealings has been reduced, thanks to the enhanced regulatory powers of the central bank since 1985 and its new systems of close scrutiny. Many firms not affiliated with a bank group have increased their market shares at the expense of rival bank-affiliated firms.[54]

Apart from student agitation against the Japanese economic presence in the early 1970s, foreign ownership per se has seldom been a policy issue in Thailand. As noted, foreign investment has been encouraged since the late 1950s. While foreign enterprises have been dominant or conspicuous as joint-venture partners in oil and gas, automotive manufacture, and other sectors dependent on foreign technologies, total direct foreign investment has remained small (less than 5 percent) as a fraction of total domestic capital formation. The relatively small role of foreign investment, compared with Thailand's regional neighbors, is another consequence of the absence of a colonial episode in Thai history.[55]

The statements in the fifth plan asserting that economic concentration and the distribution of income were national policy issues in addition to the problem of absolute poverty now look to have been politically out of phase. They were written by the technocrats, responding to the political pressures that had surfaced in the mid-1970s (and the insurgency, already collapsing when the plan was being written). While the programs aimed at absolute poverty were carried out, the government's energies were absorbed by the macroeconomic problems, of which a primary one was the threat to the financial viability of many large financial and nonfinancial enterprises. The Bank of Thailand resisted proposals that its program of soft loan accommodation for weakened financial institutions should be extended to direct assistance to individual nonfinancial companies in trouble; but neither the central bank nor the government thought that the nonfinancial enterprise sector (nor the upper income classes), under the circumstances prevailing, should be weakened further through imposition of redistributive taxation. Critics of government policy in academia and in the non-goverment organization (NGO) movement, including many who had joined the left side of the political spectrum during the years of polarization in the 1970s, focused on the adjustment of individual programs and issues bearing directly on poverty; but the Thai left, now come in from the cold, still had no general redistributive program to offer as an alternative to the mainstream agenda.

As a result, the issue of economic concentration in the modern sector has been largely ignored in recent years, and the political steam has gone out of income redistribution as a general framework for government policies. The fact that the sixth plan was silent on concentration went almost unnoticed. One exception to this apparent fading of interest might be among those army circles that have expressed the antibanking and anti–big business populism noted earlier. The Young Turks who issued vaguely populist decrees during their coup attempts have been eclipsed in the military politics of recent years. Most observers discount the alleged populism of some prominent military figures, men whose own family commercial activities place their personal interests squarely within the existing economic system. It is believed that if any of these military personalities known for past utterances against bigness achieved prime ministership, they would leave the institutional structure of the private sector undisturbed.

As the anti–big business sentiment of the 1970s receded, the Prem government was able to focus on the elevation and promotion of modern, progressive ownership and management over the "traditional" enterprise culture that resorted to tax evasion, shady practices, alleged criminal associations, and client relations with the bureaucracy to obtain access to government contracts, quotas, and other non-market-determined business. The objective was to encourage an evolution of business professionalism and of internationally accepted business norms, essential to joint ventures and to the ability of Thai business to absorb modern technology and develop competitiveness on international terms. The JPPCC dialogue, the development of graduate education in modern business management, incentives for family firms to go public with equity flotation (and disclosure) on the Stock Exchange of Thailand (SET), and the encouragement of investment by multinational corporations in joint ventures with Thai firms were among the policies used in the effort to accelerate the development of a modern business culture. While the results of this effort are not in their nature measurable, the modern business sector did surge in the 1980s, reflected in such developments as the growth in the SET listings and in the inflow of portfolio investment; the beginnings of direct investment in the United States, China, and other countries by Thai blue-chip companies; and the rise of professional business managers numerous enough to be dubbed a class. However, the blatant exploitation of office during the Chatichai administration suggests that the evolution of the professional business sector has not been accompanied by a decline in the "old-style" sector.

Parenthetically, if one moves away from the economist's perspective, it is possible to view the bureaucracy's cultivation of the modern business elite in a less favorable light. As the principal proponent and manager of the JPPCC dialogue, Secretary-General Snoh saw the development of the JPPCC and the close communication between the economic policy and business elites as "progressive" steps for encouraging private investment, putting pressure on government to reduce uneconomic interventions, and strengthening the position of the professional business class at the expense of the "old-style," rent-seeking, corrupting tycoons. While the direct effects of the JPPCC's operations were (inevitably, as in any institutional change process) mixed, they were positive enough to open this experience to criticism from a political science perspective. Chai-anan, among others, has contrasted this ensconcing of business interests in the halls of bureaucratic power with the recurrent failure of the government to create a comparable forum representing the interests of the mass of small farmers. In a political system that is still deeply flawed, in terms of institutionalizing processes for representation and influence for broad unempowered publics, Chai-anan sees the deliberate strengthening of business elite access as cementing an old bureaucratic-business alliance, widening the imbalance between the already powerful, on the one hand, and the still unorganized and excluded groups, mainly nonunionized labor and small farmers, on the other. Nevertheless, from an overall development point of view, and arguably even for the welfare of the excluded groups, the proximate objectives and accomplishments of the JPPCC innovation were progressive. Given the political realities of the time, to have delayed the strengthening of the one business elite against the other, and the creating of leverage against market-distorting government interventions, pending the establishment of comparable forums for the excluded, would have been a case of making the best the enemy of the good.

The modernization of Thai business appears to have gotten an unexpected assist in one respect from the impact of the mid-decade recession and the 1984 devaluation. I refer to the financial vulnerability of many enterprises in Thailand stemming from the common reliance on high debt-equity ratios, and from the time structure of business debt, which was typically unbalanced toward short maturities. There are important differences between large firms and smaller enterprises in terms of their access to institutional credit. These differences have usually been seen as disadvantageous and discriminatory toward the smaller enterprises, forcing them to rely on family funds and the informal credit market. However, there are indications that the recession had more severe financial effects on the larger enterprises, and among the latter, perhaps most severe on entrepreneurs most reliant on dubious financial practices. The small and medium enterprises, less able to obtain off-shore credit, were probably much less affected by the devaluation than larger enterprises caught with substantial foreign-exchange-denominated liabilities. Thus, the credit crunch of 1984, and the impact of the recession on cash flow, likely fell more heavily on the highly geared larger enterprises more dependent on formal system credit, especially the widely used overdraft accounts of one-year duration. Larger enterprises that qualified for project-based loans from IFCT, or that had access to equity financing from foreign partners, were less reliant on short-term domestic credit, but still faced an imbalance in the maturity structure of their liabilities because of the virtual absence of domestic medium-term credit sources. In any case, the modern corporate sector is thought to have come through the recession having learned of the advantages of more conservative financial management. (Companies trading on the securities exchange had reduced their average debt from 85 percent of total capitalization in 1985 to under 50 percent in early 1991.[56]) These lessons are being reinforced by the changing lending practices of the commercial banks, also more conservative as a consequence of the recession and of closer Bank of Thailand scrutiny. Previously loose insider lending appears to be under tighter, more standard criteria, while more attention is being given to borrowers' financial condition besides the traditional focus on collateral. In a number of conspicuous cases in which high-flying entrepreneurs fled the country to avoid prosecution, it was apparent that the shake-out fell heavily on enterprises prone to fraud and speculative financial practices.

Finally, two unusual Thai institutions, not much studied, should be mentioned for the progressive roles they play in the modernization of the industrial sector and the "culture" of Thai business. First is the Siam Cement Company, founded with government and royal funds in 1913. Siam Cement is the largest manufacturing conglomerate in the country, based mainly on construction materials. It has a reputation for professional management, integrity in business practice, and engineering quality. It is the venture partner most sought after by large foreign investers, and it is the number one blue-chip on the Thai stock exchange. Siam Cement serves as a kind of "flagship" enterprise for Thai industrialization. Conscious of the uniqueness of their corporation, the senior executives are public figures (one of these, Amaret Sila-on, was a member of Anand's cabinet) and apparently have managed their expansion cautiously, to avoid opening the enterprise to charges of unfair competition or of excessive preemption of opportunities for investment in new products.

Second is the Crown Property Bureau, a public agency that holds substantial real estate and industrial and financial portfolio investments, the income from which is dedicated to the support of the Royal Household. The association of the bureau with the monarchy requires its management to invest in enterprises with reputations for social responsibility, and to maintain, by implication, a continuing interest (which can be exercised through board membership) in the character of these enterprises, profitability aside. In practice, the bureau maintains a low profile and does not use its shareholdings as a basis to intervene in corporate management. The largest of the bureau's holdings are in Siam Cement and in the Siam Commercial Bank, third largest of the domestic banks. Although the manager of the Crown Property Bureau has been a civil servant, his position as an appointee of the king, and the bureau's curious position as an agency neither public nor private, according to the ordinary usage of these terms, has enabled the organization to serve an additional function of some importance for economic policy. In some of the most politically sensitive projects in recent years, involving both government and private equity, the government and the private investors have been able to finesse the question of allocating majority control (or of having a 50–50 split that could lead to deadlocked management) by having the Crown Property Bureau take up 2 percent of the equity and dividing the remainder, 49–49, between the government and private sectors. Majority ownership is therefore Thai, and the holders have been satisfied that the controlling margin was in responsible hands.

The Role of Government

In each of the components of the structural adjustment program during the Prem administration, the central strategic issue was to define the proper role of government. There was no significant debate within the bureaucracy, or at the political level, over this role as formulated in the fifth plan. Specific private-sector groups raised their objections and lobbied accordingly as aspects of the program affecting their interests surfaced and began to be implemented. But in the main, these focused objections did not address the general question of the role of government. As far as the short-run macroeconomic imbalances of the economy were concerned, it was undisputed that the public sector was the principal source of excess absorption and that the size of the public sector in the economy would have to be reduced. To achieve the industrial restructuring and export promotion objectives, the role of government would be expanded in some respects, even as its intervention would be reduced in others.

Thai technocrats were well aware of the alternative roles government had performed in Taiwan, Korea, and Japan (and the fact that all three of these economies had developed much faster than Thailand's). The Thai experience thus far had been closer to that of Taiwan than to those of Korea and Japan in this respect, with the latter governments having employed extensive "guidance" and (especially in the case of Korea) financial system development to lead private industry into preselected areas of putative comparative advantage and technological development.

Most Thai planners saw the Taiwanese model as more suitable for Thailand. Government promotion of specific industries would be the exception rather than the central pattern. In both economies, family-based enterprise continues as the dominant commercial and industrial organizational form. An effort to force-feed a shift in industrial structure in favor of products and technologies requiring large-scale organization would have been constrained by the limited Thai experience with large industrial units.

Perhaps the most striking contrast between Thailand and Korea/Japan in this respect, however, was the skepticism in Thai bureaucratic and business circles alike that government in Thailand could make the right choices if it did attempt to define putative comparative advantage and substitute bureaucratic, in place of market-determined, private choice. In the automotive case, the bureaucratic, political, and business interests pulling in opposite directions compromised on a no-change solution; the preference for avoiding an overt zero-sum outcome dominated over the efforts on both sides to pull the state toward greater or lesser intervention to determine the future of the industry. Nevertheless, even while structural adjustment called for numerous efforts to get government out of the way (e.g., reduction of regulation and arbitrary imposition of intervening rents) and to reform the incentive structure in the direction of product neutrality and reducing government protection of infant industries, the program also called for greater government efforts of a facilitating character (in export promotion services, science and technology development, etc.), and for one major exception in the Korea/Japan direction, so to speak, the leading role for government in the development of industrial projects along the Eastern Seaboard. This exception would be the first since the general withdrawal of government from industry effected in 1959. As has been seen, this foray into industrial planning was successful in its final outcome, but not before generating intense controversy that ended in a reaffirmation of the old lines between public and market-driven investment allocation, with an artful compromise in petrochemicals.

As it turned out, one of the important structural legacies of Prem's administration was a further shift toward the private sector in the balance of development responsibility. By reversing the interventionist directions of the late 1970s; by ending some of the long-standing market manipulation functions, especially respecting some key agricultural commodities; by establishing as policy (even if implementation lagged) that state enterprises should be put on a businesslike basis, privatized, or supplemented by private providers; and by admitting in the context of the JPPCC that economic growth required a diminution in bureaucratic regulation, the government was contributing to the growing conviction in Thai society that higher wisdom in national economic life was no longer a monopoly of the bureaucracy.

As a broad statement of development philosophy, the downgrading of the role of the bureaucracy in Thai economic life does not appear as such in the fifth plan or the SAL documentation. The explicit formulation of the idea of a shift in development responsibility seems to have begun to take shape under Prem II. By 1987 it was such common currency that a full statement was written into the sixth plan document. As the next defining policy on the relative roles of government and the private sector in Thailand after the statements in the first development plan and the Sarit investment legislation, this sixth plan text is worth quoting at length:

> One of the main policies of the Sixth Plan is to transform the role of the public sector (comprising the central government, local authorities and state enterprises) into that of a planner, supporter and facilitator of private sector participation. The government will withdraw from activities which can be carried out better and more efficiently by the private sector and will allow more privatization of some parts of its operation. Based on this policy, the role of the private sector is defined as follows:
>
> Encourage the private sector to assume a more active economic role especially in investment. Private investment is expected to increase at an average rate of 8.1 percent per year compared to the (actual) decrease of 0.8 percent per year of the Fifth Plan. Government investment is expected to increase by only 1.0 percent per year (the increase in the Fifth Plan was 1.8 percent).
>
> Encourage the private sector to increase its investment in such areas as transportation, agriculture, water resource development, energy, education and public health in order to reduce the burden of government. Pricing policy will be used as an incentive while government aid and subsidies are to be minimized.
>
> Encourage the private sector to participate more in the activities of the government and state enterprises through the following means: State enterprises will mobilize funds from local and foreign private sectors through joint ventures rather than through loans as has been the case in the past. The private sector will be encouraged to participate more by investing in and managing activities of the government and state enterprises.[57]

In this text the private sector is invited to invade areas of economic activity previously reserved for government. Even within the context of the Sarit policy framework, this invasion represents a sharp turn from the language in the fifth plan that set out the policy basis for the government's active role in the industrial projects then planned for the Eastern Seaboard. The fifth plan language was cautious by interventionist standards elsewhere in the Third World but had a dirigist ring by Thai standards:

> The government will promote the private sector, both domestic and foreign, to invest in the production and marketing of manufactured goods. The government will stipulate measures and regulations to direct manufacturing development according to the targets included in the Fifth Plan. In general, the

government will temporarily participate in any investment project with the private sector at the initial stage. However, the government may participate permanently if the activity is considered vital to the country's economy and security.[58]

In the end, this fifth plan industrial role applied only to the natural gas and upstream petrochemical projects, but was frustrated otherwise by the poor quality of other proposed projects and by the fiscal constraints operating in the mid-1980s. In fact, the exigencies of conservative fiscal management were a major driving force behind the policy enunciated in the sixth plan. One might argue that the government's repeated failure to achieve the revenue increase targets of the SAL and the standby, combined with its rigid adherence to the borrowing ceiling set unchanged at $1 billion for four years starting in 1985, made a powerful positive contribution to long-term structural adjustment by preventing the public sector from expanding its share of GDP, thereby keeping the bureaucracy in a contractionist state of mind.

The result was one of the most significant shifts in economic structure of the 1980s. By 1988 investment as a share of GDP had recovered to 27.5 percent, about the same level as at the beginning of the Prem government. The composition of investment changed over the period, however, shifting in favor of the private sector to the tune of about 3 percent of GDP, private investment then standing at 20 percent of GDP compared with 5.8 percent public. The shift in the structure of savings was greater still. Public savings were brought up from under 2 percent to nearly 7 percent by 1988. Taking public-sector consumption and fixed capital formation together (excluding changes in stocks and statistical discrepancies), the share of the public sector in Thailand's GDP, from an average of 21.8 percent in 1980–85, fell over 1986–88 to 15.1 percent (Table 7.3). In other words, the relative economic size of the public sector was brought down by one quarter (back to its level in 1960–64), while the private sector's command over the country's resources grew accordingly.

The common use of the term "private sector" to refer to the business community should not obscure the fact that the agriculture sector is entirely private, and that the role of government in Thai agricultural development is seen from a different perspective. The need for extensive government investment and promotional activity on behalf of the mass of small farmers has never been contested by any segment of opinion. Some of the government's interventions have been critical to agricultural growth and equity, such as the establishment of the BAAC, road building, the rubber replanting scheme, and hybrid maize adaptation. Other properly public activities have yielded low returns, such as many of the irrigation systems, and rain-fed agriculture research. On the other hand, much of the diversification in output in recent decades has been largely market-driven (e.g., cassava, fruits, and vegetables), with little or no direct government involvement.

Table 7.3

Public Sector Expenditure as percent of GDP

Period	Average % of GDP
1960–64	15.1
1965–69	17.1
1970–74	16.8
1975–79	18.1
1980–85	21.8
1986–88	15.1

Sources: 1960–79, World Bank, *Managing Public Resources,* table 4.1; 1980–88, Bank of Thailand.

The sixth plan included a "production, marketing, and employment" program that reflects both the public-sector contraction theme and the continuing necessity for government to be seen as actively supporting development activities for farmers. The objective of the program was to raise the production and export of nontraditional agricultural commodities. The program relied on the private commercial and agro-industry sectors to initiate production and conduct the processing and marketing functions. The role of government was limited to a set of support functions, "projects" using little money, with very modest physical investment.

In sum, there is no simple ideological generalization that would characterize the role of government in economic development as it has evolved in Thailand in recent years. There was a clear diminution of public-sector size and functions in the 1980s, and a further shift of conviction toward the private sector and the market as institutions more suitable and effective for propelling the development process. At the same time, within this general framework or predisposition, the government continues to be viewed as having important functions of guidance, direct investment, promotion, regulation, and service provision, depending on the pragmatic needs and nature of each sector and subsector of the economy. This may read like a banal conclusion, suitable to the postideology world of the 1990s. It emerges as a more sharply defined philosophy of economic management if compared with the Thailand of the 1940s and 1950s, or the reign of dirigism in various forms in the Third World over much of the postwar period.

The Future of Economic Policy

One might be justified in concluding that Thai policy is likely to continue along the same basic lines that have facilitated the country's relatively successful economic performance thus far. While there have been deviations, inconsistencies, and periods of drift, the continuities stand out when one takes a long view. At the risk of oversimplification, I shall summarize these continuities in one paragraph.

Abrupt swings in policy have been avoided; although often criticized as dilatory, the preference for continuity and incremental change in the decision processes has created confidence and stable expectations. Financial and monetary management has been conservative; control of inflation has been an enduring objective accorded high priority. Realistic exchange rates have been maintained in most periods. Equal importance has been given to stability and growth. Policy formation has benefited from recurrent periods of technocratic management. There have been few cases of large-scale misallocation of public resources in prestige projects yielding low or negative returns. Protection of domestic manufacturing has been relatively moderate; the economy has been relatively open and trade-oriented. Foreign investment has been promoted, and the climate for foreigners has been receptive. Government has attempted relatively little dirigism in industrial investment, through either direct administration or credit allocation. The record in market interventions (including the exploitation of opportunities for corruption and rent-seeking) is more mixed, but still relatively limited. Highly skewed distribution of land holdings has been avoided, and peasant taxation to finance industry and subsidize urban consumption has (again, by international standards) been moderate. Financial repression has been mild. There has been relatively free entry and exit in all sectors except commercial banking. Policy making has been pragmatic, little affected by ideological predispositions, and rooted in accommodation and compromise rather than zero-sum conflict resolution.

The strong performance of the economy over a long period under this policy regime does not serve as a justification for dismissing the policy omissions and failures, some of the more important of which we have discussed above. Public policy spans a very wide range of subjects, even in a relatively laissez-faire framework. It is interesting to note some of the additional problems and recommendations set forth by the World Bank in 1970 that were still lacking adequate government policy response in 1991:

1. The gap between public- and private-sector wage levels, threatening the recruitment and retention capabilities of the civil service
2. The absence of road user charges and water fees to rationalize private use of public goods
3. The low return to investment in irrigation
4. The absence of a capital gains tax that could moderate real estate speculation
5. The weakness of the fiscal powers of local jurisdictions
6. Inequities of the tax system, such as the absence of inheritance tax[59]

To this list I would add

7. The neglected urban and rural environmental problems
8. The long-standing managerial weaknesses of certain state enterprise utilities

9. Excessive protection (finally cut back by the Anand government) of an uneconomic automobile assembly industry
10. The crisis of the finance company sector, allowed to flower in the 1970s without adequate regulation or supervision
11. The glacial pace of land titling, leaving large numbers of farmers with uncertain tenure.

This is certainly not a complete list of problems of economic and social management in which Thai policy or implementation has been faulty, or where government has responded but only after avoidable delay. Nevertheless, in an international perspective, and in the light of the record of economic growth and rising per capita income, a balanced judgment would give the overall policy performance a good grade.

The success of the policy structure makes it difficult for occasional proponents of substantial alteration to make a case credible to Thai opinion. The collapse of socialist command economics, especially in Indochina, should further solidify the Thai centrist consensus. The collapse deprives the intellectual left of a credible external model and deprives the right of a credible external threat or domestic radical antagonist. There are indications that the assimilation of the Chinese accelerated during the 1980s, assisted by the more positive relationships between government and business and by the continuing professionalization of the modern business community.[60] The assimilation process has been embedding an entrepreneurial dynamism into Thai society. The broad policy framework is likely to gain increasingly strong support from the middle classes, business, and financial interests, and other elements of the Thai elite who are reaping fruits from the development process.

Despite these considerable strengths, the institutionalization of economic policy in Thailand still rests on foundations that are insecure in important respects. While the basic policy framework is unlikely to be challenged (barring serious deterioration in the international trading and financial system), the scope for policy distortions and large-scale rent-seeking, and for a weakening of policy predictability, remains wider than it would be if greater progress had been made in addressing the problems to which I now turn, that is, the legal framework, and the relationship between economic management and the political process.

Law and Development

It is a truism, of course, that the Thai legal framework relevant to economic activity has been adequate for the growth that has taken place. Although that growth has been vigorous, the legal framework in fact has been deficient. To the extent that constitutional problems and the historical weaknesses of the rule of law (respecting the parliamentary system and the processes for transfer of power) have led to recurrent episodes of political instability, these problems of legal fundamentals have had occasional direct economic impact by temporarily weakening investor confidence. However, even at a more mundane level of routine legal philosophy and practice respecting commercial activity and the operations of the market system, the legal framework has given rise to significant problems. I refer, not to the economic content of regulations that have been deleterious for growth, but to generic problems of transparency, predictability, consistency, and codification.

It is apparent that the domestic and foreign investors who have sustained a relatively high level of capital formation over the years, and who have shown flexibility under changing conditions, have not been seriously deterred or hampered by the legal framework in which they have had to operate. Nevertheless, Secretary-General Snoh introduced into the sixth plan the idea that the laws and regulations relevant to economic and social development needed to be reviewed and overhauled.[61] The brief and rather innocuous treatment in the plan document did not reflect the scope of the critique developed by the seminars NESDB had arranged, drawing on legal scholars from several of the universities. The seminars concluded that the legal system had been creating obstacles to economic efficiency and should be overhauled to better serve future economic development.

Predictability of the economic rules of the game is commonly cited as an indispensable prerequisite for a modern economy. While I have stressed the continuity of Thai economic policies, the legislative embodiment of the particulars of policy authority has been notably lacking in predictability. Also weak has been the quality of transparency that reinforces the confidence of investors and the general public in their understanding of the law and of the processes of legal formulation and implementation. Most Thai legislation is very brief, limited to granting specified ministries, or departments within ministries, broadly worded empowerment. Legislation typically contains no instructions as to when, where, or to what extent the powers granted must or must not be exercised. The departments are thereby given wide discretion to apply the law as the bureaucracy sees fit. Normally, no processes of public or parliamentary review, or limitations on regulatory discretion, are included in the empowerments. Cabinet approval of regulations is normally required, but in practice cabinet members seldom object to a regulation tabled by an issuing minister for formal approval; to do so would invite retaliation when an objecting member tabled his own regulations at some future date. Past practice is no guarantee of how any law might be implemented by a future department head. Past applications (e.g., regarding tax liabilities) can be reversed in retroactive administrative determinations. Few laws contain mechanisms for controlling abuse of discretionary powers.

It is often unclear, where there are a host of laws, regulations, and decrees applying to a particular issue, which legal level dominates in cases of inconsistency. Predictability and transparency are further hampered by an insufficiency of codification. New laws frequently contradict old ones without canceling the latter, while the absence of codification can leave it unclear to administrators and the public whether all the law, or the current law, applying to individual cases has been identified. These complexities can be compounded by overlapping empowerments in many subjects and by poor coordination and turf rivalries among competing authorities. Unfortunately, adjudication does not serve well as a clarifying process; courts are not bound by precedent decisions in similar cases.

Excessive regulation and wide administrative scope create opportunities for corruption and market intervention. When permission for some activity authorized under a law is denied, the responsible officials normally are not required to explain their decision to the applicant or to the general public. Ministries often (at their discretion) consult affected parties before issuing regulations, but not the public.[62]

Since only preliminary work has been done on the effects of these problems on the workings of the Thai economy, their overall economic significance is not clear. Despite the fact that the legal framework appears to be substantially at variance with Western structures and practice—in ways that would seem to be at least potentially harmful to economic development—the performance of the Thai economy suggests that, thus far, the weaknesses and abuses have been relatively marginal in their impact on economic processes. Between the ability of the economic actors to work the system, and the manner in which the bureaucracy administers the system (I have said nothing about the judicial processes because most disputes are settled without recourse to formal litigation), the balance between facilitation and hindrance of economic processes must clearly favor the former.

The Thai legal framework would seem to be deficient for economic processes if judged by Max Weber's view that "only a legal system that is rational in the sense that it is autonomous, consciously designed and universal in its application can be (i) precise enough to enter into the active calculations of economic players and (ii) able per se to command the general loyalties of these players."[63] In the judgment of Thai legal scholars, the Thai system is anything but precise. It may very well be that legal philosophers, and sociologists like Weber and Gunnar Myrdal, have ascribed too much importance to the formal characteristics of legal systems while underplaying the processes of informal adjustment and accommodation. With sufficient accommodation in a context of social stability, the Thai "soft state" has turned in a credible economic performance despite its apparent lack of "hard" legal rationality. Nevertheless, the problems cited by the Thai legal scholars and NESDB are serious, and their amelioration would be constructive for future economic growth. For the further pursuit of the whole subject of law and development, the Thai case appears to hold some interesting lessons.

Political Evolution and Economic Policy

The Chatichai government was commonly seen as a period of political ascendancy of business, as achievement by the business sector of full penetration or capture of the political process. However, the parties in the coalition, and indeed in the opposition, had no intellectual or substantive character. They had no party platforms that would define any of them as representing or appealing to any large societal interest group(s). They had virtually no regional or national organizational depth nor permanent membership of any size. The main parties were composed of factions that also had no basis in policy but were merely sets of patrons and clients contending for dominance, cliques led by rival politicians most of whom had to be businessmen with the wealth to help clients finance election campaigns and to cement political alliances. Further, the factions had no agenda even to pursue the interests of Thai business on a policy level, however conceived, but were distracted by the power struggles among themselves and between the government and the military, and by the pursuit of the spoils of office. In other words, although the Chatichai government was commonly seen as a businessman's cabinet, it did not represent the capture of government by business as a class.

The ability of the businessmen-cum-politicians to regain direct control of the levers of economic policy is uncertain at this writing. One of the purported objectives of the leaders of the 1991 coup was to rewrite the constitution in a way that would discourage the practice of vote-buying (the high cost of which gave provincial business interests and/or their Bangkok patrons a virtual lock on parliamentary access) and would raise the professional quality of future cabinets by separating parliamentary membership from cabinet membership. Nevertheless, the military-installed Anand government contained a number of prominent business leaders besides the prime minister himself, most of whom (but not all) had been technocrats earlier in their careers.[64] Whether or not they were technocrats earlier, these men represented a class of industrial and commercial managers who are educated business professionals, known for disinterest in partisan politics as an alternative career or as a route to insider advantage or personal aggrandizement.

The relationship between the military and the Anand government reflected a military recognition that business in Thailand is not a homogeneous or cohesive political class and does not attempt to shape economic policy as a unified pressure group. Besides those who have entered politics directly, various business interests have exerted influence on government policy through different channels, including the individual product and industry associations, the aggregative organizations like the Association of Thai Industries, the government-inspired JPPCC and provincial JPPCCs, and occasional ad hoc lobbying. Examples of the latter include (a) business community criticism of the port crane operation monopoly, granted to a private firm under the Prem government, (b) pressure the garment and textile industries exerted on the Chatichai government to accede to U.S. demands on the protection of intellectual property rights in order to avoid possible retaliation against Thai exports to the U.S. market, (c) Northeast business pressure on Prem in 1986–87 to ease restrictions on border trade with Laos and Cambodia, and (d) pressure from fourteen southern chambers of commerce in 1987 calling on the government to control crime and violence in that region.[65]

The entry of business interests and personalities into the circles of political power in the 1980s, culminating in the Chatichai cabinet, seemed to testify to the spreading conviction that economic development was creating the conditions for democratic, or at least more pluralistic, government and for the disappearance of the military coup from the Thai political stage. Development also showed signs of creating upcountry business, aware of differences between provincial and Bangkok economic interests and that these differences held potentialities for separate provincial politics, including both local politics and the representation of provincial area interests against the interests of the capital city. While the provincial chamber of commerce head, who in 1987 saw the logic of geographically decentralized power, spoke with typical Thai gradualism, the point is nonetheless valid as a recognition of an important consequence of provincial economic growth. Speaking after the provincial chambers had succeeded in getting the parliament to reject a legislative provision that would have subordinated provincial business bodies to their Bangkok counterparts (in a proposed national Council of Industries), he observed that "The opposition to the Council represents an overture to a major future change in Thai political economy. Our long term goal, to be accomplished in perhaps ten to twenty years, is to put an end to the practice of 'Thailand is Bangkok.' We will strive for a systematic decentralization of power to the provincial areas."[66]

In addition to variegation within the business community, development was seen by political observers to be creating growing pluralism and democratic "preconditions": an expanding, consumption-oriented middle class; high adult literacy; rapidly growing university-educated population; new religious movements within Buddhism offering new spiritual responses to social change; a growing nongovernmental organization (NGO) sector, especially active in rural development, in Bangkok slums, and in environmental disputes with the government; reemergence of organized pressures from rural economic interest groups; and media penetration throughout the country. Finally, there was hope that the sophistication of Thai politics would be enhanced by the appearance during the late 1970s and 1980s of a small number of younger, educated members of parliament and by the return of academics (especially political scientists and economists) to active writing and public appearance on political issues. Apart from the occasional environmental issue, however, there were few signs of a return of student political activism. It was also argued that the military were changing, becoming more professional, more susceptible to the widely held view that the coup was no longer a respectable political act and could damage the country's image and economic progress.

Economic development will continue to produce increasing complexity and diversification in Thai society, holding the potentiality for further development of interest group aggregations. The process is still at an early stage and is lagging in some respects that recall the early anthropological paradigm of the loosely structured society. In advanced industrial democracies, the NGOs play an extremely important role in both economic and political affairs. The term usually refers to noncommercial organizations independent of government control, active in virtually the whole gamut of socioeconomic and political affairs, instruments for like-minded members of the population to aggregate their influence. Apart from business and some professional and academic associations, most of this "sector" in Thailand is still in a fledgling condition. Few of the NGOs have large membership, and most of the leading NGOs working in such areas as the environment, civil liberties, and slum and rural development are identified as the creations of a handful of middle- and upper-class civic-minded individuals who believe that social reforms in Thailand can come only from systemic change generated at the top levels of the polity. There is, in addition, a large group of NGOs, including many provincially based, that is less elitist and that seeks to alleviate poverty through grass-roots work aimed at village self-reliance. This second group has served as a kind of activist refuge for people who were student radicals in the 1970s.

Among farmers, permanent interest group organizations have been limited to a very few commodities that are grown by small numbers of producers concentrated in relatively small areas. Rising village activism has been limited to ad hoc responses to single-issue, local neighborhood problems. The Bangkok middle class has created few consumer or urban-dweller organizations for the application of citizen pressure on government despite their dissatisfactions over many aspects of life in the metropolitan area. In the 1980s the revival of labor unions after the suppression in the postdemocratic period of the mid-1970s was weak except for the state enterprise sector. By the late 1980s the state enterprise union leadership appeared to have alienated middle-class opinion, thanks to their opposition to measures that would have reduced feather-bedding, or opened the way to privatization and increased efficiency. In addition, the union leadership appeared to be tools of political manipulation in matters that had no direct bearing on workers' interests. Whatever the facts may have been in these sometimes obscure incidents, the closure of the state enterprise unions by the military leaders of the 1991 coup provoked no reaction from the middle class, or even the university students, in defense of the unions' existence. The reasons behind the weaknesses of interest group aggregation in each economic sector differ in their legal, historical, and substantive dimensions, but are often ascribed, in a sociological context, to a general disinterest or aversion in the society to continuous adherence to organizations, and a tendency to suspicion of the motives of organization leaders.

The Prem government succeeded in restoring political stability because it accommodated these proliferating interests, excluding neither the military nor any of the economic interest groups from access to the political processes, and generally avoiding policies that might polarize the society. The advent of the Chatichai administration was greeted with skepticism. There was widespread speculation that the first businessman's government would succumb to coalition rivalries and fall within a few months. As the prime minister's political acumen appeared to be mastering the fissiparous forces of the coalition, the Chatichai government began to be seen as a vindication of the view that Thailand indeed had graduated from quasi-democracy under Prem to full-scale, nonauthoritarian, parliamentary democracy. The freedom of the press, which had become virtually unbridled in practice during the Prem administration, became fully established under law when the Chatichai government put through parliament new press legislation revoking the authority the police had had to shut newspapers and magazines for ill-defined reasons.

Yet, as noted, public opinion was sympathetic to the military's usurpation after the elected government's rent-seeking and political gaming had dissipated its moral legitimacy. Public opinion seemed to agree with the military that Thai democracy needed another constitutional reform. There is no doubt that the technical-legal weaknesses of the 1978 constitution contributed to the general weaknesses of the Thai political system. The commonly cited problems include the proliferation of political parties; the lack of continuity among members of parliament from one election to another; the focus of the political process on access to cabinet positions that command rent opportunities; the rising costs of election campaigns with their extensive vote-buying; cabinet control over the frequency of parliamentary meetings, which results in minimal numbers of days during a year in which parliament is in active session; and virtual absence of committee structure with legislative research and staff support. It remains to be seen if the 1992 constitution will provide a framework more conducive to parliamentary functioning and continuity.

More fundamental than formal provisions of the constitution, however, have been two problems in the body politic. First has been the continuing military claim to higher, extra-constitutional authority to intervene when the military, in their own judgment, think the basic interests of the state are being threatened. The military have taken this claim much beyond the role of a final arbiter in a time of crisis, creating development program "initiatives" from time to time (e.g., the "greening" of the Northeast), controlling certain state enterprises, engaging in private business activities, and mediating in union–management disputes, not to mention the exertion of influence over cabinet appointments and other direct political acts short of government overthrow. Second has been venality and intellectual aridity among the political parties, resulting in political cynicism among the public.

Caught in a dilemma between preference for democratic civil government and disillusionment over its episodic performances since 1932, Thai public opinion has appeared to accept the notion that the society still needs the military to play a "balancing" and correcting role, even at the price of occasional usurpations. This view appeared to be acceptable as long as the military did not overstep certain boundaries, that is, a coup must be bloodless, the monarchy must not be compromised, military leaders should be eligible for prime ministership only after retirement from active service, and any (justifiable) usurpation (hopefully rendered unnecessary at some stage by the evolution of "responsible" democratic process) must leave economic management to the civilians and set in motion an early return to parliamentary government.

Admittedly, this characterization of Thai "public opinion" prior to May 1992 was impressionistic conventional wisdom (Thailand has yet to develop opinion polls that measure political sentiment); but the gist of this impression was well stated as recently as 1990 by Sippanondha Ketudat, a prominent scientist, educator, and industrial executive. Sippanondha first lays out his view of the Thai effective polity, that is, the active participants in power and governance:

> In sharing my thoughts on . . . the Thai polity with the non-Thai reader, I must stress the importance of suspending ethnocentric value judgements based on the standards of some other culture. What I am about to say is best understood in terms of the totality of Thai culture—not some foreign culture.
>
> The ultimate essence of our polity is "nationhood, religion, and monarchy" (chaad, saadsanaa, phramahaakasad). Loyalty to these three symbols is of the highest order. The Thai people are held together by an intense loyalty to the monarchy, a loyalty supported by a strong cultural propensity toward tolerance, harmony, and compromise. The king is, among other things, the guardian of our Buddhist faith, and this serves symbolically to link polity and faith. . . . Our polity has also been preserved by its civil and military servants (khaaraadchakaan). For centuries, both civil and military officials have been bulwarks of the stability and continuity of our nation. In our long history we have never observed the sort of strict separation between military and civil officialdom that has characterized many other polities. . . .
>
> [Since 1932] the tripartite arrangement [monarchy, civil administration, and military officer corps] has been broadened by the addition of a fourth element, namely the intellectuals, including especially those educated in the West. . . . Whenever the system has gotten out of balance, there has been a gyroscopic tendency toward achieving a new equilibrium and harmony. . . .
>
> Since the mid-1980s there appears to have emerged a fifth constitutive group in the Thai polity, namely that of wealthy businessmen overtly and directly involved in elective politics.

Sippanondha then outlines a continuing role for the military as one of the components still needed at this stage of the country's political evolution:

> It is a mistake, I believe, to regard the Thai military leadership as being exclusively narrow in an intellectual sense. . . . Nor should one regard them as being exclusively rightist in political orientation. Many, especially those who have served in the poverty-stricken Northeastern countryside, are much more keenly alert to the plight of the nation's villagers than is the average Bangkok civilian intellectual. Many military officers are, indeed, pro-poor and pro-reform.
>
> But above everything else, the Thai military are pro-independence, stability, and continuity. In our history they have been a key force for equilibrium,

whenever the balance of power has leaned *either* too far left *or* too far right. True, this balancing role has been carried out, in part, by means of coups d'etat. True, too, such behavior by the Thai military has not always appeared, to the Western eye, to be very democratic or constitutional. However, given that Thai freedom is best understood in terms of the totality of Thai cultural reality, and that written constitutions are not well established in Thailand, this balancing role of the military has, in my judgment, generally served the best interests of the nation. . . .

I do see as a more ultimate possibility the gradual withdrawal of the military from politics . . . [but] only after some other set of institutions—political, educational, religious, or whatever—has matured to the point where it can provide the discipline and moral leadership needed to preserve stability and continuity.[67]

Sippanondha's model of the dynamics of the Thai polity is incomplete in an important respect. It overlooks the fact that the political role of the military has been very different at different times, depending on the extent of unity within the top army echelons. During those periods when the army has been divided among factions loyal to rival senior officers, the factional power struggles have been destabilizing to the polity. These struggles for supremacy have generally been motivated by personal ambitions, sometimes associated with policy pronouncements that have only vague associations with what one would normally recognize as an agenda of the left or right. One could hardly characterize the administration of Prime Minister Prem as unbalanced, leaning too far to the left or to the right. Thus, the two factional (Young Turk) coup attempts against Prem could hardly be characterized as efforts to return the polity to a stable center. It is a striking feature of Thai military politics that the key perpetrators of the 1981 coup were able to return from voluntary exile for a second attempt in 1985, and were then pardoned, reinstated in the officer corps, and brought into the government by Chatichai as part of his effort to counter the power of the dominant Class 5 officers. One may admire the Thai propensity to pardon rather than to exact punishment; but the leniency usually practiced toward failed military usurpers reinforces the military ideology that sanctions extralegal political intervention.

In short, for all its democratic assets—social stability, conservatism, forbearance and accommodation, the absence of deep language, religious, caste, or ethnic divisions, or severe landholding inequalities—the political system remains vulnerable to personal ambitions and idiosyncracies of senior military individuals. The economic bases for stability and continuity within the framework of the rule of law are now well developed, but the rule of law over the rule of men has yet to be attained. The Thai have managed to return to and sustain the balances Sipppanondha outlines, balances that have enabled the technocrats to sustain the continuities of sound economic management. The scope for the rule of military men has apparently been narrowing by custom and opinion, by Prem's example, by the military's 1992 debacle, and by the influence of the present monarch. But the scope for unlegitimated and destabilizing seizure of power, and of social and economic policy, remains to be finally closed off. The fact that the intervention of the throne has been imperative for restoring the balance at several critical junctures is at once a sign of instability as it has been a source of confidence. It places the ultimate stability of the polity in the hands of the single personality wearing the crown.

Even if the military were to retire to the barracks, leaving politics in favor of military professionalism, there remain the serious doubts in the minds of many Thai that civilian politics can be trusted to manage a responsible economic policy. The return of technocratic attention to economic policy under the Anand government presented the most recent contrast with the rent-seeking propensities and policy inattention to which Thai civil politics are prone. Between the dangers of allying military and political power, on the one hand, and the danger of factional civil party government descending into Philippine-style cronyism, on the other, the "quasi-democratic" system of the Prem years—with much cabinet power in the hands of appointed technocrats, under a compromise nonparty prime minister of integrity—appeals to many Thais as a middle path. If the economic performance, and behavior, of the Chuan government and its early successors can sustain the tone of responsible governance set by the Anand government, the recent swing of public preference toward parliamentary-based legitimacy and military withdrawal might solidify, creating the historic departure needed to institutionalize the rule of law.

The political orientation of the bureaucratic elite remains important, if much diminished in influence since the halcyon days of the bureaucratic polity. In chapter 4 I noted that this elite has been socialized to democratic values, but has been willing to work under autocratic regimes. Indeed, the elite has enjoyed the widest scope for policy formation during some (but not all) of the periods when parliamentary process has been either suspended or significantly constrained. To some extent, this willingness stemmed from the conviction, expressed by Sippanondha, that the society was still at a stage in its political evolution where realistic accommodation with the military was preferable to the disorder that would accompany a polarizing confrontation. There has also been an element of disdain for the self-interest of politicians, and of distaste for the "interference" into the affairs of national administration that is inherent in parliamentary politics. The failings of the parliamentary episodes were taken as justification for these attitudes, which, in a less charitable interpretation, might also be explained as simply serving the self-interest of the bureaucratic establishment.

The reality evidently is complex. As pointed out above, the technocrats under Prem and Anand pursued policies of deregulation and economic liberalization that entailed deliberate reduction in the scope of bureaucratic power and economic intervention. Thus, while the elite has flourished in Thailand's periods of autocratic government, it has also, in fits and starts, pursued a policy of reducing the power of the state, and of the state's elite officialdom, either to expand the state sector or to intervene in the operations of the private sector.

However strong or weak their individual private preferences may have been respecting democratic process, the generation of technocrats who held senior positions in the last decade—sharing power with the military except for the Chatichai years—were helping to pull the curtain down on the era of the Thai bureaucratic polity.

It would be a mistake to conclude that Thailand is an example of a generic developing country syndrome, that is, that authoritarian governance is more likely to pursue sound economic policy, while under democratic governance economic policy is more likely to fall hostage to special interests or to the avoidance of painful adjustment that might threaten electoral popularity. Such a proposition has never really been tested in Thailand. The character of governance has been very different in each of the three postwar periods of technocratic dominance over economic policy: Sarit's authoritarianism without parliament or parties; Prem's parliamentary-based coalition politics; and the Anand technocratic cabinet installed by the military during an enforced parliamentary interregnum. Although the quasi-democracy under Prem had functioning parliaments, parties, and elections, the political participation of the majority of the polity was in fact very shallow. As noted, economic development has produced increasing differentiation, and common interest groups have aggregated to form associations to influence individual economic policies and administrative actions directly affecting their interests, usually through negotiation with the bureaucracy. But most of the differentiation still lacks the institutionalized forms and representation that, in a mature democracy, function as national-level participants and pressure groups interacting with an electoral process and the executive and legislative branches of government.

Even the business groups, the most advanced and powerful aggregations, have had relatively few years of development as policy players; it must be remembered that business began to shed its "pariah entrepreneur" image only in the 1960s and achieved intellectual and prestige parity with the bureaucracy only in the 1980s. Competition among regional interests could become an important political phenomenon under future parliamentary evolution. Cohesion among members of parliament from specific areas or regions has not been a significant political factor since the parliaments under Phibun in the 1950s, in which MPs from the Northeast formed a pressure bloc. Regional, or more often subregional, political pressures have always been present and have been reflected in resource allocations at the project level (e.g., in the creation of provincial universities) and in the government's occasional forays into regional planning. But these pressures have never seriously challenged the policy, implicitly adopted by every Thai government, of offering modest location incentives, removing obstructions, strengthening institutions, and so on, but avoiding major subsidies or incentive structure distortions that would massively favor one geographic area over others.

Given the likelihood that the urban/rural and leading/lagging regional divisions will remain substantial, regional interest aggregations might well emerge as major forces in future politics.

Rural and middle-class passivity have contributed in the past to Thailand's relatively high degree of social stability. But continued passivity could become dysfunctional if the naturally centrist and moderately reformist instincts and interests of this majority of the polity remain unmobilized, thereby leaving political power to oscillate between military and political-business personalities. Economic development has been creating the pluralistic raw material for democratic politics, but there is no simple or necessary correlation between the emergence of these preconditions and the achievement of the democratic goal. If the polity cannot break out of this pattern of oscillation, future continuity of economic management will depend on the ability of the upcoming generation of technocrats to maintain its hold on monetary and fiscal policy, at a minimum, through recurrent accommodations with successive powerholders of uncertain legitimacy.

It is true that villagers have begun to shed their traditional passive acceptance of the actions of powerful officialdom, and of private economic interests, that are harmful to village welfare. However, while their new activism falls into the category of "participatory" politics, these democratic initiatives have yet to coalesce into a national-level organization representing rural interests generally. It is striking that the first entry of the rural advocacy NGOs onto the stage of national (rather than single-project) policy occurred only in 1991 as the Anand government formulated its environmental initiatives. The ability of the NGOs to play an active role in this process reflected the fact that Anand's technocrats were determined to make major policy advances on the country's environmental problems during their (perhaps last) interlude of policy monopoly. It remains to be seen if the NGOs can continue to play a national policy role by transforming "participatory activism" into effective parliamentary politicking.

While the main concern here has been with the political setting for economic policy making, it is interesting to observe how Thailand's political evolution has not conformed to the paradigms of political scientists who study developing countries. I noted earlier the artificiality of the attempts to recast Thai history in Marxist terms. As for the present state of affairs, no less a student than Chai-anan Samudavanija calls Thailand a "riddle" that he expects will become only more "perplexing" as industrialization proceeds. He finds different political science paradigms—presumably mutually exclusive modes of organization like statism and pluralism—coexisting in a melange of political structures. Many forces are pulling in different directions. "Pluralism is emerging but due to the capacity of the state to adjust its alliances, pluralism remains a phenomenon, but not a sustaining potent force to reduce the political effectiveness of the established bureaucracy." He concludes:

> Democracy in Thailand is not yet institutionalized, neither is public authority. There is co-existence of opposing forces of industrialization, democracy, tech-

nocratization and militarization interacting simultaneously, each having its own values, structure and process. So, both statism and pluralism are evolving. The only cementing force or the reference framework has been the monarchy. As long as the monarchy continues to be legitimate and strong, it could act as the center that can hold these opposing forces together. [68]

There are very few countries left in the world where constitutional monarchy serves as a deus ex machina to resolve crises while the polity continues to evolve, hopefully in the direction of democratic stability and the rule of law. In this respect, Thailand is idiosyncratic (and fortunate in the character of the present king). Otherwise one cannot help but wonder to what extent these same paradigms may oversimplify, rather than clarify, the realities of other developing countries when they too are closely observed.

I close with a few observations regarding the future role of the Bank of Thailand, one of the key economic policy institutions of the country's postwar era. The Bank of Thailand's departures from credit neutrality have set precedents that could endanger its independence and compromise its effectiveness in conducting normal countercyclical policies. The imposition of mandatory agricultural lending quotas on the commercial banks and the individual commodity rediscount facilities have created a basis for the view that a proper role for a central bank is to act as an off-budget source of finance tailored to support (with subsidies, if necessary) specific groups facing structural disadvantages or temporary hardships. The support the Bank of Thailand provided throughout the 1980s to troubled commercial banks and to a large group of finance companies that would have gone bankrupt otherwise reinforced this view, although the support in these cases was designed to prevent general loss of confidence in the financial system in addition to the (partial) coverage of depositors' accounts in the finance companies (there being no depositor insurance system in place). The bank's exposure to political pressures for direct off-budget, soft-loan schemes may be illustrated with two incidents from 1986.

In the first, the bank extended 5 billion baht in concessional credits to commercial banks for on-lending to rice millers who agreed to increase their paddy stockpiles during the post-harvest season.[69] Paddy prices decline seasonally virtually every year after the harvest begins in November. Schemes to bolster rice prices are also a regular seasonal feature of the Bangkok political scene. In this particular case, a casual discussion among senior officials of the Bank of Thailand about possible central bank action (rice price support loans being an old and recurrent bank activity) led to an unauthorized announcement by one of these officials that a support decision had been made. Despite the fact that short-term stockpiling was unlikely to have any net effect on farm income (the stockpile would merely create offsetting price reductions when released later into the local market), the bank felt it had no alternative but to proceed with the scheme; it would be open to attack if it "reneged," appearing to be refusing to "do something" for rice farmers while laying out vast sums "for the rich" through its schemes for supporting the financial institutions.

In the second case, a prominent monk known for right-wing views on secular matters suggested that the allegedly exploitative rice millers be supplanted by placing two thousand small mills in village wats around the country. A powerful military figure endorsed this idea and proposed that the mills be financed by the central bank out of the 5 billion baht rice soft-loan "fund." While nothing ever came of this proposal, it illustrated (as did the price support "fund") how the concept of central banking as a supplement to the Budget Bureau had become common currency. In the past couple of years the Bank of Thailand's management has begun to move away from selective credit allocation as a general principle. The reestablishment of central bank apolitical independence in this respect is a commendable objective of the monetary authorities. But it may be more difficult to pursue, if the political system evolves toward more democratic pluralism, in the face of the bank's long record of lending for purposes beyond those of "last resort" monetary policy.

It may seem excessively puristic to criticize the allocative interventions that have been undertaken by the Bank of Thailand. Compared with the very extensive credit allocation histories of Taiwan and South Korea, the Thai experience has been relatively limited and market-determined. Nevertheless, within the Thai context the central bank has played an unusually important role as a primary institutional embodiment of public integrity and conservative monetary management, both for the Thai and foreign business communities and for foreign governments and financial institutions. It is to Thailand's interest to avoid actions that reduce either the appearance or the actuality of the central bank's independence, including actions that would make the bank a convenient instrument for policies having no direct relevance to the bank's monetary and financial system responsibilities. Perhaps even more threatening to the bank's independence than the credit allocation issues described above was the change in the 1980s in the relationship between the bank's governor and the Ministry of Finance. Two ministers of finance (one in the Prem government, one under Chatichai) exercised their authority to dismiss a governor. The circumstances were different in the two cases, and in one case the friction between governor and minister was based more on personal chemistry and a poor working relationship than on any issue of substance.

I have noted that for most of its history the Bank of Thailand has either been left to manage its prudentiary and monetary responsibilities without political interference or been able to resist occasional political pressures, along the lines, say, of the German or American central banks. The legal position of the Bank of Thailand, however, exposes it to intervention, since the bank's governor can be dismissed by the minister of finance at will. In practice, then, the independence and policy scope of the bank has depended on the personal characteristics of the governor and the finance and prime ministers, and their relationships. (The point was illustrated in 1977 when the governor rejected pressure from the prime minister to go on television and assure the public that the economy was in better shape than it really was. The prime minister would have dismissed the governor for his refusal to make such a statement but was removed himself from the political scene by that year's coup.) The tradition of Bank of Thailand policy independence should be firmly reestablished, preferably by embodying that tradition in law.

Economic Development and Cultural Change: A Faustian Bargain?

An important conceptual accomplishment of the Prem government was to give common currency to the idea that economic flexibility was essential to Thailand's future growth. The virtue of flexibility in the economic realm is that it facilitates rapid domestic changes to cope with unfavorable external developments and to take advantage of new favorable opportunities. By the same token, however, flexibility in economic affairs implies an acceptance of the need to make social and cultural changes that are either associated with or consequences of changes in the location or nature of economic activities. In the modern world, countries have varied in the extent to which they have tried to insulate their social character and culture from the consequences of economic development and international intercourse. While Japan has certainly been experiencing significant cultural change, it is commonly cited as a country that has mastered the requirements for outward-oriented economic adjustment while remaining relatively insular and unique, and while protecting or adapting traditional mores.

Trade-oriented developing countries of Thailand's size, or smaller, would appear to be less able to remain insular. Larger fractions of their educated elites must, perforce, study abroad. Working knowledge of a major international language is more widespread. Foreign products and associated advertising are likely to have much wider impact on consumers. Thailand has been a relatively open society on all these counts and has had the additional exposure to external influences that comes with large-scale tourism. I have noted that Thai culture has historically been tolerant and assimilative, and that the successful parrying of colonial encroachment has been a source of national self-confidence. Nevertheless, although Thailand appears to be relatively untroubled by questions of national identity or loss of cultural integrity, development has had consequences that to many Thais are deeply disturbing.

Some of the social consequences would be considered unequivocally undesirable in most cultures. The character and implications of other changes are more complex and open to conflicting interpretations. This point can be illustrated, first, with a few observations on architecture in Bangkok, one of the most conspicuous and debated areas of Western influence and of Thai adaptation. The graceful forms of traditional temple and residential architecture evolved centuries ago and remained little changed until the reign of King Chulalongkorn. In the late nineteenth century, Western influence appeared in the harmonious incorporation of classical and Italianate ornamentation in some of the temple, governmental, and official residence construction of the time. In much of Bangkok, however, the traditional wooden homes have been replaced by shop-houses lacking any aesthetic identity or interest. Postwar development has reshaped Bangkok's landscape with much construction that is drab and much that, while new and even innovative, appears unharmonious, unauthentic, un-Thai—or the reverse, depending on one's point of view. One Western insight into the assimilative dimension of Bangkok's newest architecture is worth quoting as a counter to the denunciations of what modern development hath wrought upon the city:

> New large-scale commercial buildings began to spring up in the 1950s and from the early 1980s their faceless anonymity had begun to be replaced by something that, to Thai eyes, is exotically Western.
>
> [Western] classical temples have no deeper meaning or emotional resonance for them than do pagodas for us, so they can use them heedlessly, quite simply for their decorative effect and for their exotic air of Western wealth and consumer abundance. In other words their Post-Modern buildings are reverse images of ours. So far from being expressions of Western cultural dominance, they illustrate how in architecture, as in other ways, the East now exploits the West for its own ends, taking and adopting what it can use and discarding what seems immaterial.[70]

Thai musicians and artists have shown a similar capacity to adapt and innovate as they attempt to interpret the rapid changes in Thai life, or, in the case of folk and popular culture, to respond to changing tastes of their audiences. In addition, as in many cultures in recent years, modern Thai writers of fiction have found rich material in the detrimental effects of change and in the struggles of individuals and families to harmonize new ways with the traditional.

Many of the changes in recent decades are regarded by Thai and foreign social scientists as undesirable, for example, migration of young adults out of Northeast villages, growth of "mass consumption" values, decline of traditional religious practices (such as the formerly universal practice of young men entering the monkhood for a period of several months), commercialization of traditional relationships between villagers and local temples, large-scale prostitution, and sex-based tourism. Other changes might arguably be viewed as signs of social advance or social unraveling depending on one's point of view, such as the rising incidence of divorce initiated by women; the weakening of traditional animist and superstitious beliefs, integral aspects of the village social web as large numbers of youth experience Bangkok's secularism; the increase in village litigation in place of the traditional accommodating techniques for dispute settlement; and the rising disinclination among educated middle-class women to marry. The assimilation of the Thai Chinese, which most observers view as a positive social change, may be less favorably viewed by older generation Chinese. The small Hill Tribe minorities of the North are likely to lose much of their cultural individuality as they are settled and drawn into the majority economy and educational system.

Thai concerns over the social consequences of economic change extend to the transformation in rural life in particular, including changes that few would be inclined to classify as social pathologies. I refer to such things as the proliferation of TV antennas in all villages; the relentless accumulation of consumer durables and the associated implication of materialism; the decline of community labor exchange in favor of cash hiring; the reduced time villagers allocate to traditional ceremonies; the decline of the buffalo (supplanted by tractors), a central figure in the image of the traditional bucolic Thai scene; the penetration of trucks, passenger vehicles, and noisy motorcycles into the remotest areas; the replacement of thatched roofs by ugly (but long-lasting) corrugated metal sheet.

To some extent, the reservations many Thais have about the social consequences of development reflect the speed with which these changes have been occurring. A sense of this speed may be conveyed by looking at the changes that have taken place over the last ten years in the economic geography of one small changwat. Samut Prakan has been one of the fastest growing nonpoverty changwats. It has a coastline well located for the development of aquaculture and has been receiving industrial investment spill-over from Bangkok. In the decade 1975–85 Samut Prakan's provincial gross product grew 112 percent, exceeding the 85 percent growth of the economy as a whole.[71] Still, in 1982 the province was largely agricultural. The land-use pattern was dominated by rice paddies (40 percent) and fish and shrimp ponds (38 percent). Coastal mangrove swamps covered 3 percent of the land area, while the industrial area was negligible. Five years later, aquaculture had expanded to 45 percent, agriculture had dropped to 26 percent, mangrove had fallen to 1 percent, and industry had risen to about 4 percent. Part of the drop in paddy area was due to expanding human habitation. Only two years later, in 1989, agriculture had dropped further to 22 percent, mainly to make way for further habitation. Industrial land use was rising fast to 7.5 percent of the land area; mangrove swamps had almost disappeared. However, land area in aquaculture had started to decline as upstream pollutants were reducing the shrimp and fish production of downstream operators. Land conversion to golf courses was also getting under way.[72] Samut Prakan's real product per capita had doubled in this ten-year period. But the economic change had caused local external diseconomies, both private and social: the destruction of the mangrove area and its associated wood products and ecological function (as a littoral zone between fresh and sea water, hosting many marine species); accumulation of agricultural chemicals in sediment and in the human food chain; the effluent from some producers, destroying the economic value of land held by other producers.

The local economy may change at a slower pace in changwats further removed from Bangkok, but compared with the glacial rate of change out in the provinces in the century prior to World War II, village society in recent years has had to adjust to extraordinarily rapid economic transformation and to a tidal wave of intrusions of new ideas, tastes, and choices. Some village studies have observed how economic change has widened the social distance between the relatively rich and poor, caused deeper resentment, and divided the communities over questions of allocation of village funds.[73] In contrast, a recent study of an irrigation project in the Northeast (Lam Nam Oon in Changwat Sakon Nakorn) found no evidence of new social tensions despite wide income differentiations created in the past four to five years between households participating in a program of off-season production of high-value seeds and vegetables and households not included.[74]

The penetration of the modern economy to the village level has been examined in detail by a few anthropologists who have made repeat studies of the same communities, at long intervals. Perhaps the most extensive recurrent effort has been Konrad Kingshill's studies, at ten-year intervals, of Ku Daeng, a village in Chiangmai Province in the North. I include here a few passages to give a sense of the impact of economic development on everyday life in a rural community that was isolated and "premodern" when first studied in 1954.

> While the number of households increased steadily at an annual rate of approximately 1.5 percent over the thirty year[s] . . . the change in total population of the village showed quite a different pattern. During the first ten years there was a 50 percent increase . . . [followed by] a 12 percent decline in the following ten years, and a further 16 percent decrease during the decade ending in 1984. The population . . . today is only 6 percent larger than it was in 1954. The emigration pattern seems to have remained much the same over the thirty-year period, while the success in family planning must be credited for the stability in size. . . .
>
> Technological innovations. . . . From one radio in 1954 to 81 in 1964 and at least one per family in 1984. By 1974 electric lights had been installed in most houses. Within two years of the advent of electricity, television sets made their appearance. While there were no motorcycles or automobiles in Ku Daeng in 1954, by 1984 there were at least as many as there were households. In 1954 excess cash was almost entirely invested in land or livestock; by 1984 . . . mechanized agricultural implements, personal vehicles, and household appliances.
>
> Agriculture remains the basic income producing occupation . . . supplemented by cash earnings from labor, entrepreneurial activity.
>
> [E]ducation and educational aspirations have increased considerably [but] most children still leave school after the fourth grade. However . . . two members [have] university degrees and a number . . . have achieved vocational certification.
>
> The temple and work related to this institution have changed little. . . . The administrative structure of the village has shown very little change.

Women continue to play an important part in the life of the village. While a few of the sex roles have changed one way or another, on the whole the pattern of division of work and responsibility has remained the same.[75]

While Kingshill records important continuities in social life, he also observes changes. Divorce is still rare, and respect for elders and a pattern of close social cohesion remain strong, but the extended family is being replaced by the nuclear family. While religious expression and practice—the annual cycle of festivals (Buddhist, Brahman, and astrological)—have remained little changed along with the moral and behavioral framework emanating from the village wat, the worldview of the younger generation (e.g., respecting the traditional animistic elements of the syncretic village beliefs) appears to be shedding some traditional ideas.[76]

An anthropologist who has specialized in the rural Northeast, William J. Klausner, describes the changes from 1957 to 1972 in a village in the southeasternmost corner of that region:

Nong Khon, a small village sixteen kilometers from the provincial capital, Ubon, was relatively isolated from the world outside its borders. While there was an almost continuous flow of movements in and out . . . the villager's emotional, psychological and intellectual commitments and concerns remained stationary, tied to their village. The economic focus was squarely within the confines of the village and, through barter, to neighboring villages, as a cash economy had yet to insinuate itself. Today cash is very much a part of life and while there have been significant changes in the traditional economic and social setting . . . threads of continuity have preserved, to a surprising extent, the web of traditional village life.

Instead of bartering goods, one now goes to Ubon market to sell village products and buy necessary commodities. . . . . The road to town is now paved and the bus service more frequent and cheaper. . . . The mobility of youth, while bringing the village into more immediate contact with the outside world, has upset and dislocated traditional social patterns to some degree. . . . Once the gates of the village had been opened . . . it became increasingly difficult to stem the tide as the children began to pressure their parents to be allowed to work in Bangkok. . . . With each passing year, the percentage of [migrants'] income sent to their parents in the village decreased and the number of trips back to the village . . . also declined.

The pendulum has swung back to some extent as, today, the young men, at least, have found satisfying remunerative work in Ubon and are able to sleep in their village homes.

While fifteen years ago there was only one radio . . . today . . . almost every village house possesses one. Bicycles and motorcycles were, a decade ago, identified with teachers and government officials. Today, most of the young men possess either one or the other. . . . Large and, in village terms, ornate houses have been built within the past few years.

Materialism . . . is a competing force with the Wat for cash income. Recently, some villagers have even opened bank acounts.[77]

Klausner notes some of the undesirable social consequences of these changes but concludes that as of 1972 the process was not socially destructive, but was a transition that appeared to be taking place without rending the fabric of the culture:

> Petty thefts within the village, almost unknown fifteen years ago, are now a frequent occurrence.... Everywhere there is evidence of conspicuous consumption.... However, traditional entertainment forms ... still have the strongest attraction. While traditional village leadership patterns have shown marked staying power with the voice of youth yet unheard, parental authority has been compromised.... The brightest village youth are reaching beyond the village borders, and it is questionable whether they will return.... Continuity has so far held its own against the forces of change.[78]

Visiting again in 1986, Klausner recorded further signs of economic change in the improvements in housing, spread of consumer durables, family planning, and knowledge of national and world events. The culture was undergoing further change, absorbing outside elements, but it was a process of assimilative change, not destruction or replacement.[79]

Thai social scientists point out that an accurate assessment of the effects of technological change and foreign cultural penetration must balance the disharmonies, weakening of traditional interpersonal norms, growth of village crime, breakdown of the extended family, and other changes generally regretted if not deplored by most Thais, with positive effects that are reinforcing traditional culture or creating new syntheses. For example, radio and recordings have spread through the entire Northeast region many variants of the traditional musical theater (*moh lam*) that were previously known only in their isolated localities. The most skilled performers of the unique northeastern musical genre have become popular nationally only since the introduction of modern technology and a commercial entertainment industry. Local cultural centers have been set up to preserve and study local arts that might otherwise have died away with their elder practitioners. While migration and the ending of rural isolation are seen by critics as having destroyed the rustic peace of village life, they have also broken down the snobbism and prejudice that Central Plain Thai formerly held toward Northeasterners and the old sense of inferiority among the Northeasterns who used to accept Bangkok's judgment that Isan culture was backward. Tourism has encouraged the revival of local art forms, counteracting the earlier effects of development that had been weakening local interest in some of their plastic and performing arts. Tourism has also contributed to the strengthening of the Northeast's cultural status since that region contains the oldest prehistoric archeological sites in the country and the finest of the Khmer ruins outside Cambodia.

A succinct view of the reservations Thai mainstream intellectuals have over the country's development experience was given in 1987 by Anat Arbhabhirama, who, it will be recalled, has been prominent among the technocrats guiding this experience:

Development in Thailand has been gradual, moving from an agriculture-based economy to an industrializing one. Thailand's national goal is to achieve the status of a newly-industrialized country by the end of its Sixth Five Year Plan in 1991. Judging from GDP growth, we can say that the country is already better off economically. But the price we pay for this development process can be measured in terms of negative impact on our culture and the degradation of our environment.

The development process has also brought great pain to the Thai people. The widespread migration from rural to urban areas, or from urban areas to foreign countries, in search of gainful employment has led to the separation of families. Social scientists in this country have observed an increasing number of family breakdowns. The Thai extended family of three generations living under one roof, with some members working and living away from home, is being challenged.

In urban areas, where infrastructure development has been outpaced by the economic boom, cities inevitably suffer from social problems as well as air and water pollution. Witness the traffic jams and polluted canals of Bangkok. These problems are expanding with urbanization into the countryside. . . .

Telecommunications have made face-to-face dialogue unnecessary, but at a cost to human relations; personal contact and hospitality, which are cherished in Thai culture, have decreased. Now, while we may be more aware of one another's wants, we are becoming ignorant of our needs. . . .

Thai culture is also susceptible to foreign influence. Countries in stronger economic positions inadvertently impose their cultural values on the less developed ones. A case in point is the predominance of Western music in even the most remote villages of Thailand via transistor radios. Blue jeans and T-shirts are as common as traditional dress at temple fairs across the country.

However, foreign culture need not be dominant, depending on the resilience of the recipient culture. Even Thai music uses Western instruments. The lyrics, however, are still very Thai and reflect current social values.

In agricultural development, Thailand's pattern of land use is affected by fluctuating international demands. Rice has been labelled by many agronomists as an "antiquated" cash crop with a return that can hardly justify its continuing production. Hence the switch from paddy fields to aquaculture ponds, a transformation that is spreading across the Central plains.[80]

It is difficult to find any realm of discourse in Thailand, other than religion, in which deliberate, systematic, recorded efforts have been made to elaborate the ambivalent judgment Anat reflects into a full analysis of the implications of these changes. In his recent work on Thai literature, Herbert P. Phillips describes his search for material on "how Thai thinkers conceptualize the nature of the 'good life' and what they reasonably expect of themselves and of their society."

Although there is clearly some concern for these matters (mainly as specific goals, unstated premises, and asides), that concern has not yet been institutionalized into a literature of aspiration and self-assessment. . . . [T]he thrust of the Thai literary effort is toward criticizing (and to a lesser extent, approving) what is rather than toward formulating a conception of what might be reasonably sought for or attained.[81]

The one piece Phillips includes is a short "Chronicle of Hope from Womb to Crematorium" written by Puey Ungphakorn. It is a statement of what Dr. Puey thought "life was all about, and what development should seek to achieve for all." The statement is not a discussion, but a mere listing of personal desiderata. It reflects the evolution of Puey's thinking to which we have referred earlier, in which he criticized the materialism and income inequality of the initial periods of postwar development. His list of development purposes includes few references to material goods accumulation, but focuses instead on family harmony, health and nutrition, family planning, access to education and meaningful work, a society of law and order and political participation, and social security in old age.[82] While the simplicity of Dr. Puey's objectives for personal life reflects his Buddhist perspective, and explains the priority he accorded to rural development and distributive effects of macroeconomic development, he was anything but simplistic and was fully aware (as reflected in his career and writings) of the importance of modern technology-based economic growth for achieving and sustaining the range of choice and even the restrained life-style he personally valued.

The most critical assessments of the effects of economic development, and the most comprehensive efforts to cope with the impact of material change on the Thai identity and worldview, have been formulated from a religious perspective because of the central role of asceticism, self-restraint, and rejection of materialism in classic Buddhist doctrine, especially the Theravada school of Buddhism (the "southern school" followed in Thailand, Sri Lanka, Myanmar, Laos, and Cambodia). To some thinkers, the characteristics of modern economic development—material accumulation, continuous growth, the deliberate stimulation of consumption demand, the hectic intrusions and sources of anxiety of modern life—are in fundamental conflict with Buddhism. One of the most prolific of the lay Buddhist intellectuals, Sulak Sivaraksa, distinguishes between the quantitative and qualitative dimensions of modern development and criticizes Thailand for adopting Western emphasis on quantitative accumulation at the expense, or even destruction, of qualitative aspects of life. Sulak appears to draw unrealistic conclusions that would roll back the clock if translated into an actionable program:

> [E]conomists measure success in terms of increased production, and so must turn to industrialization, to the profit motive. And it is the economists who are most influential in development planning. As a result development becomes supremely a matter of economics and politics. For economists see development in terms of increasing currency and things, thus fostering greed (lobha). Politicians see development in terms of increased power thus fostering ill-will (dosa). Both then work together, hand in glove, and measure the results in terms of quantity, thus fostering ignorance (moha), and completing the Buddhist triad of evils.[83]
>
> When an economic system, based on a capitalistic market economy, requires increasing greed, both in the producer and the consumer, can any religion encourage it?[84]

> [In] the spirit of Buddhist development ... the inner strength must be cultivated first; then compassion and loving-kindness to others become possible. Work and play would be interchangeable. There is no need to regard work as something which has to be done, has to be bargained for, in order to get more wages or in order to get more leisure time. Work ethics would be not to get ahead of others but to enjoy one's work and to work in harmony with others. Materially there may not be too much to boast about, but the simple life ought to be comfortable enough, and simple food is less harmful to the body and mind. Besides, simple diet could be produced without exploiting nature, and one would then need not keep animals merely for the sake of man's food.[85]

It has been painfully obvious to Buddhist thinkers, and to many lay Thai, that the "rejectionist" position of Sulak, and even the call for restrained consumerism represented by Dr. Puey, are unrealistic in the face of rising incomes, changing tastes, and the powerful impetus to social change imbedded in the Thai economy's performance over the years. As a result, the focus of much thought has been on how Buddhist doctrine and practice might be reinterpreted, or reformed, to reestablish their pertinence to modern life for the increasingly educated and secular middle class. Part of this reinterpretation has aimed at a return to original Buddhist doctrine, cleansed of the traditional popular non-Buddhist (i.e., animist and Brahmanistic) observances seen as no longer intellectually tenable. While religious reform in Thailand (partially under the impact of Western ideas) was first undertaken by King Mongkut (prior to his accession) starting in the 1830s, the postwar period has seen probably the most extensive debate in Thai history between traditionalists and reformers, and between the established hierarchy and the founders of a variety of schools and formally constituted sects.

Without going into the doctrinal and ritualistic differences per se (especially for non-Buddhist readers unfamiliar with the wide differences between the Buddhist and Western religious worldviews), it is pertinent to give an indication of the impact of modern economic change on these challenges to traditional practices and the Buddhist hierarchy (the Sangha), and the potentialities these challenges may hold for Thai identity and social cohesion. A convenient summary of the main schools and their implications is given in a recent article by Suwanna Satha-Anand of the Chulalongkorn University philosophy department:

> [The] past two or three decades has been a dynamic period in Thai Buddhism, involving changes in all major aspects, namely, doctrinal interpretations, the *vinaya* rules of the monks, the roles of laymen, the establishment of Buddhist communities, and the incorporation of high technology in the propagation of Buddhist messages. These changes have arisen in the conditions accompanying the intensive development activities of the last 30 years, a process that has given rise to the distinct formation of an urban middle class ... [who] are very different from the rural Thai villagers who have been the major followers of traditional Thai Buddhism. The former are ... the main adherents of the three major religious movements.[86]

The three movements to which Suwanna refers are the Suan Moke Movement founded by one of the most eminent monks in Thailand, Buddhadasa Bikkhu; the Dhammakaya Temple; and the Santi Asoke Group. According to Suwanna, each group can be seen as a "reaction to the changing socioeconomic conditions of the Buddhist community and also to the inertia of the Buddhist establishment." Their attempts to offer an alternative religious framework for contemporary Thai are very different. Buddhadasa teaches a reinterpreted doctrine that is the most philosophical and intellectual. Santi Asoke advocates a "radically simple way of life," requiring "strict moral behavior from its relatively small number of followers."[87] While not as demanding as the rules for life in the monkhood, Santi Asoke's rules of behavior call for a lay asceticism at variance with the consumerism of everyday life. The Dhammakaya movement has come under severe criticism for its commercial-like marketing and fund-raising, and for "selling 'religious pleasure,'"[88] methods that have drawn large numbers of adherents. The Dhammakaya "create a novel image of Buddhism that corresponds well with the grandness of capitalism, and the concretization of Buddhist ideals also corresponds with the concrete sensual satisfactions of a consumer society."[89] Suwanna expresses confidence that the Sangha establishment will change in accordance with changes taking place in the secular world. That confidence rests on the fact that monks within the Sangha recognize the challenges posed by secular development. The point is well put by one of the leading thinkers within the Sangha, Phra Rajavaramuni:

> With the current latent conflicts unrectified under the attitude of [Sangha] indifference and inaction, the direction of Thai Buddhism seems unpredictable. Concealed behind all the conflicts is the conflict between traditionalism and modernization. Strict traditionalism becomes an extreme which not only hinders effective adjustment but also causes a reaction in the form of another extreme, usually the opposite one, that is extreme modernization. By modernization is meant good and effective adjustment to the modern changing world. But extreme modernization will go too far so as to result in secularization or even politicization. In the age of social change and political instability of today, there is a fear of overstepping from one extreme to the other. A mistake of this type would mean danger and perhaps even a discredit to Buddhism. To avoid this, the Middle Way must be secured.[90]

One noteworthy adjustment within the Sangha to modern secular conditions has been the "development monk" movement. Since the early 1960s, the two Buddhist universities in Thailand have been training young monks in modern educational, social service, and community development skills. The adoption of these practical functions adds new dimensions to the relationship between the Sangha and the rural population in particular. Having practical secular, rather than intellectual or doctrinal (or political) content, the development monk movement has gotten little attention in the literature on contemporary religion in

Thailand. Although the movement does not address the potential erosion of the traditional worldview of Thai villagers increasingly exposed to secular influence, as Klausner points out the Sangha, "through such community service, is actively contributing to improving the prospects of a more productive and creative tension between the forces of traditional religious beliefs and practice and the forces of modernization."[91]

If the modern Middle Way is not found, if the Sangha does not adjust doctrine or monk's practices, if the middle class becomes increasingly secular and merely ritualistic at best in its interest in the Sangha, if the worldview of the rural population is affected by Bangkok's secularism or by sects offering an alternative institutional framework, the establishment Sangha could decline in importance, weakening the appearance of religious unity in Thailand and calling into question the relationship among Buddhism, the monarchy, and the state that has formed the framework of national identity in modern times.[92] While the doctrinal disputes may be abstruse even to many Thai, the social and political ramifications of their outcome may be profound for Thailand's future.

I do not presume to draw any general conclusion as to the balance of positive and negative effects of economic development on the social, cultural, and aesthetic dimensions of life in Thailand. Much of the evidence is mixed. Much depends on the weights the Thais might assign to the advances in material condition, health and educational status, personal mobility, and other fruits of economic development, compared with the conflicting trends in other dimensions. However, few Thais or foreign students of Thailand are likely to disagree with the conclusion that, compared with much of the developing world (including Eastern Europe and Soviet successor states), the social tensions in Thailand do not add up to serious discontent with, or challenge to, the social system, the economic rules of the game, or the development process.

One can draw no general conclusions either about the role of public policy in responding to, or attempting to shape, social evolution. The category is too heterogeneous. Each trend or problem must be considered on its own merits. Some of the social changes that have accompanied Thailand's modern economic development, such as the mutual assimilation of the urban Thai and Chinese, are positive processes, best left outside the realm of public policy. Other large-scale social changes, such as the rise of consumerism, result from the cumulative exercise of individual preferences. On the assumption that a liberal society should permit economic development to serve individual choice as exercised through the market, these changes also are best left outside the area of government responsibility, subject to the free play of ideas.

In fact, the Thai government has been passive toward much of the social change of recent decades and is criticized by sections of public opinion for turning a blind eye, especially in the case of changes involving clear violation of law already on the books. Prostitution is one of the most conspicuous social problems largely ignored despite its formal illegality. The economics of prostitution, both its connection with tourism and its long-standing domestic role, have weighed against any effective policing despite the damage done to the country's international image. With increasing evidence that AIDS (or, more precisely, HIV-positive incidence) may be reaching alarming proportions in the general population, and possibly developing in the 1990s into a social and economic problem of greater importance than many of the economic issues discussed herein, the government began in 1991 to show signs of according AIDS the policy attention it deserved. As with the generality of economic problems, the response of public policy in new areas of social welfare or cultural stress has largely been determined by the interplay of the bureaucracy with other elites and limited organized groups. The weakness of institutional political mobilization of large publics in Thailand leaves the great majority of the polity without effective voice or participation in these realms of social policy that are at least as important as the economic realm in determining the future course of Thai life.

Afterword

In the end, it is reasonable to be optimistic about Thailand's economic future, if one can assume that the community of nations manages to avoid catastrophic changes such as a collapse of the world trading system or global climatic alteration and sea level rise. Such optimism would rest on the record of the past three decades and on the assumption that social and political evolution in Thailand will succeed in facilitating pragmatic economics in a continuing balance of growth, stability, and equity. The Thais have a playful habit of attributing their (not complete) avoidance of calamities in economic, social, and foreign affairs to the benevolence of the country's guardian angel, Phra Siam Devathirat. At least equal credit, and equal justification for optimism, must be given to the Thai propensity to translate Buddhist doctrines of moderation, of seeking the Middle Path, into their approach to public affairs. To the Westerner who often hears Thai policy makers explain policy outcomes in terms of deliberate preference for the Middle Path, it might appear that the Thai also derive their understanding of social optimality from the *Ethics* of Aristotle: "So much, then, is plain, that the intermediate state is in all things to be praised, but that we must incline sometimes towards the excess, sometimes towards the deficiency; for so shall we most easily hit the mean and what is right."

APPENDIX

Table A1

Growth in GDP, Population, and Income per Capita

	1950	1960	1970	1980	1985	1990
Index of real GDP growth	100.0	164	359	690	908	1,470
Population index	100	135	187	239	265	284
Population (millions)	19.5	26.3	36.4	46.7	51.7	55.3
Population annual growth rate	3.0	3.3	2.8	2.0	1.8	1.5
Real GDP per capita index	100	122	192	288	342	501
GDP per capita (current prices—U.S.$)	80	100	195	688	721	1,200[a]

Source: NESDB 1950–60, old GDP series; 1970–85, new GDP series; 1990, est.

a. 1989, from World Bank, *World Development Report 1990*, table 1.

Table A2

Composition of GDP (percent, current market prices)

	Agriculture	Industry[a]	Services[b]
1960	39.8	18.6	41.7
1965	34.8	22.7	42.5
1970	25.9	25.3	48.8
1975	26.9	25.8	47.3
1980	23.2	31.0	45.8
1985	16.7	34.0	49.3
1990	12.4	39.2	48.4

Source: NESDB, 1960–65, old series; 1970–90, new series.

a. Manufacturing, construction, mining, electricity, and water supply.

b. Transportation, communication, trade, banking, real estate, ownership of dwellings, public administration, and defense, other.

Table A3

Savings and Investment as Shares of GDP

	1960–65	1965–70	1970–75	1975–80	1980–85	1988	1990[a]
(1) Gross domestic investment/GDP	18.5	24.2	24.1	26.3	25.1	28.8	36.8
(2) Gross domestic savings/GDP	18.0	22.5	22.1	21.1	19.7	28.6	30.4
(3) Savings gap (1) – (2)/GDP	0.5	1.7	2.0	5.2	5.4	0.2	6.4

Source: Meesook, table 5.7; Bank of Thailand.

a. Estimated.

Table A4

Merchandise Exports Compostion (in percent)

	1960	1965	1970	1975	1980	1985	1987	1990
Major products								
Rice		34	17	13	15	12	8	5
Rubber		16	16	8	9	7	7	4
Maize		8	14	4	5	4	1	1
Tin		9	11	5	9	3	1	x
Tapioca		5	9	10	11	8	7	4
Prawns		1	2	2	1	2	2	3
Sugar		1	x	13	2	3	3	3
Canned fish		—	—	—	x	3	3	3
Textiles		x	x	x	7	12	16	14
Integrated circuits		—	—	—	5	4	5	4
Jewelry and precious stones		1	1	2	3	4	7	4
Footware		—	—	—	x	1	2	3
Miscellaneous		25	30	43	33	37	38	52
Total		100	100	100	100	100	100	100
Sector Composition								
Agricultural products[a]	90	83	69	69	47	38	28	34
Manufactures	1	5	15	20	32	50	63	63
Other	9	12	16	11	21	12	9	3
Total	100	100	100	100	100	100	100	100

Source: Bank of Thailand, *Quarterly Bulletin* (various).
a. Includes rubber, forestry.
x = Less than 0.5 percent.

Table A5

Merchandise Imports Composition (in percent)

	1965	1970	1975	1980	1985	1987	1990
Consumer goods	27	19	13	10	10	10	9
Intermediate products and raw materials	21	25	24	24	30	36	33
Capital goods	31	35	33	24	30	32	39
Fuel and lubricants	9	9	22	31	23	13	9
Other	12	12	8	11	7	9	10
Total imports	100	100	100	100	100	100	100

Source: Bank of Thailand, *Quarterly Bulletin* (various).

Table A6

Exchange Rates, Trade Indices

	Exchange Rate[a] Baht/U.S.$	Export Value (1985 = 100)	Import Value (1985 = 100)	Terms of Trade
1960	21.0	4.5	3.9	163.3
1965	20.8	6.7	6.2	165.5
1970	20.9	7.6	10.8	169.1
1975	20.4	23.2	26.6	147.9
1980	20.6	68.9	75.1	127.7
1983	23.0	75.8	94.2	108.5
1985	26.7	100.0	100.0	100.0
1987	25.7	155.1	133.1	109.6
1990	25.2	305.0	337.3	101.3

Source: Bank of Thailand.

a. End of period.

Table A7

Consumer Price Index—Bangkok (annual rate of increase)

	Percentage
1961–69 (average)	1.8
1970–73 (average)	4.7
1974	23.3
1975–79 (average)	7.3
1980	19.9
1981	13.4
1982	5.4
1983	3.4
1984	0.7
1985	2.4
1986	1.9
1987	2.6
1988	3.8
1989	6.3
1990	6.6

NOTES

Chapter 1

1. See, e.g., Caldwell, *American Economic Aid*; Muscat, *Thailand and the United States*. Also, Likhit, *The Bureaucratic Elite of Thailand*.

2. The term "vent for surplus" was coined by Adam Smith, then applied by Hla Myint to the experience of the alluvial rice plain economies, in "The 'Classical Theory' of International Trade and the Underdeveloped Countries."

Chapter 2

1. Wyatt, *Thailand: A Short History*, p. 2.

2. Ayal, cited in Chira and Medhi, *Comparative Development: Japan and Thailand*, p. 77.

3. See Chira and Medhi, *Comparative Development*, for the most recent general treatment of the Japan–Thailand comparison, including reviews of the ideas of the principal earlier writers.

4. The full exposition is found in Benedict Anderson, "Studies of the Thai State," in Ayal, ed., *The Study of Thailand: Analyses of Knowledge, Approaches and Prospects in Anthropology, Art History, Economics, History, and Political Science*. In the same volume, Sulak Sivaraksa and Clark Neher provide critical comments on Anderson's chapter.

5. Girling, *Thailand: Society and Politics*, p. 48.

6. Girling, *Thailand*, pp. 49–50.

7. Brown, *The Elite*. Brown's summary of the revisionist Thai historical school is based on the following cited works: Chattip Nartsupha and Suthy, eds., *The Political Economy of Siam, 1851–1910;* Chattip et al., eds., *The Political Economy of Siam, 1910–1932;* Suthy and Chattip, "The Rise of Dependent Commodity Production in Siam, 1855–1910," pp. 144–68, among others.

8. Brown, *The Elite*, pp. 170–73.

9. Ibid., p. 181.

10. See, for example, Chattip et al., *The Political Economy of Siam*, and Thawatt, *History of the Thai Revolution*.

11. For recent broad historical surveys, see Wyatt, *Thailand*, and Keyes, *Thailand*. The most extensive treatment of the manpower problem and its political and social ramifications is the seminal work of Akin, *The Organization of Thai Society*.

12. The most extensive modern analysis of the *sakdina* in English is by Akin, *Organization*. Keyes (*Thailand*) gives a good brief definition and an account of the controversies

over its interpretation. He notes that the *sakdina* system has been the subject of considerable controversy among scholars who have attempted to understand the social system of premodern Siam and to trace the persisting influence of this system on modern Thai society. "*Sakdina* combines an indigenous Tai term *na*, meaning 'rice field', with a Sanskrit-derived term, *sakdi*, that in India carries the primary meaning of 'energy' or 'active power' of deity. The Siamese phrase has typically been translated as 'degrees of dignity or rank . . . giving the right to rule over certain grants of land'. In practice the reference to units of land served as a unit of account for numbers of (client) persons, and not units of land per se." Keyes, *Thailand*, pp. 29–30.

13. Akin, *Organization*, p. 179.

14. Ibid., pp. 178–79.

15. Pramoj and Pramoj, cited in Ingram, *Economic Change in Thailand*, p. 61.

16. Ibid.

17. See Akin, *Organization*, for a full account of the legal distinctions between different degrees of bonded service, the rights of the indentured, the restrictions on the rights of masters, and citations from Bowring and other early observers, pp. 104–12.

18. Ibid., pp. 109–10.

19. Ibid., pp. 110–11.

20. Cited in ibid., p. 109.

21. Ingram, *Economic Change*, p. 63.

22. Akin, *Organization*, chapter 7.

23. Ingram, *Economic Change*, p. 12.

24. Ibid., p. 79.

25. Ibid., p. 15.

26. Ibid., p. 100.

27. Ibid., pp. 55–56.

28. Constance M. Wilson, "Bangkok in 1883," pp. 55–56.

29. Coughlin, *Double Identity*, p. 14.

30. Ingram, *Economic Change*, p. 211.

31. "One of the most persistent themes in [his] writings might be termed modernity—that is, encouraging, even exhorting people to act and live as modern people did in the West. He introduced surnames and coined names for hundreds of families; he refashioned the flag of Siam, replacing the old white elephant on a red field with a tricolor red, white, and blue; he introduced the first national holidays in honor of King Chulalongkorn . . . and the Chakri dynasty . . . he promoted team sports . . . worked to improve the status of women . . . arguing for monogamy in the place of widespread Siamese polygamy; and he was an ardent supporter of modern education." Wyatt, *Thailand*, p. 228.

32. Coughlin, *Double Identity*, p. 128. Coughlin suggests that Vajiravudh acquired these views from his long exposure to the prejudice of English society and to the anti-Sinic prejudice of his British advisers.

33. Ibid., p. 75.

34. Ingram, *Economic Change*, p. 170.

35. Ibid., pp. 80–81.

36. Wyatt, *Thailand*, p. 198.

37. In October of the next year the new regime succeeded in crushing, with some loss of life, a counterrevolutionary effort led by a group of royalist comanders. The entire episode took about two weeks. For a full account of the coup, the politics among the factions, and the events of the royalist reaction (which Rama IV disclaimed), see Thawatt, *History*.

38. Thak, *Thai Politics*, pp. 1–2.

39. Thawatt, *History*, pp. 94–95.

40. Phya Song Suradet, quoted in Thawatt, *History*, p. 87.

41. From the *New York Times*, June 24, 1932, cited in Thawatt, *History*, p. 93.

42. Pridi Phanomyong, from "Minutes of a Meeting of a Committee to Consider a National Economic Policy, at Paruskawan Palace, March 12, 1933." Thak, *Thai Politics*, pp. 167–69.

43. Chattip et al., *The Political Economy of Siam*, pp. 187–89. A *satang* is one-hundredth of a baht.

44. Wedel and Wedel, *Radical Thought*.

45. See ibid., pp. 23–36, and Morell and Chai-anan, *Political Conflict*, pp. 13–14.

46. The reference is to Sangop Suriyin, Chai-anan Samudavanija, and Tawee Muennikon and the publications cited in Wedel and Wedel, *Radical Thought*, pp. 36, 221–23.

47. Drawn from Wedel and Wedel, pp. 37–44. Their account is based on Suriyanuwat's writings and on Chattip Nartsupa, "The Economic Thought of Phraya Suriyanuwat."

48. Lt. Gen. Prayoon Phamonmontri, "The Political Change of 1932," in Thak, *Thai Politics*, pp. 49–50.

49. All citations from Pridi's economic plan are from the translation by Kenneth P. Landon in his *Siam in Transition*, reproduced in Thak, *Thai Politics*, pp. 109–61.

50. For example, responding to the criticism he had already heard that universal government employment would stifle research creativity, Pridi asks the reader "please do not go around saying that after this policy is in force there will be nothing left for man to do except to live in a hole and eat his rice out of the frying pan. If you will ask critics who make remarks of this sort what books they have been reading to get such ideas such as these, and will then let me know, I shall consider it an act of kindness." Thak, *Thai Politics*, p. 135.

51. Thawatt, *History*, p. 144.

52. Thak, *Thai Politics*, p. 149.

53. See "His Majesty King Prachathipok's Coments on Pridi's Economic Plan," ibid., p. 234.

54. "It is noteworthy that before Pridi set out to write the economic plan, he had often discussed with Phya Manopakorn's group the basic principles on which the plan would be based. These men had indicated their approval of Pridi's idea, and urged him to put it down on paper. . . . [W]hen Pridi finally proposed his plan to the government, it was these same men who adamantly opposed it. In view of the facts, there was some truth in the over-simplified conclusion that Pridi was lured to propose the plan by his rivals who sought to use the issue to eliminate him." Thawatt, *History*, p. 184.

55. Thak, *Thai Politics*, pp. 178–79.

56. Pridi fled into a final exile in 1949 after the failure of a coup by naval and marine officers attempting to bring him back to power.

57. Wyatt, *Thailand*, p. 253.

58. Luang Vichit's writings and career are outlined by Thak, *Thai Politics*, pp. 179–86.

59. Thak, *Thai Politics*, p. 145.

60. Ibid., pp. 180–81.

61. Wyatt, *Thailand*, p. 254.

62. deYoung, *Village Life*, pp. 107–8.

63. "Why need the Thai have gone so far as to ally themselves with Japan? Phibun and the military under his leadership either cynically judged that Japan would win the war and Thailand's best interests lay in going along with the tide or more adventurously judged that they might retain more independence, and better protect their citizens, by a friendly rather than adversarial relationship with the Japanese. Probably both considera-

tions influenced their decisions." Wyatt, *Thailand*, pp. 257–58. While Wyatt leans toward attributing the Thai government's Japan policy to a mix of motives, the considerable literature on this period falls into separate camps; some historians (and participants) assert that Thailand was realistically accommodating to Japanese power ("bending with the wind"), others concluding that Phibun and his group were supportive of Japanese ambitions in Southeast Asia for some time (possibly several years) before Japanese troops moved against Thailand. For a recent review of the controversy and a list of sources, see Benjamin A. Batson and Shimizu Hajime, *The Tragedy of Wanit, A Japanese Account of Wartime Thai Politics*.

64. Ibid., p. 263.

65. The history of the CPT is described in Morell and Chai-anan, *Political Conflict*, pp. 77–92.

66. Ingram, *Economic Change*, p. 134.

67. Ibid., p. 136.

68. Sompop Manarungsan, *Economic Development*, pp. 32–33.

69. Ibid., appendix C.

Chapter 3

1. Thawi Bunyaket was technically the first postwar prime minister, holding the position for two weeks until Seni returned from Washington in mid-September 1945.

2. The postwar premiers prior to Phibun's return to direct rule on April 8, 1948, were as follows: Thawi Bunyaket (August–September 1945); M. S. Seni Pramoj (September 1945–January 1946); Khuang Aphaiwong (February–March 1946); Pridi Phanomyong (March–August 1946); Luang Thamrongnawasawat (August 1946–November 1947); Khuang Aphaiwong (November 1947–April 1948).

3. Wyatt, *Thailand*, p. 266.

4. Thak, *Thailand*, gives a detailed account of the political events of 1957–58, especially pp. 117–50.

5. Darling, *Thailand*, p. 69.

6. U.S. Operations Mission, cited in Muscat, *Thailand*, pp. 77–78.

7. Caldwell, *American Economic Aid to Thailand*, p. 4.

8. Ibid., p. 179.

9. Loftus, "Economic Development Planning in Thailand," annex A–2.

10. World Bank, *A Public Development Program*, p. 216.

11. Ibid., p. 217.

12. Loftus, "Economic Development Planning," annex A–1, pp. 1–7.

13. This paragraph is drawn from Loftus's *Semiannual Report*, January 1957.

14. Loftus, Economic Planning Note no. 19, June 21, 1962, p. 11.

15. World Bank, *A Public Development Program*, p. 31.

16. Thak, *Thai Politics*, pp. 542–50.

17. Ibid., pp. 551–55.

18. Thak, *Thailand*, chapter 3.

19. Coughlin, *Double Identity*, pp. 132, 135–36.

20. Ibid., p. 132.

21. Ibid., pp. 136–37.

22. The principal sources include Riggs, *Thailand*; Skinner, *Leadership*; Suehiro, *Capital Accumulation*; Sungsidh, *Thai Bureaucratic Capitalism*; Coughlin, *Double Identity*.

23. Riggs, *Thailand*, pp. 251–52.

24. Skinner, *Leadership*, pp. 191–92.

25. Riggs, *Thailand*, pp. 254–97.

26. Suehiro, *Capital Accumulation*, pp. 2-38 to 2-42.

27. There appears to have been no definitive list of state enterprises. Riggs obtained a list of enterprises subject to government audit in 1957 numbering 141 "public corporations and organizations" divided among 12 ministries, largely industrial and commercial but also including utilities and cultural organizations, the State Lottery, and a few private companies (e.g., Siam Cement) in which the state was a minority shareholder (*Thailand*, pp. 305–8). Under Thai law a corporate entity is a "state enterprise" if the state holds more than 50 percent of the equity. Muscat identifies 124 organizations, including 11 in which the state holds minority interest (*Development Strategy*, pp. 296–300). The World Bank refers to "80 or more quasi-independent government organizations which are engaged in various commercial, industrial and financial activities" including the utilities and the lottery (*A Public Development Program*, p. 200). Some of the differences among these numbers result from varying treatment of enterprises grouped under holding companies.

28. Ibid., pp. 2–58, 59.

29. Sungsidh, *Thai Bureaucratic Capitalism*, provides some meager profit and loss data drawn from balance sheets and files of the Department of Commercial Registration.

30. Sungsidh cites the example of the Thaharn Co-Operation Co. (which earned profits from its favored access to rice export quotas) buying gunny bags from the Northeast Jute Mill Co. (which operated at a loss in most years in the 1950s). The jute bags were lower in quality but higher in price than bags imported from India. Both firms were owned by the Soi Rajakru group. Ibid., pp. 167–79.

31. Sungsidh cites the well-known case of Sarit's own construction firm. Details on the operations of Sarit's extensive corporate holdings became public knowledge during the course of a contest over his estate among his heirs. Ibid., pp. 191–96. Citations on most of the practices referred to in the text can be found in the sources mentioned in note 22.

32. Ibid., pp. 180–83.

33. Cited in ibid., p. 119.

34. Girling, *Thailand*, p. 76.

35. Loftus, Economic Planning Note no. 19, June 21, 1962.

36. Loftus, *Terminal Report*, pp. 10–12.

37. Loftus, memorandum to M. L. Snidwongse, Ministry of Finance, May 15, 1961.

38. Loftus, *Terminal Report*, p. 24.

39. Skinner, *Leadership*, p. 187.

40. The ease with which the same historical events can be construed as stability by some interpreters and unstable crisis by others is illustrated by the well-known essay by B. Anderson cited earlier. Anderson refers to the "image of Thai politics made popular by the work of Riggs—i.e., the 'bureaucratic polity,' a polity described as immensely stable, impervious to appeals or pressures from outside or below. Yet, if we compare the years 1782–1932 (in which seven monarchs and one regent held power—roughly 18.8 years per power-holder) with the years 1932–73 (heyday of the 'bureaucratic polity'—with twelve different men in the Prime Ministership, an average of 3.3 years per person, and no less than eight successful and many more unsuccessful coups carried out), a picture of great *instability* emerges" (original emphasis). Anderson also criticizes one of the classic models of Thai society: "His [Lucien Hanks's] discussion of the dialectic of 'merit and power' and his model of the 'entourage' have been especially attractive because they incorporated instability within stability: a ceaseless 'karmic' quest for patrons and followers, which never crystallized into stable institutions but at the same time never turned into anything new or different. . . . Instability was thus frequently read, comfortingly, to mean 'Thai-style stability'—rather than as an indicator of the crisis of the Thai state" (Anderson,

"Studies of the Thai State," in Ayal, ed., *The Study of Thailand*, pp. 216–17). Commenting on Anderson's paper, Sulak Sivaraksa wrote: "I do not see any model state nowadays—including the United States—that is stable." In a second comment, Clark Neher asserts that "Contrary to Anderson's view, there has been social and political stability at all levels of Thai society. The names of the Prime Ministers have changed, but not the fundamental nature of elite, authoritarian politics—characterized by various high-level groups vying for power, with an almost total absence of peasant involvement in central Thai politics" (Ayal, ed., *The Study of Thailand*, pp. 250, 255).

41. Evers and Silcock, "Elites and Selection," in Silcock, *Thailand*, p. 103.

42. A short biography of Dr. Puey and a personal account of his wartime activities is contained in Puey, *Puey Ungphakorn, A Siamese for All Seasons*.

43. At this writing, Puey Ungphakorn lives in retirement in London.

44. Puey, *Puey Ungphakorn, A Siamese*, pp. 303–4, 310.

45. The early history of the Bank of Thailand is summarized by Silcock, "Money and Banking," in Silcock, *Thailand*, pp. 178–80, from which this paragraph is drawn.

46. Ibid., p. 187. When he was minister of finance in 1949, Prince Viwat resigned a second time, after the government failed to adhere to its obligation to the International Monetary Fund to consult before changing the baht exchange rate.

47. There was a brief exception in 1958 when the governor who immediately preceded Dr. Puey (and who simultaneously held the post of minister of finance) was ousted and arrested for his role in a scandal involving the contract for printing Thailand's currency.

48. Puey Ungphakorn, "Address to the Thailand Management Association," (July 1967), in Puey, *Best Wishes*, p. 51.

49. Ibid., pp. 51–52.

50. Puey, "The International Economic Position of Thailand," address to the Thai Council of World Affairs and International Law (October 1969), in *Best Wishes*, pp. 43–46.

51. Puey, "The Role of Ethics and Religion in National Development," in *Best Wishes*, p. 18.

52. Ibid., p. 16.

53. Ibid., p. 4.

54. Muscat, *Thailand*, p. 106.

55. The turnkey roads (from Saraburi to Korat and from Pitsanuloke to Lomsak) contributed to the technical capacities of the Highway Department by training a large number of Thai engineers and equipment operators and by demonstrating the application of higher standard construction technology. Ibid., pp. 95–100.

56. Ibid., pp. 107–10.

57. Some of the outstanding members of this group were Boonrod Binson (electric power), Xujati Khambu (irrigation), Sippanondha Ketudat, and Kasame Chatikavanij.

58. The national account aggregates in this section are drawn from Oey Meesok et al., *The Political Economy*, chapter 3 and annex tables A.1 and A.2. Much of the production and national accounts data of the 1950s cannot be treated as having a high degree of exactitude. For a readily accessible discussion of assumptions and caveats behind the national accounts see Prot Panitpakdi, "National Accounts Estimates," in Silcock, *Thailand*, chapter 5.

59. Oey shows government capital expenditure as a percentage of total government outlays rising from a 1946–48 average of about 7 percent to a 1954–55 average of 23 percent, then receding to an average of about 16 percent in 1956–60. She cautions that data on government expenditure prior to the budget accounting reform in 1961 should be treated only as approximations. Oey, *Political Economy*, p. 4.12 and table 4.5.

60. Silcock, *Thailand*, table 6.4, p. 140. Trade and payments data were also incomplete during this period as reflected in large errors and omissions entries for several years.

61. For example, see Silcock, *Thailand*, pp. 135–36; Muscat, *Development Strategy*, pp. 128–31.

62. "Overshadowing all the individual crop possibilities is the very large potential of Thailand as a rubber producer. . . . But, as in the case of rice, achievement of anything like Thailand's potential pace of rubber expansion will require more assistance and better incentives for the rubber grower than he now receives. And also, as in the case of rice, little is now being done along these lines. Before much can be done it will be necessary first to stimulate greater administrative interest in expanding rubber production and to develop the necessary organization." World Bank, *A Public Development Program*, p. 5. "Conceivably, Thailand's rubber output could well be eight times what it is today within a few decades, although a practicable goal is undoubtedly lower. The Mission believes that rubber exports can come to rival and eventually exceed rice exports" (p. 70). In fact, rubber exports attained the eightfold volume increase in 1989 (and are likely to continue rising) when the tonnage reached 1.1 million compared with the 1958 figure of 135,000 metric tons. Rice production and exports have fared better than the bank team expected, however, and have not been surpassed by rubber.

63. See especially Ingram, *Economic Change*, pp. 87–92; Yang, *A Multiple Exchange Rate System*, chapter 3; Mousny, *The Economy of Thailand*; and Ammar, "A History of Rice Policies in Thailand," from which this summary is drawn.

64. Ammar, "A History," pp. 236–37.

65. Silcock, *Thailand*, p. 14.

66. The economically active were defined as all persons over the age of eleven years who had been employed during the year preceding the census. Principal occupation was the job in which the respondents worked for the greatest number of hours. National Statistics Office, *Population by Detailed Classification of Industry*, 1980 census, p. 4.

67. World Bank, *Thailand: Rural Growth and Employment*, p. 149.

68. Silcock suggests that the army politicians may have had private, if puzzling, reasons for wanting to appreciate the currency. *Thailand*, p. 177, from which this paragraph is drawn.

69. World Bank, *A Public Development Program*, p. 241.

70. Conversation attended by R. Muscat.

71. Thak, *Thailand*, p. 337.

72. Silcock, *Thailand*, p. 173.

73. Riggs, *Thailand*, p. 176.

74. Wilson, *Politics*, p. 277.

75. Jacobs, *Modernization Without Development: Thailand as an Asian Case Study*, pp. 80–81, cited in Morell and Chai-anan, *Political Conflict*, p. 48.

76. For a more recent treatment, see Morell and Chai-anan, *Political Conflict*.

77. Wyatt. *Thailand*, pp. 272–73.

78. Girling, *Thailand*, pp. 72–78.

79. Ibid., p. 79.

80. I have provided a detailed account of the range of activities undertaken by the U.S. aid program and the American private foundations (the latter especially important in university development and the training of Thai scholars) during this period. See Muscat, *Thailand and the United States*, chapter 4.

Chapter 4

1. Cited in Thak, *Thailand*, p. 156.

2. Ibid., pp. 156–57.

3. Ibid., p. 157.

4. Wyatt, *Thailand*, p. 281.

5. Thak, *Thailand*, p. 188.

6. Ibid., p. 208.

7. Ibid., p. 227.

8. Silcock, *Thailand*, p. 20.

9. Thak, *Thailand*, p. 225.

10. Ibid., p. 214.

11. Wyatt describes as "naive" the major Marxist work of Chit Phumisak (*The Face of Thai Feudalism*, written in 1957), the most prominent of the radical writers (Wyatt, *Thailand*, p. 271). Thak is sympathetic to Chit but is not prepared to assert that his ideas would have had much impact at that time: "It is argued that many of the radical ideas expressed in the late 1950's were not exceedingly relevant to Thai society of that period. This is debatable. What is significant is that when they were resurrected after October 1973, they became potent explanatory symbols of Thai society's problems—both from the viewpoints of their contents and symbolism of intellectual suppression" (Thak, *Thailand*, p. 215).

12. The World Bank mission was headed by Prof. Paul T. Ellsworth from the University of Wisconsin. Members included G. H. Bacon (agriculture), Romeo dalla Chiesa (economics), Jean R. de Fargues (irrigation), Andrew Earley (transportation), William M. Gilmartin (economics; chief economist), Norman D. Lees (industry, mining, power), Fritz Neumark (public finance), K. J. Oksnes (social services).

13. Board of Investment, *Expanding Private Investment for Thailand's Economic Growth*.

14. The report of the Economic Survey Group was appended to Loftus's second report to the finance minister, July 18, 1957, on file along with his other semi-annual reports in the library of the Finance Ministry.

15. Stifel, "Technocrats," p. 1192.

16. Ibid.

17. Examples drawn from Loftus, *Semiannual Report*, July 1, 1960.

18. Muscat, *Thailand*, p. 124.

19. Morell and Chai-anan, *Political Conflict*, p. 49. The classic studies of Thai bureaucratic mores include Riggs, *Thailand*; Mosel, "Thai Administrative Behavior;" Reeve, *Public Administration in Siam*; Wit, "The Thai System;" Siffin, *The Thai Bureaucracy*.

20. Excerpts from the first six-year plan, Thak, *Thailand*, pp. 228–29.

21. Abonyi and Bunyaraks, *Thailand*, p. 23.

22. Loftus, "Economic Development Planning," July 1961; *Terminal Report on the Economy of Thailand*, August 1962, annex D, p. 8.

23. Silcock, *Thailand*, p. 281.

24. Details are contained in Government of Thailand, National Economic and Social Development Board, *Evaluation of the First Six-Year Plan, 1961–1966*, chapter 3.

25. Ibid., p. B.

26. The old series showed a rise in the fixed investment ratio to 21.8 percent in 1966, smaller than the revised series, but essentially the same as a reflection of the structural shift in the distribution of expenditure between investment and consumption.

27. Examples of underperforming assets included NEDCOL (cited earlier), a wide range of state enterprises, highway maintenance equipment, irrigation water storage projects without tertiary canal systems, and underutilized provincial power-generating capacity. Muscat, *Development Strategy*, pp. 52–52, 68–69.

28. Ammar, "Stability, Growth and Distribution in the Thai Economy," in Prateep, ed., *Finance, Trade and Development*, p. 30.

29. Measures described in Bank of Thailand, *Annual Economic Reports*, 1970–72.

30. Government of Thailand, National Economic and Social Development Board, *Evaluation*, p. 7.

31. World Bank, *A Public Development Program*, p. 100.

32. Bank of Thailand, *Annual Economic Report*, 1963, p. 56.

33. Asher and Booth, *Indirect Taxation in ASEAN*, pp. 40–47, 182.

34. World Bank, *Managing Public Resources*, p. 186.

35. There are problems with these numbers (labor force surveys, themselves problematical, show significantly different numbers in 1969 and 1971 from those in the 1970 census; the 1970 census probably underestimated the work force, etc.), but the essential picture is correct.

36. World Bank, *Current Economic Position and Prospects of Thailand*, 3:55.

37. Ammar, "Stability, Growth and Distribution in the Thai Economy," in Prateep, ed., *Finance, Trade and Development*, p. 38.

38. Narongchai, "Import Substitution, Export Expansion and Sources of Industrial Growth in Thailand, 1960–1972," in Prateep, ed., *Finance, Trade and Development*, p. 276.

39. World Bank, *Managing Public Resources*, p. 186.

40. Bank of Thailand, *Annual Economic Report*, 1970, p. 60.

41. Narongchai, "Import Substitution," in Prateep, ed., *Finance, Trade and Development*, p. 276.

42. For comparative studies of the Chinese business communities see McVay, *Industrializing Elites*.

43. Loftus, *Terminal Report*, p. 25.

44. Pathmanond, cited in Oey et al., *Political Economy*, p. 5.48.

45. Pasuk Pongpaichit, *Economic and Social Transformation of Thailand, 1957–1976*, cited by Suehiro, *Capital Accumulation*.

46. Suehiro, *Capital Accumulation*, pp. 4–17.

47. Two other commercial banks, the Thai Military Bank and the Siam Commercial Bank, are normally considered private because they are operated as private, and because (since 1983 and 1976, respectively) they have raised capital by issuing equity traded in the securities exchange. Their origin and controlling interests, however, set them aside from the other banks, when looking at the financial sector from political or social perspectives, especially in the context of economic concentration. The Thai armed forces owned and controlled the Thai Military Bank (in 1988 the armed forces held about 42 percent of the bank's equity, and key management positions). Major shareholdings in SCB were in the hands of the Crown Property Bureau, the Ministry of Finance, and the Princess Mother. As with the Thai Military Bank, these holdings remain dominant although diluted by the publicly issued equity.

48. Data in this paragraph are drawn from Suehiro, *Capital Accumulation*, chapter 4, especially tables 1V–19, pp. 4–41 and 4–74.

49. Mingsarn Santikarn, *Technology Transfer*, provides detailed analysis of the joint-venture experience of the Thai textile industry, including the market-share protection motivation of the (mainly Japanese) foreign partners, and the technical and financial motivations of the Thai entrepreneurs.

50. On Japanese technology transfer, for example, see Mingsarn, *Technology Transfer*, who observes that "Japan is heavily involved in the production of standardized commodities which have low technological barriers. To compensate for low explicit cost, Japanese suppliers have to set up artificial barriers to entry by applying more stringent conditions on technology transmission than other developed countries did." Ibid., p. 144.

51. Narongchai demonstrated that the growth of domestic demand was the dominant source of growth in industrial output in the period 1960–66, while import-substitution

provided the main scope for expansion of output in the later 1960s when the domestic market was expanding at a slower rate. "Import Substitution," in Prateep, ed., *Finance, Trade and Development*, p. 275.

52. Suehiro, *Capital Accumulation*, table III-II, pp. 3–47.

53. BOI "Activity Reports" show Thai and foreign country origin only for registered capital. Registered capital typically ran around 20 percent of the total planned (equity plus debt) investment, while actual investment often differed from amounts planned. Japan, the United States, and Taiwan were the three leading foreign sources in this period.

54. For the whole year of 1972, the largest number of vehicles was produced by the Bangchan enterprise (Volkswagen), 9,000 cars and trucks. Second and third were Toyota and Isuzu, with 6,000 vehicles each. "The Automotives Industry," *Business in Thailand* (June 1973), cited in Suehiro, *Capital Accumulation*, pp. 4–35.

55. Todaro, *Economic Development*, p. 101.

56. For details on these projects, see Muscat, *Thailand*, pp. 97–101.

57. Phisit Pakkasem, "Regional Planning within a National Framework," in Prateep, ed., *Finance, Trade and Development*, p. 235.

58. When the malaria compaign was launched in Thailand and other developing countries in the 1950s, the World Health Organization and U.S. aid public health experts thought total eradication was feasible. Although eradication proved unattainable, malaria was reduced to a minor public health problem in Thailand and many other countries. Muscat, *Thailand*, pp. 87–90.

59. Government of Thailand, Ministry of Public Health, *Thailand Population Monograph*, pp. 59, 78.

60. The Potharam project experience is described in Rosenfield et al., "Thailand's Family Planning Program."

61. Ibid., p. 44.

62. Knodel, Aphichat, and Nibhon, *Thailand's Reproductive Revolution*, chapter 10, from which this paragraph is drawn.

63. Strictly speaking, these census figures understate the level of urbanization. Absent any formal definition of urban and rural residence in Thai official statistics, the urban population is normally defined as those residing in "municipal" jurisdictions. The numbers and boundaries of Thai municipalities have changed little in many years despite the growth and spread of urban areas beyond these boundaries and in urbanized settlements officially designated as "sanitary districts." Inclusion of large sanitary districts would raise the urban proportion in 1980 from 17 percent to over 23 percent. (This figure would be modestly reduced if account were taken of the rural enclaves within Bangkok and other urban areas.) Nevertheless, the point remains valid that the Thai population has remained predominantly rural.

64. World Bank, *World Development Report*, 1990, table 31, p. 238.

65. Ibid., table 27.

66. These themes are also reflected in the anthology of popular literature in English translation edited by Anderson and Mendiones, *In the Mirror*.

67. Hamzah Sendut, "City-Size Distribution of Southeast Asia," in Yeung and Lo, *Changing South-East Asian Cities*, p. 170.

68. Morell and Chai-anan, *Political Conflict*, p. 6.

Chapter 5

1. Keyes, *Thailand*, p. 83.

2. Morell and Chai-anan, *Political Conflict*, pp. 143–44.

3. Between 1969 and 1971 leaders of the Thai Contractors Association, the Thai Chamber of Commerce, the Board of Trade, and a group of 30 business and trade associa-

tions voiced their apprehension that foreign and Japanese business interests were attempting to "dominate" the Thai economy. Various Bangkok press stories to this effect are cited in Hewison, *Bankers and Bureaucrats,* p. 107.

4. Keyes, *Thailand,* p. 84.

5. Information on Royal Initiative projects is contained in publications of the Secretariat Office of the Coordinating Committee for Royal Development Project. The king's development activities are described in several commemorative publications, for example, "Illustrated Handbook of Projects Undertaken Through Royal Initiative," a publication of the Committee for the Rattanakosin Bicentennial Celebration, B.E. 2525 (1982); *His Majesty King Bhumibhol Adulyadej and His Development Work,* Coordinating Committee for Royal Development Project, issued to celebrate the king's sixtieth birthday, December 1987.

6. Wyatt, *Thailand,* p. 302.

7. Abonyi and Bunyaraks, *Thailand,* p. 30.

8. Bank of Thailand, *Annual Economic Report,* 1975, pp. 100–101.

9. Stifel, "Technocrats," p. 1185.

10. Abonyi and Bunyaraks, *Thailand,* p. 31.

11. Ibid.

12. Excerpts from Puey, *Puey Ungphakorn,* pp. 113–25.

13. Ibid., p. 139.

14. Medhi, *Institution Building,* p. 13.

15. Government of Thailand, National Economic and Social Development Board, *Fourth National Economic and Social Development Plan,* p. 127.

16. Ibid., p. 128.

17. World Bank, *Managing Public Resources,* table 5.3, p. 91. The security share would be higher if one could include expenditures on highways, remote rural roads, civic action, and other nonmilitary projects the government might not have undertaken otherwise.

18. Disbursement and loan service data by individual public-sector loan are contained in Bank of Thailand, *Annual Economic Reports,* only through 1981. The share of military credits in near-term debt service payments was probably greater than the share in total public-sector credit drawings since nonmilitary borrowing included loans (from concessional aid sources and from the World Bank and Arian Development Bank (ADB) with much longer amortization periods than the five- to ten-year repayment schedules of Foreign Military Sales (FMS) and commercial credits.

19. Morell and Chai-anan, *Political Conflict,* give a good account up to the end of the 1970s and cite references in their bibliography. Some additional materials are cited in Muscat, *Thailand.* For chronology and an analysis by one of the leading architects of Thailand's counterinsurgency tactics, see Saiyud, *The Struggle for Thailand.*

20. Muscat, *Thailand,* p. 177.

21. Silcock, *Thailand,* p. 190.

22. Ibid., p. 195.

23. Bank of Thailand, *Annual Economic Report,* 1970, p. 60.

24. Bank of Thailand, *Annual Economic Report,* 1974, p. 39.

25. Ibid., p. 73.

26. Since 1967 the Bank of Thailand was rediscounting promissory notes arising out of various agricultural transactions (crop production, fishery, animal raising, agricultural equipment). The volume of notes involved did not amount to a significant allocative magnitude. The commercial banks argued that the spread between the rediscount rate and the (concessional) maximum rate the Bank of Thailand permitted the banks to charge the borrowers was too narrow to serve as an inducement to use the facility. World Bank, *Thailand; Perspectives for Financial Reform,* p. 49.

27. Bank of Thailand, *Annual Economic Report*, 1975, pp. 40–41.

28. Ibid., pp. 41–42.

29. Bank of Thailand, *Quarterly Bulletin* 30, 3 (September 1990): 4.

30. Hewison, *Bankers and Bureaucrats.* "Even some state officials criticised the banks. Police Major-General Sangha Kittikachorn, for example, called on the government to regulate the banks' activities more closely, so that banks would help farmers instead of 'keeping in league with the capitalists and supporting the middlemen to exploit the farmers' "(p. 190).

31. "We have a very strong social commitment to Thailand.... For example, our agricultural credit business represents 13 percent of total assets and yet brings in little or no return." Chatri Sophonpanich, President, Bangkok Bank. "New Era of Professional Banking," *The Nation,* May 1986, p. 39.

32. Bank of Thailand, *Annual Economic Report*, 1979, p. 155.

33. World Bank, *Thailand: Financial Sector Study*, pp. 70–75, from which this paragraph is drawn.

34. A speech on this subject by Governor Nukul Prachuabmoh to the Thai Bankers Association in 1981 illustrates nicely the deft style of the Bank of Thailand's public moral suasion, normally taken quite seriously by this audience. "Several banks have not given sufficient attention to the need for modernising and streamlining their operations.... [One] reason could be that bankers who are also part owners of their banks have extensive involvement in many commercial and business enterprises which leave too little time for the daily management of their banks. In these cases, it could in fact be concluded that the banking business is given a lower priority compared to other businesses. The efficiency, efficacy and returns of such banks, therefore, tend to suffer in consequence. Once aware of this problem, an earnest solution should be sought by attaching greater importance to the stability and growth of your respective banks and by strengthening your management system through recruitment of professional and qualified staff. In this way, your management burdens can be alleviated for the benefit of your banking institutions and the entire banking system." Bank of Thailand, *Quarterly Bulletin* (March 1981): III.

35. In 1990 Governor Chavlit Thanachanan floated the idea of allowing new entry, not through licensing additional foreign banks, but through granting existing finance companies the right to offer banking services. "Moreover, it is our policy to merge small institutions to enhance their financial strength and ability to compete. The 'top-tier' finance companies could in fact be upgraded to become banks. This should help heighten the competitiveness of the system, which is too low at present considering that there are only 15 local banks serving 55 million population." Bank of Thailand, *Quarterly Bulletin* 30, 3 (September 1990): 4.

36. Prices of imports relative to domestic prices are also affected differentially by the so-called business tax, which is levied on the gross value of sales or turnover of businesses. However, given the varying rates and methods of application (and the relative ease of evasion by domestic producers compared with importers), it is difficult to generalize on the overall protective impact.

37. Bhattacharya and Brimble, *Trade and Industrial Policies*, p. 5.

38. Ariff and Hill, *Export-Oriented Industrialization*, pp. 81–83.

39. World Bank, *Managing Public Resources*, p. 186.

40. Bhattacharya and Brimble, *Trade and Industrial Policies*, pp. 16–17.

41. Cited in World Bank, *Managing Public Resources*, p. 188.

42. World Bank, *A Public Development Program*, pp. 98–100.

43. A major critique at this time was that of Little, Scitovsky, and Scott, *Industry and Trade in Some Developing Countries.*

44. Thailand Development Research Institute, *Financial Resources Management*, p. 99.

45. Government of Thailand, National Economic and Social Development Board, *Fourth Plan*, pp. 209–10.

46. World Bank, *Managing Public Resources*, p. 186.

47. Chaipat et al., *Lessons*, pp. 63–64.

48. Narongchai Akrasanee, "Import Substitution, Export Expansion and Sources of Industrial Growth in Thailand 1960–1972," in Prateep, ed., *Finance, Trade and Development*, pp. 257–77.

49. "Over the Plan period, the total balance of payments surplus is projected at 5,842 million baht representing an average increase of 4.7 percent per annum. This amount of surplus will give rise to an accumulation of international reserves to a level sufficient to finance 3 months' imports by the end of the Plan period. This balance of payments target will contribute to economic stabilization policy. To achieve this target, it is necessary to implement import substitution, export promotion as well as investment and fiscal plans simultaneously." Government of Thailand, National Economic and Social Development Board, *Fourth Plan*, p. 37.

50. Government of Thailand, Ministry of Finance, Fiscal Policy Office, *Study on Fiscal Implication of Investment Incentives and Promotion Efficiency*, pp. 114–31.

51. Bank of Thailand, *Annual Economic Report*, 1974, p. 91.

52. Ibid., pp. 92–95.

53. World Bank, *Thailand, Toward a Development Strategy of Full Participation*, pp. xi–xii.

54. Bank of Thailand, *Annual Economic Report*, 1977, p. 1.

55. Ibid., pp. 11–16.

56. Bank of Thailand, *Annual Economic Report*, 1978, pp. 1–16.

57. World Bank, *Thailand's Manufactured Exports*, p. 15. As this study points out, the distribution (of value-added, export values, and other measures) between agriculture and manufacturing at any time is affected by whether the initial semi-process milling (e.g., of rice and sugar) is defined as agricultural or manufacturing activity. In this case, for example, a shift of the definition of this processing from agriculture to manufacturing would raise the share of manufactured exports to total manufactures production in 1980 from 20 percent to 35 percent. Food processing still comprised nearly a third of manufacturing value-added.

58. Even after several years of rapid growth of manufactured exports, Thailand's share in total world trade in manufactures in 1983 was only 0.2 percent. Ibid., p. 15.

59. Examples would include textiles, garments, polished gems and jewelry, leather products, and furniture. Average wages of a skilled Thai factory worker were estimated even several years later (1985) at 9 percent of U.S. levels, compared with 19 percent in Singapore, 16 percent in Malaysia, and 6 percent in the Philippines. Ibid., p. 22.

60. Ibid., p. 13. The economic contribution of SMEs is likely understated since enterprises employing seven or fewer workers are excluded from Ministry of Industry registration and probably undercounted in all relevant data series.

61. For example, a World Bank study of the transport system summarized its condition as follows: "Since the mid-1960's, the Thai economy ... grew at a rapid pace and generated a high demand for transport. Roughly some 75% of total demand in 1981 was for bulk or semi-processed agricultural produce. To accommodate the growing demand, the government undertook large transport investments (in particular road infrastructure) and created a policy environment in which with some exceptions, a competitive transport industry developed. Today, all Changwats ... are interlinked with a good interregional and interprovincial communications network, and transport services have penetrated the majority of previously remote rural areas. In comparison with other similarly situated countries, the transport system is, by and large, good. There are, on the whole, no

significant physical or administrative impediments to meeting current transport demand."
Thailand: Transport Sector Review, Main Report, pp. 1–2.

62. At 14.3 percent in 1977, Thailand's ratio of central government revenue to GDP was below that of Indonesia, but above Malaysia and the Philippines. World Bank, *World Tables,* 1980.

63. One estimate put the loss of revenue in 1978 at 10 percent of the public-sector deficit as a result of the failure to sustain the petroleum product tax share of 1970–73, excluding the cost of the subsidy payments. World Bank, *Coping With Structural Change,* p. 30.

64. The ratios in Table 5.4 are based on government finance data. If various adjustments are made to the state enterprise accounts, which are incomplete in several respects, they would show higher savings rates and hence lower aggregate deficit ratios. On the other hand, if these relationships are developed from the national income account classifications the deficit ratios are higher by around 10 percent. In any case these accounting refinements do not alter the basic direction or magnitudes of these aggregates. The details are contained in World Bank, *Managing Public Resources,* pp. 65–69, 89–92.

65. Sadiq Ahmed, *Shadow Prices for Economic Appraisal of Projects.* Ahmed also gives conversion factors calculated in earlier World Bank studies and loan appraisal reports, and by other authors. The results of these other analyses are generally consistent with Ahmed's conclusions, apart from the effects of different assumptions about labor market imperfections and of differing treatment of rice.

66. The indices for selected countries are shown in Table 5.6. World Bank, *World Development Report,* 1983, pp. 59–63.

67. Calculations of David R. Dollar, recorded in Lant Pritchett, *Measuring Outward Orientation,* p. 46.

68. Giovannini and de Melo, *Government Revenue from Financial Repression.*

69. Hanson and Neal, *Interest Rate Policies,* annex 6.

70. Ammar et al., *Public Policies,* p. 10.

71. World Bank, *Thailand: Financial Sector Study,* p. 9.

72. Easterly and Honohan, *Financial Sector Policy in Thailand,* p. 35.

73. Muscat, "Government, Financial Systems, and Economic Development: Thailand," in Lee, ed., *Government, Financial Systems and Economic Development,* 1994.

Chapter 6

1. See Chai-anan, Kusuma, and Suchit, *Armed Suppression,* from which this paragraph is drawn. Also see Chai-anan, *The Thai Young Turks.*

2. Neher, "Thailand in 1987," pp. 192–93.

3. *Far East Economic Review,* March 7, 1991, pp. 17–18.

4. Ho Kwan Ping, "Thailand Inc.: An Open Door for the World's Multinationals," *Far East Economic Review,* May 24, 1980.

5. Bank of Thailand, *Annual Economic Report,* 1980, pp. 10–11.

6. Girling, *Thailand,* pp. 225–26.

7. Discussing the charge of indecisiveness, General Prem noted that a prime minister must seek compromise to maintain government unity, a situation unlike that facing a military commander. In his defense, he cited the swift actions he took in the three major crises of his administration—the two coup attempts, and General Arthit's bid to roll back the devaluation of 1984. "Management, Prem Style," *Business Review,* January 1987.

8. The example of the Bangkok bus procurement project in 1984–85 is described in "Highlights of the Year," *The Nation,* December 1985, pp. 44–45.

9. See "Indefinite Decisions: How the Government Makes Its Mind Up on Our Be-

half," "Highlights of the Year," *The Nation*, December 1985, pp. 44–46, for a discussion of the various proposals and the views of some of the participants.

10. For example, see "Asia-Euro Group Cries Foul over Skytrain Decision," *The Nation*, December 9, 1988, p. 13.

11. This and preceding citations drawn from Snoh Unakul, "Thailand: The Fifth Plan Strategy," pp. 18–27.

12. For a detailed treatment of the JPPCC, see Anek, *No More Bureaucratic Polity*.

13. World Bank, *Structural Adjustment Lending*, p. 5. The bank used so-called program loans as a form of support for the foreign exchange costs of significant economic policy changes from the very start of bank activities in 1946. Program loans were considered exceptional, however, applying to "special circumstances," and were not favorably received by bank executive directors from some of the industrial member countries. Within the year after the second oil shock in 1979, in the face of the extraordinary deterioration in the economic position of a large number of developing countries, the bank formally adopted structural adjustment lending as a major instrument. A distinction was made between program loans aimed at very short-term economic stress and SALs that would address medium-term structural change.

14. Bank of Thailand, *Annual Economic Report*, 1981, p. 134.

15. Details of the structural adjustment program can be found in Chaipat et al., *Lessons,* and in the World Bank *Program Performance and Audit Report* and *Structural Adjustment Lending* and SAL documents cited in the Bibliography.

16. World Bank, *Structural Adjustment Lending*, p. 80.

17. The possible advantages and disadvantages of rapid versus gradual adjustment programs are reviewed by Michalopoulos, *World Bank Programs for Adjustment and Growth*.

18. World Bank, *Program Performance and Audit Report*, p. 21.

19. The weaknesses of World Bank activities in institutional development were explored at length in a series of papers for a Conference on Institutional Development and the World Bank, December 1989. See especially the paper by Beatrice Buyck, "Technical Assistance as a Delivery Mechanism for Institutional Development."

20. World Bank, *Structural Adjustment Lending*, pp. 72–74.

21. For a succinct discussion of the scope of structural adjustment see Streeten, ed., *Beyond Adjustment*, pp. 1–9.

22. Ammar, "Two Excerpts from the Factbook on Rice," p. 29.

23. Tongroj, *A Land Policy Study*, p. 28.

24. The correlation between full land title and institutional credit access in Thailand has been demonstrated in Feder, *Land Ownership, Security, and Farm Productivity in Rural Thailand.*

25. Feder et al., *Adoption of Agricultural Innovations in Developing Countries,* p. 10.

26. World Bank, *Program Performance and Audit Report*, pp. 15–16. The World Bank continued to support the land titling program through a separate $35 million loan project initiated in 1985.

27. Carl Goldstein, "Thailand Starts to Save Energy: A Switch in Time," *Far Eastern Economic Review*, August 1, 1991.

28. Mingsarn, *Technology Transfer*, pp. 131–33.

29. Ibid., pp. 91–94.

30. Mingsarn noted that marketing restrictions were no more prevalent in agreements with Japanese firms up to 1975 than with firms in other countries. Ibid., p. 140. Nevertheless, it was commonly believed that Japanese firms were less forthcoming in this respect (and other aspects of commercial and joint venture relationships) than firms of other nationalities.

31. "Dr. Somsak (Tambunlertchai) and I interviewed 25 textile firms, both pure Thai

and joint ventures, in Bangkok in . . . 1979, and collected data of export performance of individual firms. We found divergent export-output ratios among these firms in 1979, although none of them exported in 1970. The divergent export performance of individual firms is partly explained by whether they specialize in the type of product in which Thailand has a comparative advantage (such as cotton and polyester-cotton staple fabrics and clothing vis-à-vis filament and polyester-rayon fabrics). But the high export-output ratio of a firm generally reflects its efforts in production and management change toward export expansion, such as concentration of production in . . . fewer items of bigger lots, stricter quality control, better coordination between factory and sales sections, and export marketing activities. In contrast to sales at protected domestic markets, steady export expansion requires certain production and management changes, a requirement which a group of firms has learned from their competition with other Asian rivals in export markets." Ippei Yamazawa, "Development Through Industrialization and Foreign Trade: Comparative Analysis of Japan and Asian Developing Countries," in Chira and Medhi, *Comparative Development*, p. 195.

32. Dapice and Flatters, *Thailand: Prospects and Perils*.

33. Data on tourism earnings are relatively ambiguous compared with other sectors. The figures for gross foreign exchange earnings are calculated by the Tourism Authority based on surveys of travellers. One estimate puts the net earnings, after taking account of tourism's import content, at two-thirds of the gross. On the other hand, the Tourism Authority's data exclude Thailand's considerable earnings from tourists' international travel costs. In the national accounts and in the Bank of Thailand's balance-of-payments data, tourism is not identified as a sector or line item as such; value-added and exchange earnings, respectively, are distributed over the standard categories in these accounts. Data on tourism is published regularly in the annual statistical reports of the Tourism Authority of Thailand.

34. See Thammanun and Sonchai, *Trade in Services*, for a brief review of tourism issues and citations of a few studies.

35. Phisit Pakkasem, *Leading Issues*, p. 160. Phisit records that state enterprises' net internally financed investment, as a proportion of their total investment outlay, fell from 47 percent in 1973 to 17 percent in 1980.

36. Ibid., p. 156.

37. Ibid., pp. 160–61.

38. Government of Thailand, National Economic and Social Development Board, *Fifth Plan*, pp. 29–31.

39. Government of Thailand, National Economic and Social Development Board, *Sixth Plan*, pp. 180–90.

40. The military were most commonly cited as the manipulators of union leadership. *Far Eastern Economic Review*, April 3, 1986, p. 59.

41. Examples of protests against "privatization" that had as yet no specific content were demonstrations in 1985 at the Tobacco Monopoly and the Communications Authority. Ibid.

42. The Nation, *Thailand, Midyear 1990*, pp. 14–16. In this case the union leadership came out against the PAT management. The PAT provided ammunition for the government side by asserting that the authority lacked the capacity to take operation of all four wharves. The port unions insisted that they had the requisite capacity. The whole episode, taking place during the Chatichai administration, took on wider political overtones when General Chavalit Yongchaiyudh stepped into the controversy to act as a mediator between the unions and the government.

43. Vickers and Yarrow, "Economic Perspectives on Privatization," p. 113.

44. Government of Thailand, National Economic and Social Development Board, *Fourth Plan*, p. 379.

45. Government of Thailand, National Economic and Social Development Board, *Eastern Seaboard Study.*

46. "Domestic equity requirements of the program were estimated to amount to about B 1.8 billion per annum, which is more than seven times the equity financing raised by the Stock Exchange of Thailand in 1980, and about one-third of the average net annual increase in the capitalization of Thai industry for the period 1978–80. . . . The program would require about B 6.2 billion per annum in loan financing, of which B 5.5 billion could be derived from foreign sources. This amounts to about 10% of disbursements of medium and long-term foreign debt to Thailand in 1981. Domestic loan requirements would represent about 6% of *total* advances to the manufacturing sector in 1980, most of which was in the form of *short-term* overdrafts. . . . [ESB] could absorb a considerable portion of *long-term* credit resources available to industrial development in Thailand, thus potentially crowding out other borrowers." World Bank, *Managing Public Resources,* p. 194.

47. Several international oil companies began exploration in Thailand in the late 1960s. The first natural gas discovery was made in 1973 by Union Oil of California in the off-shore Erawan field. Onshore delivery of gas through the pipeline began in 1981; the gas was initially used for power-generating plants near Bangkok. The pipeline was built and owned by the Petroleum Authority of Thailand (PTT), a state enterprise under the Ministry of Industry. PTT also built and operates the two gas separation plants, the first of which came on-stream in 1984. In the meantime, the ESB Committee authorized the organization of the National Petrochemical Corporation (NPC) to build and operate the olefins plant which would utilize ethane and propane from the separation plant, and in turn supply ethylene and propylene to downstream producers of various plastics and chemicals. NPC is 49 percent owned by PTT. The remaining equity was divided among the four private downstream dompanies and the Crown Property Bureau, with a small remaining share held by the World Bank's IFC.

48. The project received its first major setback in mid-1985 with a sharp fall in international fertilizer prices. None of the potential guarantors of the OECF's $85 million "yen loan" offer could be induced to carry through. In late 1985 the IFCT was pressured to serve as guarantor but insisted as a condition that NFC raise its registered capital over tenfold. Unable to obtain agreement from the private investors in the project, Chairman M. R. Chatumongkul Sonakul resigned. His successor, Kasame (Super K) Chatikavanij, succeeded in persuading the investors to double their stake but was unable to cope with the insuperable problem created by the yen revaluation, which had raised the baht-denominated size of the OECF loan nearly 50 percent, well beyond IFCT's ability to guarantee. After the cabinet affirmed its unwillingness to raise its stake, a reexamination of the project by the Chulalongkorn University Graduate Institute of Business Administration concluded that NFC would earn losses even if world fertilizer prices recovered 50 percent. Efforts in 1987 by the next NFC chairman, Aran Thammano, and the lead Japanese engineering contractor on the project, to persuade the Japanese government to offer additional financing concessions failed. In March 1988 Aran announced that the project had been shelved. *Business in Thailand,* May 1988, pp. 44–46.

49. *The Nation,* December 2, 1985.

50. A published example is the forecast prepared by the Thailand Development Research Institute in late 1985, summarized in *TDRI Newsletter* 1, 1 (March 1986): 7–8.

51. *The Nation,* May 6, 1986, p. 17.

52. To explore the potential demand for sites in ESB's proposed industrial estates, the original consultants' report surveyed a number of firms located in the Bangkok area to ascertain their interest in relocation. The survey found only lukewarm interest, not surprising given the powerful economies of concentration that have drawn industry to the greater

Bangkok area and the uncertainties surrounding ESB, then still in an early planning stage. It was clear that without financial incentives greater than those normally offered by BOI for location outside Bangkok, Thailand could expect no greater success in inducing relocation than other countries had experienced in similar regional development or industrial deconcentration schemes. Development of the ESB as an industrial area would depend entirely on the initial location decisions of new investment.

53. Corden, "Macroeconomic Policy and Growth: Some Lessons of Experience." Among the seventeen are Brazil, Chile, Colombia, India, Indonesia, Kenya, Nigeria, Pakistan, Thailand, and Turkey. Corden takes account of Korea.

54. Ibid., pp. 71, 73.

55. Bank of Thailand, *Quarterly Bulletin* 27, 3 (September 1987): 41–42.

Chapter 7

1. World Bank, *World Development Report*, 1991.

2. Bank of Thailand, *Thailand: Economic Developments in 1990*, pp. 25–26.

3. Krueger, "Asian Trade and Growth Lessons," provides a capsule summary from which I have drawn.

4. I owe these observations to Vijit Supinit, then director of the Banking Department of the Bank of Thailand, and to Olarn Chaipravat of the Siam Commercial Bank.

5. See Thailand Development Research Institute, *Thailand: Natural Resources Profile*, for a recent analysis of the state of Thailand's natural resource and enviromental endowment—soil, forest, water, and mineral resources; wildlife and conservation; urban air and noise pollution; solid waste and hazardous materials; and occupational hazards.

6. Hirsh and Lohmann, "Contemporary Politics of Environment in Thailand," p. 442. Two other projects seen as environmentally damaging also served as rallying issues for political mobilization during the "democracy period." One involved an American radar installation atop Thailand's highest mountain. The other concerned southern mining concessions granted to a joint venture with the American company Union Carbide. The radar installation was built, but the mining concession was canceled.

7. In 1986 a tantalum refinery being built on the resort island of Phuket was burned down after a series of local demonstrations. The demonstrators were Phuket residents protesting that the plant would create health hazards and pollute their beaches. Although the destruction of the plant (which has since been replaced by a new facility at Map Ta Phut) appeared to be the most violent environmental clash Thailand had ever experienced, it remains unclear whether the plant was actually torched by the demonstrators or destroyed by others using the environmental ruckus as cover for yet obscure reasons.

8. Anat Arbhabhirama, "Introduction," in the Siam Society, *Culture and Environment in Thailand*, p. xxxiii.

9. Government of Thailand, National Economic and Social Development Board, *Fifth Plan*, p. 57.

10. "The Land Wars," *Far East Economic Review,* October 31, 1991, pp. 15–16.

11. Ammar, *Labor-Abundant Agricultural Growth*, p. 40.

12. The studies are cited in the reference list under Thailand Development Research Institute, *Industrializing Thailand and Its Impact on the Environment*. See also Thailand Development Research Institute, *Thailand: Natural Resources Profile*.

13. Banasopit et al., *Urbanization and Environment*, Thailand Development Research Institute, pp. 94–95.

14. Government of Thailand, National Economic and Social Development Board, *Sixth Plan*, pp. 134–37.

15. Banasopit et al., *Urbanization and Environment*, p. 98.

16. Hirsch and Lohman, "Contemporary Politics of Environment in Thailand," p. 446.

17. "A U.S. $2 billion plan for sewage treatment plants in major cities was announced in June. Mining permits in forests are being allowed, but tougher constraints have been set to protect the environment. Unleaded fuel was introduced for vehicles and priced cheaper than other types as an incentive to users. An ambitious plan is being mapped out to establish an anti-pollution fund partially funded by polluters. And thought is being given to providing financial incentives to industries to invest in anti-pollution measures. But putting these plans into action is not assured. The current government expects to be voted out of power by April 1991. Their prospective successors have shown no commitment to the issues, neither has most of the bureaucracy." *Far East Economic Review*, September 19, 1991, p. 44.

18. Chalongphob et al., *Human Resources Management*, p. 168. The most serious (clinical) "third degree" malnutrition was below 1 percent. The measures of lesser deficiency had been brought down from 16 percent in 1981 to under 7 percent in 1984.

19. Government of Thailand, Ministry of Public Health, *Mini Health Profile*, and *The Realization of Primary Health Care in Thailand*.

20. Chalongphob et al., *Human Resources Management*, pp. 166–67.

21. For a discussion of the technical problems of defining and measuring Third World poverty, see World Bank, *World Development Report*, 1990, pp. 24–38, and McGreevy, ed., *Third World Poverty*.

22. Medhi et al., *Priority Issues*, p. 6.

23. The index of unprocessed agricultural products rose from an average of 151.5 in 1984–87 to 181.4 in 1988, rising moderately again in 1989 to 191.8 and in 1990 to 195.7. Bank of Thailand, *Quarterly Bulletin* (December 1990), table 51.

24. Medhi et al., *Priority Issues*, table 2.12.

25. Ibid., tables 2.1; 2.2; 2.5; 2.6.

26. These differentiations and changes have been documented in a set of "village history" studies by the Research and Development Institute of Khon Kaen University. In English translation, see Chulaporn, *Village History: Ban Polo*.

27. World Bank publications have argued both ways. Binswanger et al. (World Bank, *Thailand: Rural Growth and Employment*) conclude that "taxation of rice farmers probably has a regressive effect not only on farmer groups but also on wage earners" by lowering the demand for rural labor (p. 148). O'Mara and Vin Le-Si (*Supply and Welfare Effects*) conclude that real wages in Thailand are invariant with respect to the price of rice (p. 58).

28. Medhi, *Agricultural Development Policies*, p. 51.

29. World Bank, *Thailand: Rural Growth and Employment*, p. 149.

30. Ammar and Suthad, *Trade, Exchange Rate and Agricultural Pricing*.

31. Ronald Findlay, "Trade, Development, and the State," in Ranis and Schultz, *The State of Development Economics*, pp. 83–84.

32. World Bank, *Thailand, Toward a Development Strategy*, pp. 25–26.

33. Ibid., table 2.12.

34. Chalongphob, *Human Resource Problems*, p. 58.

35. The constraints are summarized in two extracts from the proceedings of a workshop in Khon Kaen University, *Rainfed Agriculture in Northeast Thailand*, ed. C. Pairintra, et al.: "The inherent fertility of most Northeast soils has long since been depleted and/or exhausted from long-term cropping without sufficient replacement of plant nutrients, and from long-term degradative processes such as soil erosion, nutrient runoff losses and organic matter depletion. Consequently, the tilth, fertility and productivity of Northeast soils are low" (p. 406). "In the future, if agricultural production is to continue to expand, and the natural resource base of the region is to be maintained or improved, then

yields per hectare must be increased. This will not be achieved in the initial phases, however, by dramatic increases in purchased inputs. Rather, attention must focus on low-cost improvements in water control such as small weirs, shallow wells and better levelled paddies, and on low-input systems of soil improvement such as green manuring, liming and more efficient use of animal manure and compost, that the poor subsistence farmers can afford" (p. 36).

36. Ammar et al., *Public Policies*, p. 21.

37. Ibid., p. 31.

38. For a recent summary of the literature and state of the art on comparative studies of income distribution, see Gary S. Fields, "Income Distribution and Growth," and the comments by Albert Fishlow in Ranis and Schultz, *The State of Development Economics*, pp. 459–85.

39. Medhi, *Industrialization, Employment, Poverty*, p. 43.

40. Government of Thailand, National Economic and Social Development Board, *Bangkok Metropolitan Regional Development Proposals*, p. S–5.

41. Ibid. p. S–11.

42. World Bank, *World Development Report*, 1990, table 31. Figures on urban population are imprecise as they depend on where the lines are drawn between community sizes defined as urban or rural. Urban population in Thailand is normally defined as residents of (legally established) municipalities. If the large numbers of relatively small towns constituted as "sanitary districts" (which are larger and possess more urban characteristics than villages) were included as "urban" along with municipalities, the urban proportion of the population would be substantially greater. Thus, the addition of the sanitary districts (with population above 5,000) to the municipal population in 1980 would raise the urban proportion from the municipal 17 percent to a total of 26 percent. (Chalongphob et al., *Human Resources Management*, p. 16.) Thai urbanization would still be low by international standards, perhaps even unchanged in its original relationship to other countries, if the definitions of urbanization were made uniform.

43. Comparisons drawn from Shlomo Angel, *Where Have All the People Gone?*

44. World Bank, *Thailand: Country Economic Memorandum*, pp. 96–98.

45. Lewis and Kapur, *The Thai Economy's Medium-Term Prospects and Challenges*, p. 27. Nepal is included as a twelfth country (its ratio was 8.1) but was put aside by the authors as extraneous.

46. World Bank, *Thailand: Country Economic Memorandum*, annex 7.

47. For fuller treatment, see Oshima, *Economic Growth in Monsoon Asia*; Nipon, *Employment in Thailand*; Pasuk et al., *General Employment Situation in Thailand*; Chalongphob et al., *Human Resources Management*.

48. World Bank, *Thailand: Country Economic Memorandum*, p. 136.

49. Government of Thailand, National Economic and Social Development Board, *Sixth Plan*, p. 34.

50. Chalongphob, *Human Resource Problems*, p. 7.

51. Thailand Development Research Institute, *The Outlook for the Thai Economy*, p. 6.

52. Bank of Thailand, *Quarterly Bulletin* 30, 3 (September 1990): 12.

53. Paul Handley, "Banking in Bangkok: Thai Officials Aim to Establish Finance Hub," *Far Eastern Economic Review*, January 16, 1992, p. 34.

54. This observation was made in 1991 by the senior economist of the Siam Commercial Bank, as cited by Richard Donor and Daniel Unger in "The Politics of Finance in Thai Economic Development," draft chapter in Lee, *Government, Financial Systems and Economic Development*.

55. For a succinct, comparative analysis, see Lim and Pang Eng Fong, *Foreign Direct Investment*, especially pp. 45–51.

56. Barton Biggs, Morgan Stanley Memorandum (no date).

57. Government of Thailand, National Economic and Social Development Board, *Sixth Plan*, p. 46.

58. Government of Thailand, National Economic and Social Development Board, *Fifth Plan*, p. 62.

59. World Bank, *Current Economic Position*.

60. Recent study of cultural change among the Sino-Thai is described in Somboon, *Religious Belief and Ceremony of the Chinese Community*, and *Chinese Community: Continuity and Change*.

61. Government of Thailand, National Economic and Social Development Board, *Sixth Plan*, pp. 172–73.

62. For a detailed presentation on the problems of economic law, see Surakiart, *A Preliminary Report on Laws and Regulations*.

63. Effros, *Financial Sector Study*, p. 3.

64. Business members of the interim government and their prior business affiliation were as follows: Prime Minister Anand Panyaruchun (Saha Union); Nukul Prachuabmoh, communications (First Asia); Amaret Sila-On, commerce (Siam cement); Sippanondha Ketudat, industry (National Petrochemical Corporation); Snoh Unakul, deputy prime minister (Bank of Asia).

65. The latter two examples are cited in Anek, *No More Bureaucratic Polity*, pp. 165–67.

66. Ibid., p. 255.

67. Sippanondha, *The Middle Path*, pp. 6–7.

68. Chai-anan, "Industrialization," p. 12.

69. Bank of Thailand, *Annual Economic Report*, 1986, p. 129.

70. Hugh Honour, "The Battle Over Post-Modern Buildings," *New York Review of Books* 35, 14 (September 29, 1988): 27–33.

71. Government of Thailand, National Economic and Social Development Board, *Gross Regional and Provincial Product*, p. 173.

72. Hastings and Chatchawan, *Integrated Information*.

73. Chulaporn, *Village History*, pp. 70–72.

74. Dolinsky, "Contract Farming at Lam Nam Oon."

75. Kingshill et al., *The Red Tomb—Thirty Years Later*, pp. 6–7.

76. Ibid., pp. 50–51.

77. Klausner, *Reflections*, pp. 132–36.

78. Ibid., p. 143.

79. Ibid., pp. 144–47.

80. Anat Abhabhirama, "Introduction," in the Siam Society, *Culture and Environment*, pp. xxxi-xxxiii.

81. Phillips, *Modern Thai Literature*, p. 44.

82. Puey, *Puey Ungphakorn, A Siamese for All Seasons*, pp. 333–37.

83. Sulak, *A Buddhist Vision*, p. 57.

84. Ibid., p. 62.

85. Ibid., p. 74.

86. Suwanna Satha-Anand, "Religious Movements," p. 396. See also Somboon, *Buddhism and Politics in Thailand;* Jackson, *Buddhism, Legitimation, and Conflict;* Jackson, *Buddhadasa.*

87. Ibid., pp. 402–3.

88. Ibid., p. 402.

89. Ibid., p. 407.

90. Phra, *Thai Buddhism in the Buddhist World*, pp. 117–18.

91. Klausner, "The Thai Sangha and National Development," in *Reflections*, pp. 152–53.

92. For a full treatment of the political role of Buddhism in Thailand, see Jackson, *Buddhism, Legitimation, and Conflict.*

BIBLIOGRAPHY

Abonyi, George, and Bunyaraks Ninsananda. *Thailand: Development Planning in Turbulent Times*. North York: University of Toronto-York University, 1989.

Ahmed, Sadiq. *Shadow Prices for Economic Appraisal of Projects; An Application to Thailand*. World Bank Working Papers no. 609, Washington, D.C., 1983.

Akin Rabibhadana. *The Organization of Thai Society in the Early Bangkok Period, 1782–1873*. Ithaca, N.Y.: Cornell University Southeast Asia Program, data paper 74, 1969.

Ammar Siamwalla, "A History of Rice Policies in Thailand." *Food Research Institute Studies*, 14, 3, Stanford, 1975.

————. *Labor-Abundant Agricultural Growth and Some of Its Consequences: The Case of Thailand*. Bangkok: Thailand Development Research Institute, no date.

————. "Two Excerpts from the Factbook on Rice." *TDRI Newsletter* 4, 2 (June 1989).

Ammar Siamwalla and Suthad Setboonsarng. *The Political Economy of Agricultural Pricing Policies in Thailand*. World Bank, 1986.

————. *Trade, Exchange Rate and Agricultural Pricing Policies in Thailand*. Washington, D.C.: World Bank Comparative Studies, 1989.

Ammar Siamwalla, Direk Patamasiriwat, and Suthad Setboonsarng. *Public Policies Towards Agricultural Diversification in Thailand*. Bangkok: Thailand Development Research Institute, no date.

Anderson, Benedict R. O'G., and Ruchira Mendiones. *In The Mirror: Literature and Politics in Siam in the American Era*. Bangkok: Duang Kamol, 1985.

Anek Laothamatas. *Business Associations and the New Political Economy of Thailand*. Boulder: Westview Press, 1991.

————. *No More Bureaucratic Polity: Business Associations and the New Political Economy of Thailand*. New York: Columbia University Press, 1991.

Angel, Shlomo. *Where Have All the People Gone?* Urbanization and Counter-Urbanization in Thailand, prepared for the International Seminar on Planning for Settlements in Rural Regions, UN Centre for Human Settlements, Nairobi, November 1985.

Ariff, Mohamed and Hal Hill. *Export-Oriented Industrialization: The ASEAN Experience*. Sydney: Allen & Unwin, 1985.

Asher, Mukul G., and Anne Booth. *Indirect Taxation in ASEAN*. Institute of Southeast Asian Studies, Singapore University Press, 1983.

Ayal, Eliezar B. *The Study of Thailand*, Southeast Asia Series no. 54. Athens, Ohio University Center for International Studies, 1978.

————, ed. *The Study of Thailand: Analyses of Knowledge, Approaches and Prospects in Anthropology, Art History, Economics, History, and Political Science*. Athens: Ohio University Center for International Studies, 1978.

Banasopit Mekvichai et al. *Urbanization and Environment.* Bangkok: Thai Development Research Institute, 1990.

Bank of Thailand. *Annual Economic Reports*, various years.

———. *Financial Institutions and Market in Thailand.* Bangkok: Agricultural Development Council, 1985.

———. *Quarterly Bulletins*, various years.

———. *Thailand: Economic Developments in 1990 and Outlook for 1991.* Bangkok, no date.

Batson, Benjamin A., and Shimizu Hajime. *The Tragedy of Wanit, A Japanese Account of Wartime Thai Politics. Journal of Southeast Asian Studies*, Special Publications Series, no. 1, Singapore (1990).

Behrman, Jere R. *Supply Response in Underdeveloped Agriculture: A Case Study of Four Major Annual Crops in Thailand 1937–1963.* Amsterdam: North-Holland Publishing Co., 1988.

Bhattacharya, Amar, and Peter Brimble, *Trade and Industrial Policies in Thailand in the 1980's: A Review and a Framework for Policy Reform*, 1986, draft.

Board of Investment. *Expanding Private Investment for Thailand's Economic Growth.* Bangkok: U.S. Investment Survey Team to Thailand, 1959.

Brown, Ian. *The Elite and the Economy in Siam.* c. 1890–1920. New York: Oxford University Press, 1988.

Buyck, Beatrice. "Technical Assistance as a Delivery Mechanism for Institutional Development: A Review of Issues and Lessons of Bank Experience." Country Economics Department, Public Sector Management and Private Sector Development Division, 1989.

Caldwell, J. Alexander. *American Economic Aid to Thailand.* Lexington, Mass.: D.C. Heath, 1974.

Chai-anan Samudavanija. "Industrialization and Democracy in Thailand." Conference paper, the Australian National University, Research School of Pacific Studies, December 1992.

———. *The Thai Young Turks.* Singapore: Institute of Southeast Asian Studies, 1982.

Chai-anan Samudavanija, Kusuma Snetwongse and Suchit Bonbongkam. *From Armed Suppression to Political Offensive.* Bangkok: Institute of Security and International Studies, 1990.

Chaipat Sahasakul, Nattapong Thongpakde, and Keokam Kraisoraphong. *Lessons from the World Bank's Experience of Structural Adjustment Loans (SALs): A Case Study of Thailand.* Bangkok: Thailand Development Research Institute, 1989.

Chalongphob Sussangkarn. *Human Resource Problems and Policy Priorities for Thailand.* Bangkok: Thailand Development Research Institute, 1988.

Chalongphob Sussangkarn, Teera Ashakul, and Charles Myers. *Human Resources Management.* Bangkok: Thailand Development Research Institute, 1986.

Chattip Nartsupha. "The Economic Thought of Phraya Suriyanuwat" (Qwankid Tang Setagit Khong Phraya Suriyanuwat). *Social Science Review* (September 1974).

Chattip Nartsupha and Suthy Prasartset, eds. *The Political Economy of Siam, 1851–1910.* Bangkok: Social Science Association of Thailand, 1981.

Chattip Nartsupha, Suthy Prasartset, and Montri Chenvidyakarn, eds. *The Political Economy of Siam, 1910–1932.* Bangkok: Social Science Association of Thailand, 1978.

Chira Hongladaram and Medhi Krongkaew, eds. *Comparative Development: Japan and Thailand.* Bangkok: Thammasat University Press, 1981.

Christensen, Scott. "Thailand After the Coup." *Journal of Democracy* (Summer 1991).

Chulaporn Chotchuangniran. *Village History: Ban Polo.* Research and Development Institute, Khon Kaen: Khon Kaen University, 1985.

Corden, W. Max. "Macroeconomic Policy and Growth: Some Lessons of Experience." *Proceedings of the World Bank Annual Conference on Development Economics*, Washington, D.C., World Bank, 1990, pp. 59–88.

Coughlin, Richard, J. *Double Identity; The Chinese in Modern Thailand*. Hong Kong: Hong Kong University Press, 1960.

Dapice, David, and Frank Flatters. *Thailand: Prospects and Perils in the Global Economy*. TDRI Year-End Conference. Bangkok: Thailand Development Research Institute, 1989.

Darling, Frank C. *Thailand and the United States*. Washington, D.C.: Public Affairs Press, 1965.

deYoung, John E. *Village Life in Modern Thailand*. Berkeley: University of California Press, 1966.

Dolinsky, Diane J. "Contract Farming at Lam Nam Oon: An Operational Model for Rural Development." East Asian Institute, Columbia University, 1992.

Easterly, William, and Patrick Honohan. *Financial Sector Policy in Thailand*. World Bank Working Papers no. 440, Washington, D.C., 1990.

Effros, Robert C. *Financial Sector Study: The Relationship between Law and Development*. Draft. Washington, D.C.: IMF, 1988.

Feder, Gershon. *Land Ownership, Security and Farm Productivity in Rural Thailand*. Washington, D.C.: World Bank, 1986.

Feder, Gershon, et al. *Adoption of Agricultural Innovations in Developing Countries: A Survey*. World Bank Staff Working Paper no. 444. Washington, D.C.: World Bank, 1981.

Giovannini, Alberto, and Martha de Melo. *Government Revenue from Financial Repression*. Working Paper no. 3604. Cambridge: National Bureau of Economic Research, 1991.

Girling, John L. S. *Thailand: Society and Politics*. Ithaca, N.Y.: Cornell University Press, 1981.

Government of Thailand, Ministry of Finance, Fiscal Policy Office. *Study on Fiscal Implication of Investment Incentives and Promotion Efficiency*. Bangkok, 1984.

―――. Ministry of Public Health. *Mini Health Profile*. Bangkok, 1988.

―――. *The Realization of Primary Health Care in Thailand*. Bangkok, 1988.

―――. *Thailand Population Monograph*. Bangkok, 1983.

Government of Thailand, National Economic and Social Development Board. *Bangkok Metropolitan Regional Development Proposals: Recommended Development Strategies and Investment Programmes for the Sixth Plan*. Bangkok, 1986.

―――. *Eastern Seaboard Study: Interim Report*. By Coopers and Lybrand Assoc., July 1982.

―――. *Evaluation of the First Six-Year Plan, 1961–1966*. Bangkok, June 1967.

―――. *The Fifth National Economic and Social Development Plan (1982–1986)*. Bangkok, 1982.

―――. *The Fourth National Economic and Social Development Plan (1977–1981)*. Bangkok, 1977.

―――. *Gross Regional and Provincial Product, BE 2528*. Bangkok, 1985.

―――. *The Sixth National Economic and Social Development Plan (1987–1991)*. Bangkok, 1987.

Hanson, James A., and Craig R. Neal. *Interest Rate Policies in Selected Developing Countries, 1970–1982*. World Bank Staff Working Papers no. 753, Washington, D.C., 1985.

Hastings, Paul, and Chatchawan Boonaksa. *Integrated Information for Natural Resources Management*. Bangkok: Thailand Development Research Institute, 1990.

Hewison, Kevin. *Bankers and Bureaucrats: Capital and the Role of the State in Thailand*. New Haven: Yale University Southeast Asia Studies, 1989.

Hirsch, Philip, and Larry Lohmann. "Contemporary Politics of Environment in Thailand." *Asian Survey* 29, 4 (April 1989).

Ingram, James C. *Economic Change in Thailand Since 1850.* Stanford: Stanford University Press, 1955.

Jackson, Peter. *Buddhadasa: A Buddhist Thinker for the Modern World.* Bangkok: The Siam Society, 1988.

————. *Buddhism, Legitimation and Conflict: The Political Functions of Urban Thai Buddhism in the 19th and 20th Centuries.* Singapore: Institute of Southeast Asian Studies, 1989.

Jacobs, Norman. *Modernization without Development: Thailand as an Asian Case Study.* New York: Praeger, 1971.

Japanese Ministry of Foreign Affairs. *Japan's ODA 1987.* Tokyo: Japanese Ministry of Foreign Affairs, 1988.

Keyes, Charles F. *Thailand: Buddhist Kingdom as Modern Nation State.* Boulder: Westview Press, 1987.

Kingshill, Konrad. *Kudaeng—The Red Tomb: A Village Study in Northern Thailand.* Chiangmai, The Prince Royal's College, 1960.

Kingshill, Konrad, Prasert Bhandhachat, and Ronald D. Renard. *The Red Tomb—Thirty Years Later: A Follow-Up Study on Development of a Northern Thai Village (Ku Daeng), A.D. 1954–1984.* Chiangmai: Payap University, 1985.

Klausner, William J. *Reflections on Thai Culture.* 3d edition. Bangkok: The Siam Society, 1987.

Knodel, John, Aphichat Chamratritirong, and Nighon Debaralya. *Thailand's Reproductive Revolution.* Madison: University of Wisconsin Press, 1987.

Krueger, Anne O. "Asian Trade and Growth Lessons." *Papers and Proceedings, The American Economic Review* (May 1990): 108–12.

Landon, Kenneth P. *Siam in Transition.* London: Oxford University Press, 1939.

Lee, Chung H., ed. *Government, Financial Systems and Economic Development: A Comparative Study of Selected Asian and Latin American Countries.* Ithaca: Cornell University Press, 1994.

Lewis, John P., and Devesh Kapur. "An Updating Country Study: Thailand's Needs and Prospects in the 1990s." *World Development* 18, 10 (October 1990): 1363–78.

————. *The Thai Economy's Medium-Term Prospects and Challenges.* Bangkok: Thailand Development Research Institute, 1991.

Likhit, Dhiravegin. *The Bureaucratic Elite of Thailand.* Bangkok: Thai Khadi Research Institute, 1978.

Lim, Linda Y. C., and Pang Eng Fong. *Foreign Direct Investment and Industrialization in Malaysia, Singapore, Taiwan and Thailand.* Paris: Development Centre Studies, OECD, 1991.

Little, I., T. Scitovsky, and M. Scott. *Industry and Trade in Some Developing Countries.* London: Oxford University Press, 1970.

Loftus, John A. "Economic Development Planning in Thailand." *Terminal Report* (August 1962).

————. *Economic Memorandum.* Various, 1956–1962, Ministry of Finance.

McGreevy, W. P., ed. *Third World Poverty.* Lexington: Heath, 1980.

McVay, Ruth, ed. *Industrializing Elites in Southeast Asia.* Ithaca: Cornell University Press, 1990.

Medhi Krongkaew. *Agricultural Development Policies and Income Distribution in Thailand.* Workshop on "Income Distribution and the Role of Development Policies," organized by the Institute of Developing Economies, Tokyo, 1985.

————. *Industrialization, Employment, Poverty and Income Distribution of Thai Households.* Bangkok: Thailand Development Research Institute, 1987.

————. *Institution Building and Economic Development: A Lesson from Rural Public Works Administration in Thailand.* Paper prepared for Seventh Biennial General Meeting on Commonalities and Complementarities in the Asia and Pacific Region, ADIPA, 1987.

Medhi Krongkaew, Pranee Tinakorn, and Suphat Suphachalasai. *Priority Issues and Policy Measures to Alleviate Rural Poverty: The Case of Thailand.* Bangkok: Thammasat University, 1990.

Michalopoulos, Constantine. *World Bank Programs for Adjustment and Growth.* World Bank Discussion Paper no. VPERS11, April 1987.

Mingsarn Santikarn. *Technology Transfer.* Singapore: Singapore University Press, 1981.

Moerman, Michael. *Agricultural Change and Peasant Choice in a Thai Village.* Berkeley: University of California Press, 1968.

Morell, David, and Chai-anan Samudavanija. *Political Conflict in Thailand.* Cambridge: Oelgeschlager, Gunn & Hain, 1981.

Mosel, James N. "Thai Administrative Behavior." In *Towards the Comparative Study of Public Administration.* Bloomington: Indiana University, 1957.

Mousny, André. *The Economy of Thailand.* Bangkok: Social Science Association of Thailand, 1964.

Muscat, Robert J. *Development Strategy in Thailand.* New York: Praeger, 1966.

————. *Thailand and the United States: Development, Security and Foreign Aid.* New York: Columbia Press, 1990.

Myint, Hla. "The Classical Theory of International Trade and the Underdeveloped Countries." *The Economic Journal* (June 1958): 315–37.

The Nation. *Thailand, Midyear 1990.* Bangkok, *The Nation.*

National Statistics Office. *Population by Detailed Classification of Industry.* Bangkok: National Statistics Office.

Neher, Clark D. "Thailand in 1987; Semi-Successful Semi-Democracy." *Asian Survey* 28, 2 (February 1988).

Nipon Poapongsakorn. *Employment in Thailand.* Bangkok: Thammasat University, 1986 ms.

Oey Astra Meesook et al. *The Political Economy of Thailand's Development: Poverty, Equity and Growth, 1850–1985.* World Bank, ms.

O'Mara, Gerald, and Vinh Le-Si. *The Supply and Welfare Effects of Rice-Price Policy in Thailand.* World Bank Staff Working Papers no. 714. Washington, D.C., 1985.

Pairintra, C., et al., eds. *Rainfed Agriculture in Northeast Thailand.* Proceedings of a Workshop at Khon Kaen University, USAID, Washington, D.C., 1988.

Panayotou, Theodore, ed. *Food Policy Analysis in Thailand.* Bangkok: Agricultural Development Council, 1985.

Pasuk Phongpaichit. *Economic and Social Transformation of Thailand, 1957–1976.* Bangkok: Social Science Institute, Chulalongkorn University, 1980.

————. *Employment, Income and the Mobilisation of Local Resources in Three Thai Villages.* Bangkok: International Labour Organisation, 1982.

————. *General Employment Situation in Thailand.* Chulalongkorn University. Bangkok: ILO-ARTEP, 1986, ms.

Phillips, Herbert P., in association with Vinita Atmiyanandana Lawler, Amnuaycaj Patipat, and Likhit Dhiravegin. *Modern Thai Literature.* Honolulu: University of Hawaii Press, 1987.

Phisit Pakkasem. *Leading Issues in Thailand's Development Transformation, 1960–1990.* Bangkok: National Economic and Social Development Board, 1988.

Phra Rajavaramuni. *Thai Buddhism in the Buddhist World.* Bangkok: Mahachulalongkorn Buddhist University, 1985.

Pisan Suriyamongkol. *Institutionalization of Democratic Political Processes in Thailand: A Three-Pronged Democratic Polity*. Bangkok: Thammasat University Press, 1988.

Potter, Sulamith Heins. *Family Life in a Northern Thai Village*. Berkeley: University of California Press, 1979.

Prateep Sondysuvan, ed. *Finance, Trade and Economic Development in Thailand: Essays in Honour of Khunying Suparb Ossundara*. Bangkok: Sompong Press, 1975.

Prayad Buramasiri and Snoh Unakul. "Obstacles to Effective Planning Encountered in the Thai Planning Experience." *The Philippine Economic Journal*. 4, 2 (1965): 327–40.

Pritchett, Lant. *Measuring Outward Orientation in Developing Countries*. Working Paper Series 566, World Bank, Washington, D.C., 1991.

Puey Ungphakorn. *Best Wishes for Asia*. Bangkok: Klett Thai Publications, 1975.

————. *Puey Ungphakorn, A Siamese for All Seasons*. Bangkok: Komol Keemthong Foundation, 1981.

Ranis, Gustav, and T. P. Schultz. *The State of Development Economics*. Oxford: Blackwell, 1988.

Reeve, W. D. *Public Administration in Siam*. London: Oxford University Press, 1951.

Riggs, Fred W. *Thailand: The Modernization of a Bureaucratic Polity*. Honolulu: East–West Center Press, 1966.

Rosenfield, Alan, et al. "Thailand's Family Planning Program: An Asian Success Story". *International Family Planning Perspectives* 8, 2 (June 1982).

Saiyud Kerdphol. *The Struggle for Thailand*. Bangkok: S. Research Center, 1986.

Siam Society. *Culture and Environment in Thailand*. Bangkok, 1989.

Siffin, William J. *The Thai Bureaucracy: Institutional Change and Development*. Honolulu: East–West Center Press, 1966.

Silcock, T. H. *Thailand: Social and Economic Studies in Development*. Durham: Duke University Press, 1967.

Sippanondha Ketudat, with Robert B. Textor. *The Middle Path for the Future of Thailand*. East–West Center and Chiang Mai University, 1990.

Skinner, G. William. *Leadership and Power in the Chinese Community of Thailand*. Ithaca: Cornell University Press, 1958.

Snoh Unakul. "Thailand: The Fifth Plan Strategy." *National Development Strategy of Thailand*. Bangkok: National Economic and Social Development Board, no date.

Somboon Suksamran. *Buddhism and Politics in Thailand*. Singapore: Institute of Southeast Asian Studies, 1982.

————. *Chinese Community: Continuity and Change* (in Thai). Bangkok: Chulalongkorn University, 1987.

————. *Religious Belief and Ceremony of the Chinese Community* (in Thai). Bangkok: Chulalongkorn University, 1986.

Sompop Manarungsan. *Economic Development of Thailand, 1850–1950*. Bangkok: Institute of Asian Studies, Chulalongkorn University, 1989.

Stifel, Laurence D. "Technocrats and Modernization in Thailand." *Asian Survey* 16, 12 (December 1976).

Streeten, Paul, ed. *Beyond Adjustment: The Asian Experience*. Washington, D.C.: IMF, 1988.

Suehiro, Akira. *Capital Accumulation and Industrial Development in Thailand*. Bangkok: Chulalongkorn University Social Research Institute, 1985.

Sulak Sivaraksa. *A Buddhist Vision for Renewing Society*. Bangkok: Thai Watana Panich, 1981.

Sungsidh. *Thai Bureaucratic Capitalism*.

Surakiart Sathirathai. *A Preliminary Report on Laws and Regulations Concerning Natural Resources, Financial Institutions and Exports: Their Effects on Economic and Social Development*. Bangkok: Thailand Development Research Institute, no date.

Suthy Prasartset and Chattip Nartsupha. "The Rise of Dependent Commodity Production in Siam, 1855–1910." *The Review of Thai Social Science* (1977): 144–68.

Suwanna Satha-Anand. "Religious Movements in Contemporary Thailand." *Asian Survey* 30, 4 (April 1990): 395–408.

Thailand Development Research Institute. *Financial Resources Management*. Bangkok, 1986.

———. *Industrializing Thailand and Its Impact on the Environment*: (1) Dhira Phantumvanit and Theodore Panayotou, "Natural Resources for a Sustainable Future: Spreading the Benefits"; (2) T. Panayotou and Chartchai Parasuk, "Land and Forest: Projecting Demand and Managing Encroachment"; (3) Sopin Tongpan et al., "Deforestation and Poverty: Can Commercial and Social Forestry Break the Vicious Circle?"; (4) Sacha Sethaputra et al., "Water Shortages: Managing Demand to Expand Supply"; (5) T. Panayotou et al., "Mining, Environment and Sustainable Land Use"; (6) Duangjai Intarapravich et al., "Mineral Resource Development: Making the Best of a Limited Resource." Papers prepared for the Thailand Development Research Institute 1990 Year-End Conference, Bangkok, 1990.

———. *The Outlook for the Thai Economy*. Bangkok, 1989.

———. *Report of the Seminar on the Liberalization of Laws and Regulations for the Promotion of Private-Sector Activities for Economic and Social Development*. Bangkok: UN Development Programme, 1988.

———. *Revision and Development of Rules and Regulations Governing Commercial Banking Practices in Thailand*. Bangkok, 1987.

———. *Thailand: Natural Resources Profile*. Bangkok, 1987.

Thak Chaloemtiarana. *Thailand: The Politics of Despotic Paternalism*. Social Science Association of Thailand. Bangkok: Thammasat University Press, 1979.

———. *Thai Politics, 1932–1957*. Vol. 1. Bangkok: Social Science Association of Thailand, 1978.

Thammanun Pongsrikul and Somchai Ratanakomut. *Trade in Services*. Background Paper no. 5. Thailand Development Research Institute 1989 Year-End Conference, Bangkok, 1989.

Thawatt Mokarapong. *History of the Thai Revolution*. Bangkok: Thai Watana Panich, 1983.

Tipsuda Sundaravej and Prasam Trairatvorakul. *Experiences of Financial Distress in Thailand*. World Bank Working Papers, Working Paper Series 283, Washington, D.C., 1989.

Todaro, Michael P. *Economic Development in the Third World*. New York: Longman, 1981.

Tongroj Onchan, ed. *A Land Policy Study*. Bangkok: Thailand Development Research Institute, 1990.

Turton, Andrew. *Production, Power and Participation in Rural Thailand*. Geneva: United Nations Research Institute for Social Development, 1987.

UN Industrial Development Organization (UNIDO). *Thailand*. Industrial Development Review Series, 1985.

Vichitvong na Pombhejara. *Pridi Banomyong and the Making of Thailand's Modern History*. Bangkok.

Vickers, John, and George Yarrow. "Economic Perspectives on Privatization." *The Journal of Economic Perspectives* (Spring 1991): 113.

Wedel, Yuangrat, and Paul Wedel. *Radical Thought, Thai Mind: The Development of Revolutionary Ideas in Thailand*. Bangkok: Assumption Business Administration College, 1987.

Wilson, Constance M. "Bangkok in 1883: An Economic and Social Profile." *The Journal of the Siam Society* 77, 2 (1989).

Wilson, David A. *Politics in Thailand.* Ithaca: Cornell University Press, 1962.

Wit, Daniel. "The Thai System." In *A Comparative Study of Local Government and Administration.* Bangkok: Thammasat University, 1961.

World Bank. *Coping With Structural Change in a Dynamic Economy.* Washington, D.C., 1980.

————. *Current Economic Position and Prospects of Thailand.* Vol. 1. Washington, D.C., 1970.

————. *Managing Public Resources for Structural Adjustment.* Washington, D.C., 1983.

————. *Program Performance and Audit Report; Thailand—First and Second Structural Adjustment Loans. Report No. 6085. Washington, D.C., 1986.*

————. *A Public Development Program for Thailand.* Baltimore: The Johns Hopkins Press, 1959.

————. *Report and Recommendation of the President of the IBRD to the Executive Directors on a Second Structural Adjustment Loan to the Kingdom of Thailand.* Report P–3481-TH, March 1983.

————. *Structural Adjustment Lending: A First Review of Experience.* Report No. 6409, September 1986.

————. *Thailand: Country Economic Memorandum; Building on the Recent Success—A Policy Framework.* Washington, D.C., 1989.

————. *Thailand: Financial Sector Study.* Washington, D.C., 1990.

————. *Thailand; Perspectives for Financial Reform.* Washington, D.C., 1983.

————. *Thailand: Rural Growth and Employment.* Washington, D.C., 1983.

————. *Thailand's Manufactured Exports; Key Issues and Policy Options.* Washington, D.C., 1985.

————. *Thailand, Toward a Development Strategy of Full Participation.* Washington, D.C., 1980.

————. *Thailand: Transport Sector Review, Main Report.* Washington, D.C.,1984.

————. *World Development Report.* Various years.

————. *World Tables.* Washington, D.C. Various years.

Wyatt, David K. *Thailand: A Short History.* London: Yale University Press, 1984.

Yang, S. C. *A Multiple Exchange Rate System.* Madison: University of Wisconsin Press, 1957.

Yeung, Y. M., and C. P. Lo. *Changing South-East Asian Cities.* Singapore: Oxford University Press, 1976.

INDEX

ROBERT J. MUSCAT is executive director of the Institute for Policy Reform in Washington, D.C. He has been a visiting scholar at the East Asian Institute of Columbia University, and has served as economic adviser to the Thai government's development planning agency, as undersecretary for economics in the Malaysian Ministry of Finance, and as a program policy director for the UN Development Programme. In the U.S. Agency for International Development he held positions in Southeast Asian, Latin American, and African missions, and was AID's chief economist in 1972–75. His recent publications include *Thailand and the United States: Development, Security and Foreign Aid* and *Cambodia: Post-Settlement Reconstruction and Development.*